Letters to Molly

Edited by Ann Saddlemyer

The Belknap Press of Harvard University Press

Cambridge, Massachusetts, 1971

Letters to Molly

John Millington Synge to Maire O'Neill

1906–1909

Remembering Joey

Contents

Introduction xi

Acknowledgments xxv

Chronicle of Events, 1905–1909 xxvii

Manuscript Locations and Code to Description xxxiv

Letters to Molly 1

General Index 321

Illustrations

John M. Synge, from a drawing by John Butler Yeats, December 1905, in the possession of Professor D. J. Gordon. Courtesy of M. B. Yeats and Anne Yeats. (University of Reading photographer) *Page iii*

Maire O'Neill, from the painting by John Butler Yeats, 1913. Courtesy of the Abbey Theatre, Dublin, and M. B. Yeats and Anne Yeats. *Page iii*

Molly Allgood, about 1906. Courtesy of the National Library of Ireland. (Photograph by Dane Campbell Studio, Sidney, British Columbia) *Page xi*

Maire O'Neill as Pegeen Mike in *The Playboy of the Western World*, 1907. (Photograph by Lafayette of Dublin) *Page 1*

Synge at thirty. Courtesy of Mrs. L. M. Stephens. (Photograph by Dane Campbell Studio, Sidney, British Columbia) *Page 83*

Synge in 1906. Courtesy of Mrs. L. M. Stephens. (Photograph by Chancellor, Dublin) *Page 83*

Maire O'Neill, about 1907. Courtesy of the National Library of Ireland. *Page 83.*

Riders to the Sea, 1906, with Maire O'Neill, Sara Allgood, and Brigit O'Dempsey. Courtesy of the National Library of Ireland. *Page 83*

Molly Allgood, about 1907. Courtesy of Mrs. Morton Hague. *Page 235*

Spreading the News, 1907, with Sara Allgood, Brigit O'Dempsey, and Maire O'Neill. (Photograph by Dane Campbell Studio, Sidney, British Columbia) *Page 235*

Molly Allgood, about 1909. Courtesy of the National Library of Ireland. (Photograph by Dane Campbell Studio, Sidney, British Columbia) *Page 235.*

John M. Synge to Molly Allgood, 14 September 1908. By permission of Trinity College, Dublin. (Photograph by the Green Studio, Dublin) *Pages 279–280*

Maire O'Neill's contract, made out by J. M. Synge as Director of the Abbey Theatre. By permission of the Abbey Theatre, Dublin. (Photograph by Dane Campbell Studio, Sidney, British Columbia) *Page 311*

Molly Allgood, about 1908. Courtesy of the National Library of Ireland. (Photograph by Dane Campbell Studio, Sidney, British Columbia) *Page 312*

John M. Synge, from the painting by John Butler Yeats, 1908. By permission of the Municipal Gallery of Modern Art, Dublin. (Photograph by Dane Campbell Studio, Sidney, British Columbia) *Page 312*

Maire O'Neill as Deirdre of the Sorrows, 1910. Courtesy of the National Library of Ireland. *Page 319*

Map

County Wicklow. Drawn by Samuel H. Bryant *Page 5*

*"Little Heart you dont know how much feeling I have for you. You
are like my child, and my little wife, and my good angel, and my
greatest friend, all in one! I dont believe there has been a woman
in Ireland loved the way I love you for a thousand years."*

(Synge to Molly, 4 December 1907)

Introduction

For Molly Allgood, who as "Maire O'Neill" became one of the leading actresses of Dublin's Abbey Theatre, John Millington Synge created two of his most famous characters and wrote some of his most moving poetry. Because of her he became estranged from his family and frequently risked the displeasure of his powerful colleagues, W. B. Yeats and Lady Gregory. Yet despite the fact that their engagement was public knowledge, there are no references to it in the early biographies and memoirs, and even when Yeats finally published extracts from a diary written at the time of Synge's death, Molly is mentioned mainly as an obliging provider of "pre-visions." Synge's older brother restricts himself to discreet references to a photograph; and his closest friend, Stephen MacKenna, who with his wife frequently entertained both Synge and Molly in their home, protects him to the extent of removing with the scissors all references in letters to marriage plans.[1] Not, in fact, until David Greene and Edward Stephens published their biography in 1959 could we grasp the significance of this alliance to Synge's development as man and artist, and the insight it offers into the politics and problems of the Abbey Theatre.[2] But even this biography makes use of only a small percentage of the letters, and so here for the first time we are privileged to observe the whole man.

It is possible that the letters collected here, spanning the entire period of their relationship and reflecting all its moods and turbulence, are the only ones still in existence. A large number of them were purchased from Molly herself by Edward Stephens, Synge's nephew, for safekeeping; the last small bundle recently unearthed included a copy of Synge's will and an envelope containing a lock of his hair, cut by Molly at his deathbed. But except for a few hasty lines, or the occasional angry word scrawled on the bottom of Synge's letters to her, Molly's responses do not survive. Always protective, he apparently destroyed them before entering Elpis Nursing Home for the last time.

1. See W. B. Yeats, *The Death of Synge: Extracts from a Diary Kept in 1909* (Dublin: Cuala Press, 1928); Rev. Samuel Synge, *Letters to My Daughter: Memories of John Millington Synge* (Dublin and Cork: Talbot Press, 1931); "Synge to MacKenna: The Mature Years," ed. Ann Saddlemyer, *Irish Renaissance*, eds. David Clark and Robin Skelton (Dublin: Dolmen Press, 1966), pp. 65–79.
2. David H. Greene and Edward M. Stephens, *J. M. Synge: 1871–1909* (New York: Macmillan, 1959).

It is a devastating comment on the mores of the age that Synge should have had to write so many letters in the first place. But he was a theatre director and she was only a member of the company; her first walk-on part was in *The Well of the Saints,* the first play with which Synge was actively concerned in production, and it was not until she created the part of Pegeen Mike in *The Playboy of the Western World* that she became a serious rival to her sister, Sara Allgood. Furthermore, it is evident that Lady Gregory and Yeats disapproved of fraternization; it could and did lead to serious disruption and confusion of responsibilities. Nor could their backgrounds have been more different: Synge, the son of a barrister and landowner, descendant of bishops and academics, graduate of Trinity College Dublin, a cosmopolitan who could read six languages and for many years spent half of his time in Paris; Molly on the other hand the product of a mixed marriage, both in race and religion, daughter of lower middle class turned working class, her education consigned to the cursory attentions of an orphanage and supplemented by the nationalist fervor of the period. The differences culminate in one of age: when they first fell in love, Synge was thirty-five, Molly was nineteen.

What did they have in common? What he made them share—their art, his natural world, his experiences, and an intensity of emotion heightened on her part by the excitement of life and on his by an obsession with sickness and death. One of the earliest poems addressed to her, probably late in 1906, indicates his keen awareness of the bitter-sweetness of their love:

> To you Bride, Nora, Kathleen, Molly Byrne,
> I of my age have brought the pride and power,
> And seen my hardness in your sweetness turn
> A new delight for our long fame a dower
>
> And now you bring to me your young girl's pride,
> And sweeten with your sweetness all my days,
> Telling me dreams where our red lips have cried
> The long low cry that folds all earthly praise.
>
> And so in all our lot we hold a mart,
> Of your young joy and my too gloomy art.[3]

3. Quoted by Elizabeth Coxhead in *Daughters of Erin* (London: Secker and Warburg, 1965), p. 186.

Synge had been in love before. Just as he was to capture the brilliance and poignancy of his love for Molly in the lyricism of *Deirdre of the Sorrows* and draw the spectrum of love and jealousy reflected in his letters in the characters of Conchubor, Naisi, and Owen, so too he preserved the frustrations of his early love for Cherrie Matheson in his first play, *When the Moon Has Set.* Cherrie too had accompanied him to art galleries and listened to him talk about art and poetry; she once joined Synge and his mother for a holiday in County Wicklow. But, unlike Molly, she could not accept their religious differences—she and her family were Plymouth Brethren; he was a nonbeliever—and refused his proposals of marriage (one made on his behalf by his mother), eventually marrying a teacher of the same faith who took her to South Africa.[4] Hurt and angry, Synge had the last raw word in *When the Moon Has Set,* where Sister Eileen (of an undetermined religious order) is swayed by the lengthy arguments of her earnest nature-worshipping cousin, Colm Sweeny (recently returned to Ireland from Paris), to exchange her religious vows for an emancipation "more exquisite than any that is possible for men who are redeemed by logic." The play ends with a symbolic marriage rite later echoed in the first act of *Deirdre of the Sorrows:*

> "I, the male power, have overcome with worship you, the soul of credulous feeling, the reader of the saints. From our harmonized discord new notes will rise. In the end we will assimilate with each other, and grow senseless and old. We have incarnated God, and been a part of the world. That is enough. [*He takes her hand.*] In the name of the Summer, and the Sun, and the Whole World, I wed you as my wife. [*He puts the ring on her finger.*]"[5]

After Cherrie's refusal, Synge allowed himself several mild relationships with women he met during his years on the continent, but apart from a brief unrequited infatuation for Margaret Hardon, a young American studying in Paris, epistolary warmth never led to anything more serious than sincere friendship, and passionate out-

---

4. Cherrie published her reminiscences, signed "C. H. H[oughton]" in "John Synge as I Knew Him," *The Irish Statesman,* 5 July 1924, pp. 532 and 534.

5. *J. M. Synge Plays, Book I,* ed. Ann Saddlemyer (London: Oxford University Press, 1968), p. 177; an earlier two-act version of the play contains even more autobiographical references.

bursts seem to have been confined to his notebooks.[6] Valeska von Eiken, youngest of the sisters with whom he boarded when a music student in Germany, remained a close confidante to whom he could turn in the last months of his life; the art historian Hope Rea visited him at least once in Dublin and they corresponded spasmodically. That he could also be a charming conversationalist is proved by the affection with which even the nurses in the Nursing Home regarded him. Many years later Sara Allgood recalled his "beautiful . . . dark grey eyes" and the ease with which the company addressed Synge in preference to the other more dignified directors.[7] Certainly by the time Molly Allgood walked on to the Abbey stage for the first time, Synge was a lonely man almost despairing of ever achieving the ideal love he sought to match the perfection of his artistic yearnings. Here the letters speak for themselves as the love affair traces a pattern from querulous distrust on both sides to the carefree happiness of the summer in Wicklow and, finally, the confident acknowledgment of the last months.

But even before they met, Synge was suffering from the Hodgkin's disease that was to prevent their marriage. Characterized by painless, progressive enlargement of the lymphoid tissue, the disease may not have been identified until a casual examination by Oliver St. John Gogarty in the summer of 1907,[8] although ten years earlier the first apparent manifestation, a large lump on the side of his neck, had been removed by surgery. Similar swellings continued to plague him, but with his strong physical constitution he suffered no pain until the disease entered its final stage with the tumor which began to bother him late in 1907 and which was discovered when the doctors operated four months later. It is obvious, therefore, that the frequent discomfort Synge complains of in his letters to Molly was not merely the result of a highly strung constitution or innate morbidity: that annoying cough, the mysterious recurring fevers which more than once made him suspect tuberculosis, even the dark skin

6. See especially "Vita Vecchia" and "Etude Morbide," *J. M. Synge Prose*, ed. Alan Price (London: Oxford University Press, 1966), pp. 16–36.
7. From an unpublished memoir in the possession of her niece Mrs Morton Hague, Oakland, California.
8. Greene and Stephens, *J. M. Synge*, p. 273n.

pigmentation that partially hid his pallor, are all symptoms of the creeping disease.[9]

Synge was also used to the close attentions of a devoted mother, and his letters to Mrs. Synge reflect the demand for concentrated sympathy he was to expect of Molly. For although travel both in Europe and the west of Ireland had freed him from too much dependence on his mother, since his father's death in 1872 and the ill-health and asthma he suffered as a child he had become accustomed to being the center of attention. Family concern was intensified when at sixteen he renounced any formal religious belief, a few years later seriously considered music as a profession, and finally joined the nationalist literary movement. Mrs. Synge's letters to her other sons reiterate her prayers that "poor Johnnie" may return to the fold, and the Reverend Samuel doubtless spoke for the entire family when he wrote of his brother,

> There is little use in trying to say what if our father had lived might have happened different to what did happen. But I think two things are fairly clear. One is that as your Uncle John grew up and met questions that he did not quite know how to answer, a father's words of advice and instruction would have made a very great difference to him. The other thing is that probably our father would have arranged something for your Uncle John to do besides his favourite reading, something that would not have been too much for him but would have brought in some remuneration at an earlier date than his writings did.[10]

However, despite his nationalist tendencies and the indifference to religion which separated him from the rest of his family, Synge was dependent on their financial backing in order to live in the way that he wished. And except for two brief periods during his last years, Synge made his home with his mother, next door to his sister and her barrister husband; another brother, Edward, whose job as land

---

9. M. M. Wintrobe, "Hodgkin's Disease and Other Conditions Chiefly Affecting Lymph Nodes," *Principles of Internal Medicine*, ed. T. R. Harrison (Toronto: Blakiston, 1950), pp. 1225–1228; references are made to the stages of Synge's illness in Greene and Stephens, *J. M. Synge*, pp. 43, 70, 117–118, 210, 247, 254, 263, 280, 284–289 and 297–299.
10. *Letters to My Daughter*, p. 145.

agent frequently meant the supervision of evictions, lived nearby; and his oldest brother Robert returned from Argentina in time to see Synge die. It is hardly surprising that the family disapproved of his alliance with a young actress who, to make matters worse, was as careless about money as he was.[11]

Molly, too, lived with her widowed mother, but here the similarity ends. Although biographical material on the Allgood family is scant, apparently life with mother, grandmother, and seven brothers and sisters was high-spirited, inclined to play and laughter and patriotic fervor.[12] Molly's mother, Margaret Allgood (c. 1860–1928), née Harold, was of Irish-Danish descent and Roman Catholic; Margaret's parents had run a second-hand furniture shop on the Liffey quays, and it was Margaret's mother whose maiden name O'Neill was to provide Molly with a stage name and both her actress granddaughters with an ideal model for character parts. George Allgood (c. 1855–1894), a printing compositor, was a dour Orangeman whose insistence that his children have a Protestant upbringing was countered by his wife's equal determination not to deprive them of their Roman Catholic heritage. Their oldest child Margaret (1879–1959) married early and became Molly's refuge during the long struggle to have her engagement acknowledged; later, after separating from her husband, Peggy moved to London and became active in the suffragette movement. However, Peggy's lasting memorial remains Synge's spirited prayer for vengeance against "the sister . . . who disapproved of 'The Playboy,'"[13] and in later years Molly and Sally casually disclaimed any close connection to Peggy by introducing her at their London parties merely as "Mrs Callender." Sally (1883–1950) and George were followed by Molly (1887–1952) and Harry; despite their early Sinn Feinism, both brothers were killed while fighting for the British in 1915. Of the three youngest, Tom became a Trappist monk, while Johanna (Annie) and Willie led quiet lives as civil servants in Dublin. In this lively, quarrelsome household, Molly was considered gifted, lazy, and "wild." After her father's death she was placed in a Protestant orphanage, but soon ran

11. See Greene and Stephens, *J. M. Synge*, p. 284, and passim; also below pp. 77, 108.
12. I am indebted to Elizabeth Coxhead's chapter on Sally and Molly in *Daughters of Erin* and to Mrs Morton Hague, Peggy Callender's daughter, for biographical information.
13. See below, pp. 116, 118.

away, was then apprenticed to a dressmaker, eventually worked in a shop, and finally, closely chaperoned by her grandmother, joined her older sister in the Abbey Theatre company in 1905.

From the very beginning she made an impression. Early in January 1906 Frank Fay describes her to Lady Gregory as "a very determined young lady"; certainly she was soon promoted from crowd scenes to bit parts, and later that same month took over the role of Cathleen in *Riders to the Sea*. By February it was already apparent that Synge and Molly were strongly attracted to each other; many years later Dossie Wright, Synge's most hated rival, recalled his surprise at discovering the usually reserved Synge sitting with his arm half round her.[14] On 10 March 1906 Synge wrote to Lady Gregory, "I have just performed the delicate operation of getting Sara Allgood out of Nora Burke's part—where she was impossible—and getting Molly Allgood in. Molly A's voice is too young for the part but she feels it, and has some expression."[15] A week later Synge again accompanied the players on a one-night stand, this time to Dundalk, and if his fellow directors had any doubts about the relationship between Synge and Molly these were rapidly dispelled on the lengthy tour of Scotland and northern England in June and July. In her list of complaints against the company in general and Mr. Synge in particular Miss Horniman, the theatre patroness, observed tartly to Yeats, "three months of one girl on his knee doubtless leads him to wish for a change."[16] Privately, Lady Gregory also commented to Yeats, "Synge is evidently quite useless . . . and his behaviour with Molly Allgood must have helped to destroy discipline."[17] This was the last tour Synge took with the company, but by then his engagement, if not yet formally announced, was tactfully taken for granted. In September of that year Synge's American friend Agnes Tobin wrote, "Please give many messages for me to both Mr Fays and to the Miss Allgoods. I shall never forget how beautiful that dear girl looked at dinner with her wreath—it was something to burn candles before."[18]

14. From an unpublished note by E. M. Stephens in possession of Mrs Lily Stephens.
15. Quoted in *J. M. Synge Plays, Book One*, p. xx.
16. Gerard Fay, *The Abbey Theatre Cradle of Genius* (Dublin: Clonmore and Reynolds, 1958), p. 107; the letter was written 17 July 1906.
17. From a letter in the Berg Collection, New York Public Library, July 1906.
18. Letter in the possession of Trinity College Dublin.

But by then, too, the letters—and the quarrels—had begun in earnest. A fragment scrawled on a scrap of paper and brusquely signed "J.M.S." echoes the tenor of their correspondence during that first year, as the two proud lovers struggled toward an understanding: "I was awake nearly all night—you know why—and I am not good for much today. Is that the way you are going to comfort me and help me in my work?"[19] It also becomes obvious that by the end of 1906 the marriage, and perhaps even a date for it, was agreed upon; Synge's letters from his cousin Edward's house in Surrey speak of making the dreaded revelation to his own mother and perhaps dropping in on Molly's "unbeknownsted." But there is no reference to an actual confrontation with Molly's family (other than the gradual winning-over of Sally), and again and again frenzied plans for the wedding are followed by silence. Why the delay? One can only surmise: Synge's uneasy health, or Mrs. Allgood's intractable refusal to give consent (Molly's move to the Callenders' seems to have been because of rows at home over Synge), or their continual penury. There were at least three postponements in 1907, the most puzzling in December. In the spring of 1908 arrangements seem to have been made, and Synge actually took rooms in Rathmines in order to qualify for the Registrar's Licence, but plans were once again deferred when he entered Elpis Nursing Home at the end of April. By the middle of 1908 the letters cease to mention any immediate prospect of marriage, and Synge's form of address may unconsciously indicate resignation as "Dearest Changeling" alternates with "My dearest child." When marriage is mentioned again it is in the shadow of death, and uppermost in his mind is the material care he can now promise Molly, no matter what might befall them.

It is always unwise, however intriguing, to speculate about what might have been. But it is obvious, with the extent of the correspondence before us (one-sided as it is), that it would be unfair to underestimate the positive qualities of their relationship and the strength Molly's love provided. For not only did she inspire two of his finest plays, but her outgoing personality, her love of life, even her scatter-brained, impulsive ways were the qualities Synge took most delight

19. This undated fragment is in the possession of Trinity College Dublin.

in. Yet he constantly demanded that this contrary, charming creature whose emotional outbursts equaled, sometimes surpassed, his own, play Galatea to his Pygmalion. Molly's activities, choice of friends, dress, reading, in fact her whole style of life, are subject to the closest scrutiny and bluntest comment. Again and again the letters echo the ideal which forced him to polish and re-write his plays:

> I hate to preach at you, or schoolmaster you,—I like you so perfectly as you are—but you must know, that it will make life richer for both of us if you know literature and the arts, the things that are of most interest to me and my few personal friends, that you'll know one of these days.

It could not have been easy for a young girl, no matter how engrossed in her first love, to satisfy such obsession with perfection. When one considers in addition the vast difference in artistic temperament, the endurance of their relationship is even more impressive: Synge, the self-conscious, introspective craftsman whose sense of irony pervades and often shapes even his most tender love letters; Molly the instinctive, sometimes careless, nearly always impatient, frequently brilliant mimic. And both admitted to violent fits of temper.

If Synge's pet name for Molly, "Dearest Changeling," reflects her mercurial nature as well as her art, his own signature is equally revealing. First use of the "old Tramp" follows naturally from their private rehearsals of *The Shadow of the Glen* early in 1906, but the image of the wandering vagabond is a significant symbol in both his art and his life. The playboy, tinker, and vagrant of his plays seek the richness of a life beyond the narrow horizon; the Tramp and beggar sing sweetly of nature's wildness and grandeur, delighting equally in the cry of the heron and the south wind of the glens. The vagabond of Synge's essays is also in tune with Nature, but, equally significant, he is frequently the gifted younger son whose prospects are not of this world. It is not surprising therefore that the happiest moments Synge and Molly shared were in his beloved Wicklow hills, strolling along deserted country roads, lying in the heath eating *fraughans* (Molly's "little purple grapes"), sauntering down under the stars into Kilmacanogue or Enniskerry, taking tea in country cottages. The summer of 1907 offered still greater luxury, several weeks (staying for

propriety's sake in separate cottages) in Glencree, where with not a
house or cabin for the full twenty-four miles of wandering road
between Laragh and Loch Bray, they could be themselves with neither
director, player, mother, sister, nor time itself to mar their joy. Not
until the last months of his life, when he wandered moodily through
the woods of Coblenz, would Synge again capture the lush growth he
celebrates in Deirdre's lament.

After so much illness, so many disappointments and fears, the end
came surprisingly quickly. On 22 February 1909 Molly returned from
a week's performances in Manchester to realize for the first time that
Synge was dying. (Ironically too, for the first time, the Synge family
opened its ranks, for during Molly's absence Synge's sister kept her informed of his condition.) On 23 March, Yeats wrote to Lady Gregory, "I
have just met M. in the street and I saw by her face that she had bad
news. She told me that Synge is now so weak that he cannot raise himself on his arm in bed and at night he can only sleep with the help of
drugs. For some days he has been too weak to read. He cannot read
even his letters. They have moved him to another room that he may
see the mountains from his bed."[20] The next day he was dead.

"Poor Molly is going through her work as always. Perhaps that is
best for her," Yeats confided to his diary. True to her promise, she
did not attend the funeral.[21] But less than a week later she appeared
in two plays by newcomers to the theatre, Lennox Robinson and
Norreys Connell, and in August that year had the satisfaction of
reducing Bernard Shaw to tears over his own creation, "The Woman,"
in *The Shewing-up of Blanco Posnet*. Finally, on 13 January 1910, she
appeared as Synge's Deirdre; not only did she help direct the play,
but she worked with Yeats and Lady Gregory to assemble the thousands of typescript pages into some kind of manageable draft. Her
name continued to appear regularly on Abbey Theatre programs until
1911, but by then she had enchanted another brilliant, highly strung
young writer, the *Manchester Guardian* critic, G. H. Mair. Lady Gregory
reported to Yeats in November 1910, "I took Miss O'Neill to the
dressing room today and asked about her engagement. She says it is
true 'in a way'. I asked what way. She said she has allowed Mair to

---

20. Letter in the Berg Collection, New York Public Library.
21. See "A Question" and the letter below, 2 October 1908, p. 283.

be engaged to her, at the same time that she is not engaged to him!"[22]
The marriage, which took place in June 1911, was a happy one and
produced two children, Pegeen (Mary Marguerita) and John Dunbar.
Molly returned to the Abbey occasionally, but spent more time in
provincial repertory and on the London stage. Finally, in 1913, she
made her first trip to America, playing in George Birmingham's
General John Regan.

Molly's strength as an actress continued to grow. In 1917 Yeats
wrote to Lady Gregory from London: "Miss O'Neill gave a wonderful
performance yesterday of the old woman in *Tinker's Wedding,* most
poetical, and distinguished and yet such an old drunken good for
nothing."[23] Two years later, when seeking a Decima for his *Player
Queen,* Yeats commented, "Miss O'Neill is an exquisite actress in
dialect. I have never yet seen her equally good out of it. In dialect
she is the one poetical actress our movement has produced."[24] But
the frenzied social life of London was too much for her; she took to
drinking heavily, and her personal life grew even more chaotic and
tempestuous. Mair died in 1926, after a long illness, and six months
later Molly married her old Abbey Theatre colleague, Arthur Sinclair ("Mac"). Together with Sara Allgood they toured America in
Juno and the Paycock and *The Plough and the Stars;* eventually, however, quarrels led to a separation and Molly was once again alone.
Her son, himself a talented writer, was killed while training with the
R.A.F. in 1942. After touring briefly with her mother, Pegeen aban-
doned the stage to become a script writer. Molly continued to live
mainly in London, constantly on the edge of poverty, but often at work
in stage, film, or radio, and always with the keen zest for life that had
attracted Synge to her so many years before. She died 2 November 1952
after collapsing while rehearsing for a radio version of *The Silver
Tassie.*

Although Molly has been dead for almost twenty years, and
Synge for over sixty, one cannot help but feel distress at the violation

22. Letter in the Berg Collection, New York Public Library.
23. Letter dated 22 January 1917 in the Berg Collection, New York Public Library;
see Lennox Robinson, *Ireland's Abbey Theatre* (London: Sidgwick and Jackson, 1951),
pp. 191–192 for another description of Molly's acting.
24. Letter to W. S. Kennedy, 21 January 1919, quoted in *The Letters of W. B. Yeats,*
ed. Allan Wade (New York: Macmillan, 1955), p. 654.

of his most secret self through the publication of these letters. But Fanny Brawne's admission to Keats's first biographer holds even more truth today, "If his life is to be published no part ought to be kept. back."[25] And it is easy enough to take advantage of Molly's pride and generosity of spirit to assume her approval—she who admitted shortly before her own death, "To me he was everything, in his work and personality. Today he still remains the same to me."[26]

*   *   *

Of the four hundred-odd letters in this volume, only one is typed; the others were written by hand in pencil or ink on any paper available. In order to preserve as much of the flavor and immediacy of Synge's letters as possible, I have transcribed grammatical errors, dashes, marginalia and all. Although Synge was a careless and emotional writer, there are few spelling errors (the most significant being his chronic inability to spell "changeling" correctly); where misspellings might lead to false identification, proper names have, however, been silently corrected. Nothing has been deleted, and, where possible, words struck out by Synge himself have been deciphered and inserted in angle brackets. Since many of the earlier letters are undated, a certain amount of inspired guesswork has been necessary, and this is indicated by a question mark; fortunately the letters occur so frequently that there are usually enough cross-references to help place them in order. Occasionally separate parts of one letter turned up in different collections, and this too is indicated in square brackets. Apart from the Greene and Stephens biography of Synge, an invaluable reference has been the daily chronicle of the Abbey Theatre itself, faithfully and minutely recorded by the theatre architect, Joseph Holloway. Without the aid of "Impressions of a Dublin Playgoer" many letters and more references would have remained enigmatic.[27]

25. Quoted in *The Letters of John Keats,* ed. Maurice Buxton Forman, 4th ed. (London: Oxford University Press, 1952), p. lxiii.

26. Sean O'Mahony Rahilly, "Synge and the Early Days of the Abbey," *The Irish Press,* 21 April 1949.

27. The almost indecipherable 221 volumes, preserved in the National Library of Ireland, have recently been edited by Robert Hogan and Michael J. O'Neill. Their first selection, *Joseph Holloway's Abbey Theatre* (Carbondale and Edwardsville: Southern Illinois University Press, 1967) has been followed by *Joseph Holloway's Irish Theatre,* vols. I–III (Dixon, California: Proscenium Press, 1968–1970).

Acknowledgments

The collection and publication of these letters has been made possible only by the cooperation and encouragement of a great many people. Mrs. Lily Stephens first suggested the task and provided the bulk of the letters as well as much background material. Miss Edith Synge solved many obscure family references and together with her brother John Samuel Synge granted permission to quote from their father's memoirs, *Letters to My Daughter*. Miss Pegeen Mair offered helpful advice concerning her mother's biography, and Mrs. Morton Hague, Molly's niece, provided further details of family history. The late Mrs. W. B. Yeats was a constant source of advice and encouragement; Miss Anne Yeats and Senator Michael Yeats granted permission to quote from their father's writings. Professor David H. Greene allowed me to use the material he had already quoted in *J. M. Synge 1871–1909;* Miss Elizabeth Coxhead offered advice, encouragement, and permission to quote from material published in *Daughters of Erin*. Major Richard Gregory discovered further new material and granted permission to quote from Lady Gregory's unpublished letters. Miss Christine Hayden offered valuable memories of acting with Molly; Professor D. J. Gordon provided the unpublished drawing of Synge by J. B. Yeats.

I wish to record my thanks also to the following people for their help in countless ways: Dr. William Benzie, Miss Sharon Brown, Dr. and Mrs. Andrew Carpenter, Dr. Joan Coldwell, Mr. Padraic Colum, Mr. Alan Denson, Mr. Gabriel Fallon and the directors of the Abbey Theatre, Mrs. Anthony Farrington, Mrs. Mary Hirth, Dr. Robert Hogan, Dr. A. J. Hutchison, Dr. Anthony Jenkins, Mrs. A. LeBrocquy, Professor A. J. McClean, Mr. Alf MacLochlainn, Mr. Niall Montgomery, Miss Hilary Pyle, Dr. Gordon Ray, Miss Georgiana Remer, Dr. Lola Szladits, Dr. Manfred Triesch, Miss Ethna Waldron, Mrs. A. Whitfield.

Letters reproduced are in the possession of Trinity College Dublin, the Academic Center Library of the University of Texas, and the National Library of Ireland; I appreciate the willing cooperation of all three institutions. Permission to quote has also been granted by the Henry W. and Albert A. Berg Collection of the New York Public Library, Astor, Lenox and Tilden Foundations.

Work was first begun on this edition while I was a John Simon Guggenheim Memorial Foundation Fellow and it was completed with the aid of a Canada Council Fellowship. I am grateful to both foundations as well as to the University of Victoria.

I am pleased also to have this opportunity to record my appreciation of the cooperation and courtesy of the staff of the McPherson Library of the University of Victoria, especially the Reference and Special Collections Divisions.

A. S.

University of Victoria
Victoria, B.C., Canada

Chronicle of Events

1904

27 December	opening of the Abbey Theatre with first performances of *On Baile's Strand* (Yeats) and *Spreading the News* (Lady Gregory)

1905

4 February	first performance of *The Well of the Saints* (Synge); Molly Allgood's first walk-on part
15 February	Synge moves from rooms in Rathgar to his mother's home, 31 Crosthwaite Park, Kingstown
25 March	first performance of *Kincora* (Lady Gregory)
25 April	first performance of *The Building Fund* (William Boyle)
4–11 May	Synge on fishing trip in Donegal with his brother Robert
3 June–3 July	Synge and Jack B. Yeats tour the Congested Districts for *Manchester Guardian*
9 June	first performance of *The Land* (Padraic Colum)
2? August–16 September	Synge visits Kerry and the Blasket Islands
16 September	Synge attends a policy meeting at Coole with Yeats and Lady Gregory
22 September	Irish National Theatre Society becomes a limited company with W. B. Yeats, Lady Gregory and Synge as Directors, W. G. Fay as Stage Manager and Frank J. Fay as Secretary; seven players resign in protest
23–30 November	company on tour to Oxford, Cambridge, and London
9 December	first performance of *The White Cockade* (Lady Gregory)

1906

12 January	Max Meyerfeld's translation of *The Well of the Saints* performed in Berlin

[1906]

20 January	first performance of *The Eloquent Dempsey* (Boyle); Molly takes over role of Cathleen in *Riders to the Sea*
6 February	Synge takes rooms at 57 Rathgar Road
7 February	Karel Musek's translation of *The Shadow of the Glen* performed in Prague
19 February	first performance of *Hyacinth Halvey* (Gregory)
26–27 February	Synge accompanies players to Wexford
10 March	Molly takes over role of Nora Burke in *The Shadow of the Glen*
17 March	Synge accompanies players to Dundalk
16 April	first performance of *The Doctor in Spite of Himself* (Molière-Gregory)
23–30 April	company on tour to Manchester, Liverpool, and Leeds
15 May	company plays in Dundalk
26 May	seceders found The Theatre of Ireland with Edward Martyn as President, and Padraic Colum, Thomas Keohler, George Nesbitt, Dermot Trench, James Cousins, Helen Laird, Padraic Pearse, and Thomas Kettle on board of directors
26 May–9 July	Synge accompanies players on tour (managed by Alfred Wareing) to Cardiff, Glasgow, Aberdeen, Newcastle, Edinburgh, and Hull
9 July	Synge moves with his mother to her new home Glendalough House, Glenageary, Kingstown
12 July	company plays in Longford; Molly stops off in Balbriggan on her way back
17–18 July	Synge joins Yeats, Lady Gregory, and Willie Fay for policy meeting at Coole
24 July	Karel Musek arrives for a two-week visit to Ireland
25 August– 12 September	Synge in County Kerry
mid-September	company plays in Galway
1 October	W. A. Henderson takes up duties as Abbey Theatre Secretary
13 October	Abbey Theatre "At Home"

20 October	first performances of *The Gaol Gate* (Gregory) and *The Mineral Workers* (Boyle)
29 October	W. G. Fay and Brigit O'Dempsey are married in Glasgow
22 November	Molly visits Synge at Glendalough House for the first time
24 November	first performance of *Deirdre* (Yeats) with Miss Darragh in title role
30 November–14 December	Synge visits his cousin Edward Synge in Surrey
1 December	Abbey Theatre institutes Saturday matinées
8 December	first performance of *The Canavans* (Gregory) and revised version of *The Shadowy Waters* (Yeats) with Miss Darragh in title role

1907

4 January	rehearsals for *The Playboy of the Western World* begin
26 January	first performance of *The Playboy*, disturbances in audience; Boyle and Colum withdraw their plays in protest
28 January	new general manager Ben Iden Payne has arrived but stays for only six months
4 February	*The Playboy* debate, Synge home ill until 11 March
23 February	first performance of *The Jackdaw* (Gregory)
9 March	first performance of *The Rising of the Moon* (Gregory)
16 March	first performance of *Interior* in translation (Maurice Maeterlinck)
1 April	first performance of *The Eyes of the Blind* (Winifred M. Letts) and a revised version of *Deirdre* (Yeats) with Mona Limerick (Mrs. Payne) in title role; J. M. Barrie and Charles Frohman visit the theatre but are unrecognized
3 April	first performance of *The Poorhouse* (Lady Gregory–Douglas Hyde)
27 April	first performance of *Fand* (Wilfrid Scawen Blunt)

[1907]

11 May–17 June	company on tour to Glasgow, Cambridge, Birmingham, Oxford and London
30 May	Synge visits Jack Yeats in Devon
8 June	Synge joins company in London
28 June-28 July	Synge in Glencree, County Wicklow; Molly is with him except for 11–23 July
29 July–10 August	Abbey Theatre open; Henderson resigns as Secretary
11–25 August	company on tour to Waterford, Cork, Kilkenny, and back to Cork
13–26 September	Synge in Elpis Nursing Home for removal of the swollen glands in his neck
3 October	opening of the Abbey Theatre season with first performance of *The Country Dressmaker* (George Fitzmaurice)
11 October	professional matinée at the Abbey for Herbert Beerbohm Tree
12–16 October	Synge visits Kerry but asthma forces him to return to Dublin
25 October	professional matinée at Abbey for Mrs. Patrick Campbell
31 October	first performance of *Dervorgilla* (Gregory)
15 November	professional matinée at Abbey for John Martin Harvey
21 November	first performance of *The Unicorn from the Stars* (Yeats-Gregory)
24 November–15 December	company on tour to Manchester, Glasgow and Edinburgh; trouble flares up between the players and Willie Fay

1908

6–10 January	company on tour to Galway
13 January	W. G. Fay, Frank Fay, Brigit O'Dempsey and Ernest Vaughan resign
2 February	Synge takes rooms at 47 York Road, Rathmines
3 February	Henderson is reinstated at the Abbey as Business Manager

13 February	first performances of *The Man Who Missed the Tide* (W. F. Casey) and *The Piper* (Conal O'Riordan)
19 March	first performances of *The Pie-Dish* (Fitzmaurice), *The Golden Helmet* (Yeats) and *Teja* (Sudermann-Gregory; directed by Synge)
4 April	first performance of *The Rogueries of Scapin* (Molière-Gregory), directed by Synge
20 April	first performance of *The Workhouse Ward* (Gregory)
30 April	Synge enters Elpis Nursing Home for abdominal operation 5 May; is there until 6 July
14 May	first performance of revised version of *The Well of the Saints,* with Molly as Molly Byrne
29 May	first performance by the company of *The Scheming Lieutenant* (R. B. Sheridan)
10–16 June	Molly and Sally visit the Wrights in Balbriggan
6 July	Synge convalesces at his sister's home, Silchester House, Kingstown
3 August	Abbey open for Bank Holiday
13 August	Synge returns to Glendalough House
24–29 August	Abbey open for Horse Show week
3–9 September	Abbey open for British Association Week
16–19 September	company performs in Galway during Exhibition Week
1 October	first performance of *The Suburban Groove* (Casey)
6 October	Synge visits the Von Eicken sisters in Coblenz, Germany
8 October	first performance of *The Clancy Name* (Lennox Robinson)
15 October	first performance of *When the Dawn is Come* (Thomas MacDonagh)
26 October	Synge's mother dies
7 November	Synge returns from Germany
9 November	Mrs. Pat Campbell performs in *Deirdre* (Yeats)
29 November– 5 December	company performs in Belfast

1909

21 January	first performance of *The Miser* (Molière-Gregory)

[1909]

2 February	Synge enters Elpis Nursing Home
14–22 February	company plays in Manchester
11 March	first performance of *Stephen Gray* (D. L. Kelleher)
24 March	Synge dies
1 April	first performances of *The Cross Roads* (Robinson) and *Time* (O'Riordan)

Letters to Molly

Manuscript Locations

NLI   National Library of Ireland (photographic reproduction only)
TCD   Trinity College, Dublin
Texas Academic Center Library, University of Texas
AS   Ann Saddlemyer

Code to Description

encl enclosed with preceding letter
frag incomplete letter
GS   letter referred to in David H. Greene and Edward M. Stephens,
     J. M. Synge 1871–1909 (New York: Macmillan, 1959)
tel   telegram

[*NLI*]   57 Rathgar Road
                                 Saturday [*spring 1906*]

Dear Molly

I am going out tomorrow, so, if it is fine, meet me at ten minutes
past ten at *Harcourt Street.* Dont be late

                                 Yours
                                 J. M. Synge

[*TCD/GS201*]   Glendalough House
                                 Glenageary
                                 Kingstown
                                 (Monday) [*16 July 1906*]

Dear Molly

I saw Frank Fay today and heard from
him that you had come back to Dublin
instead of going to Sligo, and that you had
gone now to Balbriggan[1] for a week. I have
been wondering what had become of you it
seems strange that you would not send me
a line to tell me where you were. If I had
known you were in Dublin I might have
seen you on Saturday. I go down to Lady
Gregory's tomorrow morning for a week[2]
and then come back here to meet the Bohemian who is to arrive on the 24th.[3] I
hope I shall see you then before I set off

again. I hope you are enjoying yourselves, I have been dull enough
these days here.

I was at the Espositos last night they are full of the Trinity Show.[4]
This address will always find me.

                                 Yours ever
                                 J. M. Synge

P.S.   I wonder if this will find you?[5]

1. A small coastal resort 22 miles north of Dublin, where another member of the
company, Dossie Wright (1887–1952) had relatives.

2. Yeats and Lady Gregory had called a Directors' meeting at Coole Park, Gort, to discuss reorganization of the Abbey Theatre company; W. G. Fay went down on the 14th, and Synge joined them on the 17th, but stayed two nights only.

3. Pan Karel Musek, actor and stage manager of the National Theatre in Prague, had translated *The Shadow of the Glen* and *Riders to the Sea* into Bohemian. *The Shadow of the Glen* was produced by "The Bohemian Dramatists Club" at the Inchover Theatre in Prague on 7 February 1906.

4. Signor Michele Esposito (1855–1929), Italian pianist, composer, and teacher, had been professor of pianoforte at the Royal Irish Academy of Music since 1882, and conductor of the Dublin Orchestral Society since its establishment in 1899. His compositions include *Deirdre*, a cantata for solo voices, chorus and orchestra (1897); *The Postbag*, an operetta with libretto by A. P. Graves, produced in London in 1902 by the Irish Literary Society; a string quartet; a sonata for violin and pianoforte; a sonata for cello and pianoforte; an "Irish" Symphony which was awarded the Feis Ceoil prize in 1902; music for Douglas Hyde's *The Tinker and the Fairy* (1910); and an overture for Shakespeare's *Othello*. Madame Esposito translated *Riders to the Sea* into Russian and French, and their daughter Vera acted with the Abbey company under the name "Emma Vernon" until she moved across to the London stage in 1905.

5. Molly has written *Idiotic* across the top of this letter.

[NLI]   Glendalough House
                                                                   Glenageary
                                                                  Kingstown
                                                            July 19th [1906]

Dear Molly

I have come back as I had nothing more to do at Gort when we had once arranged everything. I enclose a fragment of a letter I began to you last Thursday. I got your card this morning forwarded to Lady Gregory's before I left. I asked you not to send me post cards to avoid gossip please dont do so next time. Did you get my other letter. I heard accidentally of your walking arm in arm with Wright at Longford. Is that true? Please let me know when you are coming back to Dublin. The Bohemian comes next Tuesday I believe.

                                                              Yours ever
                                                              J. M. Synge

[AS/encl]   July 12th [1906]
Dear Changling

I suppose you are getting into Longford by now, I've been feeling very lonesome all the morning thinking of you posting away over Ireland without me.[1] I had a lot to say to you yesterday before you went off but I couldn't get an opportunity. It doesn't much matter however as you know all I had to say. The Bohemian man Musek is his name is coming here on Tuesday, and then I suppose I'll go to Lady Gregory's for a while but after that I dont know yet where I'll turn to. I am writing this on the chance of getting your address but I wouldn't be surprised if you've forgotten mine. I've just written five letters so I'll write no more to you now

1. The company frequently played one and two-night stands throughout the south and west of Ireland. See "Chronicle of Events."

[TCD/GS202]

Glendalough House
Glenageary
Kingstown
Thursday night [19 July 1906]

Dear Changling

Why dont you write to me? We have not seen each other for ten days and I've had nothing from you but a few wretched lines on a post card. It makes me imagine all sorts of things when you are so queer and silent. I have a lot of things to tell you about my talks with Lady Gregory and Yeats but I will let that wait. Also the story about Wright which came out at a moment and in a way that was peculiarly painful and humiliating to me. Why—However I did not start this letter to scold you as I'm better again though I have been more distressed about it than I can say.

I think I am going to stay about Dublin for the present and finish my play¹ so I may see a good deal of you this next while, when you come back and the Bohemian goes. When my play is finished I'll go off myself for a while; I think to the Blasquet Islands.

I came up with Fay² yesterday and he, I think, went to Enniscorthy in the evening. He got influenza or something at Gort and was ill for two days. We have arranged the affairs of the company satisfactorily on a new basis and everything is going to be much more regular and orderly than it has been so far. That is our only chance.

Friday morning

I have got your letter at last—and I am much better. I think about you a lot indeed I'm nearly always thinking about you in one way or another, but my thoughts aren't always pleasant ones as Cardiff and other incidents come up in spite of me. I'm glad to hear that you are lonesome its very good for you. I wonder in the end if you will stay out there a week or a fortnight. I thought I heard some of them saying that Lady Gregory was sending Sally[3] the money she had lost. *Dont say* anything about it, of course, unless it comes. I am longing to have a good walk with you again, but of course you should stay on the fortnight if you are able. I shall probably be very busy next week with the Bohemian. Is Wright at Balbriggan too as he met you at the station?

I am sending you one of my photos, not one of the good ones, as one has gone to an Australian paper, and I am giving the other to my nephew to photograph again. I'll give you a better one when I get it. You dont seem to have got the letter I sent to your Dublin address on Tuesday, but it doesn't matter as there was not anything in it. I am afraid the letter I wrote you yesterday wont have made you happier, so I am sending this off early to cheer you up. You see I began it last night as I had begun to relent.

I dont know whether I shall stay here to work at my play, or get lodgings somewhere. It is not very convenient here as I have to walk a quarter of a mile to my sister's for every meal, and one gets tired of it.[4] Now good bye to you and be good and lonesome and write to me again at once if you want another letter as much as I do.

Your old Tramp alias Dan Burke![5]

1. *The Playboy of the Western World,* begun in September 1904.
2. William G. Fay (1872–1947), stage manager and leading actor of the company which grew out of his nationalist group, the Irish Dramatic Company.
3. Molly's older sister Sara Allgood (1883–1950) had been acting with the company since 1903 and was by now the acknowledged leading lady.
4. Mrs. Synge had taken a house in County Wicklow for the summer, where she was joined by her older son Samuel who was home from China with his wife and baby daughter. While his mother was away Synge had his meals at his sister Annie Stephens' home on Silchester Road nearby.
5. The Tramp and Dan Burke were both characters in Synge's play *The Shadow of the Glen* (see Introduction, p. xxi).

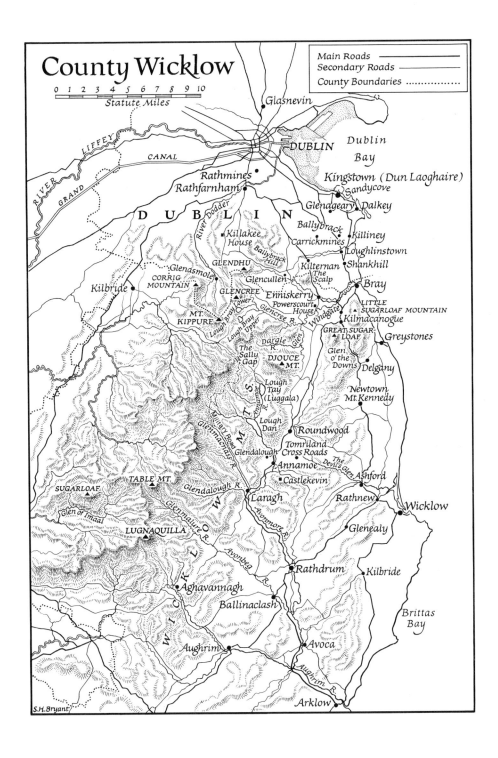

County Wicklow

0 1 2 3 4 5 6 7 8 9 10
Statute Miles

Glasnevin

LIFFEY

CANAL

RIVER

GRAND

DUBLIN

Dublin Bay

Rathmines
Rathfarnham

Kingstown (Dun Laoghaire)
Sandycove

D U B L I N

Glenageary Dalkey

River Dodder

Killakee House

Ballybrack
Carrickmines
Killiney
Loughlinstown

GLENDHU

Ballybrack Hill

Glenasmole
CORRIG MOUNTAIN

GLENCREE

Glencullen

Kilternan
The Scalp

Shankhill

Kilbride

Glencree R.

Enniskerry

Bray

LITTLE SUGARLOAF MOUNTAIN

MT. KIPPURE

Lough Bray Lower
Lough Bray Upper

Powerscourt House

Windgate

Kilmacanogue

Dargle R.

GREAT SUGAR-LOAF

The Sally Gap

Glen

DJOUCE MT.

Greystones

W I C K L O W   M T S

Glen o'the Downs

Delgany

Lough Tay (Luggala)

Newtown Mt.Kennedy

Lough Dan

Roundwood

Glenmacnass R.

Tomriland Cross Roads

Glendalough

The Devil's Glen

Ashford

Annamoe

Castlekevin

Rathnew

SUGARLOAF

TABLE MT.

Glendalough R.

Laragh

Wicklow

Glen of Imaal

Avonmore R.

Glenealy

LUGNAQUILLA

Rathdrum

Kilbride

Avonbeg R.

Brittas Bay

Aghavannagh

Ballinaclash

Avoca

Aughrim

Aughrim R.

Arklow

S.H.Bryant

[AS]
                                              Glendalough House
                                              Glenageary
                                              Kingstown
                                              Friday night [*20 July 1906*]

My dear little Changling

I am writing this to you in my bed at one o'clock as I am not able to sleep and I wont have time to write to you tomorrow as I am going to Wicklow to see my old mother. I got your second letter this evening. It seems to have been a different occasion of walking with Dossy Wright that I heard of—some time when he had B. O'D[1] on one arm and you on the other—so I was more hurt than ever. As for your excuse you are as well able to keep on your feet as any one I know, and even if you weren't a sprained ankle is a trifle compared with what you have made me suffer. Why I have felt the whole thing so much is of course, that it seems as if you have been doing all the little things you know I cannot bear as soon as ever you get away out of my sight. Dont you want me to have full trust in you, changling? Dont you know that a suspicious love is more degrading than ennobling? and yet everytime just as I am beginning to trust you fully—I always trust you in one sense—you do some foolish thing that upsets everything again. However let us drop the matter for the present. We are fond enough of each other, I am sure, to get these things right by degrees. I had a long ride today up by the lower end of Glen Cullen and Kilternan (where we once walked from Carrickmines). It was a very beautiful day here with a wonderful lustre in the sky and a clear blue sea. I read your little letter up there in the hills and I felt overjoyed that I have got you. I have had a lot of trouble and lonesomeness in my life, changling, and for God's sake dont disappoint me now. Perhaps you think I am too strict, but it is really only a little outer dignity and loyalty that I ask you for beyond what I have got already. These little loyalties are not unimportant as they are a part of the courtesy and therefore of the comeliness of love, and unless love is kept courteous and comely it loses its 'humaness' and cannot be trusted to last through life. Polished wood wont rot, and it is the same with polished love. Surfaces are not important in themselves but if the surface goes the heart rots—

This is d—ly philosophical but it's a roundabout way of saying you must see Dossie hanged before you take his arm again. Dont imagine that I'm trying to copy your handwriting, but I've a cramp in my back and my hip's asleep on me from writing sideways with my paper on my pillow. By the way dont think that I signed myself 'yours *etc.*', mine was 'yours *ever*', a very different story!

The cocks are crowing themselves hoarse under my window so I'd best ring down the curtain and have a sleep

Believe me
my worthy changling
Yours fervently
J. M. S.

Is that any better?
P.S. Saturday morning. I am to meet Musek the Bohemian on Tuesday at 12 o'clock so I dont know yet when we'll be able to meet. I need not say it will be as soon as I can manage it. I hope you got my letter and photo all right.

J. M. S.

1. Brigit O'Dempsey had recently joined the company.

[*Texas/GS204*]

Glendalough House
Glenageary
Kingstown
Tuesday [*24 July 1906*]

Dear Molly

Will you and Sally come to the Abbey about 4.30 on Thursday to meet Karel Musek the Bohemian. I am going to ask F. Fay and Darley[1] to come in too. He wants to hear the keen and see some of our Aran dresses etc.

He brought me a most flattering letter from his director calling me chèr maître—(dear Master) and telling me he is going to put on the 'Shadow' next winter in their regular repertoire at the *National Theatre* —which will mean royalties! Musek himself is going to do Micheal Dara. They have £12,000 from the government to play with and all scenery and light, so they can afford to do things well!

Could you and Sally bring in means of making tea and cakes *at my expense* on Thursday? If its a bother dont mind and we'll let him starve, if it isn't perhaps you might tell Mrs Martin[2] we're coming. So that she may have clean cups!

I hope you weren't too tired after your walk, and that you got home safe. We had a great day!

Yours ever
J. M. Synge

1. Frank J. Fay (1870–1931), with his brother Willie was responsible for the formation of the company and was at that time one of the principal players and the verse-teacher. Arthur Darley (1873–1929) was theatre violinist until the autumn of 1906 when a small orchestra took over under the direction of G. R. Hillis. Darley, a collector of traditional Irish airs, had studied at the Royal Irish Academy of Music with Synge, where they had both belonged to the student orchestra.

2. Mrs Catherine Martin acted as Abbey Theatre caretaker from its opening in December 1904. Her reminiscences were published in *Ireland's Abbey Theatre: A History* compiled by Lennox Robinson (London: Sidgwick and Jackson Ltd., 1951), pp. 67–69.

[*TCD/GS205*]

Glendalough House
Glenageary
Kingstown
July 27th [*1906*]

Dear Molly

Saturday and Sunday are bad days for the country now so I think we wont go out till Monday or Tuesday. I'll write you a line again to fix the time. Please let me know what I owe for the tea, it was very nice. I liked your dress very much, but I'm not quite sure of the hat. It is very smart and becomes you, but I'm inclined to think it is just a shade too fly-away. I'll make up my mind when I see it again. I wish you'd write me a line to keep me going till we meet. I'm trying to work but I'm unsettled and I'm not making way with anything. If I dont make way next week I'll go off to the west maybe and rest myself. I must go sooner or later so it would be as well to get it over.

Did you get my last letter to Balbriggan?

Your old Tramp

[*TCD*]   Glendalough House
                                            Glenageary
                                   Saturday [*28 July 1906*]

Dear Molly
    I meant that Sunday and Saturdays were bad for our outings
because of the crowds in trains and in the glens. However I am longing so to have a walk with you that we will go in spite of them tomorrow *Sunday*. Come down from Westland Row to Bray by the train that
goes from W. Row at a *quarter to 12* (taking a return ticket to Bray) and
I'll join you in the train at Sandycove or Glenageary. That is if it is
fine of course. I hope you will get this in time, I suppose you will. I
dont think my letter to Balbriggan was very business like, yesterday
evening I nearly died of 'lonesomeness' so I am as badly off as you are.
                                   Yours ever and always
                                          The Tramp
P.S.   I am not sure whether you will get this letter so I will not wait
for you in Bray, so dont miss your train. I enclose 3/0 two for the tea
and one for your train, J. M. S.

[*TCD*]   [Glendalough House]
                                   Tuesday [*31 July 1906*]

Dear Molly
    I have only a moment to write a business line.
    Will you and Sally please meet me tomorrow at the Abbey between
3 o'clock and half-past to go through the clothes. I have asked Colum
to come at 4 o'clock, but it would be best if you would come earlier
so that we could sort the things out first. I have got a list from Lady
Gregory of the things she paid for so it will not be difficult.[1]
    I believe Musek comes back on Wednesday; I suppose in the eve-
ning. I am afraid I'll be with him on Thursday, but when he goes
we'll have a long day in the country.
                                   Yours lonesomely
                                          J. M. S.
If you cant come tomorrow please send me a card tonight to say so, if
possible. J. M. S.

1. Those members who had seceded when the company was reorganized in September 1905 as a limited company and with Miss Horniman's subsidy became professional, had formed a new dramatic society, The Theatre of Ireland, in May 1906 with Edward Martyn (1859–1923) as President and Padraic Colum (b.1881) as Secretary. The Abbey Directors granted the seceders £50 from the theatre funds and all the peasant costumes made by the original company with the exception of those paid for by Yeats and Lady Gregory. Maire Nic Shiubhlaigh describes the secession and the fortunes of the Theatre of Ireland in *The Splendid Years* (Dublin: Duffy, 1955).

[*TCD/GS205*]   Glendalough House
                                                 Friday [*3 August 1906*]

My dear Changling
     I was with Musek all day today and I am to see him again *tomorrow (Saturday)* so I cant go to walk with you. However my cousin[1] is not coming down till Monday so I can go on *Sunday if it is fine*. Will you come down by the *quarter to* ELEVEN from Westland Row? I will join you like last time at Glenageary or Sandycove, and if you are not in the train I will take it for granted that you are not coming. It is better to get off an hour earlier as I must be home a little earlier in the evening. You can send me a line if you feel disposed to say if you are coming, and anything nice that you can think of. I'm fagged out with my efforts to amuse Musek all day, he goes away tomorrow evening. I like him very much but it is hard to talk to him continually as his English is so uncertain.

                                                 Your old Tramp
                                                 J. M. S.

1. Probably his childhood friend Florence Ross (1870–1949), daughter of Mrs Synge's sister and a frequent visitor to Glendalough House. See Synge's *Autobiography, Collected Works: Prose*, ed. Alan Price (Oxford University Press, 1966), pp. 6–9.

[*TCD/GS206*]   Glendalough House
                                                 Tuesday night [*7 August 1906*]

Dear Changling
     I have just got your little note. I waited about in my sister's garden till it was near the post hour, sitting on a dark seat by myself under a

chestnut-tree and feeling very lonesome. My sister was going about with her husband watering their flowers, and the nephews were doing other things and I wanted my changling to keep me company and to cheer me up. Then I came home here and presently the post came. Changling do you think I can live on 'little purple grapes'?[1] If you want to write such little notes I must have them by the *half dozen* at least. What are those few lines for a very starving man? I wanted to hear how you got home, and how you supped, and how everybody's temper is, and what you did yesterday, and what you read or didn't read, and God knows what, and yet you're too lazy to tell me! What there was, was very tasty so I wont scold you this time, but the next time I want a good fat letter with talk in it, that I can chew the cud with at my ease. I haven't taken any steps yet about going away, so I dont know when it'll come off. I have been hammering away at my play till I am dizzy but it is too hot and I am not doing much good. My brother[2] is to be here tomorrow morning I believe, I am rather amused at the prospect of our talk, I dont mind him a bit.

Wednesday

My brother has been here but it was something else he wanted to talk about that hadn't any thing to do with you. I will write and tell him some day I think. I did not get a good opportunity or I would have told him today. You know I am longing to see you but I do not know if we could manage it tomorrow. My cousin has put off her coming home till tonight—so I may have to attend her tomorrow it is a nuisance. I'm half afraid we wont meet till Sunday, or shall we take Saturday instead?

If you will write me more I'll write you more; at present you dont deserve it. You'll hear from me again very soon in any case about our walk. I'm sorry to write to scrappily but I mean a great deal more than I find the right moment to say.

Yours always
The Tramp

P.S.   Write to me again tomorrow please. *Dont forget.*

1. Molly's term for the *fraughans*, small blue berries that grow among the heather.
2. Probably Samuel Synge (1869–1951), who published *Letters to My Daughter: Memories of John Millington Synge* (Dublin:Talbot Press, 1932).

[*TCD/GS206*]   Glendalough House
                                               Glenageary
                                         Friday 10th [*August 1906*]

My dear Changling

  I have been looking out all day for a letter from you but none has
come. The last post hasn't passed yet so one may come still. I have
missed you this week somehow more than ever before but I have kept
valiantly to my work and I have got through a great deal. It is wonderful how the play begins to grow in one's mind when one gives one's
whole time to it, after a few days of misery the ideas begin suddenly
to come of themselves and then all is plain sailing. Why didn't you
write to me yesterday? I meant to write you a nice letter this evening
that would please you, but my head is too tired. I wish to Heaven this
play was finished. Now it's nine o'clock so I'll stop a moment to see
is a letter is coming, if it comes at all it will be here soon _____

No letter, I'm curiously disappointed I made sure you would acknowledge the book I sent you yesterday, but may be it has not reached
you.

  Will you come down by *the quarter to eleven* train *from Westland
Row on Sunday* and let us have a good walk. I will join you as before.
Come unless it is really wet as I suppose it will be our last chance
before I go away Send me a line if you can

                                                Yours ever
                                                  The Tramp

I dont know why you will not write to me, it is very strange

[*Texas*]   Glendalough House
                                         Wednesday [*15 August 1906*]

Dear Changling

  I was very glad to get your note yesterday, but I have not had time
to write to you and even now I am in a hurry.

  I understand that I am to go to tea with you tomorrow (Thursday)
at 4 o'clock. If anything has turned up to keep you busy at that time
send me a line—*posted early*—or a wire, please, to put me off. I am
not going away this week so I hope we may have another walk next
Sunday. We might go up Big Sugar Loaf perhaps.

I had F. J. F[ay] out here last night and we had a pleasant talk. Excuse this hasty business line as we are to meet tomorrow.

Your old

Tramp

I was in the Scalp[1] this afternoon and stood *lonesomely* under a tree in a big shower I hope tomorrow'll be fine so that I may admire your roof!

1. *The Scalp* is a narrow gap in the rocks through which the main Dublin-Enniskerry road passes, about two miles north of Enniskerry.

[*TCD/GS207*]   Glendalough House
                    Friday night [*17 August 1906*]

Dearest Changling

I'm very dejected tonight again I dont know why except that I'm dead tired and that I was annoyed and bored to death at dinner by a foolish lady who was praising the English and abusing the French. I dont fit well in to that family party somehow, they are rich and I am poor, and they are religious and I'm as you know, and so on with everything. I used to feel very desolate at times but now I dont so much mind as I've a changling of my own to think about and write to. I dont like hanging about their house as a poor relation—although I am a paying guest—as I know that they—or most of them—in their hearts despise a man of letters. Success in life is what they aim for, and they understand no success that does not bring a nice house, and servants, and good dinners. You're not like that are you? I wish we could keep each other company all these evenings. It is miserable that we must both be lonesome and so much apart. I hope you'll read steadily when I'm away. I hate to preach at you or schoolmaster you,— I like you so perfectly as you are—but you must know, that it will make life richer for both of us if you know literature and the arts, the things that are of most interest to me and my few personal friends, that you'll know one of these days.

It is quite an autumn evening here tonight cold and blustery. I like autumn but I always get a pang of regret when I feel that the summer is over. I have just been having a little walk by myself in the dark and I have a greater yearning than I can describe to you, to have you with me, to make much of me, and cheer me up.

Your old Tramp

P.S.   Remember you are to come down by the quarter to eleven on Sunday. Dont miss it, if you are coming at all. I hope it may be fine enough for us.

J. M. S.

[*TCD/GS207*]

[*Glendalough House*]

Monday night [*20 August 1906*]

Dearest Changling

I've written the letter to Kerry and I feel lonesome at the thought of it. I hate the thought of leaving you for so long especially as you will have this tour with no one to look after your comfort. Please go home to your people as soon as you can after I am gone and make it up with Sally. She is your natural companion in the company and it will be very unpleasant on tour if you are not on good terms. For the sake of *my* ease of mind do make it up if you can.¹

I am writing this letter to put with some books I'm sending you tomorrow. I meant really to tell you only how nice you were in the Green Room today. Will it make you vain if I tell you I felt proud of my little changling she looked so pretty and quiet and nice. I think mountain air and little purple *grapes*—not papers mind—must be the natural food of changlings they seem to agree with you so well! Or— to carry out the contrasts of my play—would you rather have the pig's leg, you spoke of with such fond enthusiasm last night?

I hope you'll like the books, please treat them kindly. Do you thing I'm a fool to spend my time writing to you—six hours after I leave you—when I ought to be reading? If I'm a fool now its folly to be wise.

Your old Tramp.

Can you read all this?

---

1. After a quarrel with Sally, apparently over the relationship with Synge of which neither family approved, Molly had moved from her mother's home at 37 Mary Street to stay with her sister Peggy (Mrs. Tom Callender) at Park Chambers, 13 Stephens Green North. The company planned a tour of Galway and the west in September. See Introduction, p. xviii.

[*TCD/GS208*]

c/o Mrs. Harris
Mountain Stage
Glenbeigh
Co Kerry
[*27 August 1906*]

Dearest Changling

I enclose a lot of scribbles to you that I did out on the rocks today
and yesterday. Tell me if you can read them and if you care for more.
They are a bit scrappy I fear. It isn't an easy place some how to get
time to write I am nearly always out or talking to someone, and when
I come in and sit myself down I dont seem to be in the right mood. I
have been in moods since I came here, however, that were very right
indeed. I wish I could have written to you then. You would have
been very pleased I think with what I had to say.

I had a very good journey down on Saturday and I felt in great
spirits, I was so pleased to have you to think about. I had a honey-
moon couple opposite me in the train. The good lady's wedding ring
was too tight for her and her finger was puffed up double its size,
above the ring which of course they could not stir. Unless they look
out she'll lose her finger.

I got a great welcome from them all here and although I'm very
lonely at times I'm glad to be here. It is very heavy and close today,
and I've got a bit of a headache so dont mind the thinness of this
letter. I'll send you a fine one one of these days. Be good, and write
me a long letter. I daresay I'll be back in three weeks.

Your old Tramp.

[*Encl*]

Dearest Changling

I'm out sitting on the cliffs over the sea, on Sunday morning in a
gale of wind with rainbows, and clouds & showers and sun flying
over me. It's just 11 o'cl. the time of our train at Sandycove! What a
pity you aren't here with me, you'd enjoy it all so much. An old man
I know came into the kitchen last night and shook me by the hand:
"A 100,000 welcomes to you", he said, "and where is the Missis?"
"Oh" I said "You'll have to wait till next year to see her"!

There is an old tramper staying in the house who is eighty years
old and remembers the famine and the Crimean War. He is one of the
best story-tellers in the county and he told us some last night in

Irish. He says he used to be good at it but he has lost his teeth now and he isn't able "to give them out like a *ballad.*" This morning when I went in to the kitchen he was sound asleep on the wooden settle in his bare feet with nothing over him but his coat.[1]

This perfectly fresh wild beauty of the sea and sky is a delight to me, but it makes me sick when I think that you are left behind, and of all the more or less vulgar or beastly talk of Mac,[2] and his friends that you are more or less forced to listen to. Read your Arthur, that will keep your mind full of wild beautiful things like the beauty of the world. When I had to live in London I always kept some book like "Arthur" on my hands and found it a great plan for keeping myself up when I was in ugly surroundings.

Monday

I'm out again on my perch over the sea. This morning there is a dead hot calm, with heavy clouds, and I can hear the sea birds clapping their wings in the cliffs under me. The air is full [of] the smell of honey from the heather, and there is a seal sneezing and blowing in the sea just under me. It is all wonderful & if I only had my changling with me! I am thinking of you a great deal and I have bad fits of loneliness. Never mind every day now is bringing us nearer, and there's a great time coming!

1. Synge describes this incident in his article on West Kerry for *The Shanachie* (see Oxford *Prose,* p. 263).
2. Francis Quinton McDonnell (1883–1951), who acted under the name Arthur Sinclair, was a member of the company from December 1904 until he led a mass resignation of the players over St. John Ervine's management in 1916. He became Molly's second husband in 1926.

[*TCD/GS208–9*]

c/o Mrs Harris
Mountain Stage
Glenbeigh
Co Kerry

Tuesday [*28 August 1906*]

Dearest Changling

All your letters have come this morning, you know they couldn't come any sooner as there are only the three posts in the week. I am delighted to hear from you. I am very lonesome too, and not very well. I dont know which of them to answer first. Yes, dont let us squabble any more, it is a wretched degrading sort of business. I am very glad to hear that your people are coming round. Sally shook me very cordially by the hand when I told her I was going away to Kerry for a month. I think she sees that she has been making rather a fool of herself, and I'm sure she'll be all right now. We are all fools at times so we cannot blame her, and you know I've great respect for her in many ways.

I am very glad you saw the flats, but you do not say a word as to how you like the place now you have seen it. Dont talk about it by the way or you'll have the Fays down there and then we could not go. It is too soon yet I think to take one, I would rather see them for myself first, and in any case I could not pay four or five months rent for nothing, and in the end perhaps see some thing else that would suit us better. Even if they are not to be had when we want them people are sure to be moving in and out continually so we would be sure to get a nice one in the end. Are Peggy and Tom[1] going to settle there? The most charming relations if they are *too* near are in the way at times. However we'll have a good look at them when I go home and then we'll see what to do.

Dont be alarmed about turning into a saint I dont think there's much danger! I had no opportunity to speak to Fay about your teeth so I'll write about it when I am writing to him next. I daresay I shall only stay here for three weeks after all, in which case I'll be back in a little more than a fortnight, so cheer up!

I haven't touched my play since I came down. It is too hot somehow to sit over it in the house, and my head is aching a good deal so I think I'll be the better for a bit of a rest. You'll get this I suppose on Wednesday morning and I ought [to] have an answer on Thursday. There is no post here tomorrow, or Friday. The letter you wrote yesterday was in time so you'll easily be able to catch the post.

This [is] a dull sort of letter I'm afraid but I'm writing it in a hurry to have it finished before my dinner as I will be going out afterwards and I can post it then. I'm thinking of you a great deal, and I hoped for a photo this morning I think you had better send me the two and I can keep the two of them at least till I go home.

Write as often as you can, it does me good

Your old Tramp.

This is a beautiful day and the country is wonderful I wish you were here to enjoy it with me. I can only half enjoy it now by myself. Never mind we'll have great walks presently.

1. Molly's sister and brother-in-law, Mr. and Mrs. Callender.

[TCD/GS209]   [*Kerry. 28 August 1906*]

Dearest. I am lying in one of the most beautiful spots in the whole world, with my head in among the heather that is fragrant with honey. I have masses of mountains all round me and a wonderfully blue sea and sky. Down in the valleys a number of little people are working at their oats and hay, the women looking so comfortable in their little red petticoats and bare legs. Wouldn't we be happy, changling, if we could live like that?

I posted a letter to you ½ an hour ago—not as nice a one as you deserve—and now I am at it again! Although I am lonely and depressed these days I am glad I have come out here to see all the glories of the world. I am out on a ride now over a high mountain gap—the Windy Gap—and I am resting in the heather on my way up. I'm off again—— ——

I have come out through the Gap & I am resting again. I have Carrantuohill on my left—the highest mountain in Ireland—full of ragged peaks with white cloud twisted through them like a piece of lace. Just under me there is a great basin, six miles across, full of woods and rich bogs and a blue river and lake. Outside it there is a circle [of] grey mountains.———

I'm resting again, now down among the woods. The richness and colour and sweetness of every thing is beyond words, at least beyond any hasty ones I can write now. It almost seems as if you were riding with me today I am thinking of you so much. Dear Changling! You do not know what I would give to have you with me here—— It is good for anyone to be out in such beauty as this is and it stirs me up to try and make my Irish plays as beautiful as Ireland—I wonder

if you could act a *beautiful* part? If it was in your compass—as we say
of singers—I think you could. We must try you.

                                                    Tuesday night
This isn't much of a letter but perhaps you will like to have it, so I'll
post it tomorrow on my way to the fair—I start early. I hope you aren't
disappointed that I have not decided on the Coombe¹ it is too soon.
You were good not to go out wandering on Sunday. Good night,
changling, I'll soon be back again. Your old Tramp.

---

   1. The old part of Dublin near St. Patrick's Cathedral where restoration was taking
place and new flats were being built.

[*TCD*]   [*Kerry*]
                                      Thursday [*30 August 1906*]
Dearest
    The post man has just walked in over the hill with your two letters
—by the way the Post Offices have just sent out notices that if
people persist in putting stamps on *the backs* of *their letters* they will
decline to deliver them, that wouldn't do!
    I'm afraid I'm spoiling you by writing to you every day—I wont
keep it up after this week, so be prepared! I didn't write any thing to
you yesterday (though I posted Tuesday's notes) as I was out at Killorglin fair¹ in the morning and then up into a mountain pass—on my feet
in the evening. The fair was very amusing as usual and I met a great
many country people that I knew. I saw three lustre jugs in a little
crockery shop, and I'm going to buy them—or at least two of them—
for *our* use! They are worth 2/6 I believe in Dublin, and it is well for
us to have something that we can *pawn!*
    I wonder what *Madame Giraffe*² would say to me if she thinks Fay
too poor. That's the Giraffe's doing you may be sure. I am glad Miss
Yeats was friendly to you, she likes you, she told me so six months
ago. She is extremely nice I think, if you—I wont finish that it was to
be about your millionaire. N.B. Dont take my spelling for gospel
sometimes I make my words French by mistake. I wonder what will
become of me if you all go to America and leave me behind. Do you

take that into your consideration? That would mean 6 months instead of three weeks remember!

Last night I was out on my little hill over the sea about nine o'clock in the moonlight. It was extraordinarily peaceful and grand and I was wondering how you were getting on in the Abbey (it was rehearsal time) listening to the blather of Mac and Co. My walk yesterday afternoon too was wonderful, I was high up on a mountain path looking down a thousand feet of sloping heather into the sea. Then there was Dingle Bay perfectly calm and blue, and in the background another line of mountains ending with the Blasquet Islands about 15 miles away. I was up there till sunset and the colour was strangely beautiful. After all while the fine weather lasts it is better to spend my time in places like that than to be fumbling over my play. So far I haven't looked at it, and I am not sure that I will, there is too much movement in this cottage somehow to get my mind to work. I am getting good from this change I think though I get a sort of Hay-fever at night that worries me. What is worse since last year my bed has got full of fleas—saving your presence or absence—and they bite me nearly into a fever, I killed three or four last night and I saw a lot more that got off!

Do you know Joy,[3] Colm's friend? He was to be at Killorglin these days and I wrote to him there, but have not heard so I suppose he has gone. He is one of a family of 17 and his mother died two or three months ago, as another was coming! His father is a publican in Killorglin, but is paralyzed or something and never appears! It is an extraordinary story—told me by a little Killorglin girl of ten who is staying here—you had better *not* repeat it. Now will that suit you for today's letter? I dont know, by the way, whether you will get this tomorrow or not as I am going to post it in Cahirciveen M. Doul's Cahir-Iveraghig[4]—and I may not catch the post. I cannot go down to the Glenbeigh post every day.

Your old Stager.

---

1. The famous "Puck Fair," held each August in Kerry.
2. This might refer to Annie E. F. Horniman (1860–1937), the English friend of Yeats who built the Abbey Theatre and financed the company in support of his aims until increasing disharmony between herself and the directors forced her to turn to Manchester, where she founded the Gaiety Theatre repertory company in 1907; she finally withdrew her subsidy in 1910 when the Abbey Theatre remained open on Edward VII's death.

3. Maurice Joy (1884–1944), a poet-friend of Padraic Colum and one of Horace Plunkett's secretaries for several years, edited *The Irish Rebellion of 1916 and its Martyrs* (New York: Devin-Adair, 1916).

4. Martin Doul was a character in Synge's play, *The Well of the Saints;* Cahir-Iveraghig (city of Iveragh) is pronounced Kȧhir ēevráu-ig, the 'au' as in "caught."

[*TCD/GS209–10*]
c/o Mrs Harris
[*Kerry*]
September 1st [*1906*]

Dear Changling

Your note—a short one—has just come. I sent you a long letter on Thursday—posted in Cahirciveen which does not seem to have reached you when you wrote yours. Tell me if you got it all right. I'm sure I'm writing you about double as much as you write me, amn't I? I have just heard that the MacKennas[1] are in Dublin for a week and want to see me. I shall be very sorry if I miss them. I have written to Fay on the teeth question and I hope he will devise something. What would you say if I was to turn up in Dublin this day week? It is possible I may go up then as I am not very well, and I find I cannot possibly work at my play here. I woke up the othernight feeling that you were in difficulty or danger or something and I didn't like it, so I was glad to hear this morning that you are all right. Of course you wont go with Power[2] unless your sisters go. I am disappointed at getting such a scrap of a line from you this morning, and now I cannot hear again till Tuesday. Well if you dont write to me! you know our bargain. Joking apart I've three more letters to write so this must do you for today.

Your old T.

P.S.   I've got my other letters written so I may come at you again. I think it's a shame for you to send me such a scrap with a whole side of the paper untouched! I bathed yesterday in the sea for the first time for about 25 years, and found it delightful. I have bathed and learned to swim in Wicklow rivers but the blue fresh sea some how is far more exciting. I was afraid to stay in more than a minute or so as I have a sort of asthma and I didn't want [to] make it worse. These moonlight nights here are most wonderful. Last night when I was coming back from the cliffs about 9 o'clock I came on the little girls belonging to this house and two or three others, and I got them to dance and sing Irish songs to me in the moonlight for nearly an hour. They were in bare feet of course, and while they were dancing a little divil of a brother of theirs kept throwing in dried furze-thorns under their feet, so that every now and then one of them would go lame with a squeal. I am glad you like *Catriona*.[3] Wont the Arthur books keep you going for a while still? Have you read any of the second volume?[4] Have you read Shakespeare? Remember in three little weeks there'll be another new moon, and then with the help of God, we'll have great walking and talking at the fall of night. Do write me some decent letters before Tuesday's post.

J. M. S.

1. Stephen MacKenna (1872–1934), journalist and translator of Plotinus, was one of Synge's closest friends. They had first met in Paris about 1897; MacKenna married Marie Bray, an American pianist, in 1902 and at this time he was still special correspondent for the *New York World*, a post he was shortly to give up. See "Synge to Mackenna: The Mature Years," *Irish Renaissance* (Dublin: Dolmen Press, 1966), pp. 65–79.
2. Ambrose Power joined the company in the autumn of 1904.
3. A novel by Robert Louis Stevenson, published in 1893 as a sequel to *Kidnapped*.
4. Presumably tales of the Arthurian cycle or Malory's *Morte Darthur,* although the books cannot be identified; Synge was familiar with all the major versions of the Arthurian story, see above, p. 16.

[*TCD*]   c/o Mrs Harris
                                                      etc. [*Kerry*]
                                     Tuesday [*4 September 1906*]

Dearest Changling

No letter has come from you. I can hardly believe that you have not written, so it is perhaps the postman's fault, he may be drunk after the races yesterday or God knows what. As soon as I get my dinner I'm going down to the post town to make the divil's own row. I have invented seven new curses—for my private prayers of course only— during the last hour and a half. Tell me when your sister goes to the Hospital, and when you go back to your people. Am I to go on writing to P[ark] Chambers after you go back, it seems rather absurd?

I'm a good deal better and I dont think I'll go home at present, not at least till my three weeks are up. I am only here ten days now but it seems an age. I have not even opened my play yet, after all it is far more important for me to be out in the fresh air now, getting a stock of health to carry me through next winter, than to be finished with the play a few weeks sooner or later. I am in such a rage now with this postman or whatever it is that I cannot write. Fortunately I have some scribbles to send you that are more likely to please you.

Your T.

What about the photos?

If you have written to me since please write by return and tell me when and where you posted it. If you have *not* written, if it is *your* fault——————!!!![1]

---

1. Across the top of this letter Molly has written the word *reconcile*.

[*Encl/GS210*]   Sept. 3.1906

D.C.   I couldn't write yesterday or today—at least couldn't post to you —so I've come down now under the cliffs—right on the edge of the sea—to watch the sunset and tell you my news. I've been at races today near here, at Rossbeigh with Philly Harris, the man of the house, and some of his family. They—the races—were run on a flat strand when the tide was out.[1] It was a brilliant day and the jockeys and crowd looked very gay against the blue of the sea, but somehow all the movement and festivity made me miss *someone* even more than I do when I'm out alone in the hills so I got rather dejected. I think I'm getting lonesomer every day, I wonder if you are? I suppose we'll survive two or three weeks more?

It is wonderful out here tonight. I told you I'm on the edge of a long bay with mountains on both sides. The sun sets over the sea now right at the mouth of it, and throws the most marvellous lights and shadows on the hills that I am facing. The bracken on them is turning red the last few days, which puts a sort of warm bloom on them in the late evening light. Between them and me, of course, there are 8 or 10 miles of fresh purple sea with sea gulls and cormorants and one seal that is watching me. You remember how we enjoyed the smoky back-yard kind of sun we had at Whitty Bay so you can fancy how you'd like this radiant place if you were here! I could write sheets to you about the wonders I see day by day, but it is as well to wait till you see them for yourself some day.

Tuesday (morning)

I'm out on the road above the cliffs that I was under last night, waiting for the post—with letters from you I hope—and watching the people picking Carragheen moss.[2] Dozens of men & women are out in the sea up to their waists—in old clothes, poking about for it under the water. They only find it at the lowest spring tide so the sea is far out and as smooth as a lake. It is a day with thin grey clouds wonderfully clear and silent & beautiful but I can just hear the voices of the people talking and laughing in the sea under me. My poor changling to be shut up in Dublin when I am in such a divine place! Found your letter all right after an hour's hunt in Drunken Postman's pocket. Thanks. Tell me all about Dossie mind.

1. Synge describes this incident in more detail in his article for *The Shanachie* (see Oxford *Prose*, pp. 263–264).
2. A variety of seaweed (*chondrus cristus*) exported for commercial use as a gelatine and also used for medicinal purposes, see Oxford *Prose*, pp. 269–274.

[*TCD/GS210*]

c/o Mrs Harris
[*Kerry*]
Thursday [*6 September 1906*]

Dear Changling

I have just got your little note. That is strange news about B. O'Dempsey. I wonder how it will end, I have no news of it from the others.[1]

Now about yourself. We talked over your staying on at St[ephens] Green by yourself as you know. You agreed not to stay there as I did not like it for you. Now at the LAST moment you tell me that you are going back of your definite word, and going to do what I asked you not. What does it all mean? Do you think—I had better not write what I think. I am too distressed. You seem determined that I am never to TRUST you. I do not so much mind your staying on as the way you

seem utterly to disregard your word. If there is any reason for you
to change your plans why do you not give it to me. I am very unwell
and now very wretched. I am going home in a few days.

Yours J.

Surely you might have had the courtesy to consult me at least about
your plans!

P.S.   You can write here again as I do not leave till next week.

Later

P.S.   Dearest. Perhaps you understood that our bargain was that you
should not stay on in the Green *unless* your mother agreed. If so,
though, that is *not* my recollection of what passed, it makes things a
little different, if your mother really agrees.

   Why are you staying on? I dislike EXTREMELY the idea of your being
there as a sort of caretaker. In any case it is outrageous that you should
make these plans without letting me know. I cannot understand why
you treat me so badly.

J. M. S.

Please write by return The thought that I cannot trust you is anguish
to me. You have finally ruined my holiday.

---

1. Willie Fay's courtship of Brigit O'Dempsey was being opposed by her family; at
this time rumours claimed that she had resigned from the company and returned home.

[*TCD/GS210*]

[Kerry]
Saturday [8 September 1906]

Dearest

   The post has passed the first post since I left Dublin with no
letter from you. I expect to go home on Tuesday evening or Wednesday
morning next so please WRITE here again. I am very unwell—nothing
at all serious but an ailment brought on by the damp, and unsuitable
food, that causes me intense pain at times, I nearly fainted yesterday
I was so bad—however I always get all right at once when I get back
to civilization. I suppose you have taken what I said badly, it is vain
trying to write of these things. We can talk it over next week together.
I was very unwell while I was writing, and, as you must have seen, it

was a shock to me to think that you made nothing of what we had talked of so much. Believe me, dearest, as always

your old T.

Is it not cruel of you to leave me without a letter? I have no news of the Directors or the affair of B. O'D.

Yours
J. M. S.

Write me a nice letter *by return.* I will call for it at the post town on Monday.

[AS]
Glendalough House
Glenageary
Kingstown
Wednesday [12 September 1906]

Dear Changling

I got home this morning, and I hope I'll soon be all right again. Very many thanks for the tie which is admirable. I cannot write you a letter today, this is merely to announce my arrival. If I feel well enough I shall probably be in at the Abbey tomorrow. (Thursday) Shall I see you then I wonder. Wont it be fun to see ourselves again?

I have not heard whether the Galway tour is on next week or off. You are all great hands at *not* Spreading the News![1]

Yours
J. M. S.

1. The title of one of Lady Gregory's most popular plays.

[TCD/GS211–12]
[Glendalough House]
18th.IX.06

Little treasure of my soul

I am delighted with your picture, it is very pretty and distinguished though it does not of course quite give your expression—photographs seldom do that.

I was very pleased with you the other evening, you were very self-possessed and charming, and got through very well, I think, considering your inexperience. Isn't Miss Tobin nice?[1] I have to go to Waterford with her tomorrow for the day—she wants to see the place as some of her people come from there—and she does not like going alone, so she asked me to go with her. Today I have to work at my play— I am getting very unhappy about it as it wont come out right. I am beginning to fear there is some inherent defect in the story as I am treating it. I am at my wits end with it. Tonight I may go to see *Mrs Tanqueray*[2] at the Gaiety I am not sure, Thursday please God I'll see you, I am famishing, it is heartrending as you say. I nearly went in to call on you on Sunday I got so lonesome. Never mind next Sunday we'll have a *long long day* in the Mountains. Could you come by the quarter to *ten* train the days are so short now? I have a very old friend to see this week—she is over from England for a few days only—and I may wire to you on Thursday to have tea and cakes for her at the Abbey. She is a writer on art.[3]

I am much better again now, nearly well in fact. You have no idea how much I have suffered. Good bye, my treasure, till Thursday I suppose

J. M. S.

I am sick and tired of this sort of thing. I think in a week or two we had better make ourselves "official" and then defy gossip. I may drop in and see your mother some day *unbeknownsted!*

1. Miss Agnes Tobin (1864–1939), daughter of a prominent San Francisco banker, Richard Tobin, had given a dinner for Synge and the principal players. A poet and translator of Petrarch, she spent much of her time in Britain, where she became a close friend of Alice Meynell, Arthur Symons, and Joseph Conrad (who dedicated *Under Western Eyes* to her and "her genius for friendship"). On this visit to Dublin the Abbey players undertook a copyright performance of one of her plays; later the Directors contemplated producing her translation of Racine's *Phèdre*.
2. *The Second Mrs. Tanqueray* by Arthur Wing Pinero, was produced at the Gaiety Theatre by Olga Nethersole's company.
3. Probably Hope Rea (b.1860), whom Synge had met in Florence in 1896. Author of *Tuscan Artists, Their Thought and Work* (London: George Redway, 1898), and individual studies of Donatello, Rembrandt, Rubens, Titian, she later published several folk miracle plays.

[*TCD*]

[*Glendalough House*
18 September 1906]

Dearest

I have just got your note. I hope my letter has reached you by this time and made you all right. I was thinking of going to town yesterday that is chiefly why I did not write to you, the rest was laziness. Your photo only came last night at 9.30 and I wrote to thank you this morning so I dont think I was very bad was I? Dont think for a moment that I take offence at imaginary trifles, or that I would leave your letter unanswered for a reason of that kind. You may be sure when I have anything I dont approve of I'll let you know fast enough.

I'm very sorry indeed that I have made you uneasy, you must have seen by my note this morning how far you were from knowing the real state of things when you said that I didn't seem to want to see you or hear from you. Since I was away I seem to value you more profoundly than ever, you need never doubt me, my little heart, if you treat me well. I put up your photo last night on a stand next my bed so that it was the first thing I saw this morning. Good bye

J. M. S.

[*AS*]

[*Glendalough House*]
Friday [*?21 September 1906*]

Dear Changling

I have no paper[1] and I am in no humour for writing so this is merely to carry out my half-promise and to bid you good day. I am still under the cloud you put over me in the Park, I hope it may wear off before tonight.

Dont forget Sunday by the quarter to eleven from West R. I hope to Heaven we may have a good day.

J. M. S.

Evening—The cloud is lifting again. Am I too hard on you, treasure, for your little sins? If I am forgive me.

---

1. The letter is written on the back of a page from one of the final drafts ("G" 18 September 1906) of Act I of *The Playboy*.

[*AS/GS215*]   [*Glendalough House*]
                                        Saturday. 7.A.M.
                                        In my little Bed
                                        [*?22 September 1906*]

My Own

    I dont suppose I shall get a word with you tonight, and I will not
be well enough I fear to walk tomorrow, so I want to write you a line
to thank you for your notes. Dearest, yesterday morning I sat down to
write you a letter that would have made your hair stand on end, but
fortunately when I got the pen in my hand I wrote to Germany
instead. I was greatly troubled all day—far more so than you imagine
—by our quarrel on Thursday. And my first impulse was to give you
a terrible scolding but I am going to drop my dignity and appeal to
you instead. Dont you know, changling, that I am an excitable, over-
strung fool,—as all writers are, and *have to be,*—and dont you love
me enough to be a little considerate, and kindly with me even if you
do not think that I am always reasonable in what I want you to do?
Surely you wouldn't like to worry me into consumption or God knows
what? And with the continual, deadly strain of my writing I haven't
much health over to shake off the effect of these hideous little squab-
bles that harrass me indescribably, because my own darling, I love
you indescribably. When you know how my whole heart has gone out
to you, why do you speak to me as you did on Thursday, or break
your word to me as you did a few days before? We may have a beautiful life together, but, if we are not careful, we may put ourselves into
a very hell on earth. Do let us be careful.

                                  J. M. S.

[*TCD/GS212*]   [*Glendalough House*]
                                Monday night [*?24 September 1906*]

My dearest Changling

    I believe I promised to write to you today, and I am a man of my
word so here goes!

    I have just been out having a little turn on my cycle in the twi-
light, which was very clear and quiet so I am in a peaceful mood.
What shall I say about our squabble last night? It haunted me and

distressed me more than I expected. I could not go to sleep thinking of it last night, and it was back into my head before I could get my eyes open this morning. You gave me an utterly hard hostile look, when I tried to put things right that is not pleasant to think of. Some people seem to be able to have disputes and forget them but I am not like that so we must not do that sort of thing again. Please write me a good letter tomorrow, when you get this, that will put me to rights again.

As to the matter we fought over it was small in itself, but such things mean a great deal. We can talk it over better than we can write of it, I am always afraid to say much in a letter, letters are so easily misunderstood by a little over emphasizing some thing that is really put lightly.

When am I to go to tea with you? On Wednesday afternoon I suppose you will be rehearsing. I could go on Thursday instead if you are free then. Let me know in time.

I was sorry to leave you so soon today but as you refused to have tea with me there was nothing for it. I was rewarded for my industry in coming home to work by getting some of the best speeches down that I have got hold of since I began work this time. Dont forget to write to me *at once*

Your old Tramp

[*TCD/GS212*]   [*Glendalough House*]
Thursday [*?27 September 1906*]

Dearest

I am getting on well again today, and I have just got your note, thanks. You ought to have some smelling salts to hold under F. J.'s nose when he goes to sleep!

You made me a wee bit uneasy last night, dear Heart, by some of your talk, and the moods you told me of. I thought you had come round altogether to like the sort of life you'll have with me best—the life I mean that we have out on the hills, and by the sea on Bray Head and in the art we both live for—but if you begin again hankering after commonplace pleasures and riches and that sort of thing we shall both be made wretched. I do not mean of course that we want to be poor or that we shouldn't amuse ourselves, but I fear there is something a little different in your head now. Write me a nice letter, my own heart, and cheer me up again. I dont really believe that it's anything more than a passing whim, but I'd like you to tell me so again. I have often told you that I am sure with a little care we may have a beautiful life together, but that a little carelessness—especially with you as you are so young and so quick and an actress—might easily ruin our happiness for ever. Forgive this preaching, my life, I dare say it is very absurd.

Your old Tramp forever.[1]

---

1. At the bottom of this letter Molly has written *peculiar* twice.

[*TCD/GS213*]

[*Glendalough House*]
Saturday [*29 September 1906*]

Dearest.

I was taken with a very lonesome turn last night, on my way home. It is painful being so near you and hardly seeing you at all. This state of affairs cant last much longer, only I dont want to start making fusses till my play is off my hands. I had no notion that you had such a beautiful voice, at least, it seemed beautiful to me. I liked your whole show of Mary[1] except one gesture that seemed forced. You see Darley is quite friendly. I knew he was, when in his ordinary humour.

By the way I was unspeakably pained and offended by your note, and P.O. that I got on Thursday night. What have I done that you should write to me as if I was a dunning Jew? It was well your second letter came or I'd have been raging all day yesterday.

I'm not at all well, inside, I'm sorry to say—it is the worry of my play that is knocking me up I think—but I hope I'll be all right tomorrow. Please come down as usual by the *quarter to eleven train,* I'll be able to get as far as the train in any case and go to Bray with you and back. That is of course if it is *not a wet day.* It is looking doubtful this morning, but the glass is high and it may clear off again. I hope to go in this evening if I am not too unwell, but I shall be much occupied with a not very pleasant job.[2] I've had a long morning at my play, by

degrees the unfinished pages are getting fewer and fewer—Thanks
be to God—

Good bye my own little treasure, till tomorrow with the help of
God—(tonight doesn't count)

Your old T.

P.S.   If my ailments get *much* worse I'll write tonight to put you off,
but I dont think that will be necessary.   J. M. S.

Did you get the book?

P.S.   Little Heart. Some times I haven't any words deep enough and
tender enough to tell you all I feel for you. I am ashamed of my arid
little letters when I have posted them, and of my foolish tempers, sometimes, when I bid you good-bye. But dont doubt your old Tramp. Anything that is profound, you surely know, cannot be expressed easily,
and our feelings, little heart, are profound indeed!

---

1. Molly had a leading role in Lady Gregory's one-act play *The Gaol Gate*, in which
she sang a keen composed by Arthur Darley.

2. Yeats and Lady Gregory were both away from Dublin, and Synge was responsible
for arranging the new season with the recently hired Business Secretary, W. A. Henderson (who was also Secretary of the National Literary Society).

[*Texas*]

[*Glendalough House*]
Thursday night
7.30 [*?4 October 1906*]

Dearest

Just a line of greeting. I have been slaving off and on all day and
now I am going down to the pier. Fancy, two days more and then
Sunday! How I look forward to it! I hope rain or Jack Yeats[1] wont stop
us. Could you come by the quarter to ten next time do you think? I
want to take you to Enniskerry on the long car[2] and then to Glen Cree,
it is a lovely place and I'd like you to see it before the autumn is over.

I am going to make Christy Mahon come in dressed as a jockey
from the mule race in the third act, wont Fay look funny!

This is a miserable scrap but excuse it I'm wearied out. Till the Day
of Judgement and after it.

Your old T.

1. Jack B. Yeats (1871–1957), artist-brother of the poet, lived in Devon but frequently visited and exhibited in Ireland. He and Synge had toured the Congested Districts of the west of Ireland in July 1905 for a series of illustrated articles for the *Manchester Guardian,* and had remained friends ever since; see Oxford *Prose,* pp. 401–403.

2. The long car, an uncovered four-wheeled horse-drawn car in which the passengers sat in two rows back to back, made regular journeys from Bray station to Enniskerry by way of the Dargle Glen and Powerscourt Demesne; see pictures from the Lawrence Collection, National Library of Ireland, in Patrick Flanagan, *Transport in Ireland 1880–1910* (Dublin: Transport Research Associates, 1969).

[*TCD/GS263*]

[*Glendalough House*]
Saturday Morning 12.30
[*6 October 1906*]

Dearest

When I got home last night I saw to my horror a letter lying on the table which I made sure was from Jack Y. When I opened it however it was only from my cousin, about Monday, so, so far, I am free for tomorrow. Please come by the *quarter to eleven tomorrow Sunday,* I am tired this week and I think that will be early enough for both of us as we are working so hard!

You must not mind if I seem a little distant at the Theatre, every one is watching us, and even when we are publicly engaged I do not care to let outsiders see anything. Isn't that the best way? Remember what a public nuisance Fay and Co. became! Last spring we had to do our talking in the Theatre as we did not see each other elsewhere but now, thank God, we can have our talk on green hills, that are better than all the green rooms in the world. Please dont be hurt, I am only defending myself because you said I wasn't nice last night! Twenty two hours and a half, the Devil mend them, till we meet again. Your old

J.M.S.

You had better look in your letter box tomorrow morning in case I should be stopped still. I hope I wont.

[AS]   [*Glendalough House*]
                                              Monday night 12.30
                                              [*8 October 1906*]

Dear Heart

I have been in bed for half an hour and I've suddenly taken a
notion that I must write you a line before I go to sleep. My little
treasure if you knew how I longed to have a little chat with you all
the evening but it wasn't possible. I wonder if you felt I was neglecting you? It couldn't be helped. Perhaps you'll think I'm an ass to write
to [you] so soon when I've nothing to say except that you're my only
changling and I'm always thinking about you, and yearning to be with
you even when I seem to be taking no notice of you at all.

Be good and faithful to your old Tramp and we'll have great times
yet. I dont know why I am writing all this. A thousand blessings on
you

                                              J. M. S.

[TCD]   Glendalough House
                                              Wednesday [*10 October 1906*]

Dearest

Would you like a walk with your old Tramp *tomorrow? Thursday.*
I will go up by the train that gets in about 20 minutes to three, and
I'll go to the bridge between *Capel St.* and *Parliament St.* at *three
o'clock (tomorrow-Thursday)* If you're there we'll take an outing either
to Lucan, or by the Palmerston tram to the Dodder and so to the glens.[1]
If you are *not* there, I'll take it you cant come and I'll go and see Jack
Yeats If they have a rehearsal of the Gaol-Gate[2] or anything tomorrow
afternoon, so that you cant come, dont trouble about it, and we'll have
our walk some other time. If it is wet—regularly wet—I wont be
there. You wont get this till tomorrow morning so there wont be time
for you to answer. It will not matter if you aren't there, but as I do not
know whether you can come I will not wait after five past three, and
if by any chance I am not there then dont wait for me. It is not a
pleasant place. I've a lot of nice things to say to you but they'll do
tomorrow. Ever your old

                                              J. M. S.

1. Among the Dublin Mountains beyond Rathfarnham on the outskirts of Dublin are Glendhu (the Pine Forest), Glenasmole ("Glen of the Thrushes"), and Glencullen.
2. Lady Gregory's play was first produced October 20th.

[*TCD/GS213*]

[*Glendalough House*]
Thursday [*11 October 1906*]

Dearest

What a Day! No chance for our walk. I shall be at the Abbey tomorrow afternoon and perhaps evening, so we'll meet then.

I have had a very nice letter from my brother he seems quite pleased. I wish you could see him before he goes away. He is to be here I believe tomorrow morning and will stay about a week, then to China for seven years.[1]

How are you feeling? Wasn't it strange how I felt your depression and got up in the middle of the night to write you a letter of consolation. It wont be my fault if we aren't happy changling, and I'm sure it wont be yours so please God we're safe.

Ever, my own dearest, your old Tramp.

1. Samuel Synge and his wife were both medical missionaries; see *Letters to My Daughter*, p. 130.

[*Texas*]

[*Glendalough House*]
Saturday *Midday*
[*?13 October 1906*]

Treasure

I am sending you a line to remind you of tomorrow, I am so afraid you might forget!! Do not come of course if it is a wet day, but if it is raining *at a quarter to ten* and clears up before a *quarter to eleven* come then. I have had so much letter-writing to do this morning—for the Theatre—I have not had time to touch my play. I am going to the Tree show, I think, this afternoon. I dont want to go a bit but I think I ought to pay my respects to Wareing.[1] I may want his help some time.

The weather glass is rising so perhaps it will be fine tomorrow Please Goodness it will. I hope we will not make any mistake, some-times it rains in Dublin and is fine here or the other way round. Look in your box again tomorrow morning, and be very happy. So till ten tomorrow good bye

Your old Tramp

1. The impresario and director Alfred Wareing (1876–1942) had managed the Abbey Theatre company's first extended tour earlier this year when Synge accompanied them to Cardiff, Glasgow, Aberdeen, Newcastle, Edinburgh, and Hull from 26 May to 9 July 1906. At this time Wareing was business manager for Herbert Tree; in 1909 he founded the Glasgow Repertory Theatre; from 1918–1931 he directed the Theatre Royal, Huddersfield; from 1931–1933 he was librarian of the Shakespeare Memorial Library, Stratford-on-Avon.

[*TCD*]

[*Glendalough House*]

Monday [*?15 October 1906*]

Dear Polly

I enclose the immortal ballad—It will do to sing by and by if I get too stiff to stand on my head.

I find there is more work than I thought to be done on the second Act of my play so I'll have to make another desperate go at it this week, last week somehow I didn't get much done

I hope you aren't tired after yesterday. I had a great sleep last night and I feel ready for a fine week's work. This afternoon I was through the edge of Bray on my cycle along a bit of the road we were on last night. It was hard to believe it was the same place. You've made me want to act by telling me I couldn't be understood. Fiddle de-dee! Dont you remember how clear I was when I was teaching you Nora B?[1] Perhaps I'll see [you] tonight, perhaps I wont be in till Wednesday.

Good bye dearest your

J. M. S.

[*Encl/GS214*]

The NEW ORIGINAL BALLAD of MISS POLLY POP-GUN . . .
Young Polly Popgun and her man went out one autumn day,
When hips and haws and blackberries their millions did display.

Then he and she did quarrel sore upon a mountain lane
And first she swore and then she bit and then to ease her pain
A black and bloody smudge she laid upon her lovers cheek
Who stood upon the pathway there in patience mild and meek,
And then in passion and in pride she snivelled loud and long
Till all her griefs he squeezed away upon his bosom strong.

1. Molly took over the role of Nora Burke in *The Shadow of the Glen* on 10th March, 1906 (see Introduction, p. xix).

[*TCD/GS214*]

[*Glendalough House*]
Tuesday [*16 October 1906*]

Dearest

Your note has just come. I've been hard at work all day—except of course for my outing, when I came in for a big shower in Glen Cullen and got soaked to the skin. I have not had a word with my brother yet, the days seem to slip by and I never see him alone. I am very bothered with my play again now, the Second Act has got out of joint in some way, and now its all in a mess. Dont be uneasy changling, everything is going on all right I think, I will go and see your mother soon. I dont much like the job so I keep putting it off. Besides of course I'm very hard at work again now, as if possible I want to read my play to the Directors next week. Wont it be a blessing if I can finish it then? I felt very lonesome today up in the country without you. I half thought of going in to town to take you for a walk but I thought it better to stick to my work. I dont know when I shall be in. When I go in the afternoon I nearly always get to the Abbey before *three,* so dont wait for me in that stuffy hole. I may be in tomorrow possibly, but it is not likely. If my letters keep you late in the morning, I'll have to knock them off again!!! I am sorry you are getting back into your bad ways. You want someone to look after you eh? This letter wont do you much good I'm afraid but I'm very tired. Good bye Pop Gun.[1]

1. The letter is unsigned and across the top Molly has scribbled in pencil: *you may stop your letters if you like. I dont care if I never heard from you or saw you again so there!*

& please dont let thoughts of me come into your head when you are writing your play. It would be dreadful if your speeches were upset   I dont care a 'rap' for the theatre or anyone in it the pantomime season is coming on & I can easily get a shop; in fact I shall go out this afternoon & apply for one.

M. Allgood

[*TCD/GS215*]   [*Glendalough House*]
                                                                Thursday [*18 October 1906*]

Dearest

 I'm looking forward to a luxurious shave by and by. I didn't thank you for the admirable article because my speeches of gratitude to you dont 'come off'.

 By the way I think we made more of the Fay incident last night than it deserved. He really said very little. If he says anything more I have my answer ready—only please keep good time and please be civil to him—civil I mean as you would be to the manager of any other business you were in. You'll never get a perfect manager till you go to Heaven, and W. G. is a good fellow at bottom—you have often said so—

 I have done a good morning's work, and ended my second act again, I think nearly right this time. How is your tooth-ache? my brother is off in town again today so I have not been able to ask him. He is extremely busy, of course, these few days bidding good-bye to all his friends. This is a lovely clear day I wish we were going out, we could have done so only for this *Oedipus* dinner with Magee.[1] I've an idea for next Sunday that we might meet at Carrickmines and walk round through the mountains to Rathfarnham, I must measure it on the map to see how far it would be? We mustn't tire you too much as you have the long week's playing before you! I saw in the *Mail* a lot of ads of rooms for 5/0 a week, in fairly good localities, I'll *soon* be after them. I hope you are in good spirits. Keep cheerful its the best way

Ever your old Tramp.

P.S.   You cant write sentimental letters I find in the morning! I'm sending you a little book I promised you long ago. Please take great care of it and let me have it when you have read it.

1. William Kirkpatrick Magee (1868–1961), Irish essayist who wrote under the pseudonym of "John Eglinton," was Assistant Librarian of the National Library, and

editor with Frederick Ryan of the short-lived "Magazine of Independent Thought," *Dana* (1904–1905). The Directors discussed producing a translation of *Oedipus* by him, but apparently nothing came of the plan.

[*TCD*]

Glendalough House
Friday night [*19 October 1906*]

My own Treasure

I have just got home and found your little note! What a pity it was that I had to spoil our pleasant evening by letting you go home by yourself! I could not get rid of Stuart,[1] but I went after you as soon as I could, with him. I saw you in the distance and hurried after you. Just as we were overtaking you, you turned into a chemist's I said "There's Miss A. going home alone," and made a run to catch you, but you shut the door in my face!! I had told him I was going by the 10.45 train so I couldn't wait for you.

Darling when I think of your little smiles today I am carried away with delight. It was worth being lonely for years and years because it has made me value a priceless love like yours more than other men could do. Isn't it glorious that we have found each other I will be very careful not to let my little Changeling be lonesome any more, and not to hurt her little feelings. My own darling please be careful too. Of course you wont go to Power's dance, the thought would be ANGUISH to me!! It's foolish but that [is] how I'm made. I know you are not likely to want to go, but I've just put this in as I heard Sally asking Power to take the two of you, and perhaps you might have let her persuade you without thinking how much it would hurt me. I dont know what would become of me if we quarreled now, I feel as if we knew each other too well to quarrel any more. You hardly know, my own changling, how entirely you've got hold of your old Tramp by the heart. I am sometimes frightened when I think what it would be to lose you. We wont talk of such things. Come down *by the quarter to eleven on Sunday* if fine, unless you hear to the contrary. Ten thousand blessings on you

Your Tramp

1. Probably the Bob Stewart mentioned in Joseph Holloway's *Journals* as a regular attender at the Abbey (see Introduction, p. xxiv).

[*TCD/GS216*]   [*Glendalough House*]
                                                Sunday [*21 October 1906*]

Little Heart

　　Another wet day for us! It was as well maybe as I'm not very
flourishing and a long walk wouldn't have been the best thing for me.
I wasn't well enough to go in last night and I am not sure that I'll get
in tomorrow, by Tuesday however I ought to be all right, as there is not
much the matter with me.

　　Little Heart, this morning I was brimming over with tender things
to say to you, but I didn't write them, and now I've forgotten most of
them. I was going to tell you how proud I was to be a man of letters so
that I could write my little changling things other men wouldn't know
how to get into words. That's a good idea, I think, worth putting into a
sonnet if I get the mood. Then I was going to talk about other profound
things that I've forgotten altogether. These two idle days I've had time
to think and you've never been out of my mind! I've felt very happy
to have a little changling of my own to think of, even though I've been
lonesome, and longing to have you here to pet me and keep up my
spirits.

　　I've a new idea. Do you think you could write a little comedy to
play in yourself; say about your life in the convent school? I could give
you a scenario, would not it be fun, and then you'd be able to patronise
Miss Darragh,[1] and Mrs Bill Fay and the lot of them. I'm sure you've
as much humour as Lady Gregory, and humour is the only thing her
little farces have. Or could you write a comedy about the women at
Kilmacanogue (that's how it's spelled) or about some incident of your
early career? The one thing needful is to get hold of some little centre of
life that you know thoroughly, and that is not quite familiar to every
one. I'm sure your old grandmother would be a lovely character in a
play. Think about it, little heart, and, when you're acting, notice how
the scenes etc. are worked out, one into the other. This is all a wild
idea, but it would be fun to try; no one would know but ourselves and
of course I'd help and advise you. You could write out your MSS on the
typewriter, so all is complete!

　　I wonder how the show went last night I suppose I shall hear from
you tomorrow. By the way what afternoons are you free this week? Our
best way would be to meet at Carrickmines and have a walk to Kilternan and round about, and then I could send you back by Harcourt

Street again, and wander home here. I believe my brother goes on
Thursday. I have not had a word with him yet on 'Ourselves', we are
both so busy I never see him except at meals. He is in town nearly
every day bidding people goodbye and so on. I dont know whether I
shall be able to post this tonight. It is very wet and I dont want to give
myself a chill. I hope I shall hear from you tomorrow morning, and that
it will be a nice letter.
Ever, my little Heart, your old
                    Tramp

---

1. Florence Darragh, stage name of Letitia Marion Dallas, was brought over from
England by Yeats to play in his *Deirdre* on 24 November, 1906, and the revised version of
his *Shadowy Waters* on 8 December; but Synge and Lady Gregory disliked her acting, and
she left before the end of the year. A friend of Miss Horniman, she became a member of
the first repertory company at the Gaiety Theatre, Manchester, and died in 1917.

[*TCD/tel*]   Kingstown 22 October 1906 10.35 A.M.
Allgood Care Callender Park Chambers Stephens Green North Dublin.
Congratulations Much better Synge

[*TCD/GS216*]   [*Glendalough House*]
                    Monday morning [*22 October 1906*]
Little Sweetheart
    I cannot tell you how delighted I was to get your letter this morn-
ing. I am much better—nearly all right again—but I will not go in
tonight unless I feel quite fit.
    I am in a great hurry with this as I want to catch the early post.
You'll be expecting something. I am delighted to hear of the success of
everything. When I read of the compliments you got I had tears of
pleasure in my eyes to the wonder of my family. Yes you have a lovely
voice, I think, it will be worth anything on the roads
    Now I must run. I posted my letter to you in Dalkey myself on
Saturday, I went round there in the afternoon and was the worse for it.
Goodbye, dearest till very soon, I hope. Write if I dont go in tonight
                    Your old Tramper

[*TCD*]   [*Glendalough House*]
                                                    My Bed
                                        12.30 [*?23 October 1906*]

Little (or big) Heart!

Did you think I neglected you tonight? My poor little heart I couldn't help it, I had a lot of business to talk with WBY etc. When he and I went across to the tea-room he launched out into *your* praises, in quite a pointed way as if complimenting me also. He says you are curiously charming in Boyle and he cannot make out how you do it as there is so little in the part.[1] He said a lot more nice things about your cleverness and imagination that I wont tell you. I think our troubles are nearly over with the help of God! Come down in good time tomorrow (Wednesday) I shall be there from 7.20 I think. We might manage a walk perhaps on Friday. I feel as if my little illness and our last letters have made us nearer than ever.

Good bye J.M.S.

1. *The Mineral Workers,* a play by William Boyle (1853–1923) in which Molly played the small role of the daughter Kitty, was first produced with *The Gaol Gate* on 20 October.

[*TCD/GS216*]   [*Glendalough House*]
                                          Thursday (afternoon)
                                            [*25 October 1906*]

Dearest Pop.

Come down tomorrow (Friday) if you can by the *quarter* to two from Westland row, taking 3rd return to Bray. I will join you at Glenageary and we can have four hours together. You can go back to Dublin by the train I went up by last night, that will be time enough I suppose. Get your dinner of course before you come.

I showed my brother your photo today he beamed at it most cordially and said with conviction "Thats a *very nice* face."[1]

Also I heard people in the Tea-rooms last night saying how good the "younger girl" was in *The Gaol Gate.*

Now are you buttered up enough for one day?
I've a crow to pluck with you all the same, Miss P.P.!
In a hurry
      ever yours
         Tramp
P.S.   Of course tomorrow depends on a fine day. Dont come if wet there would be no use.

---

1. See *Letters to My Daughter*, p. 125.

[*TCD/GS217*]
                    [*Glendalough House*]
                    Friday [*26 October 1906*]

Dearest
    Rain again! I wish you'd pray that it may be fine on Sunday, I dont know what'll become of us if it's wet!
    My brother went off last night. It was very sad seeing him going off on the boat for seven years—he is one of the best fellows in [the] world, I think, though he is so religious we have not much in common. My old mother bore up wonderfully well, though she cried a good deal of course after he was gone. She kept saying now and then, "It seems so hard that I must live without him". The whole thing gives me a 'grief-lump' in my throat!
    I found your little note waiting for me when I came back from the boat, and it pleased me very greatly. It made me feel the way I felt long ago in Wexford when you were so nice and good, before we got into the Cardiff complications and all the little troubles we have had since. If you like to thank God in my name for having given you to me you can, I feel nearly ready to do it myself today I am so happy and pleased with you. I'll be up tomorrow evening,—this evening I must stay with my mother,—and then please Heaven we'll get our walk on Sunday. Good bye my little heart
             J. M. S.

Do you realise how free you'll be when *Deirdre*'s on?[1] I hope there'll be a moon then!

---

1. Molly did not perform in Yeats's *Deirdre,* which ran for two weeks from November 24th.

[*TCD/GS217*]   [*Glendalough House
30 October 1906*]

Darling

I was very delighted to get your note this morning. I expected it last night, and was disappointed. I dont know whether I shall be in tonight or not. I wrote to Yeats asking him to fix a directors' meeting for various matters and he has not answered me, so I am not very eager to go in till he does so.

I had a dreadful turn of despair over the *Playboy* last night—it seemed hopeless—but I have come through the difficulty, more or less, that was in my way. I am feeling very much 'done up' with it all and I fear I cant leave it for a walk this week. It is too bad, but I must get done with the thing or it will kill me. I am sorry to hear that you are having gloomy dreams, you must be done up too. I am too worn out to write much of anything to you now, but if you had seen my misery when the post passed last night without a letter from my little Changling you would forgive me. I dont know what will become of me if I dont get the *Playboy* off my hands soon, I nearly wrote in to them last night to ask them to put on *The Well of the Saints* instead of it in December so that I might have a few months more to work at it but I dont like the thought of having it hanging over me all this winter when I ought to be so Happy! Parts of it are the best work, I think, that I have ever done, but parts of it, are not structurally strong or good, I have been all this time trying to get over weak situations by strong writing, but now I find it wont do, and I am at my wit's end. It's well I have the thought of you to comfort me! or I dont know what I should do. Write to me very often your letters are my only comfort.

Ever my little Heart your J. M. S.

[*TCD/GS217–18*] [*Glendalough House*]
Nov 1st [*1906*]

My little Life

Yes, you have comforted me a good bit. I like being lectured and
I'll try and keep up my spirits and work ahead. I have heard from
Yeats and I am to be in tomorrow afternoon, and probably evening so I
shall get my eyes on you again. This is a wretched day, it is well we
had not arranged for a walk. I half hope I have got over the weakness
in my Second Act that has been worrying me so much, but it is too
soon to say with certainty. Any little change seems a great improvement at first, but after a while you find out that it is the novelty only
that is taking you, and that in reality the 2nd state is worse than the
first. I hope the next play I write I'll have you at my elbow to advise
me and cheer me up. I have no one out here to talk over my troubles
with and I get frightfully depressed. What a lot of things you got the
Fays![1] I will give him a copy of the *Well* [*of the Saints*] too to make up
for the smallness of my subscription. I wonder shall we get a word
together tomorrow, I shall probably be dining with W. B. Y. *and her
Ladyship*

We'll have Sunday again soon in any case with the help of God.
That is something to look forward to!

Yours forever
J. M. S.

1. At a reception for Willie Fay and Brigit O'Dempsey who had been married in
Glasgow on October 29th.

[*TCD*] [*Glendalough House*]
Saturday [*3 November 1906*]

Dearest

I've had a great morning's work my play is getting on. Two or
three more weeks ought to finish it. I am going in tonight, but I write
this in case by any chance I should not get a word with you. Please
come down tomorrow—if it is not a wet day—by the usual train at

a *quarter to eleven.* The weather is looking very uncertain but we must hope for the best. It cant always rain!

I am very glad that you liked *Aucassin and Nicolette,*[1] it is a very beautiful little thing, I think, filled with the very essence of literature and romance. Keep it of course as long as you want it. Then I will poke out something else for you.

Did I send you *The Ordeal of Richard Feverel,* by Meredith before I went to Kerry? I was looking for it the other day to send it to you but I couldn't find it.

Pray for tomorrow.

> Ever yours
> J. M. S.

1. Synge might have come across this thirteenth-century legend of Provence in lectures at the Sorbonne in 1895; a brief account is given by Petit de Julleville in *Histoire de la litterature francaise* (Paris, 1896), which also gave him the *fabliau* on which he based *The Well of the Saints.* Walter Pater also discussed the tale in *The Renaissance* (1873, 1877), and the English translations by F. W. Bourdillon (1887, 1897) and Andrew Lang (1887, 1896) were well known.

[TCD/GS218]   [*Glendalough House*
                                                 5 November 1906]

Little Heart

I am just off to the post with the Aran book proofs[1] so I have only time to write you a hurried line in spite of all your injunctions! I feel in great form after yesterday and I have had a good morning's work. I hope you aren't the worse. There was a very bad thunder storm in Kingstown—much worse than what we got—about five o'clock—the flashes we saw I suppose in the Rocky Valley.[2] We got off very well. Let me hear from you soon.

My mother asked me again if I was alone, and I said I had 'a friend' with me. I must tell her soon. Do you really want more books. I will send you as many as you like but I dont want to plague you with books that you have no time to read. Remember to get *Cuchulain of Muir-themne* from the library and read "The Sons of Usnach" in it. It is charming.[3] Now ten thousand blessings on you I'll write more the next time

Your old Tramp

---

1. *The Aran Islands* was being published by George Roberts of Maunsel and Co.
2. By Great Sugar Loaf in the Wicklow Mountains near the tiny village of Kilmac-anogue.
3. Translated by Lady Gregory and the source of Synge's next play, *Deirdre of the Sorrows*.

[*AS*]

[*Glendalough House*]
Tuesday [*?6 November 1906*]

Dearest

This is a mere line. I was too occupied with my play to go in last night, but hope to be in tomorrow or next day, and in any case on Friday to meet Henderson. I am working now at very high tension and if I can keep it up perhaps I shall have finished in a fortnight. Wont that be great? I do not know whether I shall be able to walk on Thursday or not. I am rather afraid of taking my thoughts off my work even for one evening. Hadn't we a *splendid* day on Sunday?

Ever yours
J. M. S.

[*TCD/GS219*]

[*Glendalough House*]
Tuesday night [*6 November 1906*]

Dearest

I am so very sorry to hear of the pain in your back. Is it quite gone? I blame myself very much for taking you such a long way when you weren't very well. Do let me know tomorrow how you are. I feel uneasy about you. I did not let myself believe all the talk you made the other night but it did trouble me a bit so I am glad you have disowned it. I am dreadfully busy these days I have a book to review for the *Manchester Guardian*,[1] and a lot of proofs to correct for my Aran book, and of course the P.B. To make matters worse a spring has just broken

in my typewriter so I dont know what I shall do. I may have to go to
town with it tomorrow morning and I may look in at the Abbey but I
dont know. I want to read the P.B. to the Directors and Fay on Thursday
or Friday so I dont know about a walk, in any case we cannot go unless
you are *quite* well. Let me know. I am too tired now to write any thing
of interest. Did you go to the conversazione at the National Literary
[Society]? I had a bit of a ride this afternoon and I was wishing you
were there to enjoy it the air was so beautifully clear. I wonder what
I shall think of Miss D[arragh]. You will be very unwise if you let her
see that you dont like her. She is playing her game, and you had better
play yours. I mean that you should be affable, and reserved at the same
time, so that she will not know whether you like her or not. That is the
wisest plan, though it is not easy perhaps for little changlings! Now
take care of yourself and let me know how you are. Excuse this matter
of fact note I am writing against time and I am very tired.

Yours forever

J. M. Tramp

I've found the little spring of my T.Writer so I may be able to patch it
up myself for the present. *Remember to write* tomorrow

---

1. Of Stephen Gwynn's *The Fair Hills of Ireland,* which appeared on 16 November.

[AS/GS219]   [*Glendalough House*]
Nov. 8/06

Dear Heart

    I am greatly relieved to hear that you are better, I got very anxious
last night when no letter came. Of course I will keep myself free for
Sunday so that we may walk if it is fine. We had better take the quarter
to eleven train as you have a show on Saturday night. If your back is
not well of course we wont be able to go very far, you had better ask
Peggy[1] if she thinks you are well enough for a long walk. *The Playboy*
is very nearly ready, I am writing to Lady Gregory by this post to ask
her to fix a time for me to read it to them. Then there will be the job of
making a clean copy. My M.S. at present could not be read by anyone
but myself, it is all written over and corrected and pulled to bits. I will

send you the *Cuchulain* please take great care of it, as it is a presentation copy from Lady Gregory. Have you finished *Aucassin and Nicolette?*

What wretched weather it is! My mother is in bed with a very bad cold, I hope I wont get it. I sent off my review to Manchester yesterday, and got more proofs to correct. I am kept busy! I hope you are taking care of yourself and not sitting too much in the Green Room with the window shut. Remember if your health gives way we wont be able to have our long walks. It is only very strong women who can walk as you have been doing, so you must keep very strong, changling.

What are you changing about now? You seem greatly impressed with your changable attributes! Forever

J. M. Tramp.

P.S. This reads very scrappily I fear, but it means well, when my morning's work is over I am always too tired to write to you as well as I would like. Forgive my tired brains![2]

---

1. Molly's sister, Mrs. Callender, with whom she was still living.
2. At the top of this letter Molly has tried three times to spell *Prague*.

[*AS/GS220*]   [*Glendalough House*]
                                      Saturday [*10 November 1906*]

Dear Molly

I got your letter all right last night, and the letter and paper that you forwarded me. The letter was an invitation out to dinner on Sunday evening, but of course I have refused it. Your letter wasn't a bit nice, I wish you wouldn't write like that it makes me feel queer. You were in a mighty hurry to take it for granted that I was going to have a reading of the P.B. on Sunday and to spoil our walk!

I dreamed about you last night—a very nice dream I think—but I have got it mixed up. I dreamed also that Tolstoi—the great Russian writer came to our plays with two Japanese to see *Riders to the Sea,* and that there was a very bad house. I could not write a nice letter this morning to save my life—it shows how little right I have to scold you for yours—I slept very badly, and I am tired and dull. You dont want me to invent sweet speeches when I'm not a bit sweet do you? We'll be able to see more of each other now, I hope, as the P.B. is nearly done, that will be a blessing. Come tomorrow, if fine, by the *quarter to eleven* please, I wish to God I could say something nice to you, but your letter and some things you have hinted (or seemed to hint) have frozen a little layer of ice round my old heart which as you know very well is a mass of love for my little changeling.

Your old T.

P.S.   Dont imagine I'm huffed or anything, little heart, I'm only weary.

[*TCD/GS220*]   [*Glendalough House*]
Saturday afternoon
[*10 November 1906*]

Little Heart
    I wrote you a crusty sort of note this morning when I was tired and in a bad humour. I have taken a holiday from my work today and now —at 5 o'cl.—after a cycle ride through Kilternan, and the Scalp and Enniskerry, I'm in the best of humours and I could write you nice things till you were tired of them. What a pair of asses we are! We are so fond of each other and we get on so beautifully when we like, and still we keep pulling each other's hair, and saying stupid things till we both get miserable. It is such a pity that we cant have sense be-cause we both know quite well I think, that we are all in all to each other, and will be so always. We must see more of each [other] if we can manage it now, and I think that will make things smoother. This last tiffette—by the way—was your fault wasn't it? It was a very slight affair in any case, and you were very good last night. I believe it is that wretched Playboy who has been making all the mischief, it is unnatural that we should be so near each other, and still not be able to see each other oftener. We'll change all that with the help of God. I suppose you will get this tomorrow morning on your way to meet me. That we may have a fine day! Now goodbye my own little treasure and forgive my growls.

Ever your Tramp.

A quarter to eleven on Sunday remember from W. Row.

[*TCD*]   [*Glendalough House*
                                          ?12 November 1906]

Dearest
  I am in great form today for my work. So much so that I am not
going in to town to see this old play of [Markievicz?][1] I hope you got
home all right. I had the best sleep I have had for weeks and I feel
in great spirits. The P.Boy is very nearly done I think this week should
get me through with it! Wont that be great? I shall be in tomorrow or
next day most likely, in any case, I'll let you know of my movements of
course, we must try and fit in a walk this week, I suppose there will be
a rehearsal on Wednesday evening?
  This letter will be *thick* enough I hope![2]

                                          Ever your Tramp

  1. As no play sponsored by Count or Countess Markievicz was produced during this
season, Synge may have meant to write Martin Harvey, whose company was performing
in *The Corsican Brothers* at the Theatre Royal. See below.
  2. It is written on a postcard.

[*TCD*]   [*Glendalough House*]
                                          Tuesday [*13 November 1906*]

Dearest
  I was delighted to hear yesterday that you are well again. I did not
think I could hear from you so early in the day, but I waited about all
the same, cleaning my bicycle and fiddling about. Then just as I had
given up hope and was going out a postman rode up to the gate on a
bicycle and handed me your letter. I hadn't time to answer you yesterday as I have been working at my M.S. for the reading tonight. Unfortunately I have a cold and am very hoarse and unwell so I wont be
able to do myself justice, I fear. My cycle blew up yesterday so I went
down by the sea instead of riding and sat down in the cold wind like
an idiot. I feel very depressed and anxious about tonight, a great deal
depends on this play I think. I got a very gushing letter from George
Moore last night praising my "Vagrants of Wicklow" up to the skies.[1]
Did you see what Martin Harvey said about *Riders* in his speech in to
day's paper?[2] I do hope my *Playboy* will come off.

I am so glad we are not going to quarrel any more, of course as we have such *strong wills* once we decide not to quarrel we wont quarrel! Isn't that so? I awoke very early this morning and thought a lot and happily about you and our arrangements before I got up. I should think in another ten days I shall have done all I can do to *The Play-Boy* and then we'll come to business. I have a lot of proofs to correct today and I am so anxious about tonight I have not much peace of mind to write nicely to you. If I get a very bad cold out of this how shall I post your letters? Dont be alarmed if you [are] a day or two without news. I'll try and let you know tomorrow how the play goes.

This is a poor sort of note I'm afraid but it is not wanting of feeling, little treasure, that makes it so. It is only my weariness and fears about tonight. Goodbye dear heart, and be good to your

Old Tramper

1. Synge's essay had been published in the Autumn 1906 issue of *The Shanachie*. George Moore (1852–1933), the novelist whose early participation in the Irish Dramatic movement resulted in the ill-fated *Diarmuid and Grania* (written in 1901 in collaboration with W. B. Yeats) and the entertaining trilogy, *Hail and Farewell!* (1911–1914), had written in praise of *The Well of the Saints* and was to support *The Playboy* later.

2. John Martin-Harvey (1863–1944) frequently presented new productions first in Dublin. A long-time disciple of Sir Henry Irving, he was knighted in 1921; in 1907 he contemplated producing *The Playboy*, but decided against it. *The Irish Times* for 13 November 1906 quotes from his speech to the Ladies' Auxiliary of the Lifeboat Saturday Fund: "Mr Harvey then spoke of Mr Synge's masterly little play, entitled *Riders to the Sea*, which had been produced on Saturday night last in the Abbey Theatre, as one of the strongest object lessons in the perilous nature of the life of those who 'go down to the sea in ships.'"

[*TCD*]   [*Glendalough House*]
                                        Friday [*16 November 1906*]

Dear Heart

I've had a bad turn enough, but I'm much better though I'm in bed still. I may get up for a while this evening but I am not sure yet. Dont be uneasy about me, dear heart, it is only a bout of influenza, made sharper by my trip to town Tuesday when it was coming on and the excitement of the "reading". I would give the world and all to see you, but I'm afraid we cant well manage it. I couldn't of course have you up here and downstairs we'd have to face the whole crowd,—my cousin is staying here now—and my sister and elder brothers and nephews are all in and out.[1] We would have no peace or satisfaction I'm afraid, and so alas! you had better wait. I hope I shall be in town again by Monday or Tuesday, but if I am not I will arrange for you to come down some way or other, so that I may have a look at my little changling again. Dear Heart write to me every day, I lie here listening for the postman's knock. I think of you a great deal and changeling I love you infinitely. I cannot write any more now. It tires me and I have a line to write to Lady G.

> Ever my dear Heart
> Your old Tramp

1. Florence Ross came to Glendalough House on 15 November and stayed for several months. Robert Anthony Synge (1858–1943), an engineer, had returned home from the Argentine and taken a house at 32 York Street, Kingstown; Edward Synge (1859–1939), a land agent, had a home in Bayswater Terrace, Sandycove; Annie Isabella Synge Stephens (1863–1944) lived around the corner in Silchester Road; her two sons, Francis Edmund (1884–1948) and Edward Millington (1888–1955), were frequent visitors at Glendalough House.

[TCD]

[*Glendalough House*
18 November 1906]

Dearest.

It is cruel—cruel—cruel—to leave me without a line from you when I am so ill and miserable. Did you not get my letter asking you to write to me every day? I am very unwell, we got the doctor out from Dublin to see me last night.[1] He hopes I will soon be all right. I am to go in to him on Wednesday or Thursday. Are you offended by my last note or what has happened? I was so weak when I was writing I could hardly hold the pen. I am to stay in bed all day today   what a change from the Sundays we have had!

You have no notion, darling of my heart, how much and how tenderly I think of you. You must not be uneasy about me. I am mending now, and in a few weeks, I hope, I'll be as well as ever. It is all that accursed Playboy. There is no chance now of putting him on in

December. Why dont you write. I wish I had asked you to come down today in spite of everything. When I put you off coming, I felt so weak I didn't feel capable of making the explanations a visit would have entailed

Yours forever

J. M. Tramp

1. Dr. Alfred R. Parsons of Dublin, 27 Lower Fitzwilliam Street.

[Glendalough House]

Tuesday (afternoon)

[20 November 1906]

[*TCD*]

Dearest

Thanks for your two letters. I enclose a scrawl I wrote yesterday morning when the post passed and left me. Even when your note came at 2. yesterday I was a little disappointed that you had written so few lines when you had all Sunday on your hands. I got all the earlier ones last week, and was delighted to get them. I am up now again, and have been downstairs for a while. If you come—I leave it to yourself, you know I will be overjoyed to see you—you might come by the quarter to two from W[estland] R[ow] to Glenageary, and go home by the quarter past three in time for your rehearsal. If you come to Glenageary station ask for Adelaide Road. Turn to right down it towards the sea. Our house is a good bit down on the right, the last house before a big bare field. "Glendalough House" is on the pillars of the gate, but very faint. You could also come by tram and walk *up* Adelaide Road, when our house would be the first big house on your left, but the trams are very slow and cold.[1]

I am a little better today I think but it is very tedious. If I am well enough I go in to the doctor on Thursday or Friday afternoon. Perhaps you could meet me at W. Row and walk as far as the Doctor's with me. I will let you know if I can what time I am going. My dear old love how hard it is to be parted for so long. I promise I'll take more care from

this to the Day of Judgement and let my plays take [care] of themselves. By the way if you come give a nice little double knock! I wonder
if I shall get out soon. I am afraid of this cold weather and I am weak
still I am afraid to write too much for fear of making my head ache.

Good bye dearest

J. M. Tramp

1. He drew a diagram of Adelaide Road showing the location of the house.

[*Encl*]
Monday morning
[*19 November 1906*]

Dearest.

Why dont you write? This morning I made fully sure of a long
loving letter When the post knock came I hammered on the floor with
my stick for the servant and told her to get me my letter, but she said
there was none for me. I turned over then in my bed and said to myself
that now I had better try and die quickly as my little changeling had
turned against me or something terrible had happened. These disappointments I need not say are very bad for me. Why do you torture
me? Little soul I did not know till these days how utterly I am wrapped
up in you. Yesterday I thought in spite of all that you would come and
see me. I suppose my letter stopped you. I am very weak still Even
writing these few lines makes my heart thump. What times are you
free this week? I cannot live without you much longer Why—why—
why did I make myself ill like this just as life had become a delight and
a blessing to me for [the] first time in my life.—I wont post this till I
see if a letter comes from you at two o'clock. If none comes I'll faint
with agony. I give my letters to you to my mother to send to the post,
and she knew, I think, that I was expecting you yesterday but we do
not speak of you yet. I'm too shaky.

[*TCD/GS221*]   Glendalough House
                                          Thursday [*22 November 1906*]

Dearest

I am afraid you must be ill again as you have not turned up I hope
you are not bad. Tomorrow I am going in to the doctor so do not come
then. Saturday also is a bad day and the Fays are likely to come out on
Sunday. I will let you know what we can do. I shall be uneasy now till
I hear that you are not ill. I feel very much upset watching out for you
these two afternoons and trying to keep the coast clear so that I might
see you quietly in our dining room. It would almost be better to send
me a wire to say you cannot come than to leave me in such suspense.
However I'm not the worse, I think. I've been out for a little today,
but I felt very weak on my legs. I showed my mother your photo the
other night and told her you were a great friend of mine That is as far
as I can go till I am stronger I am thoroughly sick of this state of affairs
we must end it, and make ourselves public. Be sure to let me know how
you are.

Good bye dear heart,

Your Tramp.

[*TCD/GS222*]   [*Glendalough House*]
                                          Friday [*23 November 1906*]

Dear Heart

I am not quite sure that you are going to meet me today so I had
better send you a line. I felt quite cheered up by your little visit yesterday, and I think I am a lot better today. It was too bad that I had to let
you trot off so soon, but it couldn't be helped. A whole pack of them
were waiting to have tea in the room where we were, and besides by
the time my cousin's[1] visit was over too I was dead fagged out. I hope
you will meet me this afternoon. It is curious what a little thing checks
the flow of the emotions. Last evening because there was a sort of
vague difficulty or uncertainty about our positions in this house we
were as stiff as strangers. I felt beforehand that it would be like that,
so I was not disappointed, and I am *delighted* that you came. I do
things gradually by nature and we have made a great step in the right
direction. It is much better to let my mother get used to the idea by

degrees than to spring it on her too suddenly. I wish you could have seen your solemnity as you walked into the room yesterday with your long coat and glasses, you looked like a *Professor of Political Economy* at the very least. Your little visit has made this room more interesting than it was yesterday, and I have the pleasantest remembrance of every little thing you said. I hope to Heaven the doctor will not find much the matter with me today.

How did you get home? As soon as you were gone I began imagining that you would get into the wrong train and be carried off to Bray and then have no money to take you home. I saw you as plainly as possible standing in your long coat on the platform in Bray explaining your case to the Station Master and porters! It looked very funny. Dear heart I wish I had you here every day what a difference it would make

Tenderly your
J. M. Tramp

I had a letter from Miss Tobin this morning she heard from Sally that I was ill.

1. Edward Synge (1860–1913), the etcher whom Synge had known in Paris, was visiting Dublin and invited Synge to return to Surrey with him to recuperate.

[*TCD*]   [*Glendalough House*]
                                  Friday Night [*23 November 1906*]

Little Heart

This is my second letter to you today, I'm afraid I'm spoiling you! Well I had to wait *two* long hours before I saw the doctor so that it was a quarter past five when I got away. I am grateful to you for coming to meet me I liked you (in spite of your hat) more than I am going to say. But to get to the point. The doctor says I've got on very well, but I've a very slight irritation on one lung still, so it is well for me to be careful, and he advises me to put off *Playboy* and to go to England for a fortnight. So, dear heart, I think I'll go for your sake as much as for my own. You would not like me to knock up regularly would you? The other day when I felt so very ill I kept wondering over and over what my poor little changeling would do if I died and she was left to fight along by herself. I dont like to think of it. You would get along well I dare say, but it is lonesome to think about. However I'm all right again and you'll have me back to you in two weeks ready for walks and mountains, and all our tramping as before. Please tell me as soon as you can what times you are free next week, I must have one little outing with you *before* I go.

I hope you weren't hurt by my sayings about your hat! Remember I'm so proud of my little changeling that I wont let anyone spoil her, not even you!! But forgive me, it wasn't nice of me to go on so much about it when you had taken all the trouble to come down and meet me. I'm afraid I cant see you on Sunday. I am a bit feverish still and I must be very quiet for a couple of days My cousin is coming out here that day. I hope I shall see you on Monday or the day after. Write me a long letter Ever yours

J.M.Tramp

[Glendalough House]
Saturday Morning
[24 November 1906]

[*TCD/GS222*]

My dearest

I am much better today, I think, but I feel very sad, somehow, at the thought that I am not to see you till Monday or Tuesday. I am much more "lonesome" now than when I was really ill. My little life how fond I am of you! I wonder if you are tired of all the times I tell you that. When you begin to be tired of it tell me. Dont you think I am right to go to England and get strong again? Mind you write a full real letter today or tomorrow or both, at least send me a line today if you have not time for a long letter. You will have plenty of time for that tomorrow. I wonder what you will do all day. I shall be thinking of you. When I go to England I'll write to my mother and tell her all. I am afraid I might say something too violent if we talked it over at first as I lose my temper so easily.

Forever and ever, my heart's light,
Your old T.

[*TCD/GS222*] [*Glendalough House*]
Saturday [*24 November 1906*]

My Heart's Joy

Thanks for your note—a very nice one—which I got this morning. My mother is too shy to say much about you, but I think she is pleased. She said you seemed very bright and she hoped I had asked you to come down again on Sunday and cheer me up. I said I hadn't but I would write. Today she has reminded me several times not to forget my note to you. So come down tomorrow (Sunday) by the *quarter to three*, like yesterday and we'll have another little chat If I can think of a suitable excuse I'll write to F. Fay and put him off coming tomorrow. I'm not quite up to entertaining him in any case.

The doctor says I am going on well, getting better slowly. I am not sad except at moments when I get depressed by being ill so long, and not able to see you. Now this must go to the post so that you may have it before you go to bed. Thousands of blessings

from your old Tramp

[*Texas*] [*Glendalough House*]
Tuesday [*27 November 1906*]

Dearest

I forget whether I promised to write to you today or you to me. I was none the worse for our nice little walk yesterday, and I hope to be in at the Abbey tomorrow night. I am to go to the Nassau [Hotel] to finish reading the *Playboy* in the afternoon and I suppose they'll keep me to dine. Then on Thursday I think I shall [have] to take my cousin round to see old Yeats[1] and on Friday I'm off, so it was well we had our time yesterday. Let me know however, what time you are free the next two days in case, by any chance I should be able to arrange to see you again. I am sending you a couple of books tomorrow—two very well known novels that everyone reads, and that will amuse you I think. You had better keep the other books till I come back. You may like to dip into them again. I have been thinking about you a great deal, and very *happily* since yesterday—as I always do for the matter of that. I have just taken a notion—*dont tell any one*—that it would be grand if we could get the place you are in now when the Callenders go.

I wonder if it would be possible. Something you said about the mountains made my mouth water. Goodbye my little heart till tomorrow night. I hope you have written.

Your old T.

1. John Butler Yeats (1839–1922), whose studio was in No. 7 Stephens Green North.

[*Glendalough House*]
Thursday [*29 November 1906*]

Dear Heart

I only slept for an hour and a half last night—I was even worse than in Cardiff—and I feel very much done up today. I wrote you a letter at four o'clock in the morning and another at ten, but I am not going to send you either of them at least not today. They are sad, not cross, ones, but I think my poor little changling was sad enough herself last night, so I do not want to sadden her more. I need not tell you how much I have suffered. You must see yourself how strange it all looked to me but I am telling myself that you are not experienced in the ways of the world and that I must not blame you for what you do in haste only. Why did you try and hide it, that is the worst of all? I am almost frightened sometimes when I think how wildly I love you. My life is in your hands now, as well as my honour. You will very soon send me into my grave if you do not begin to act like a woman who loves—instead of the way you are doing. This was meant to be a cheerful letter, but I'm afraid it can hardly be called that. I am not well. The Playboy is rather a weight on me too, he is not turning out well. I am getting depressed again now so I had better come to an end. My address will be from tomorrow

Wintersells Farm
Byfleet
Surrey. England.

Please write to me very often and very nicely. Oh my little Heart *why* do you torture me?

Your old Tramp.

I send you some of the verses as I promised. Remember they are not particularly good examples of my verse although my heart is in them. *Write.*

[AS/encl]   [29 November 1906]

NB To be read last, but followed by p. 4. over again!
Dear Heart

It is four o'clock in the morning but I cannot sleep my mind is so full of misery. To think that the one evening in five weeks that I was able to go into the theatre you should go and leave me for hours, listening to every footfall with a sort of lump in my throat. And for such a reason! And the very day you wrote me a letter so filled with promises. I wish to God I had never been born. I did not allow myself to think anything while I was waiting in the theatre. I had begun to trust you so completely. You must know as well as I do the low scurrilous thoughts medical students and their like have when they dangle after actresses! And to think that after all our walks among the quiet mountains, you should face that! [deletion] I wish I had died last week when I was so ill. It would have saved me the anguish I am feeling now. Do not think that I want to pain you. It is only because I love you so profoundly, that I feel as I do. You have my life and honour in your hands now, as well as your own, and oh my treasure for God's sake dont ruin our lives by the want of a little thought and a little will. I feel broken down and infinitely wretched. I wish I was not going away I would like to see you again my heart's light! before I go but that is hardly possible.

[10 a.m.]

Such dreary thoughts to haunt me. Do not think I am making too much of what has happened. Taking it at the lightest it is much more than a trifle. If you had told me in the Green Room that you were going it would have been quite different.

I do not know whether I am right in sending you the letter I wrote last night in bed. Perhaps it is as well that you should know something of what I have suffered. Dear Heart wont you be better when we are married?

I wonder if I shall hear from you at two o'clock.

My address in England will be

> Wintersells Farm
> Byfleet
> Surrey. England.

Later.[1] I've had a good walk and I feel more cheerful again. Little Heart it frightens me sometimes when I think how wildly I love you. Oh do be a little more careful or you will kill me quite certainly. I do not think I ask you anything that it is not reasonable to ask and yet–!

I send you three[2] of the old verses you may like to have them for old time's sake though you must not take them as specimens of my verse writing. They were really improvisations. Two others I have about you are better, but you could not read them they are so much pulled about. If you will write me a really nice letter every day when I am away perhaps I shall be able to do something with *The Playboy* still. I suppose I shall hear from you today. Yours ever.

> Tramp.

[AS/encl]
> I knew all solitude, it seemed,
>   That any man might know,
> —Dead year passed year—and then I dreamed
>   I could find comfort so.
>
> But now if you and I apart
>   Must pass two days or three,
> ⟨Then I in my own lonesome heart
>   Seem lost eternally.⟩

(or) *Then in the desert of my heart*
>   *I perish utterly.*[3]

We came behind the rain from Murphy's inn
And saw the splendour of the night begin,
Behind bare sycamores, that in the west
Clung to the sky like lace about the breast
             Of Women richly dressed.

We heard the thrushes by the shore and sea,
And saw the *golden* stars nativity,
      in the furze we met
Then ⟨seemed as best within⟩ a lonely cloud
Of strange delight, where birds were singing loud,
The rest was silence, with the smell
⟨Of furze and grass, and buds that swell⟩
            in its
Of golden ⟨In⟩ honey's   golden well.

And then I asked why with your lips to mine
Had all these glories added eight or nine
New volumes to their glory? Were stars made new
Because your little lips were round and true?
                land
I asked what change you'd wrought in ⟨earth⟩ and sea
This more than Earthly Paradise to wake for me?
With what new gold you'd cased the moon, ·
With what new anthems raised the river's tune?
And why did every sound with rapture break
While my two lips were on your honied cheek?[4]

1. The beginning of the page 4 he refers to following *NB* at the top of the letter
he enclosed.
    2. He apparently decided to send only two poems. Both are typed with manuscript
alterations in ink.
    3. Molly has written above the second version, *I like this the best*. For a later version
still of this poem see *J. M. Synge Poems,* ed. Robin Skelton (Oxford University Press,
1962), p. 41.
    4. This version is quoted in the Oxford *Poems,* Appendix B, p. 113.

[*TCD*]   Glendalough [*House*]
                                                        [*30 November 1906*]
Dearest
    Forgive me, I am just off   my car is coming. I love [you] more
[than I can] say so be happy till I come back to you   it will be very
soon   write at once
    With a thousand blessings

                                                    Your old
                                                    Tramp

[*TCD*]   City of Dublin Steam Packet Company
                                         Royal Mail Steamer *Munster*
                                                [*30 November 1906*]
My dearest Soul
    I am off in the Mail and as it is going to be very rough I am writing
before every one gets sick. I was so sorry to hear this morning that
you are unwell. Do take care of yourself, above all dont smoke much,
it upsets your nerves and heart always if you are unwell. Forgive me
for seeming hard on you. I will explain what I felt some other time.
Now I only want to tell you how completely I am yours. Do let us be
wise and open. Can you wonder that I felt upset and queer when you
went off so secretly the only night in five weeks—and after such a
bad illness—that I got in to see you.
    Little Heart I am going to write to my mother now when I get over.
Wouldn't it be lovely if I could get you down to stay with us at
Christmas for a week. What walks we would have, and what talks over
the fire! I feel very sad going away from my little changeling even for
two weeks. I hope the next journey I set out on will be a very different
one!!
    How I wish I could put my arms round you now and make every
[thing] right again. But—there was a roll I am going to catch it!
Forgive me again dear heart and remember if you have suffered so have
I, intensely and terribly.

Let me have a long loving letter every day   then I will come back
well and happy and we will be always together. How I wish I was
coming back instead of going away

Yours tenderly and forever
J. M. Tramp

[*TCD/GS223*]

Wintersells
Byfleet
Surrey
England
Dec 1st [*1906*]

Dearest Heart,

I have been thinking about you a great deal on my journey. I hope
you are feeling all right again. I got over very well but I was rather
fagged when I got here at eight o'clock in the evening. It is a nice old
house and very nicely furnished in a quiet artistic way. I have been
looking through a number of my cousins pictures this morning and
admired them greatly. I wish he would give me some. I wonder how
your Matinée will go off today, I do not feel that it will be much of a
success. I suppose you will let me hear how it goes.[1] I do not quite
know if I shall be able to get a letter to you every day here as we are
some way to the post. I will try. I suppose you will get this on Sunday
morning. I hope you will take a quiet day and rest yourself reading
your books. Dont take too many cigarettes mind. I am writing under
difficulties today as my cousin is fussing about at my table, and
'checking the flow of my emotions'. But never mind I am overflowing
with them all the same, dear heart. Your little letter yesterday made me
very sad whenever I read it. But between ourselves I dont quite see that
I am the one to be blamed. If you had been very ill, and if you came
up to see me before you went away for two weeks, what would you
think if I went off to spend the evening with say a ballet-girl, and left
you walking up and down the Green [Room] wondering what had
become of me? would you have been quite pleased with me when I

came back, ⟨and gone home quite happily.⟩ However, I do not want to
scold my little changling anymore. When you are unhappy I feel like a
hangman. I am depressed today I seem so far away from you. But still I
think for your own sake as much as my own I was right to come over
and pick myself up. Dear heart let this be our last misunderstanding,
tell me always all you are thinking and doing, as I tell you what I do.
Is that much to ask you? And for God's sake keep clear of the men who
dangle after actresses. I know too well how medicals and their like
think and speak of the women they run after in Theatres, and it wrings
my heart when I think what that man may be saying and thinking of
my little changling, who is so sweet and so innocent and whom I love
so utterly. [*Synge's deletion*] Get yourself well and strong, my own
little heart, before I go home, and we will have a happy Christmas—
happier than anyone else will have in Ireland or out of it. Do write to
[me] often. I feel so lonely here. I think it will help my work however
to have a change of ideas. I have been thinking a lot about our future.
I think you may turn out a very fine actress—if you can only preserve
your sincerity—and if the Abbey breaks up at any time I cannot of
course ask you to give up your art. We shall have to live in London
part of the year, and I think as my wife you will have more chance than
you would have by yourself,—I know so many writers etc. in London
—of getting parts in the intellectual plays at the Court[2] or elsewhere.
Then when we had a little money we'd go off to our own mountains
and worship the moon and stars! Wouldn't that be a nice life? Keep
your health sound, and keep your *distinction* of mind and all will be
well. I cannot tell you how I love you good bye for 13 days

Your Tramp

1. This was the first matinée performance offered by the Theatre. Saturday matinées
were then introduced on a regular basis, with occasional extra "professional matinées"
during the week to enable other visiting companies to see the Irish Players.
    2. The Court Theatre in Sloane Square, under the management of J. E. Vedrenne and
Harley Granville-Barker from 18 October 1905 till 29 June 1907, produced plays by Bernard
Shaw, John Galsworthy, Granville-Barker, Ibsen, and other modern playwrights.

[*TCD/GS223–24*]   Wintersells
                                                      Byfleet
                                                      Surrey
                                                      Dec 2nd/06

Little Heart
    I was delighted to get your note this morning and to hear that you
are getting on well. I could not post a letter here today—there was no
post out after ten o'clock—so you will have no news of me tomorrow
(Monday). I wonder how you have passed your day, and if you care at
all for the books. I have been dodging about in and out most of the
day, and for a while sitting in my cousin's studio at the end of the
garden while he was working at his etchings. He is very kind, and I
cant help pitying him living here by himself with no one to talk to
except his dog. It reminds me of my life before I had a changling to
look to, and make much of—when she is good! It is strange what a
difference you have made in my life, I used to be infinitely lonely,
though I was so used to it in a way. How did you like the last verses
about my lonesomeness? I sometimes wish that you had had some
experience of lonesomeness before we met, it makes one value real
fellowship more deeply. Try and write me a long letter the next time
with talk in it so that I can talk back to you, as there is no news here
to tell you. My cousin—Edward Synge is his name—has a great many
books and I have been dipping into a number of them. It is about six
now, and I am alone in his library with his dog, and he is down in his
studio. I dont go down between four and dinner (at 7) so I have time
to dream and write and think about my changeling. It is a beautiful old
room full of cupboards and alcoves with bookshelves, and a lot of
valuable etchings that he has bought or been given. I like these sort
of times, when one can simply sit and think about all one has done
or left undone, and all one is going to do. I wish we could make
ourselves a beautiful home like this. It is a help, I think, to one's mind
to have everything about one quiet and uncommon and beautiful. My
next play must be quite different from the *P.Boy*   I want to do something quiet and stately and restrained and I want you to act in it. I
think I will work more easily when I have you at my elbow to advise
me, and when we are in our own little abode. I think we ought to [be]
able to make it nice. I have books that are not common and pictures

that are not common and I'll have a little wife who is altogether unheard-of(!) I mean unlike anyone that has ever been—so we shall be well away from all good commonplace people. I wonder if you'll think this a very rambling letter. If you do you can write me another as rambling as you like. Isn't that fair. I got the last batch of proofs for *The Aran Islands* this morning so it ought to be out now before very long. I am beginning to feel very ambitious again. That is a good sign I think. My cousin here is just beginning to get real success now with his work and he is more than ten years older than I am, so if I dont kick the bucket I ought to be able to do good work and plenty of it still. You must help me and keep me up to it. How do you like *Deirdre* now that you have seen it so often?[1] I wonder shall I have a letter from you tomorrow morning.

[*Encl*]   Monday [*3 December 1906*]
My Treasure

I got your second charming letter this morning, and it filled me with joy. I will write and tell Lady Gregory as soon as she goes home for Xmas about the 15th of this month. That will be the best way I think. I wrote the enclosed yesterday, and I am in a great hurry now to go off to the post so I cannot put much into this line. I am always thinking about you and wishing I was home again. I am not very well as I have got a sort of asthma at night that disturbs me a good deal. Take care of yourself Dear Heart and be quite well when I get back. I am to lunch with Miss Tobin—did I tell you—some day this week. You need not be jealous! No one will run away with me.

I am so sorry you will have no letter today. It could not be helped as the posts are bad here on Sunday.

With endless love

Your old Tramp
J. M. S.[2]

1. Yeats's *Deirdre,* starring Miss Darragh.
2. Molly has written *frivolous* at the bottom of the letter.

[*TCD/GS224*]   Wintersells
                                                Byfleet
                                                Surrey
                                                Dec 4 [*1906*]

Dear Heart

Another letter this morning. I am so glad to see that you are cheerful again! I have not written to my mother since Saturday, but I will
tell her in my next letter. I dont know whether it would be any use to
write to your mother, I should think it would do as well to go and see
her when I go over. I am not very well yet as I have a sort of asthma
at night that gives me a nasty cough. I haven't been able to do anything
to the Playboy yet, next week I hope to work at him.

I often read over your little letters and they seem to do me good.
I think of you a great deal and I get very lonely sometimes. Two other
cousins were down here yesterday—sisters of the man I am staying
with—one of them is a hospital nurse, the other a writer, who does
school histories and that sort of thing.[1] They are very pleasant and
kindly both of them. I have not heard yet from Miss T[obin] what day
I am to lunch with her. It is half-a-crown for a return to London so I
cannot go up very often, although I am so close. I am glad you had such
a good matinée. I am beginning to count the days till I see my little
changling again. This is Tuesday, and on Friday half the time will be
over. Is not that a comfort? I hope we shall have a fine Sunday, two
days after I go back so that we may have a long day together. Dear heart
we must be careful now   another quarrel would kill us.

I am certainly stronger today, so I hope in ten days more I shall be
all right. Good bye and be good   I fear I am late for the post though
I have been writing in a hurry. There is not much in my letter but I
suppose you are glad to hear

                                                Your old Tramp.

1. Margaret Bertha Synge (1861–1939) published, among other children's stories and
histories, *Cook's Voyages* (1892), *A Book of Scottish Poetry* (1897), *A Child of the Mews*
(1896), *The Story of Scotland* (1896), *The Life of Gladstone* (1898), *The Life of General Charles
Gordon* (1900), *The Story of the World for the Children of the British Empire* (1903), *The
World's Childhood: Stories of the Fairies* (1905), *A Short History of Social Life in England*
(1906).

[*AS/GS225*]

Wintersells
Byfleet
Surrey
Dec. 5. Wednesday [*1906*]

Little Heart

No letter from you today! The last I got was written on Sunday, and this is Wednesday. I have felt uneasy all day, wondering if you were ill, or if anything had gone wrong. I hope I shall hear tomorrow morning, it is evening now.

I am afraid some of my last letters may have seemed cold in comparison, with the full and loving ones of yours that I was answering, but you are too wise I think to mind even if they seemed so. It is sometimes hard here to get a good time for writing and in a strange place one's mind is a little distracted with the new people one meets.

I dont know how I have lived so long without you, for you are a part now of every thought and feeling that I have. It is evening now and E.S. is down in his studio so that I am alone again in the library I told you about. I have opened the end window—it is a long narrow room with a window at each end—so that I can see the stars we used to walk about under, a long time ago! All that we feel for each other is so much connected with this divine world, that our particular affection, in a real sense, must be divine also. What is there in life, dear heart, to come near our walks down that winding road from Enniskerry when the stars themselves seemed like little candles, set round our great love that is more priceless than they are. The stillness of this dim room puts me into a sort of dream. Would to God that you were here that I might put my arms round you and feel that the reality and mystery of our love is stronger even than dreams. (I wonder am I writing nonsense? It sounds uncommonly like it)

Talking of dreams. I dreamt last night that I introduced you to my brother, and that he began at once retrimming your hat! The last thing he would notice. I dreamt also that Mac. and O'Rourke[1] fluffed so badly at the Abbey that the curtain had to be dropped on them! What a step from the sublime to the ridiculous!

[*TCD/GS224/Encl*] Thursday [*6 December 1906*]

Dearest

Your rambling letter came this morning. Why didn't you write to me on Monday when you'd nothing else to do? How do you manage to write backwards I've tried to do it and I cant. Between ourselves it is very ugly. I dont mind the blots   the 'J' is certainly an improvement.

Why do you think Miss D[arragh] 'knows'? I wrote to you last night a letter which you'll find with this. I'm writing now in the garden in a sort of old Green House (that has only the roof and end left standing) so that I may get the air. It does not help letter-writing to have your paper blowing up every minute. Your letter was pretty 'rambling', but I know it is not easy to write good letters always when one writes often, and I want to hear from you very often indeed. I am going to write to my mother tonight. About yours is more difficult. I felt it hard somehow to write on such an important matter to a person I dont know. As soon as I speak to her I will *feel* how to put things, but my mind becomes a blank when I think of writing to her now, and I am afraid my letter would be stiff or awkward. What do you think? I am not very well. The asthma has left me with a heavy cough, so that I am not much the better yet for the change. However I am picking up now I think, and I hope to look into the *Playboy* tonight or tomorrow. Tomorrow week I go home!!!

Your old Tramp.[2]

1. Joseph A. O'Rourke (1882–1937) had recently become a member of the company; he remained until 1916 when the players seceded under Arthur Sinclair and founded the Irish Players.
2. Molly scrawled *presume* twice at the top of Thursday's instalment.

[*TCD/GS224–25*] [*Wintersells. Byfleet. Surrey*]

Friday Night [*7 December 1906*]

Dearest

Your note written on Tuesday evening came this morning—why it took so long on the way is best known to itself—and was very welcome.

It was a nice note. I wonder what put it into your changeling's head that I want you to be 'serious'. The lighter your little heart is the better —the only thing I dont like is a certain cheap, commonplace, merriment which is at times strongly felt among 'the company', but which you are naturally, thank God, quite free of. A kind of restraint in one's merriment—a restraint I mean not in the degree of it, so much as in the quality—gives style and distinction without taking any joyousness away. In a way I do perhaps want you to be serious, that is I want you to take serious things seriously, and to look where you are going so that you may not be a mere weather-cock twisting about after every breeze that blows on you. This isn't a lecture mind, but you mustn't get it into your head that I am a morose tyrant. Surely we are merry enough when we are out having our walks and taking our little teas at Kilmacanogue (i.e. Kilmaconic) aren't we?

I have posted the letter to my mother today! So that is done. I will write to yours also if you like. I spoke about it in my last letter, and I'll wait to hear what you say in answer.

I went up to London today and lunched with Miss Tobin, she was very nice and kind. There is not of course the remotest sign of flirtation about us but I like her greatly, and value her friendship. She has taken a great liking to you and Sally. She says she would hardly know me I have changed so much since the summer, and I look so thin now and generally unwell. That is not very encouraging, is it? Your last letter was the right kind of thing as it is possible to answer what you say. You say that I'll think you sentimental because of what you write about the verses. It is hard to define sentimentality, but you may be quite easy in your mind, you are not sentimental, and never will be in the sickly sense of the word. A full vigorous affection does not get sentimental, it is only sickly, inactive half-and-half people who are really attacked. A true affection naturally occupies itself with the little things as well as the big things that concern it, but it does not grow any less healthy for that reason.

I am glad you were at *Don Giovanni*. We must hear a lot of good music together. There are so few ways of enjoying the arts in Dublin, I feel I have been foolish to neglect music so much. Is this letter too philosophical for you? If it is, tell me, and I'll write you next time about 'Jones', E. Synge's dog, and the 'Encumbrance' as we call the housekeeper's Baby!

Saturday Morning

Your note of Thursday has come this morning. It cut me like a knife. It brings tears into my throat when I see you trying to pick a quarrel with me again so soon after what has passed, and when I am so far away from you, and so utterly unwell. I have never said, or thought for an instant that you were either *'silly'* or 'sentimental'. I have written as best I could in any time that I could find, and fagged off to [the] post with my letters to you in all weathers. If you do not care to have them I am sorry I took so much trouble.

Your old Tramp

P.S.   Later.
You must know that you are never out of my mind, and that I love you as the very breath of my soul. It is perhaps because I am a writer that I am not able to write about this profound passion and love that I am filled with, except at times when I feel I can express it worthily.

When I get a loving letter from you I am full of joy for the whole day. But when you write as you have just written I feel utterly broken down.

Tramp

Dear Heart why do you write so snappily when you know how much it hurts me. If you only could know how I lie awake at night counting the hours till I get back to you you would know how unjust you are. This is Saturday I get back on Friday.

[TCD/GS225]

[Wintersells. Byfleet. Surrey]
Monday [10 December 1906]

Dear Old Changeling
Many thanks for your letter this morning. I wrote you a long one on Wednesday or Thursday that you dont seem to have got. Also a 'grumpy' one on Saturday that I suppose you got yesterday. I am

better I think on the whole and I go back on Friday so do not post to
me after 6.0′c. on Wednesday. Write as much as you can before that
I live on your letters. I have not heard yet what my mother thinks. Why
am I to put off telling Lady G.? I thought you wished it. Dear Heart
I am looking forward to fine walks during your holidays. Unfortunately
the P.Boy is hanging over me still   I haven't been well enough to do
much to him since I came over. There is a sort of open Green House
in the garden—did I tell you before?—where I sometimes sit and work
at him. I often dream of you now, pleasant little dreams but nothing
remarkable. It shows how much I am thinking about you. I got the
Irish Society all right. You come out very well but I am jealous of the
public getting *my photo,* that was promised to me for my exclusive use.
A woman was murdered in the village half a mile away from here last
night. They are making a motor-race course all round this house and
there are a lot of cut-throats about. Now, dearest, I'm afraid I must take
a turn at the PlayBoy so I'll have to leave you with this shabby note.
It is a shame but I cant help it   I've been busy all the morning with
last proofs etc. of the Aran Book. With a thousand blessings

                                             Your old Tramper.
P.S.   Now for a galloping Post Script. I've been through Act I. It is
good I think and only needs a little more revision. I wish I could say
the same for Act III!

Write me *one* more nice *loving* letter *at least* before I go home so
that I may have happy meditations on my long solitary journey on
Friday. Your last ones dont make me as happy as those you wrote first.
Perhaps it is my fault as I may have been too businesslike on my side
of the correspondence.

It is a glorious day here but very cold. I am nearly frozen in my
Green House, but still it is pleasanter than indoors. I wonder if you
got my last letter but one. I thought it would please you, and still (if
you have got it), you do not say a word about it. I wonder how *The
Canavans* are going.[1] You might send me a paper or two if you can
afford it!

Your old T.

1. Lady Gregory's new three-act play was produced for the first time on 8 December.

[*TCD/GS225*]   [*Wintersells. Byfleet. Surrey*]
                                                  Monday Evening
                                                  [*10 December 1906*]

Dearest Heart.

This my second letter to you today. When I am writing quickly in the morning to catch the post I do not seem to be able to say anything that is worth saying. It seems a very long time since our last walk which was only a fortnight ago, but I have never known days go so slowly as these have gone. Why do you say you had to stop writing or you would say something that you did not want to say?

I feel low and uneasy—I do [?not] know why—since your letter on Saturday. My own heart, do let us make our love a deep and certain thing with no room in it for uneasiness or misgiving. You know how lonely I have been, and how I have taken you into the very essence of my life. I do still believe that our love will be a joy and blessing to us, Dear Heart [*Synge's deletion*]—I cannot write this evening I keep wondering what you were going to say and why you do not want me to tell Lady G. when you have asked me so often to do so—

Why are you so changeable when you know how much it hurts and harms me?

I dare say that this is all my own folly and depression, and that all the time you are the best little changeling in the world, but people who have had influenza are very easily depressed so I have a good excuse if I am foolish. Wont it be a blessing when we are together again? That is our only cure I think. I tremble sometimes when I think how much power I have given you over my life, and how recklessly you often use it. "I had better stop or I shall say something I dont want to say"!! That is a quotation

There are only four more days now till I start back again. That is a blessing! Remember to write me a *beautiful* letter to cheer up my cold lonely journey.

                                    J. M. S.

Post early on *Wednesday*.

[NLI/encl]   *[Wintersells. Byfleet. Surrey]*
                                                Tuesday morning
                                                Dec *[11]*th/06¹

My thousand Treasures

    I opened your letter this morning with terror—I knew I deserved a
scolding and I was afraid I was going to "catch it". You let me off
very well and I am in wild good spirits now. Dear Heart in four Days
—damn them—I will be in the Seventh Heaven again, with my little
changling, my little jewel, my love and life, in my arms! Is not that
something to live for. Dearest if you could see how I get up thinking
of my little changeling, and go to bed thinking about my little
changeling, about her little baby nose, and her little eyes, and her little
voice, and her little bull-dog chin, and all her little soul and body that
is mine forever!

    Dear Heart, Dear Heart, Dear Heart if you knew how much you are
to me! How I see you waiting for me at the door of the scenery room,
and sitting on my knee among the quiet woods, and putting a new life
into the stars and streams and trees and Heaven and Earth and all that
therein is for me! I had better stop I think or I might blaspheme God
in my love for you.

    I send some lines I scratched off last night if they make you smile
remember they are a first draft only.² I send also a foolish letter I wrote
last night. Now for the Play Boy—God confound him!

                                    Goodbye my own dearest Heart.
                                        Your Tramp.

Many thanks for all your news. It interested me greatly. I fear you are
right about Yeats' plays. Good bye again, my single darling love, my
treasure of life.

---

    1. Synge misdated this letter December 10th.
    2. Perhaps the poem quoted by Elizabeth Coxhead in *Daughters of Erin* (London:
Secker and Warburg, 1965), p. 187, given to her in typescript by Molly's daughter Pegeen
Mair, which seems to refer to the incident of the medical students:

    I brought you where the stars and moon of night
    Filled earth and air with dreams of strange delight,
    I taught you notes of blackbirds, wrens and larks,
    And showed you ruddy buds with curious marks,
    I made you listen to far wings of rooks,

And held you in my arms in mossy nooks
And then I thought my long long waiting done
As sick me watch the rising of an autumn sun.

And then I saw you go your own sure way
To oily men made rich with cheap display.
So I go lonely to the lonely hills
Where still the fragrant air my breathing fills,

And I lie low with many a deadly weed
And write a heavy curse to fill my creed
And cry for some hot brand to seal my lips
Which my wild madness laid upon your finger tips.

[TCD/GS225–26]   Byfleet
                                  Surrey
                        Thursday [13 December 1906]

My Dearest,
    This is a line merely to thank you for papers and your note. I was
in London yesterday—lunching first, with Miss Tobin, then with her to
a show of my cousin's pictures, then to dine with *him* at an Irishman's,
called Stopford,[1] talking till one o'clock at night, sleeping there and
back here today about two o'clock when I got your note. I am off for
Ireland tomorrow morning. I am terribly afraid I may be a good deal
taken up with the Directors on Saturday and perhaps on Sunday—
you know they are both leaving Dublin very soon. However in any
case we shall have good times next week. I am inclined to shout with
delight at the thought of going back to you.
                                        Your old T.
                                        Turn over

P.S.   I heard from my mother. She says she thought 'the friend' I have
been walking with was a man, but that my showing her the photo and
the letters that came so often when I was ill made her think there was
some thing. Then she says it would be a good thing if it would make
me happier, and to wind up she points out how poor we shall be with
our £100 a year. Quite a nice letter for a first go off. So that is satisfactory

Good bye till Saturday, afternoon or evening or both. I would like
to go in early on Saturday but there would be no use as I shall be
tired after the journey

Your T.

1. Edward Adderley Stopford (1843–1919), a tea merchant and wood carver living in
Weybridge, Surrey; later he moved to Frankfort Avenue, Rathgar, and worked with Horace Plunkett in the Irish Agricultural Organization Society.

[*AS/GS205*]   Glendalough [*House*]
                                             Monday [*?17 December 1906*]
Dearest
    I feel as if I could hardly wait till tomorrow I am so eager to see
you again.
    I have had a little ride round by Bray, it was a most wonderful
evening, and I never felt so happy between the memory of yesterday
and the hope of tomorrow. What a joy to live in a place where the
twilights are so glorious, and where I have such a little friend to share
them with me. We'll make the old romances come to life again.
    I hope you weren't tired after our beautiful outing.
    Meet me tomorrow *Tuesday Wet* or *Fine* at Westland Row Station at
2 o'clock. I'll be there unless I wire; if you cant come please wire to
me before 12. Please dont be late it is such a wretched place to wait.
Ever and Ever your old Tramp
I've thought of a very nice present for you!!!!!

[*TCD/GS226*]   Glendalough House
                                                            Wednesday
                                                            Dec. 19/06
Sweetest Heart.
    Do you remember that I told you once—in Liverpool I think—that
the love of a man of 35 was a very, or at least a rather different thing
from that of a man of 25? I was making a mistake. Last night I felt all

the flood of fullness, and freshness and tenderness that I thought I had half left behind me. I can say now very truthfully that I have never loved anyone but you and I am putting my whole life now into this love.

I have no cold today after all and I have had a good morning's work at the *Playboy,* I am going out now for a turn on my bicycle and then I am going to work again. I am sorry I did not arrange to see you some time today. It is hard to be a whole day without you when you are so near, and your whole time is free.

My mother enquired quite pleasantly about our walk and where we had been, she is coming round to the idea very quickly I think, but still it is better not to hurry things.

Meet me tomorrow at the same time and place 2 oclock, Westland Row and dont be late as we could so easily miss each other in that big station.

I hope you are not tired. Good bye dearest Heart

Your old Tramp

[*TCD*]   Glendalough House
Friday Night
[*21 December 1906*]

Sweetest Heart

I am very sorry to say that I think I should stick at the *Playboy* all day tomorrow so that we shall not meet till Sunday. It is a nuisance, but I know you feel as much as I do how important it is that I should finish my job. My typewriter broke down this morning a little before twelve so I had to go into town and get a new spring put into it after lunch. Then I bought you a dear little watch,—dear in every sense— saw Old Yeats, and came home too late to get through much work.

I heard from Musek last night, the letter was waiting for me when I got home. He sent me post-card photos of the Bohemian Nora and Dan Burke. *The Shadow* is to go on there in March.[1]

Dear Heart come down by *the quarter to ten* from Westland Row on Sunday—second class—to Bray as usual. We will have a great day. Of course do not come if it is wet. Write me a nice letter when you get this

so that I shall have it tomorrow night to cheer me up after my days'
work. Hadn't we a lovely time yesterday. I think you'll like the little
watch.

Forever your old Tramp

You had better put out your little head when you come to Glenageary
there are so many seconds it would be hard to find you.

1. *The Shadow of the Glen* was not finally produced at the National Theatre in Prague
until 22 August 1907.

[*TCD*]   [*Glendalough House*]
                                              Xmas night/06
Dearest
    This has been a long day without you, and, alas, there will be
another like it tomorrow. I worked at the *Playboy* till half past one, and
then we all went up to dine at my sister's. There were 10 of us in all
and we had a pleasant dinner. My mind kept straying away to my little
changeling and wishing she was there too. After that I went for a walk
with one of my nephews and then back there for tea. Now at last I have
come home with my mother and I have a moment to write to you. How
have you passed the day Dear Heart and what presents have you got?
I got two pair of stockings from my mother—in addition to the gloves,
—a book from Florence Ross, a can of cigarettes from the nephews, a
tie-pin from my little niece and two ties, so I am well made up. I gave
Florence and the nephews and niece little books that I had, *and didn't
want!* Isn't that a good way to give your relations presents.
    You will say this is a dull letter but it cant be helped as I am
stuffed up with plum pudding and cake, and have been doing gym-
nastic tricks for the boys into the bargain till my head is singing. Next
Xmas I hope my heart will be singing too, with my little changeling to
trot round. Dont the days seem long now when we are apart?
    I hope your cold is well again, and that your spirits are tip-top.
    With ten thousand blessings
            Your old Tramp
I'll let you know *if I can* what time I'll be at the Abbey on *Thursday*

[*TCD/GS227*]　　　　　　　　　　　　　[*Glendalough House*]
　　　　　　　　　　　　　　　　　　　Thursday 27/XII/06

Dear One

I got your little note this morning. I am sorry mine did not reach
you sooner I wrote it on Xmas and went out and posted it that evening
in all the rain. I suppose it was delayed in the post—I went to the
Abbey today at 3 o'clock but found nobody. I could not let you know
before-hand as I did not know when I was going in. I have had two
hard days at P.B. and I am very tired again. In the evenings now I am
reading Petrarch's sonnets, with Miss Tobin's translations. I think I'll
teach you Italian too so that you may be able to read the wonderful
love-poetry of these Italian poets Dante, and Petrarch, and one or two
others. You are more interested in the natural and human side of art
than in the very exalted or poetical—you liked the Dutch pictures, the
other day, for instance, better than the Italian ones,—. That is as it
should be, and I am the same I think. Still we both have a poetical
strain in us, and we should take care of it—as one takes care of some
rare flower in one's garden, that dies easily and leaves one the poorer
forever. You feel as fully as anyone can feel all the poetry and mystery
of the nights we are out in—like that night a week ago when we came
down from Rockbrook with the pale light of Dublin shining behind the
naked trees till we seemed almost to come out of ourselves with the
wonder and beauty of it all. Divine moments like that are infinitely
precious to us both as people and as artists I with my writing and you
with your acting, and by reading what is greatest in poetry or hearing
what is greatest in Music—things like the Messiah—one trains one's
soul, as a singer trains his voice, to respond to and understand the
great moments of our own lives or of the outside world. I think people
who feel these things—people like us—have a profound joy in love,
that the ordinary run of people do not easily reach. They love with all
their hearts—as we do—but their hearts perhaps, have not all the stops
that you and I have found in ours. The worst of it is that we have the
same openness to profound pain—of mind I mean—as we have to
profound joy, but please Heaven we shall have a few years of divine
love and life together and that is all I suppose any one need expect.
I am growing sure of one thing and that is that we are not going to
destroy this divine love that God has put between us by the wretched
squabblings and fightings that seemed to threaten us at first.——

I wonder will all that make you laugh I am in a dreamy sort of mood sitting over the fire by myself. So excuse me if I write like a fool—

I hope I shall see you tomorrow I shall be in I think, but I dont know when—I dare say in the evening.

Good night my priceless changeling

My heart's treasure

J. M. S.

Synge at thirty

Synge in 1906

Riders to the Sea, *1906*

Maire O'Neill, *about 1907*

[AS]   Glendalough House
                                                  January 1st 1907

Dearest Heart

This is the first letter I have written this year, and the first time
I have written the new date—as it [is] right they are *for you*. My toe is
rather better, but still so tender I think I had best keep it quiet tonight.
Tomorrow I have a lot of things to do in town if I am well enough and
of course I shall be in for the night shows but I do not see any way of
getting you to meet me as I am so uncertain in my movements. Next
week please God we'll manage better. I came home last night in wonderful good spirits. The air and moon were beautiful walking down
from the train and New Year bells were ringing all round, and I remembered how good you had been and I was in great delight. The III
Act is coming out all right and all will be well I hope. How did I ever
live so long without a little changling? You are in every thought of my
life now, and may it be so for ever! If I can give you happy New Years
you'll have them as long as I am on this side of the grave. So good bye
and a thousand blessings on you

                                                  Your Tramp.

[TCD]   Glendalough [*House*]
                                                  Jan 4th/07

Dear Heart

I have a little cold so I could not go in last night, and I will not go
tonight—I think—or perhaps tomorrow. I am not at all bad but I do
not want to be laid up again just as the rehearsals are beginning.

Write me a *very* nice letter when you get this to cheer me up. I am
inclined to get very depressed when I think of my poor little changeling
going home all by her little self. Be very good, and think about me a
great deal. I am very much disgusted that I cant go in for the *Playboy*
Rehearsal this morning. It is a great nuisance. However its well I'm
not worse.

My cousin Florence Ross was at the Abbey last night with one of
my nephews and another cousin. They liked the shows very much
indeed, and they tell me there was a fairly good House.

I am scribbling this in a great hurry as the servant is going out to the post in a few minutes, so do not be surprised that there is so little depth in it. You must be learning to understand all I mean now before I say it.

I will try and get in tomorrow.

With a thousand loves

Your old Tramp.

Be careful with your cues etc and dont get into a row with Fay while we are all scattered.

I am writing about a *flat* I saw advertised in the paper today! Isn't [it] time for me to make a move?

[*TCD*]

[*Glendalough House
7 January 1907*]

Sweet Heart

I am so anxious to hear how you are. I had my ear cocked at the door all the morning till your note came to Fay. If I had known you were not coming I would have gone part of the way to the Hospital with you. Wasn't it curious how we met. I had just left my bicycle at Rudge's (at the Grafton St. corner) to be mended and then I thought I'd walk as far as Dawson [Street] to see if I could see you, and pop out you come![1]

I hope you are resting well today, and that you will be in great form tomorrow. I shall be in tomorrow at eleven. If you aren't able to come out I'll go up and see you in the afternoon. I must know how you are.

We had a good rehearsal. This first act anyhow goes swimmingly. I am longing to hear you in Pegeen Mike with the others. If your eye doesn't get better soon I'll have to go and teach you your part myself, so as not to tire you by reading it. No word from the Flat-man! I wonder why he advertises if he will not take the trouble to answer would-be tenants. Take care [of] yourself my treasure for my sake, and your sake, and the Abbey's sake.

Your old follower forever

J. M. S.

I have found my papers that were lost!!! Is that thanks to St. Antony?
Do get well Dear Heart

1. Rudge, Whitworth Cycle Company Ltd., had a shop at No. 1 Stephen's Green.
Molly was still staying with the Callenders at Park Chambers, 13 Stephen's Green North.

[*TCD*]   [*Glendalough House*]
                                                       Monday evening
                                                              7/I/07.

Darling
    I must write you another line so that you may have something to
cheer you up when you awake tomorrow morning! I am troubled to
think of you lying there all day with no one to cheer you up. I hope
you wont go down to the Abbey tonight, you must have a rest to set
you up.
    My toe is very sore again tonight but I'm going off to the post in
spite of it so that my little changeling may have her note tomorrow
morning. I am taking in the 3rd Act of *PlayB.* tomorrow and I believe
I am going to lunch with W.G. and then work at it all the afternoon
with Frank, so that there may be no delay. I dont feel quite so sure of
the third act as of the others. I have been a little hurried at the end of it.
However it will play all the faster. Sweetheart be sure you do *everything*
the doctor tells you so that you may get well *quickly.* If you are laid up
for long what will become of your old Tramp. I hope you will have a
long sound sleep tonight and be much better tomorrow. You have such
a strong healthy constitution I am sure you will get well very fast once
you begin.
                                    With many blessings your old T.

[*TCD/GS237*]   [*Glendalough House*]
                                                     Saturday Jan. 26th/07

My Heart's Delight
    A thousand thanks for your little note. I was not, of course, angry
with you last night but I felt queer and lonesome all the same on my
way to the train. I am afraid it is not very likely that we shall get away

together tonight, so I must send you all my blessings by post, or at least by letter.

I am not very bad, but, if anything, my cough is worse than it was yesterday so I do not know what to say about our Sunday walk. Unless I say something definite to you tonight you had better *not* come down tomorrow. It makes me sick to think of passing the long day without you, but it would be much worse if I got regularly laid up again, and did not see you for days like the last time. If it was not Sunday I would ask you to come out here, but that is not possible so many of my people will be here.

Fancy! I am thinking more about being without my little changeling tomorrow than I am thinking about the P.B. All the same I most fervently hope it will go off well and be a credit to both of us.

With endless love
Your old Tramper

[*TCD/GS238–9*]

[Glendalough House]
Sunday
Jan. 27/07

My Treasure

I have been awake most of the night, so I am rather worn out and it is as well that we are not going out as we would be sure to tire ourselves. It is curious how much I have changed. Last year I would have been as happy as possible among my books for a long Sunday morning, but now I am so lonesome I dont know what to do with myself. I wonder how you feel today. You played wonderfully I thought last night, and everyone was delighted with you. Now for a secret. When you went over and sat down by the fire showing off the Mrs Siddons side—or Mrs Sheridan which was it—I heard a man behind me saying "What a beautiful girl!"——! Wasn't I telling you, and you a fine handsome young woman with a noble brow?

I wish I had you here to talk over the whole show last night.[1] W.G. was pretty fluffy, and Power was very confused in places, then the crowd was wretched and Mrs W.G. missed the new cue we gave, though she can hardly be blamed for that. I think with a better Mahon and crowd and a few slight cuts the play would be thoroughly sound. I feel like old Maura today "Its four fine plays I have though it was a hard birth I had with every one of them and they coming to the world."[2]

It is better any day to have the row we had last night, than to have your play fizzling out in half-hearted applause. Now we'll be talked about. We're an event in the history of the Irish stage.

I have a splitting headache, and worse luck I have to go in and talk business with Lady Gregory half the day. She got an important wire from Yeats, so she came up in a hurry last night and we have to talk today. There is nothing new, only details of what we had on hand before. If I get an opportunity I think I'll tell her about *us*.

Dearest treasure you dont [know] how you have changed the world to me. Now that I have you I dont care twopence for what anyone else in the world may say or do. You are my whole world to me now, you that is, and the little shiney new moon, and the flowers of the earth. My little love how I am wrapped up in you! It went to my heart to desert you last night but I could not get away from Lady Gregory. There is the quarter to eleven bell ringing! That is usually my signal to put on my shoes and start for our walk. It goes through me. Perhaps we may get a walk tomorrow, or in any case on Tuesday. Now the P.B. is off we are more our own masters, thank Heaven, though I have still an article to get written before Feb. 1st. I am starving God help me. Now good bye my own soul, till tomorrow. I would take this and put it into your post box, but I dont know which it is. I suppose if I wire to you tomorrow morning you could come down the quarter to two to Bray and have a little walk. I may be too busy of course or too unwell. Goodbye again

      Your old Tramp

---

1. *The Playboy* opened on Saturday, 26 January, to an uneasy audience, and by the third act the audience's reaction had become so violent the noise drowned out the final speeches. Joseph Holloway later reported in his Diary that Christy Mahon's reply to the Widow Quin had set the protestors off: "It's Pegeen I'm seeking only and what'd I care if you brought me a drift of chosen females standing in their shifts itself, maybe, from this place to the Eastern World", the speech "made more cruelly brutal" by W. G. Fay's substitution of "Mayo girls" for "chosen females". Molly played Pegeen Mike; Sara Allgood played the Widow Quin, Ambrose Power Old Mahon, Arthur Sinclair the publican Michael James, Frank Fay Shawn Keogh, J. A. O'Rourke and J. M. Kerrigan the two farmers Philly Cullen and Jimmy Farrell, and Brigit O'Dempsey, Alice O'Sullivan and Mary Craig the village girls. It was not until the end of the week that the play received a fair hearing, and the entire run was beset by disturbances.

2. Synge is parodying the tragic speech by old Maurya of *Riders to the Sea*.

[*TCD*]   [*Glendalough House*]
                                                      Thursday
                                                      Jan [*31st*] /07[1]

Dear old Changeling

We see so little of each other now we'll have to begin to write letters to keep our spirits up, till we get a little peace again. Wont it be wonderful when we are out again in the twilight with ourselves only, and the little shiney new moon sinking on the hills? I have been lying half asleep all day trying to rest myself and my cough has been rather bad—it is getting worse bad cess to it—I am going in tonight but I wont go tomorrow, perhaps, if things are quieter. Then I'll have to lie up again on Sunday and keep myself for next week.

I have been longing to have you here with me today to pet me and make much of me. I hope you are feeling better today, you looked tired yesterday. This is a foolish empty note I fear, but I fancied you might like to see that I am thinking about my little changeling in spite of all the fuss.

I suppose you'll get this tomorrow morning

                                                      Your old Tramp.

1. Synge misdated this January 30th.

[*TCD/GS244*]   [*Glendalough House*
                                                      1 February 1907]

Dearest Heart.

I was delighted to get your envelope today. Cheer up, my little heart, the P.B. will soon be getting his rest I hope, and then, we'll be able to see a lot of each other till we get everything fixed up. These two days I have had at home by myself I have been thinking about you a very great deal—I am always at it—and wishing I had your little voice to cheer me.

I hope we may be able to [get] a little walk on Sunday if I go on getting better but, of course, I will not be able to go far. I am sorry Peggy is bothering you, when you have so much to tire you without that. Did you fight about me?

I am getting a little better I think but I am sore all over from coughing. It gets very bad in the night sometimes. The mountains looked lovely today. I cannot tell you how much I longed to be away among them again with Pegeen Mike.

I suppose you will think this is as poor a note as the one I wrote last night. You mustn't mind if it is. It is my head that is heavy not my heart. I wonder shall we be able to get away for a supper together tomorrow if I am up for the matinee.

You dont know how much I admire the way you are playing P. Mike in spite of all the row

> A thousand thousand blessings
> Your Tramper

[TCD]   [*Glendalough House*
                                                5 February 1907]

Dearest Life

I heard the post man's knock up the road today beyond this house and I was just beginning to curse etc like a gaudy officer when they came up with your note to my great joy. I am in bed still but I may be up tomorrow I dont know yet, I would give the world to see you, but you had better not come tomorrow as I may not be up. Perhaps you might come on Thursday I will let you know again. I will tell them you are going to help me to type my article[1] that I have to have [finished] this week!

I am thinking about you all the time, though even if I had you here I could not talk much I am so hoarse and wheezy. F Ross went away this morning and the other one[2] comes tomorrow Worse luck. It is a great plague to have semi-strangers here when one is ill. I laughed at the story of your attacking the poor orphan with a bottle   I wish I had seen it! I think the debate was a mistake.[3] Yeats forgets that our opponents are low ruffians not men of intellect and honesty with whom one can reason. Good bye my treasure for another day or two. What hours are you free? Be sure you write to me again tomorrow. I'll worry myself ill if you dont.

YOUR OLD TRAMP

1. Probably "The People of the Glens", published in *The Shanachie,* Spring, 1907.
2. Another cousin, Mrs. Frank Dobbs, and her little boy.
3. Yeats arranged for a public debate on "The Freedom of the Theatre" on 4 February with "Pat" (P. D. Kenny) in the chair; it too broke up in disorder.

[*TCD/GS253*]   [*Glendalough House*
                                                      6 February 1907]

Dearest Love

Many thanks for all your little notes, they are the only comfort I have. I am afraid I am worse today instead of better, and I feel very down indeed. Did I tell you that we had the doctor out from Dublin to see me on Monday evening? He says there is nothing serious the matter but that I must lie up for a few days till I get over this cough. Oh what fools we were to go and sit in the Park that cold day, and then come back on top of the tram and bring on all this misery and separation. Unless I am much better than I am today there would be no use in your coming out tomorrow. If I am really better I may possibly wire to you before *one* tomorrow, asking you to come out in the afternoon. If I dont perhaps you will be able to come on Friday instead. It seems years since I saw you, my own little heart. I am delighted to hear about the rise in your salary. I knew there was talk of raising them sometime, but I did not know it would be done so soon.

I feel as 'blue' as F. Fay today. I got the three papers all right thanks and a letter from Lady G. also telling me about the evening. I am glad I was not there I would have got into a towering rage.

Go on writing to me, dear heart, as often as you can, every line you send is a joy to me

                    Your old Tramp.

[*TCD*]   [*Glendalough House*]
                                              Thursday [*7 February 1907*]

Dearest Life

You mustn't dream of being uneasy about me, there is not any thing serious the matter only a tedious bronchitis (i.e. chest cough) the sort of thing I've had scores of times in my day. I am up again for a while today but I am glad I did not ask you to come out, as talking makes me cough, and coughing hurts me as if I had ten scarlet divils twisting a crow-bar in the butt of my ribs.

Will you come and see me tomorrow (Friday) if you are free. Come down by the quarter to two or the quarter to three, and be prepared to see a poor sick man with a beard on him—God forgive him—and a wheesy chest. Of course if you are wanted for rehearsal dont come, but I dont suppose they can want you just then. Dont bother about your dream, I'm not going to die yet—with the help of God, and I am really not seriously ill. You have been very good with all your little letters, and I am very grateful. So goodbye till tomorrow

Now this must go
Your old Tramp.

[TCD]   [*Glendalough House*]
Friday [8 February 1907]

Dear Heart

Instead of being downstairs today I am in bed again with feverish headache. It is too bad. I got your letter last night but none today. Of course I will lend you the money with a heart and a half, but you'll have to wait for a few days till I can get it out of the Bank. I hope to God I shall be well enough to be about by Sunday. I feel wretched today. Write me nice letters Dear Heart and keep me alive.

Your old Tramp.

[TCD]   [*Glendalough House*
9 February 1907]

Dearest Heart

I had a very bad night last night and I am staying in bed today to try and shake off my cough. I was delighted to get your note this morning. Be sure you write to me every day while I am ill. I think I am getting better now but I'm very shaky still, and I cannot write much to you, although I'm brimming over with things I would like to say. I will not, of course, be able to walk tomorrow. Write me long letters I cannot do more than this scrawl today.

A thousand blessings from
Your old Tramp.

I wish I had you here to read to me and look after me. I feel very flat after all the excitement

J. M. S.

[TCD]   [*Glendalough House*
                                                          10 February 1907]
Dearest Heart

I am a great deal better I think today, but I am staying in bed still, and possibly tomorrow also. I felt very gay this morning for a while but now, I am infinitely depressed and infinitely weary, lying here day after day. I half wish I had asked you to come down today, but if you had I'd have talked, and made my throat worse, so perhaps it is better as it is. This day four weeks was the day we had our last walk. Do you remember in Glen Cullen, where we sat on the top of the bank?

I wonder when I'll be about again, it is 20 years since I have had such a bout of it as I am having now so you must not think that this is a usual occurrence. When—at what hour?—do you have your verse classes with F.J.F.? I want to know what afternoons you are free next week, none at all I suppose between the rehearsals and classes, but perhaps you could come down after your class, or on Tuesday evening. I may be up then. I could have written you a nice letter if I had had a pen this morning, but now I am too wretched, so excuse this dreary scrawl. I think of you a great deal and I dont like the thought [of] America. I hope it wont come off just yet. W.B.Y. came yesterday but I did not see him. Goodbye Dearest

Your old Tramp.

[TCD]   *[Glendalough House]*
                                              Monday *[11 February 1907]*

Dearest

    I got no letter this morning and I felt very upset. It seemed strange that you should pass the whole day without writing a line. A letter has come now by the 2 o'clock post, to say that you dont want to come and see me. I dont understand it at all. I was going to ask you to come on Wednesday—my mother suggested the same thing—but of course if you dont want to come I wont press you. As I say it seems very strange —I am up now in the little front room. It is pouring rain and I feel very lonely and weak, sitting here by myself.

    I wrote to you yesterday as usual and had it sent to the post. I am sorry it has not reached you.

    In a week, I hope, I shall be about again.

                                 Your old Tramp

P.S.   Why wont you come and see me? You'll make me as ill as ever, if you upset me like this.

P.S.   This is a nasty sort of production I am afraid. Forgive it I am very weak and I suppose very foolish. I am sure you will come!

I am a good deal better I think if it will only last. How are you dear Heart? What hour is your class on Wednesday.

P.S.   You'll be able *to pull my beard* next time!

[Texas]   *[Glendalough House]*
                                              Tuesday
                                              12 o'c.
                                              [12 February 1907]

Dearest Pet

    I am sorry I wrote you a 'grumpy' letter yesterday, I am so worn out, a little thing upsets me. This morning I have been in terrible pain, —with the ailment I had in Kerry,[1]—since four o'clock. At eight I thought I heard the post pass without coming here, and I gave myself up for lost, and broke out into a cold sweat of misery all over; I thought you had only written me one line in two days instead of two letters every day as you did, and I was in despair. Then the servant brought a letter and I went wild with delight. The second time I read it I found it was written on Sunday, so your Monday letters are due still.

If you could have seen me raging this morning when I thought you had forgotten me you would not ask if I am tired of you or your notes. Poor Heart, dont you know they are the one joy I have? That I live on them? Perhaps you think my letters have been cold, but remember I have been almost too ill to write them at all. I think you make very few slips in spelling now, I daresay not more than I do, and your notes are charming always, like your own little self. Isn't that a nice compliment? Alas St Antony I am afraid doesn't like the job of curing me. I dont think I ever in my life had such pain as this morning. Otherwise, the cough and all, are much the same, not really better to any extent. It is heartbreaking. I dont know what to say about tomorrow, perhaps I shall hear from you at two o'c.

Later

Your letter has come. Yes I was a silly ass to kick up such a row about nothing, but you know my folly, so you should have told me *why* at once.

I am up again now a little stronger than yesterday, but, God knows, wretched enough. ⟨I am afraid, my life, it would be better after all to put off your visit to Friday, I am bitterly sorry but with my [throat] still so bad I should not talk at all, and with this turn of my Kerry ailment⟩ on me I do not know how I may be tomorrow—(My mother has been in and we have talked your visit over) the verdict is *you are* TO COME, and if I am not up to much I'll send you off in an hour—(of course I wont) or we'll wire to you, to the Green before one o'clock. So come along and God speed you, by the quarter to three as usual. That is something to look forward to—!!

So goodbye for 24 hours from now your train is just passing up—

Your old Tramper——

---

1. In a letter to Lady Gregory on 21 February, Synge wrote, "It has been extraordinarily tedious, first bronchities, then laryngitis, and then worst of all a sort of dysentery, which was very bad."

[*TCD*]   [*Glendalough House*]
                                                  Tuesday [*12 February 1907*]

Dearest Life

God reward you for all your notes! I live on them. F.Fay hasn't turned up yet, I hope he wont come tomorrow, you must come in any case and we'll have to chance it. Come by the quarter to three.

I dont know how I am I feel very wretched and my breathing is very bad. I fear we'll have the doctor out again. Miss Horniman wrote to say *The Playboy* was 'splendid', and I am to make haste and write another play. She wants to make peace, I suppose. I have written to thank her a little dryly. I wish I could get better, day after day with no change is fearfully depressing. Be sure you come tomorrow. I cant get on another day without you. I think of nothing but my little changling.

Your old Tramp

[*TCD*]   [*Glendalough House*]
                                                  Thursday [*14 February 1907*]

Dearest Life

Thanks for notes and dream—I wonder who the grey mare was!

I had a bad night, and I am staying in bed the whole day today, the doctor did not come yesterday, but is coming tonight instead. The turn I had yesterday has passed off—more or less—, but it has weakened me very much, and made my cough worse again.

I feel terribly wretched today, and inclined to blaspheme creation, and all that is in it except a Changling. I am afraid there is no use in bringing you down tomorrow, it would be better, I think, if you would come on Saturday, when there is some chance of my being a little better. I suppose you are free on Saturday afternoon. A thousand blessings Dear Heart, on you, and your kind eyes, and your little notes, and your love that is such a joy to me. How did I live without you?

Excuse this scrawl I cant write easily in bed. Good bye sweet Heart, I'll write to you of course tomorrow, and you'll come on Saturday.

Your old Tramp.

[*TCD*]   [*Glendalough House
                                            mid-February 1907*]

Dearest Love

I am better today, and the pain in stomach has stopped at last.
You know this last turn I have had I brought on myself by taking too
many pills and too many oranges, I hope it is over now. You mustn't
be uneasy. I have a little bronchitis, and a little laryngitis—a dryness
in my throat—brought on by being out and talking so much, the P.B.
week when I was ill already. The laryngitis is a very slow thing, the
doctor says, so I must have patience a little longer. If my stomach will
get will now, I hope I shall get better steadily now. It has nothing
whatever to say to my neck. W.G. is a little ass very fond of talking
wisely about things he knows nothing about. It is a very simple operation getting these lumps out. The last time, when they were much
bigger than they are, now, I was perfectly well in ten days. So you
see you needn't mind him.[1]

The doctor says that on account of my throat I should talk as little
as possible for a few days so you had better not come and see me—I
fear—for a day or two yet. I doubt that I shall be up tomorrow, I am
afraid of upsetting my stomach again. Take care of *yourself.* Goodbye,
dont be anxious.

                                            Your old Tramp.

1. The large swelling on Synge's neck was a symptom of Hodgkin's disease, or
lymphatic sarcoma. He had previously been operated on 11 December 1897, the incident
which he described in his essay "Under Ether" (see Oxford *Prose,* 39–43). His recurring
fevers, and perhaps the stomach ailments, were also symptomatic of this disease (see
Introduction, pp. xvi–xvii).

[*Texas*]   [*Glendalough House*]
                                            Friday [*22 February 1907*]

Beloved

Thanks for your two letters, a nice one this morning, and your
answer to my sermon, not altogether a reassuring answer by the way.
It is a healthy sign enough to be eager for adventures, so long as one
has the precaution to have the right sort of adventures, and so long as
one does not get flighty.[1]

I am getting on slowly I think in the right direction, but very slowly. My mother has knocked up now and is in bed too, so we are a dreary household. I have been trying to work today at the wretched article for the *Shanachie*,[2] but I am hardly able for it, and I have got very depressed. Thanks very much for the books and papers. They came last night about eight o'c, and I have finished one of them already, *The Master of Ballantrae*. I should think Sunday would be the best day for you to come down to see me again. You asked twice whether you should come today, but of course there was no time to answer. I think Sunday will do best, if I [am] not ill again which Heaven forbid.

Your old Tramp.

1. According to Mrs Synge's diary, Molly had been out visiting Synge at Glendalough House on Wednesday, 20 February.
2. *The Shanachie,* an "Irish Miscellany" edited by Joseph Maunsel Hone (1882–1959), one of the owners of Maunsel and Company and later biographer of Berkeley, Henry Tonks, W. B. Yeats, and George Moore. The quarterly lived for only six numbers, summer 1906 to winter 1907, but published essays by Synge in every number but the first one.

[*TCD/GS220*]   [*Glendalough House*]
                                         Friday Night
                                       [*?22 February 1907*]

My little Pigeen
    Your little midday note has come. Please, it was *I* who was the *'hurt'* one, by rights, this time. You didn't say a word about coming down today, till it was too late, obviously, to arrange it! So we're both hurt—ingeniously enough—we're clever at it—and we're therefore quits! I am glad your little note came, it has cheered me up somehow again, and we'll look forward to Sunday, with the help of God. Of course you were right to tell me what was in your little scatter-brain, and I'd be much more hurt, profoundly hurt, if I thought you didn't tell me all you think of.
    I, and some other people of *genius* I have known, in my youth nearly always got a wild impulse to wander off and tramp the world in the spring and autumn, the time the birds migrate, so as you're a genius too it's right and proper that you should have the impulse.

We're all wild geese, at bottom, all we players, artists, and writers, and there is no keeping us in a back yard like barndoor fowl. The one point is that when we fly it should be to the North Sea or the Islands of the Blessed, not to some sooty ornamental water in some filthy town. Now my geniusette are you satisfied?

[*TCD/Encl*]   Saturday
Dearest
    I wrote the enclosed last night. Your other note and card have just come! You should know by this time that I write to you every day and that my letters sometimes catch the 4 o'c post here, so that they reach you in the evening, and sometimes—more often—miss it and do not reach you till the next morning. I hope you will come and see me tomorrow by the quarter to three train. My mother is in bed still and will be in bed tomorrow so ask for me.
    I am a little better but not much. It is very depressing, and instead of being sorry for me, and writing me cheerful letters you go [on] as you have been doing. It is too foolish to annoy me.
    Dont miss your train tomorrow
    Yours as always
        J. M. Synge

[*TCD*]   [*Glendalough House*]
                                            Monday [*25 February 1907*]
Dearest Pigeenette
    I got your note all right this morning, I have been in great spirits too since your visit yesterday. I am getting on well still, and I am hard at work on my *Shanachie* article today. I typed three pages this morning, and I am going to do three more now, so that I hope to finish it tomorrow. Hone has kept back *The Shanachie* a whole month on my account. Isn't that a compliment? If I wasn't in too good a humour I'd scold you *fiercely* for throwing aside *The Master and Man,*[1] and reading instead that commonplace trash you were at yesterday. It makes me sad to think that you find more pleasure in such stuff.
    I think now the cold is gone I'll very soon be well, we'll hardly know ourselves when I'm about again, and we can go off to see how

Clencullen is, and Miss Fluke, and Bray Head. My mother is in bed still, but she is getting better. I want you, please, to send me tomorrow's (Tuesday's) *Freeman*, they have a lecture on the Western Peasant at the I.N. Literary tonight, and I know that means abuse of me, which I always enjoy.² I feel very happy and very wicket, I wish you were coming today. Goodbye my best one, be good,

Your old Tramp.

P.S.   I enjoyed your visit last night to no end. It is a blessing that all last week's nonsense has blown away. Let us keep it off in God's name

Amen.

1. A story by Count Leo Tolstoi which had been published separately several times since its first English translation in 1895.
2. *The Freeman's Journal and National Press,* edited by William Brayden, had attacked *The Playboy of the Western World* as "unmitigated, protracted libel upon Irish peasant men and, worse still upon Irish peasant girlhood . . . this squalid, offensive production, incongruously styled a comedy in three acts" (28 January 1907). At the meeting of the Irish National Literary Society on 25th February, its president Dr. George Sigerson (1838–1925), Professor of Botany and Zoology at University College, Dublin, and translator of Gaelic poetry, read a paper on "The Peasants of the West." According to Joseph Holloway, Yeats was present at the lecture but left before it was over.

[*TCD*]

[Glendalough House]
Monday 3 P.M.
[?25 February 1907]

Dearest Love

Your note has come by the midday post. I hope you are not getting my cough, that would be too bad! I was a little tired yesterday, and I got very depressed after you had gone—I felt so lonesome—then I picked up heart again, and I was saying to myself all the evening, what a little god-send you were, so pretty, and so kindly, and so clever, and so sensible, and such a baby, and so fond of the world, and so fond of an old T---p [*Synge's deletion*],—and I got very happy again. I'd like to thank God for giving me such a soul's treasure as you are to me, and I kept wondering last night how I had lived so long without you. I couldn't live without you now, not for a month. It is funny about what you made me think by holding these terrible secrets over my head! Of course you were right to tell me what you did yesterday, and it would be best—if [it] is worth while—to tell me anymore little troubles you have of the same kind. Why shouldn't I know everything that has to do with you? I dont like being kept out in the cold. However we wont bother ourselves about trifles we've had enough of that.

   This is a badly written and disjointed sort of letter. I am not much better yet I am afraid, it is appallingly slow. F Ross has just been up paying me a visit, but I feel very sad at having to pass the day without my own little changling. I wish you weren't so far away so that you could look in at me very often—three or four times a day—wouldn't that be better. I have an overwhelming thirst to be out with you again in the quiet glens, and a warm sun in it and the spring birds. Well in a week or two please Heaven we'll be off again. The thought of it keeps me up through the weary day. You dont know what it is to be shut up like this day after day when I am so used to tramping on the hills. Write me a nice letter next time, my soul's light, and cheer me up. I wish it was Wednesday.

Your Tramp

[AS/GS254]

[*Glendalough House*]
Tuesday 2 o'c.
[*26 February 1907*]

Dear Heart
   No letter today! and I am disappointed. However I got your note last night so I must not complain, you have been very good to me. The books haven't turned up either. I suppose they hadn't them in stock. There is a post-knock just as I had given him up! I have read your note twice, and I am quite happy again—I was just beginning to go down, down—down.

   I worked too hard at my article yesterday and I had a visit from Roberts[1] and between the two I gave myself a headache which I have still, so I do not feel so gay as I did yesterday.

   I would not bother about your parts. You have played lead in the biggest play of the season, so that ought to satisfy you for the time being. We have to try and get something out of Mrs F. as we have to pay her. She will never do much but with practice she may improve

for the small parts she has to get. Work hard as you say and sooner
or later you will get the position you deserve whatever that may be.
You have made your place in the peasant plays, and you may I dare say
do the same in verse. But you will never reach the very top in either
unless you read plenty of what is best and train your natural instincts.
There is a sermon!!

I hope to finish my article today or tomorrow in spite of my head.
They have sold 200 P.B.s in a week, i.e. £20 worth of which my share
is £3. That is not bad. My mother is better but in bed still. Come
tomorrow, quarter to three as usual. I shall be on the lookout for you.

Your old T.

1. George Roberts (1873–1953), managing director of Maunsel and Company and
publisher of *The Shanachie;* he contributed four poems to *New Songs,* edited by George
Russell (Æ) (Dublin: O'Donoghue, 1904), and had been Secretary of the Irish National
Theatre Society before its re-formation as a limited company in September 1905.

[*TCD*]   [*Glendalough House*]
Saturday [*2 March 1907*]

Dearest Life

Another disappointment! I am very feverish still so I cannot get up
tomorrow. I hope I shall be able to see you by *Monday* or *Tuesday.* The
Doctor is coming out again today to have a look at me. I dont think I
am quite so bad as I was yesterday. Thanks for your letters, my sweet
life. Dont be uneasy about me. It is only influenza I think. I cant write
any more. With infinite love

Your old Tramp.

Read Milton tomorrow and be cheerful my cough is nearly gone so I
will soon be well now.

Later Your morning's letter has just come. You needn't be uneasy
Dear Heart, this will pass off in turn. I am intensely sorry not to have
you tomorrow, but it is quite out of the question I fear. It is too, too
bad. T.

Write me a good letter tomorrow and post it yourself.

[*TCD*]   [*Glendalough House*
                                           ?3 March 1907]

My dear Life
    I am *very decidedly* better today, thank Heaven, but I am very weak
after all the fever. I hope I shall be able to see you in a day or two.
                                           Your old Tramp
I am afraid to write much for fear of bringing on the fever again.

[*TCD*]   [*Glendalough House*]
                                           Monday morning
                                           [*?4 March 1907*]

My dear Love
    I think it [is] you who [are] the cruel one! You must know I would
give anything to see you, but I have been too ill, the excitement of a
visit from you—it is bound to excite—would have made me much
worse. It would be different of course if you were staying here. I dont
wonder you were uneasy—we were all uneasy—but that is not my
fault. You might have pity on me instead of scolding me. However,
dearest Heart, we wont fight. Today thank Heaven the *fever is entirely
gone,* so I hope I shall be up tomorrow. I am dreadfully weak, I have a
sharp headache and the sweat is running down my face with the exer-
tion of writing these few lines. That is only natural of course, as I have
had no solid food since Friday. I feel otherwise wonderfully better.
Perhaps I shall write to you again today. I am sending this early to let
you know I am so much better
                                           Your Tramp

[*TCD*]   [*Glendalough House*]
                                           Tuesday [*5 March 1907*]

Dearest
    I am a little doubtful whether or not to write to you today as you
seem to say you are coming down for F. Fay['s] book. However I will
write a line in case you do not come. I am getting on very well now,
and I am to get up tomorrow I hope, I was not allowed to do so today

by the Doctor. He says it is of the GREATEST IMPORTANCE that I should not get a return of the fever, so that I must stay very quiet indeed for a few days. He examined me very carefully on Saturday from Head to Foot and could find nothing really the matter with me, but the fever was terrible on Saturday night, the highest I have ever had. So you will understand, sweetheart that it is as much as my life is worth to tire myself or worry myself in any way. So let us be careful. You ask if you may come down today, with your usual blind indifference to the fact that it is impossible to answer you in time. Do use your little head! Tomorrow I fear would not be a good day to come as I shall be getting up for the first time and I shall be very shaky and wretched, besides my brother[1] has to telephone to the doctor about me tomorrow afternoon, about 3 or 4, and he will be in and out all the afternoon. You will not mind waiting a day or two longer now you know I am going on well. Words could not tell you what I suffer in the way of dullness and impatience at having to lie here all day by myself, without my little changling, that is, but that makes it all the more important that I should stay quiet and get well this time. I wonder when you'll get this.

You can see by my writing how much stronger I am today, Thank Heaven. What has St. Antony been at these days?

Ever your old
Tramp.

1. Robert Synge had spent most of his time at Glendalough House during his brother's illness.

[TCD/GS254]   [*Glendalough House*]
                                     Wednesday [*6 March 1907*]

My dearest old Heart

I have now three letters to answer—as I wrote to you yesterday before the 2 o'cl letter came. I seem to have quite a lot to say. First [of] all I am up and dying to see you, and I suppose I am better though I am very shaky. I am very sorry about your eye. I wish you would go to Swanzy,[1] I am sure it wont get well by itself, and if you take it at once it will get well much faster,—perhaps after one visit. Do be wise!

If you did use your little head,—[*Synge's deletion*],—your little head is little use!!! You wrote late on Monday and I got it on Tuesday at nine o'clock, I might have wired for you, but could not get a letter written and posted before ten in my present state. You might have guessed that!!! Of course, dear Heart, you should go to Glen Dhu with the others on Sunday if your eye is well enough. I would be a brute indeed if I objected to your going. I know you wont let them walk arm-in-arm with you or anything of that kind, and I hope when you are coming back you will keep with the crowd. It would give me pain to think of you walking through OUR ROADS in the twilight with anyone else! If your eye isn't better come to me instead. When I came to the part in your letter where you spoke about our last walk up there, and the beauty of the mountains yesterday, a wave of anguish came over me, I got a lump in my throat, and the next thing I had tears streaming down like a baby. There in my bed I cannot even see a bit of sky or a cloud. That [is] what comes when you are as weak as I am, and as wretched. Will you come and see me, Dear Heart, I cant live any longer without you. Come tomorrow or Friday only let me know, by posting before eleven. Tomorrow you ought to go to Swanzy I am sure.

I am very sorry I forgot to thank you at once and properly for the *Ireland*.[2] It slipped out of my poor weary head when I was writing. I was very glad to get it indeed, though I'd like to strangle the wretch who took that photo of you Goodbye dearest love

Your Tramp

1. Henry R. Swanzy, (later Knighted), M.G., F.R.C.S.I., surgeon at Royal Victoria Eye and Ear Hospital, whose office was at 23 Merrion Square North.
2. A monthly magazine published in Dublin.

[*TCD*]

[Glendalough House]
Thursday [7 March 1907]

Dearest

Your letter has just come, thanks. The Doctor came soon after you went last night. He said I was much better and that if I wasn't feverish I was to go down stairs today and *out* on Friday. Unluckily I *am* more feverish today, so I am in *our* room still. I shall be down stairs tomorrow however so I am afraid we wouldn't enjoy ourselves if you came out. I shall make some excuse for sitting up here on Sunday so that will be a better day for you to come. I felt worlds better for your visit yesterday. Now I hope I shall be all right very soon indeed, and then we must see each other every day.

Your dreams are funny indeed! I dont remember mine now except very occasionally. Sweetheart I wish you were here today, the afternoon here over the fire is so different, when I have you to make much of me. I told the Doctor there was some talk of the Co. going to America soon and he said that would be just the thing for me, and that if I got the glands out of my neck and then had a sea voyage and change I would be a[s] strong as a horse! I wonder if there is any chance of it— I fear not. If I could lecture it would be another thing, but unfortunately that is not in my line.

Write a lot, my dearest life, and let us live on letters till Sunday. I wish you could have seen me through the key-hole yesterday when I found you hadn't come by that train. I nearly got a fit with despair. I think we should soon be married, we are too long this way already. Dont you think so?

Now goodbye for this time I wonder will this reach you tonight or tomorrow morning. I hope I shall have another note tonight. Ever and ever your old Tramp.

[*TCD*]   [*Glendalough House*]
                                    Friday [*8*] March [*1907*]¹

Dearest Heart

I am as happy as the Lord God today. Do you remember the plaintive way I talked about getting consumption yesterday? Well the reason was—I may as well tell you the whole story—the doctor in order to see if he could find out the cause of my fever last week, was examining the stuff I coughed up to see if there were the tubercular microbes in it, and he was so long letting me know that I was getting uneasy. I heard this morning, however, that none could be found, so I am all right, and in ten days, please Heaven, I shall be trotting you about as usual. This is the third time they have tried to find the tubercular microbes in me and they have always failed utterly so if Peggy says again that I am tubercular you may tell her to HOLD HER GOB!

I am in great form today but I am not going out till tomorrow as a precaution. I delight in the memory of seeing you yesterday sitting among my books. Be sure and let me know about Sunday, though of course you can come even if I dont expect you, for instance if the morning turned out too wild for your walk. I hope the Sunday after you will be out with your Tramp again. How we will enjoy it!! Dont leave me with too few letters whatever you do or I'll get ill again. I have a whole lot of books of poetry out of my press this morning and I am delighted to be able to read them again; when I am ill I have not the energy. Do read the good books I lend you instead of that dressmaker's trash! Write me a good cheering letter to put me finally in Heaven. I wish I could see you today!

with blessings
your old
Tramp

1. Synge has misdated this letter *Friday 10 March.*

[*TCD/GS256*]   [*Glendalough House*]
                                                Saturday March 9th/07

My dearest Love

I have four letters to answer this time. You are very very good to me, and I am very grateful! The tour is a surprise, I dont think it can be settled, as you seemed to say in your letter of last night, or I should have heard something of it. I knew London was being negotiated about, but I had not heard of the others. A good deal of it, you may be sure, is W.G.Fay! I should go with you most likely to Oxford and London but not further, I think, not certainly if Miss Horniman is going.

Today I am writing with a sharp pen and it feels horrible I cant get on at all with it. As to your head this time you wrote *yesterday* of Sunday—as tomorrow! and hoped it would rain. I dont think you ought to go to the Glens tomorrow after all this rain, at this time of the year they do not dry up after rain, and even if it is a fine day Glen Dhu will be like a wet sponge. So that if you go you may expect to have your shoulder in your ear on Monday! If you dont walk out there come down by the quarter to three. I hope it will be too wet for your expedition partly because I want to see you here, partly because I dont like the thoughts of your going to the glens without me. Do you understand that feeling? cant you get a pain in your stomach or something tomorrow? However it doesn't really matter much one way or other. I have not got out yet as it was too wet today, and yesterday I wasn't let, but I am getting on well and feeling more myself. Tell W.G. I would be glad to see him any evening after eight, but that the afternoon is uncertain. I hope I shall often be out now. I fully agree that the third Act wants pulling together. I hope if they go on tour Power wont be able to go, so that we may get a decent Old Mahon. It would make all the difference in the world.

My mother was talking the other day about our marriage, and how we intended to get on. She is still rather frightened at our poverty, but she is much more rational about it than she was. You must have charmed her! By the way I've a compliment for you. The last Sunday that you came I happened to see you passing from my top window, and you *walked* very prettily indeed. Quite charmingly. Keep to your low heels now, and dont spoil it, there is nothing so charming in a woman as an easy and graceful walk, and there is nothing more rare! So my dear old love you may be proud of yourself. I wonder if this will seem a nice letter to you? I am in too good spirits to write anything very deep, but, dear Heart, the depth is there, and it is filled with happy thoughts of you. I hope I shall see you tomorrow, but do whatever is best.

Your old Tramp.

P.S.   I think you should date your letters. They are all in a jumble now and I dont know which is which. Thanks for the stamps.

[*TCD*]   [*Glendalough House*]
                                                March 11th [*1907*]

Dearest Life

I have had no letter from you today so far. I have been working at my article nearly all day and I am dog tired I hope I shall not be the worse. It is finished now and going to the post. How did you get on last night with the Fays? You must excuse this scrawl I am really too tired to write. I had a nice little walk this morning for ¾ of an hour the air felt beautiful and spring like I was wishing I had you with me, now good bye till tomorrow I['ll] try and write you a nice letter then

Your old Tramp[1]

1. Molly has scribbled *appalling* twice at the foot of this letter.

[*TCD*]   Glendalough [*House*]
                                                   March 12th [*1907*]

Dear Heart

Your note has just come at two o'clock, with the proofs, thanks. I like the serious one best, I will show you which it is when you come down again. I am not at all the worse for my day's work yesterday. I was out for nearly an hour this morning, and I was going out again after dinner, but it came on to rain just as I was going out on the steps. I did not work at my article for the sake of Roberts and Co., but for the sake of the two good guineas that it will bring in to me. Still I admit I was a fool yesterday, and I worked too hard. Will you come down and see me tomorrow by the quarter to three? If you can and will, let me know by the early post that you are coming. I expect F.J.F. down this evening after supper to have a talk. I heard from him last night, in answer to my letter. I am not in a good letter-writing humour to-day, I suppose because I am disappointed at not getting my second walk. I have a horrid lot of letters to write and I keep putting them [off] in the most hopeless way. I shall never get them done at this rate. I wish you were here this afternoon I am dejected and heavy, and I want someone to cheer me. The birds are singing a great deal all round here now, it makes me sad when I cannot be out along with them enjoying the showers as much as they do. Perhaps we shall be able to have a little walk on Sunday, but it will only be a little one. I have a nasty cough still and till it is gone I cannot do very much. This will not be a very fat note but there is a mighty lot in it I have [written] so closely with this small pen. I am thinking about you a great deal. There is the cook going to the post this must go. Hope to see you tomorrow

Your old Tramp

[*TCD*]   [*Glendalough House*]
                                                           March 14th [*1907*]

Dearest Heart

I am better today and I am thinking of going out for a turn. Had
you very long to wait for your train last night? I did not see your train
going up, I suppose I missed it as I was walking about the house. I
shall have a long dull afternoon today with no one to talk to. I feel
woefully stupid with nothing to say. I am writing to Combridge[1] for
5/0 worth of books, is not that extravagant? I suppose I wont get them
till after the bankholiday on Monday.

I had a kind letter from Miss Tobin this morning. She is very keen
about Frohman[2] and seems to think it will come off. It is very hard
luck that he is not to see *The Well of the Saints,* so if there is any
money made out of the tour I shant get much of it. I dont think I'll go
out after all I've got a headache, and I dont feel very gay. I haven't
heard from you yet but the post will soon come now I suppose unless it
has passed. I'll wait to finish this till I know—— ——.

No letter! I feel disappointed and uneasy. I hope you are not unwell.
Even if you are dont leave me without news of you. I cannot get on
without hearing from you. Now I shall be in low spirits—or in lower
spirits, they were not very high!—all the afternoon. Perhaps I shall
hear at six o'clock

                                        Good bye my dearest love
                                        YOUR OLD TRAMP

   1. Combridge & Co., Limited, a bookshop at 18 Grafton Street, which later also
provided books for James Joyce in Trieste and Paris.
   2. Charles Frohman (1860–1915), the well-known American manager, was interested
in producing the Abbey Players on an American tour; his visit to the Theatre with
James Barrie on 1st April 1907 went unnoticed. He was one of the casualties, with Lady
Gregory's nephew Hugh Lane, on the *Lusitania*.

[*TCD*]   Glendalough [*House*]
                                                           March 15 [*1907*]

Dearest Heart

Your letter came yesterday by the 6 o'clock post, and the second
one this morning. I half hoped I would get one today at two to say
that you were coming down this afternoon to see me, but the post

man just sailed by on his bicycle and made my heart sink within me. So now we must wait till Sunday! For my sake—I was going to say for Heaven's sake but I think you mind me more—be careful with the flaming cauldron tomorrow in *Baile's Strand*.[1] If you burned yourself and got laid up now what would become of us. I am sorry to hear that your sister is so unwell, but as you are not accustomed to illness perhaps she is not so bad as you fear. I hope she will soon get better. I am not making much way, in fact I have felt (and feel) very poorly. I went out yesterday after all, and again this morning, and possibly I shall take another turn this afternoon, though I am inclined to be feverish again. Did I tell you that I heard from Henderson acknowledging the cheques. He says that five years ago he got into bad health something the way I am, and that the doctor made him take a sea voyage with the result that he has been quite well ever since! He added at the end "What fine times we had with the *Playboy!*" Little hypocrite!![2]

I am doing my all and utmost to make this a *corpulent* letter for you, and with the Help of God I'm getting on wonderfully. I got a wire from George Moore last night asking me to dine with him on Saturday, but of course I wont be able. Can you read that last word? I am beginning not to be able 'to stick' your writing. Today for instance you say, apparently, that as Mrs P.[3] is ill *Dancy* has asked Sally to understudy? What does that mean? I wont be able to go in tomorrow for the show as I half hoped. If W.B.Y. is over and you hear that he is coming to see me let him know that I am visible in the evenings, but in the afternoon I am *often* out walking! Poor old love I wish you were coming down today, I dread these long afternoons, I keep going from book to book seeking rest and finding none. This morning I have been reading Walter Scott's Diary during the last 9 years of his life, when he was getting old and had lost immense sums of money. It is wonderful stuff full of humour and cheerfulness. Now it is your turn to write me a fat letter. You should have all the news instead of

> Your old Tramp till death
> us do part.

---

1. At Miss Horniman's suggestion and with the reluctant agreement of his fellow directors, Yeats had hired a new manager, Ben Iden Payne (b. 1881), to produce the verse plays, but after staging Yeats's *On Baile's Strand, Deirdre,* and *The Hour Glass,* Maeterlinck's *Interior,* and Wilfred Scawen Blunt's *Fand,* Payne returned to England and became

manager of Miss Horniman's Manchester Playgoers' Club in July 1907. He went to
America in 1913 and became a producer for Frohman and others; from 1934–1943 he was
director of the Shakespeare Memorial Theatre at Stratford-on-Avon.

2. According to Joseph Holloway, the Abbey Theatre business secretary did not
approve of Synge's plays. Henderson's scrapbook, *The Playboy and What He Did,* is now
in the National Library of Ireland; he wrote a long flattering article on Synge when
Maurice Bourgeois' biography appeared in 1913.

3. Mrs. Payne, who acted under the stage name Mona Limerick, was to play the
lead in the revivals of Yeats's plays this season. She later created the role of Sarah Casey
in the first production of *The Tinker's Wedding* in London, 11 November 1909.

[TCD/GS256]   Glendalough House
                                                          March 16th/07

Dearest Heart

I was very glad to get your letter this morning, and I will expect
you tomorrow at three as usual. I feel in a bad humour this afternoon
because it has come on to rain so that I cannot get my little walk as I
hoped. I wasn't very flourishing last night, but I am better again today,
although I dont feel that I have made much progress since last Saturday.
It is slow work. I dont think I need write you a 'fat' note today as I
shall see you tomorrow, and I dont get any very fat ones from you.
I would like to work at something or other today but I suppose I had
better not till I am stronger. It is a dreary time. I never had such an
experience in my life before. It is well I have you to come down and
see me sometimes. This is a miserable dismal scrawl I am afraid, well
what can you expect from a poor fellow shut up here looking out back
and front at wet roofs and dank drizzling rain? Thank Heaven I'll have
you to cheer me tomorrow.

                                        Your old woe-begone Tramper

[AS/GS256–7]   Glendalough Ho.
                                                          March 18th/07

Dearest

You were not five minutes gone last night when W.G. and Mrs F.
turned up. We had a long chat and I heard all the inner news which
do not definitely reach you. Nothing is settled—as I thought—about

the tours. I hear however that they are showing Frohman *one* play of mine *Riders,* five or six of L G's and several of Yeats. I am raging about it, though of course you must not breathe a word about it. I suppose after the P.B. fuss they are afraid of stirring up the Irish Americans if they take me. However I am going to find out what is at the bottom of it and if I am not getting fair play I'll withdraw my plays from both tours English and American altogether. It is getting past a joke the way they are treating me. I am going to write to "My dear Friend"[1] again to tell her how I am getting on, and let her know incidentally what is going on here. I dont think she will be pleased. She, I imagine, does not worship Lady G. I have no letter from you today as there are no posts owing to Bank Holiday. I do not know whether I shall get to the doctor or not tomorrow so there is no use asking you to meet me. I am getting on well but my cough is very bad still.

> "Yours affectionately"
> Your old T.

1. Miss Tobin.

[TCD/GS257]   Glendalough House
                                               March 19th [1907]

Dearest Treasure

I congratulate you about *Fand* though I wish it was a better play and more 'actable' verse. Still it shows that you are rising in the estimation of every one.[1] You should read the story about Fand, on which the play is founded in *Cuchulain.* It is called "The Only Jealousy of Emer", I think, there are beautiful passages in it, which you should delight in, but as a story it is rather incoherent. I cannot of course go to the doctor today as the weather is so bad, so I must go tomorrow. If it is fine I shall go up by the train that gets to Westland Row *at two minutes past two*. If you are quite free then you might meet me and walk up with me, but dont miss your dinner or anything. I will not wait for you, of course, so it will not matter if you do not come.

I did not mind your 'huff' it was too utterly silly. The Fays went away at 9.30, and of course I was tired, however as I told you I was

glad to see Fay and to hear all the news. You mustn't be foolish like
that it is too ridiculous. I haven't written to Miss Tobin yet, but I am
going to. If Frohman is genuinely afraid of taking my work for fear of
making a row with the Irish Americans then, of course I have no cause
to be annoyed with the directors. But if as I understand the tour is
going largely for the cultivated University audiences in America it is a
very different matter. My cough was very bad last night, and my head
feels shaken and weary so I cannot write much Good bye dear Heart

Your old Tramp

1. Molly had been given the title role in Blunt's two-act play, to be performed
20 April 1907.

[*TCD/GS257*]   [*Glendalough House*]
March 21st [*1907*]

Dearest Heart

It was well I did not ask you to wait yesterday. When I had been
in the waiting room about ten minutes the doctor telephoned down
from I dont know where to say that he had been called away to Lucan
and would not be back till 3.30. So I had to sit it out. It was nearly a
quarter to four when I got in to him at last. He says I am going on well
and as the cough leaves me I may gradually get back to my ordinary
ways. I am as deaf as a post in one of my ears today, I dont know
whether it is cold or a lump of wax. It is a nuisance and makes me feel
lopsided, and wretched.

I have written to F.J.F. for a list of how many times *Spreading the
News, The Shadow* [*of the Glen*], *Kathleen* [*ni Houlihan*] and *Riders* [*to the
Sea*] and *Baile's Strand* have been played in the Abbey since we opened.
I expect their pieces have been done at least three times as often as
mine. If that is so there'll be a row. I am tied to the company now by
your own good self otherwise I would be inclined to clear away to
Paris and let them make it a Yeats-Gregory show in name as well as in
deed. However it is best not to do anything rash. They have both been
very kind to me at times and I owe them a great deal.

I could have written you a very pretty letter last night but I was too tired and lazy, and now, alas, I am in a bad temper with my ear! My mother was enquiring about your temper today, she says my temper is so bad, it would be a terrible thing to marry a bad-tempered wife!! If she only knew! Your letter has just come. You told me you would not come till FRIDAY, and I believed you. So it is well you did not come today without letting me know as I should have been *out,* and what would you have said then?

I wonder if Glasgow is real! The doctor advises me to have my operation early in May, so that would fit in while you are away. I must go in some time and see them at the Nassau.[1] I dare say I could get in on Saturday but I am not very keen to, except for the *Interior* which would interest me of course. I must go out now dear Heart and post this so that you may get it tonight. I *may* meet you *tomorrow* in the station or in the little lane outside. I suppose you will come by the quarter to three if *you are not coming let me know* by the early post. We shall have Sunday in any case I haven't written to Miss Tobin yet, I am so lazy

Your old Tramp

I am glad they are fining you, you DESERVE IT SO RICHLY![2]

---

1. When she was in Dublin on Abbey Theatre business, Lady Gregory stayed at the Nassau Hotel.
2. In what proved to be an unsuccessful attempt to discipline the company, Willie Fay imposed a system of fines for poor attendance or unpunctuality at rehearsals.

[AS/GS258]

[Glendalough House]
Saturday [23 March 1907]

Dearest Heart

No letter has come from you today so I really dont know where to write to you. I suppose I better try Mary St., but I wont put anything priceless into my letter for fear it should not find you. You will come of course tomorrow whether you get it or not, at least so I hope. I am better and stronger today I think than I have been yet, though I am still deaf and coughing badly.

I heard from F.J.F. last night and got the list of plays put on. I have not come off so badly—largely no doubt because I was always there to fight my own battle and did so—as I thought, and I have decided to make no row for the present at least. This American tour is of course very important, and I dont want any one to be able to say I wrecked it by forcing on my unpopular plays. I dont think it is wise to leave me out the way they have done, but let them take the responsibility, my plays will get their chance in the long run. Now I'm going out for another walk and I'll keep all sorts of nice things to say to you tomorrow.

Good luck
Your old Tramp

[*TCD/GS260*]   Glendalough [*House*]
March 25 [*1907*]

Dearest

This is just a 'how-do-you-do' as nothing new has happened since last night. I have written a lovely curse on the 'flighty one'[1] but I'm half-afraid to send it to you. How did you get on last night I wonder. I was thinking about you. I am getting on all right and had quite a longish walk this morning, still my cough is damnable at times. I went over a back part of Killiney Hill or rather Ballybrack Hill this morning and had a wonderful view of the mountains, and our chimney, and the Sugar Loaves, it made my heart jump within me. I wonder when we shall get away to them again!

I thought a lot more over my play last night, and got some new ideas. I think I'll make the old woman be the mother of the man the saints killed, instead of his own mother, she might be a heathen and keep up a sort of jeering chorus through it all. However I cannot decide anything yet.[2] You'll say this is the dullest letter you ever got from me, and—for once—you'll be perfectly right. Letter-writing seems flat work after yesterday!

Your old Tramp

1. Molly's sister Mrs Callender, who disapproved of *The Playboy*.
2. No scenario resembling this plot has been found among Synge's papers.

[*Texas/GS260*]

[*Glendalough House*]
March Twentysomething
[*26 March 1907*]

Dearest Heart

I got no letter yesterday and no letter on Saturday so I hardly think you deserve one every day. However the one I got this morning was very nice so I'll forgive you. I'm amused but not surprised to hear that you and Mrs Callender are as good friends as ever. I haven't finished her curse yet, so it'll be a rich one. I have written another little poem about you and your troubles, that promises well. You'll have to try and do something poetical every week to keep up my stock in trade. It is—the poem—a little obscure and I dont know yet if it is any good; small affairs like it always seem pure gold when you do them first and then a week later you find they're poor stuff after all. I'm too lazy to type it so here it is

> May one sorrow every day
> Your festivity waylay,
> May seven tears in every week
> From your well of pleasure leak,
> That I signed with such a dew
> May for my full pittance sue
> Of the Love forever curled
> Round the Maypole of the world,—
> — — — — — —
> Heavy riddles lie in this
> Sorrow's sauce for every kiss!

That'll want seeing to but there's a poem in it or I'm the more mistaken.[1] I wish you'd read a lot of verse I want some one who can tell me when—if ever—my verses are good. That is a thing I cannot do for myself and I've got to find out. Treasure I love you like the dew of Heaven. God be with you. Come down tomorrow as usual.

Your old Tramp.

1. See Oxford *Poems,* p. 51, for the final version Synge published in the Cuala Edition two years later.

[*Texas*]   Glendalough House
                                      Thursday [*28 March 1907*]

Dearest Heart

   I hope you got home all right. I fancy I am a little better today, but
I'm not sure it is so terribly slow. I am writing this in rather a hurry as
I am going out for a walk again this afternoon, and I dont want to be
too late. I am re-writing my curse and making it much better, I wish I
dared to make it thoroughly wicket then it would be lovely.¹ I must
write to Yeats this evening to tell him I cannot go to their meeting on
Saturday. I hate this sort of cloudless east wind weather, there is so
little colour or life about anything. I suppose you hardly know the
world well enough yet to know the difference between an east wind
and a west wind! I'll soon teach you when I have you in my care. I am
sending this to Molly Street I suppose you'll get it tonight. I expect a
letter from you this evening. I hope it'll be a nice one and better than
this.

                             Forever your old
                                  Tramp

   1. Two early versions of this poem are printed in the Oxford *Poems*, pp. 49–50; the
final version published in Yeats's Preface to the Cuala Edition, 1909, reads:

   To a sister of an enemy of the author's who
        disapproved of 'The Playboy'

   Lord, confound this surly sister,
   Blight her brow with blotch and blister,
   Cramp her larynx, lung, and liver,
   In her guts a galling give her.
   Let her live to earn her dinners
   In Mountjoy wifh seedy sinners:
   Lord, this judgment quickly bring,
   And I'm your servant, J.M.Synge.

[*TCD/GS261*]   Glendalough House
                                           March 29th [*1907*]

Dearest Love

   I got your note last night and I hope you got mine. I did not think
of asking you to come down today. I am sorry not to see you, but I am

not feeling very flourishing and perhaps it is as well for me to be quiet today.

Dear Heart your letter last night upset me very much—I know you did not mean it to—and I did not go to sleep till nearly 3 o'clock this morning. It is a long way to Glendalough three or four hours each way, and you would not get back till late at night, it is of course *impossible* that you should go off that way with those four louts. Mac would certainly be drunk coming home, and you know how Power goes on—with Mrs Callender for instance! It is a disgusting excursion on Sunday as everyone gets drunk. Surely you must have known that I would not be able to tolerate the idea of your going off that way with four men!

I am very wretched and very unwell, I may go up to the doctor tomorrow—I am not sure—in any case come to me on Sunday as usual, dearest love, and comfort me again. I wonder if I shall ever get well

Your old Tramp

[*TCD*]
[*Glendalough House*]
March 30th [*1907*]

Sweetest Heart

I am just going out for my little walk so I had better send you a line, though it must be a very short one. I am not worse today, but my throat is very hoarse again. If I had been as much better as I hoped a week ago I would have got you to come down early tomorrow and take my walk with me and spend the day, but as I am not able to talk much with my throat you had better come, please, in the afternoon as usual. I cannot tell you how overjoyed I was to see you coming down the road yesterday! It was so good of you to come. I wasn't feverish last night!

Some one sent me a paper from the Abbey with a favourable notice of *The Playboy*. They are mounting up. It must be very dull in Dublin today it is black enough out here. This will not be good weather for Glendalough, it is probably raining out there.

Till tomorrow
with infinite blessings
Your old
Tramp

[*TCD/GS261*]   [*Glendalough House*
                                                        30 March 1907]
                                                         Afternoon

Dearest
    Your letter has just come. *I* cannot decide whether you are to go
or not!
    If you think you promised to go, and they want you to go, and you
want to go, you had better go, though you are not bound to go and you
can so badly afford it. I wont be hurt.
    I have just heard from Lady G. that Yeats wants to come and see
me *tomorrow afternoon.* I am asking him *to come,* so I shall not be alone.
I would not be surprised if she comes too. Of course if you had been
coming I would have put them off.
    Dear Heart you are utterly mistaken in thinking that I do not trust
you. I trust your little heart and soul utterly, but I do not trust your
judgement and your knowledge of the world, that is all and that is not
your fault. If you go for God's sake take care of yourself if you go on
the lakes, or into St. Kevin's bed.[1] I dont know when I shall see you
now, I suppose on Wednesday. I feel a queer sad feeling that you are
going to see the Wicklow lakes for the first time without me. That is
selfish and foolish I suppose
                                    Your old Tramp.

    1. A hole or excavation in the rocky face of the cliff about thirty feet above the Upper
Lake at Glendalough.

[*TCD*]   Glendalough House
                                                        March 31st [*1907*]

Dear Heart
    Thanks for your letters. I am a little less well today and I am not
going out. I feel profoundly miserable, you promised to come and comfort me today when everyone is away holiday making and then! However that is foolish talk. I was very tired after F.J.F's visit last night, and
I slept very badly. Now I have to face W.B.Y. today and I am quite unfit
for it.

I am going to the doctor on Tuesday so do not come and see me till Wednesday I must try and go away some where I will never get well at this rate. I suppose I shall not hear from you now till Tuesday as to-morrow is a holiday. I hope you are having a good time. Oh God I wish Yeats wasn't coming today I am so utterly wretched.

Those lines of that poem I showed you in my book have stuck in my head. They seem to fit me!

"Oh have my grave in readiness
Fain would I die to end this stress."[1]

Forgive this contemptible sort of whinging. I am so lonely and miserable I cant help it, if I am to write at all.

Your old Tramp

Dont let this rubbish upset you I suppose it is because I am so ill that I am such an unreasonable ass. You are quite right to amuse yourself I dare say. Be good sweetheart.

1. The poem "Of Misery" by T. Howell, first published in *The Arbor of Amity* (1568):

Corpse, clad with carefullness,
Heart, heaped with heaviness,
Purse, poor and penniless,
Back, bare in bitterness,
Lips, laide with loathsomeness;
Oh, get my grave in readiness,
Fain would I die to end this stress,
    Remédiless.

[TCD]

Glendalough House
April 1st [1907]

Dearest Heart

Your letter last night has made me very uneasy. You must see a doctor that is all about it. You should not have gone to the Fays when you were tired, it is getting past a joke when you cannot even say 'No' to an invitation to tea. I hope you went to Swanzy today you must get your eyes *cured* this time, or you will have endless trouble. I am much better, only that I am so distressed about my poor little changeling. Send me a note by return when you get this to say how you are. If you became an invalid now what would become of us? I blame myself terribly for taking you those long walks in the summer, you should not have let me when you were not well.[1]

We had better not walk tomorrow as you have two rehearsals, so come *here* by the quarter to three as usual. Perhaps I shall meet you in the little lane beside the station and take you for a little turn if you are well, if you dont see me come on here straight away.

I do hope my dearest love you are better again. I am so unhappy about you.

Your old Tramp.

P.S.   Your letter of this morning has just come. I am so glad you are better. However you had better be very quiet for a day or two. I wonder if you make too much of your pains. I dont understand the way you go up and down! However I am glad you aren't so bad as I feared. I wrote half my next *Shanachie* article this morning and didn't feel much the worse so my strength is coming back all right. Take care Sally doesn't tell our affairs to the company. It is better to keep quiet. T.

---

1. Molly matured unusually late and suffered considerable pain with her menstrual periods.

[*TCD/GS262*]   Glendalough [*House*]
                                                       April 2nd [*1907*]

Dearest Heart

I was very glad to find your letter waiting for me when I got home. It was a nice one.

I would like to wring Boyle's neck. The last time I saw him he was all cordiality, inviting me to stay with him, and Heaven knows what, and now he turns on me and attacks me scurrilously in the papers. I'll roast him yet.[1]

The doctor says I am getting on well, and that I am not to take my temperature any more at present or bother myself whether I am a little feverish or not! He advises me to go away for a week to Lucan or Rostrevor, which I may do. I am going to see Lady Gregory on Friday

morning, so if you can come down and see me *tomorrow Thursday*
afternoon as usual. Let me know by morning post if you are coming.
I am coughing away like the mischief today, but I do not feel worse.
My cousin[2] has given me *one* of his pictures in the Academy will you
go in and see which of them you like best!
P.S.   I forgot you are not free these evenings next week will be time
enough.

Your old TRAMP

1. William Boyle had withdrawn his three plays from the Abbey Theatre repertoire
during *The Playboy* riots; now, on the occasion of Frohman's visit to Dublin, he reiterated
his stand and again attacked Synge's play in an article for *The Catholic Herald* of London
which was reprinted in *The Evening Telegraph* in Dublin.
2. Edward Synge.

[*NLI*]
Glendalough House
Glenageary
Kingstown
6th April/07

Dearest
    I did not get home from town yesterday till four o'clock and it
came on so wet then I wasn't able to send out a letter for you. I will
not go in to town today the weather is so bad. They want me to make
up the number for a meeting of the old I.N.T. Society,[1] but I'm not
going to risk knocking myself up again for all the Societies in Europe.
Isn't that right? I was very glad to get your letter last night and the
verses which I rewrote *at once*.[2] I will try and post this to the Theatre
before 4 so that you may get it tonight. Will you come down tomorrow
by the *quarter to two,* I will meet you at the station and take you to
Bray, if it is fine, if not come on here. If you cannot do that will you
send me a line *tonight* please. I will take *your* ticket from Glenageary, so
please dont miss your train. We will have a lot to talk over tomorrow,
as I heard a great deal yesterday. I counted up my money last night, and
if all goes well I think we shall have £150 for our first year, if we get
married soon, that is £3 a week.
    Goodbye till tomorrow
Your old Scamp.

[*Encl/TCD*]

Is it a month or a year's pain since I
Watched with my chosen how red twilights die,
When her soft fingers, neck, soft arms, and chin
Made all the bars that fence God's glory in,
And her young voice, tempered to twilight's key,
Brought back my spirit its lost liberty,
Till the stars' vault, half-shrinking, seemed to crush
Our boundless joy, who went in lanes of slush
Kissing from ear to ear, from throat to brow,
Losing the past and present in one radiant NOW.
Till we went silent to the spattered train,
That led us to the city, and mere life again.

---

   1. The original organization after Yeats gained control of the players was "The Irish National Theatre Society." In September 1905 a limited society was formed with Yeats, Lady Gregory, and Synge as the Directors. Apparently the earlier organization was occasionally invoked for business decisions.
   2. Probably a version of "Is it a Month" (see Oxford *Poems*, p. 52 and Appendix A, p. 107), dated 14 May 1907 by E. M. Stephens, but more likely belonging here.

[*TCD*]   Glendalough House
                                         8th/iv/07

Dearest
   I hope you are not the worse for our walk and that you have been to Swanzy this morning. I felt a lot better last night than I have done yet, the little trips seem to do me good. If it is fine today I may go to Bray again, but I think it looks rather doubtful.
   I got an invitation from Madame Esposito this morning to dine there on Thursday evening but I will not go as I am not well enough yet I think to be out at night.
   I began fiddling with my Kerry article this morning I shall easily get it done I think, but I have got uncommonly lazy I have been off work so long.
   I wonder shall I hear from you today. I have written the verses again, your criticism is useful!

                                       Your old Scamp

[*TCD/GS263*]   Glendalough House
                                 Wednesday [*?10 April 1907*]

My own dearest

I have been to the doctor and he says that there is nothing the matter with my lungs, that they are stronger in fact than they were a few years ago. He thinks however that I ought to get the glands out and recover myself a bit before I get married. That is reasonable enough as it would be wretched to knock up again after that affair. Meet me to-morrow at *2 o'clock at Westland Row* if it is fine and we'll go up towards the glens for a change we haven't been there for an age now. *If I am not there* or if it *is wet come down here—to the House—*by the *quarter* to *three.* That way we cannot miss each other. It seems very hard to have to put off our wedding again, but it will only be I hope till the autumn or early winter. I will take a 'digs', 'our digs'! when I come home from my summer outings and then it will be ready for us as soon as we are ready for it. What Heaven that will be, my sweetest little heart, it seems almost too beautiful to be possible but we'll make it possible all the same.

The Holidays are a great problem. Would Sally come with us if F.J.F. came? I dont know about your coming here yet. I'll find out to-night, and tell you tomorrow.

Excuse these tags of paper I cant find anything better for the moment. Till tomorrow my dear love, good bye

                                 Your old Tramp

[*Texas*]   [*Glendalough House*]
                                 Saturday
                                 13.IV.07

Dearest

What a day! Of course I cant go in, so Payne will have to decide about Power. I am just as glad. I hope you were not tired last night, we had a good little time on Killiney Hill, hadn't we? There is no use getting up anything 'out of the way', for tomorrow the weather will be so uncertain, and everything will be so wet. Come down by the quarter to two,—you had better come second, to Glenageary—if it is fine I'll meet you with tickets to Bray and we'll go on. If I am not there come on down to the House. If it is wet come by either the quarter to two or to three which ever suits you the best. Excuse this bit of paper Ive run out so that I haven't enough to go on with my article. You must get me some on Monday morning, I'll give you the money tomorrow. I've been thinking I'll have a book for my birthday present, there is one that I want badly

I had a card from Payne this morning urging me to go in today about *The Hour Glass* but the weather is quite impossible.[1] I've been working at my verses all the morning, it is a waste of time but it amuses me. I must have this ready in case anyone goes to the post. Be sure to be *in* the quarter to two if it is fine.

A thousand blessings,
Your old Tramp
J. M. Synge

1. Yeats, Lady Gregory, and Robert Gregory were holidaying in Italy and Synge was in charge of the Theatre until their return on May 22nd.

[TCD]   Glendalough Ho.
                                                           16/IV/07
Dearest

I expected you down today so I did not write to you yesterday. Didn't you say just before I got out of the train on Sunday that you would come down on *Tuesday?* I waited about for you half the afternoon, and met the three train but there was no sign of you. Did I mistake Tuesday for Thursday or the other way round?

This is my birthday, where shall we be the next one? Eh? I think my mother forgets it she has not said anything about it.

I got the paper all right thanks, and I thank you in anticipation for the book. I may be going to town tomorrow but it is quite uncertain, and so is the time so I cannot arrange to see you,—besides I have too many things to do.—Come down by the quarter to *two* on *Thursday* and we'll go to the Dargle if it is a fine day! Let me know if you will come.

Yes we had a great time on Sunday. Yesterday I went to Killiney in the train and walked up through the Brides Glen a bit towards the—(our)—chimney and then back again. It was nice but lonesome.

I have only six pages more of my article to do now. I hope to finish it on Thursday morning. I am afraid you wont get this till tomorrow morning, as I say I expected you today so I did not write.

Your old Tramp.

[*TCD*]
Glendalough Ho.
April 17 [*1907*]

Dearest Love

Your letter came last night—it was a foolish bungle that we made about yesterday. Was [*it*] your fault or mine? The book came last night, it is charming inside and out, many thanks dear Heart. So I shall meet you at the quarter to two tomorrow with tickets for Bray. If by any chance I'm not there of course you are to come on here. I am just off to town now to *shop*. It is a nuisance, but it must be done. I had a hateful dream last night about you and Dossy. You are unwise to encourage him the way you do when you know I dislike it. I haven't anything very much to say today, but to send you my love and blessings. I am getting on all right but still coughing. I'll shave now and see if a letter comes from you by the two post before I go out.——No letter so good-bye till tomorrow come here if it is wet, will you?

Your old Tramp

[*TCD*]
Glendalough House
Saturday [*?20 April 1907*]

Dearest Heart

I feel lonesome these two long days without you, and I feel a little hurt, I think, that you did not choose to be with me, instead of with the crowd, when we have just been separated for so long, and are going to be separated again, in a few days, for a couple of months more. Have you heard about Glen Cree? If you go there I will try and find lodgings in the neighbourhood, I think, for the fortnight you are there, wouldn't that be great? I expected a letter from you last night and this morning but none has come. F.J.F. came out to see me last night in low spirits as usual, poor man, he seems to have no way of spending his holidays. I had a long letter from Lady G. last night with important news, I will tell you some of it when I see you tomorrow.

Will you come down by the quarter to eleven tomorrow, if it is *fine*. I will meet you in the station lane and take you for a little walk, and then back *here* to lunch and to Bray afterwards. If it is wet come down by the quarter to two and come here to the House. I wish it was tomorrow I have to go for another long lonely walk today God help me, when you're off amusing yourself—!!

Your old Tramp

[*TCD*]   Glendalough House
April 25 [*1907*]

My sweet Pet

How is your eye. Be sure to go [to] Swanzy tomorrow, or I'll roar and rage.

I got a tram last night down Brunswick Street and caught my train by about a quarter of a minute, so I was here in good time for supper. The evening was beautiful when I got out of the train, colours, like what we saw on Sunday, over the trees and blackbirds singing every-where. I pitied my poor changeling shut up with a lot of——in a fusty theatre. I sometimes wish you weren't an actress! I found my new suit here when I came home—I haven't opened it yet, and some of the Aran Books from Roberts. By the way if you have really ordered those pictures of Jack B. Y's we must keep them, dont mind my little burst of temper—I am very grateful to you for thinking of getting them for me, but I have been getting a little bit scary about your extravagance lately that is why I blew up. Dont mind it—that is dont mind it this time, but be very economical in future.

I have just finished my article and I am posting it with this. I hope it will be a success. Remember to talk about the Aran Book a lot so that people may buy it. If it fails financially it will be a serious matter.

Your old Scamp.

I found the enclosed photo in an envelope. Do you know who it be-longs to? If it is yours you cant value it much as you never missed [it] all this time. I'm wounded etc.

[*TCD*]   Glendalough House
                                              Saturday [*27 April 1907*]

Dearest

I have just got your letter. I was in town today till nearly 3 o'clock, and then I came home and worked. As you dont want to walk tomorrow you had better come down by the *quarter to four* and come here to [the] house, and then *stay the whole evening* with me over the fire. My mother says you are to stay for supper Isn't that fun?

I am sending this to post now in a hurry.

Here is a GREAT SECRET *The Playboy* is to be done in Edinburgh on your tour. *Not a word to anyone.*

                                          Till four tomorrow
                                              Your old Tramp

[*TCD*]   Glendalough Ho.
                                              May 3rd [*1907*]

My Dearest

I got your note at two o'clock today, and now I dont know whether I shall be able to post this tonight, or not, as the weather is so bad. I hope you are feeling better again by this time. My throat is better but my cough is rather worse than it was last week so I must be careful. I dont know what to say about tomorrow. There is no use going to the Dargle as there would be *too* many people there if it [is] fine—there always are on Saturdays,—and I dont think you should walk far yet. On the other hand if it is very fine it would be a pity not to meet, so if the day is *really fine* meet me at Tara St. at five minutes *past two*. If the weather is not good I wont go ⟨so you need not wait if I dont come in that train.⟩ You will not have very far to go back if I am not there. If you dont feel well enough for a walk send me a wire in the morning.

I have just got a good review of *The Playboy* written by H. Jackson,[1] one of the men who had supper with us in Leeds—the night you were so depressed! I also got a letter from a man in Bohemia—not Musek— who wants to translate *The Playboy* into Bohemian.[2] So you see Christy is making his way.——

I have just got a card from Payne to say that he is coming to see me tomorrow morning. IF he runs me late for my train I shall go by the next that gets to Tara St at *20* minutes to *3* so meet that *too* if fine.

　　　　　　　　　　　　　　　　　　　　　　　　　Your old Tramp.

This is a dull note that's because I'm trying to think a better plan about our trains but there is none. We are both lonesome these times, but I hope it wont be for long now. T.

---

1. Holbrook Jackson (1874–1948), essayist, editor, and bibliophile, who later included a chapter on Synge in his book of essays, *All Manner of Folk* (London: Grant Richards, 1912); he was editor of *The New Age, T. P's Weekly,* and *Today,* and among other works published *William Morris, Craftsman-Socialist* (London: Cape, 1908), and *The 1890's* (New York: Kennerley, 1913).
2. Permission was not granted since Musek requested translation rights to *The Playboy* also.

[*Texas*]　　　　　　　　　　　　　　　　　　　　[*Glendalough House*]
　　　　　　　　　　　　　　　　　　　　　　　　　Saturday Night
　　　　　　　　　　　　　　　　　　　　　　　　　[*4 May 1907*]

Dearest

　　My old aunt is still here so if it *is wet* tomorrow *do not come*. Of course if you come and for any reason I am not at the station come on here. If you are not in the quarter to *two* train I will go on to Bray and wait for you there till the next train. But I hope you wont miss your *quarter to two.*

　　I think we ate too many chockolats today. I felt very queer on my way home. What a tussle we had!

　　I had a letter from Lebeau[1] tonight. He is delighted with *The Playboy.* I will show you his letter tomorrow. By the way it looks as if tomorrow would be fine so I hope we shall have a good walk. Take a good rest in the morning.

　　These fights make me feel intolerably wretched.

　　Goodbye my dear old Heart

　　　　　　　　　　　　　　Your old
　　　　　　　　　　　　　　Tramp

1. Henri Lebeau, a young Frenchman whom Synge had met in 1905, published an article on *The Well of the Saints* in *Revue de l'art dramatique,* April 15, 1905, which prompted Max Meyerfeld to translate the play into German. Synge corresponded with Lebeau until his death.

[*TCD/GS266*]

[*Glendalough House*]
May 12th [*1907*]

My own dearest Heart

I got your two little notes yesterday, and they brought tears into my gizzard! I have been going about since yesterday morning feeling as if I had one of those iron balls we saw in the convict ship tied to each of my legs and another hanging on my heart.[1]

Last night I got into such a dead abyss of melancholy I got scared so I am trying to be cheerful—but not succeeding very well. This is a desperately wet foggy day so I shall be sitting here now for hours and hours by myself, it's horrible. I wonder how you got across, it must have been calm enough, but I fear you must have had fog, and perhaps been delayed. I was thinking about you whenever I woke in the night, and almost wishing I had an old pal, of a St Antony I could ask to take care of you. I stuck up five photos of you along the table in front of my bed so I had quite a little picture-gallery of changlings to look at this morning. Yesterday afternoon I took the first bicycle ride I have had for months—since I was ill—up through Carrickmines and Kilternan—do you remember Kilternan?—and then down through the Bride's Glen, and past the little house in Loughlinstown where we had tea and jam-roll. It was a beautiful evening and I kept saying to myself whenever I heard a blackbird or a thrush or a yellow Hammer, "How Molly'd enjoy this." What would become of us if you had to go to America? And yet you were longing for it, you little scamp!

I remind myself today of Darley writing his long letters last year on tour, I rather despised him then for writing so much but I'm wiser now, God help me. I am going to the doctor tomorrow and then I'll either have the operation, or go away to Jack Yeats, I cannot stick on here doing nothing in particular for a long weary month. I wrote to Oxford yesterday to say I would *not* go there. If my neck is as bad as it is now I would not care to go and stay with strangers—I mean—I feel rather queer with this unsightly lump in my lug—and if I have the operation done now of course I would have no chance of being well enough to get to Oxford at the beginning of June.

My dear heart you dont know how much I love you. Do be good to me and come back soon as nice and natural and simple as when you went away. I will send you a bundle of books tomorrow, you have *Ivanhoe* to start with so I did not send them yesterday. I will write again as soon as I hear of your arrival in Glasgow. I have written to F.J.F. this morning also to patch up our fight the other day. I dont want him to be nursing his wrath against me all through the tour.

My God how shall I get through this long lonely day! I'm a fool, at my age, amn't I? Goodbye my own dearest love.

Your old Tramp.

1. The players had left 11th May on a five-week tour of Glasgow, Cambridge, Birmingham, Oxford, and London.

[TCD/GS266]

[*Glendalough House*]
Kingstown
Monday May 13th/07

My dearest Love

No letter today, I am greatly disappointed! I made sure of having one today as you promised to write yesterday.

I went for a long lonely walk yesterday—(it cleared in the afternoon) up along the lane that runs beneath *our* chimney and then down to Killiney station and home by train. I enjoyed myself for a while as the day was beautiful and the birds were singing but then I got very lonely and dejected on my way home. In the evening I read Shelley's *Epipsychidion*—a curious love poem, and thought about you

Today I went to see Mrs Payne after dinner but found the house locked up, so I went on to the Exhibition[1] for a while. I didn't enjoy it very much as I was lonesome again but there are good things in it. The Somali village especially is curious. A bit of the war-song the niggers were singing was exactly like some of the keens on Aran.

This evening after supper I have been for a little walk up towards Killiney hill as it is a lovely evening, but there is a cloud on me and I could not enjoy it. It is curious how your going has upset me altogether; I hope I wont be like this all the time you're away!

I heard from the *Manchester Guardian* this evening asking for more articles, which is a good sign! I suppose now (it is nine o-clock) you are in the thick of your first evening's bill I wonder how things are going.

I wont write any more to you tonight and I hope I shall hear from you tomorrow morning. I hope you got the letter all right that I sent off yesterday.

[*Encl*]   Tuesday

Dearest Heart

Your little note came this morning and did me a world of good. *Be sure* to write to me so that I shall get a letter every day. Please go on being "awfully good", if you possibly can.

I am so glad that you had a good journey over but you must be careful not to smoke too much if your hand is shaking it is very bad for you, your heart will begin to shake next, and that, I can tell you by sad experience, is a most horrible sensation.

It is twelve o'clock now and I have been hard at work all the morning so I am too tired to write very much. I am going to the doctor this afternoon or tomorrow to settle my programme, and then we'll know what we can do. I dont see why I shouldn't leave the operation over till the autumn. I think that would be the best way and then our coast would be clear. I am counting the days till I see you again. Half a week is gone now, and four weeks will bring us together again. It is hard to be parted from you, when I have been so much alone. Take care by the way that you dont let grease paint into your eyes. If they got sore now you might lose your sight or Goodness knows what before the tour was over

Good bye my Dear love write often and fully to your old

                                                                    T.

1. The International Exhibition was held at Herbert Park, Ballsbridge, from 4 May to 9 November 1906; it was visited by the King and Queen in July, and when it closed over 2,750,000 visitors had registered attendance.

[*Texas*]   [*Glendalough House*]
                                    Tuesday evening May 14th 1907

My dearest Love

To my great surprise and delight a second letter came from you at two o'clock (I posted a letter to you at 12 o'clock today) just as I was getting ready to go out for a bicycle ride. I went up through the Bride's Glen into the Scalp, and then I sat down and ate one of your oranges (can you read that?) and read your two letters again. My good little heart! Then I went on to Enniskerry and up past the church, and then along the upper road—you remember where we heard the thrush singing so beautifully—and down into Bray and home again through Ballybrack. The weather was perfect. All the trees in fresh green and a wonderful blue on the mountains—a summer blue that looks as if you could take it up in your arms. I was only trundling along on the roads so I could not enjoy it, as *we* might have done. That is not much news to tell you; do you care to hear where I ride to every day?

I am glad to hear that you like your 'digs'. I hope Sally wasn't *rude* to Payne. *You* ought to invite him in to tea another time to make up. It is much better to be polite 'always and ever', even if it is a little inconvenient. Told shortly in a letter the story of turning him out looked queer! Dont be offended, my old heart I'm not scolding. If I dont comment on what you tell me, and, vice versa, we wont have stuff always for our letters.

Did I tell you that I heard from Lady G? There was not much in it. I have put up three novels for you and I'll send them off tomorrow. *Tess* [*of the D'Urbervilles*] is the most interesting. Have you read any of *Ivanhoe?* Do you like it? I hope I'll have another letter from you to-morrow morning. Then I'll finish this. It is nearly bedtime.

I sent off the books today.

[*TCD/Encl*]   Wednesday (afternoon)
Dearest Love

I have just come back from town—the doctors—and found your letter waiting for me. I suppose it came at two after I had gone out.

The doctor seems to think well of me on the whole and he has given me some medicine to take for my neck. He says if it goes on well there might be no harm in leaving the operation over till *after* my summer holiday, in any case although I could hardly get it done now and be ready to face London, I would be well enough after a fortnight he thinks to go to the West. So we might have three of your five weeks. I haven't made up my mind yet about Jack Yeats! Perhaps I'll go perhaps not.

I enclose a little poem[1] to you I began last night, and part of my letter I wrote then. Why dont you tell me all you do morning and afternoon, that would help you if you find it hard to fill up your letters!

I dont think my picture can be on view now, it was in a special show of Patterson's pictures which was probably only for a week or two.[2] I heard from F.J.F. this morning he said he had been looking at a Rossetti picture in Sauchiehall street. Have you seen it? I am writing this in a hurry as I am going to post it now. I saw Roberts today and he says Aran Book is going very well. That is good. I told the doctor I was going to be married. He laughed and said "Well you're a great sportsman to go and get married before you've made your name!" He meant I would be hard up. Goodbye now sweet Heart

YOUR OLD SCAMP

1. Probably the following poem supplied to Elizabeth Coxhead by Molly's daughter, Pegeen Mair, and reproduced in *Daughters of Erin,* pp. 186–187:

With one long kiss
Were you near by,
You'd break the dismal cloud that is
On all my sky.

With one long kiss
If you were near
You'd sweeten days I take amiss
When lonely here.

With one long kiss
You'd make for me
A golden paradise of this
Day's beggary.

2. James Paterson R.S.A. (1854–1932) did three studies of Synge: a drawing (now in the possession of Mrs. L. M. Stephens) in 1906, which was reproduced as the frontispiece to Vol. IV of the 1910 Collected Edition; a photograph in 1908, which was reproduced as the frontispiece to Vol. I of the 1910 Collected Edition and also to the Oxford *Poems;* a painting in 1913 done from photographs and personal reminiscence, reproduced as the frontispiece to Maurice Bourgeois, *John Millington Synge and the Irish Theatre* (London: Constable, 1913).

[*TCD/GS266–67*]   Glendalough House
                                    Thursday evening. 16–5–07

My dearest Love

I got your nice little letter all right today (2 o'clock) before I went
out for my cycle ride. I have posted no letter to you today, as I wrote
pretty late yesterday, and I think it is better to keep this and post it
to you pretty early tomorrow so that you will be sure to get it on Saturday—your last day in Glasgow. I am much more cheerful now and I
have got over my depression though I am lonesome of course. This
was a beautiful grey day and I had a pleasant ride up through Kilternan
and then up a hill (that we have not been on together) which joins
the lane where we saw the little tinker camp on our first walk. The
furze all down the lane was magnificently golden and the mountains
very blue and beautiful behind it. I got home about five, had some
tea, and then worked for a while on a Wicklow article for the *Guardian*
first of all, and for a Wicklow book afterwards. I have written in all
about 1300 words today, that is, typing out stuff from my notes taken
on the spot. That is a good day's work isn't [it]? Do you know what?
I've an idea! Go out when you get this and buy a good thick square
note-book with a strong cover and begin to keep a journal of your
tour writing down everything as it comes helter-skelter, especially the
small things. Say what sort of landlady you have and what she says
to you, if it is funny, what you have for dinner, what your dressing
rooms are like and your journeys etc. Will you do it? At the least you
will find it intensely interesting and amusing reading ten years hence—
and later (if not now) when you are touring in Ireland, and you have
caught the knack, you will write stuff about places like the Wexford
Theatre that, *with my help,* you will be able to sell. Wouldn't that be
fun! The public are very ignorant about the inner side of the smaller
theatrical life, and very curious about it, so such articles would be
sure to go, if you put enough little details in them to make the thing
individual. I mean thousands of people travel from Glasgow to Cambridge (we know all about that), but no one knows what you are
having for dinner tomorrow, so to start with you have an unknown
fact, and unknown facts are interesting.——————

You will say this is a dull letter, will you? This is my fourth to
to Glasgow so I dont think I have done badly. You have been very

good. I will not write again now till I hear of your arrival in Cambridge and get your address. Be sure to send it. Then Monday is a holiday so there may be a delay. My dear Heart dont forget to be very dignified and good on your long Sunday journey! You dont mind my reminding you, do you? You know what a little madcap you are! Friday 12.30 P.M. I have been working all the morning at a ballad for two voices for you and F.J.[Fay] to recite if it comes off. I got your photo this morning in *S*[*preading*] *the News,* many thanks. I am so glad to have it to add to my *changling gallery.* I showed it to my mother she was greatly amused by it.[1]

You dont tell me enough what you do all day and every day. Do you go out much? Who do you go with? What do you do? You know everything that I have done since you went and I only know that you were out once before breakfast—a very Wonderful thing!—and that you went once to a gallery. I am not asking, of course, because I am uneasy but simply because I want to be able to follow my little changling along and know what she is doing. I wont post this till I see if I am to have a letter by the 2 o'clock post. I am sending you an unfinished copy of the verses I quoted to you on our wet walk please be very careful not to lose them. Did you like the others.[2]

[*TCD/Encl*]   Friday
                                                 2 o'clock

Dearest

Your letter has come and it is a very nice one. Yes you are telling me every thing this time. Are the whole company in your house or how do they know what you have for dinner? I am glad to hear that the houses are not so bad.

Let me know your address in Cambridge as soon as you can, and I'll write to you my poor pet. I am glad you seem lonesome, so am I. This will be a *fat* letter.

                                                 Your old
                                                 TRAMP

P.S.   I hope *you* wont take to card playing. *Please dont!*

[*TCD/?encl*]

                    Irish Stage - Land
                    by Miss Maire O'Neill

(or–by J. M. Synge   (N.B. if we write this we can
and Another)   get it into *Manchester Guardian*)
Journey to a southern town (Wexford but you dont name it) the gathering in Harcourt Street, the excitement of starting, the clear winter's
morning, as you pass down through Carrickmines, Bray and Greystones. The bewildered old woman who sells us apples in Wicklow.
Then the company gets tired looking out of the window and they sing
songs –

      (give Molly McGuirk ⎫ and any other
        You gay old Turk⎭ quaint ones

You pass on and arrive in Wexford. Dinner. Visit to little theatre
describe Wexford Theatre, entry etc. Rest and hurried tea before the
theatre. Describe dressing room, the feeling of the audience, the
striking matches in the gallery, describe how you come out go up the
shaky stairs into the balcony and what you see there. The turmoil of
packing after the show.

    Then take some other tour and run all the other interesting ex-
periences you have had engine driver etc into it. In this you can end
by the late supper in Dundalk the long wait for the train at three
o'clock, the dancing in the dim light, the going out into the grey dawn
the sun rises as you get into the deserted station; you walk up and
down; then train comes; you have glimpses of magnificent bright
morning; you go to sleep and wake in Dublin.

    1. The Directors had picture postcards made of scenes from various plays in the
repertory (see illustration p. 235).
    2. Probably the following lines preserved among Molly's papers now in Trinity
College:

    You're herewith summoned, for the longest day, (i.e. June 21st)
    To come back, changling, while the woods are gay,
    To Wicklow, and the Dargle, and Glen Cree,
    And all the little nooks you've loved with me. . . .
    I think the furze will be half-faded then
    But I know many a far-off hilly glen
    Where we may catch the summer's last full hour
    And smell again the primrose, violet and cuckoo flower. . . .

    And wont you love to stretch in fresh, green grass
    And watch the little clouds and shadows pass
    And show your new-found wisdom of the wren's
    And swallow's songs. . . . . (the rest is not written yet)——

[*TCD*]
Glendalough House. Kingstown. Dublin
Wednesday morning
May 22nd/07

Dearest

I got your long and interesting letter last night (Tuesday night) and was very glad to hear that you were safe in Cambridge. What a journey you had. I meant to warn you before you started not to go out from your lodgings without making sure you knew the name and address— as you did in Newcastle dont you remember?—and now you have done it again! I suppose experience will teach you. There is nothing new here. It is very cold and I am rather worse in consequence. I rode too far on my cycle before I was used to it, and hurt my leg so I stayed at home all day on Sunday, and to make things worse my eyes have got sore—nearly as bad as yours so I was not very gay. On Monday I went —walked—to Killiney and back by train. Then yesterday I went to Bray by the quarter-to-two—it seemed strange not to find you in the train waiting for me—and walked up the road we went on our last walk, then down to the lower road and up the hill into the lane where the old cross is and so back to Bray for the five train. It was cold and wretched and I did not enjoy it at all.

You have not told me yet who was sharing your digs in Glasgow? You say in your last (from there) that you sat up talking after Sally went to bed, but you do not say with whom so I am puzzled. You told me before you went that the men were not going with you. *Please explain fully.* This kind of mystery troubles me, *more than I can say.*

I had two friendly letters from Miss Horniman yesterday. A great deal depends—as to future tours—on the impression she gets of the acting and what she calls the '*discipline*' of the company—*this is strictly between ourselves*—the acting in our peasant plays is all right, I hope the discipline, the orderliness, of the company is the same. How are W.G. and Mrs F behaving themselves this tour? You had best be steadily polite—I dont mean effusive—to Miss Horniman if you come in contact with her. It is the only way to keep oneself right. One gets into the way of wearing a sort of mask after a while, which is a rather needful trick.

It will be a fortnight in two days since we saw the last of each other. It seems—to me at least—unconscionably long. This is the dullest letter I have sent you yet, but I am heavy and unwell so you must not mind. Remember to take care of yourself at the end of this week.

I am writing to Jack Yeats today to see if he can have me for a week or so before I go to London. I want a change badly. I forgot to tell you of my doings on Saturday. My leg was a little sore before dinner so I thought I would take great care of myself I dodged up on my bicycle just above Shankhill—a place between Bray and Loughlinstown—then I sat in a sunny ditch and read for an hour in the East wind—it was then I got cold in my eyes—and at last set off home. My leg was very stiff so I was going very slowly when pop my back tyre blew up with a bang. I had only 35 minutes then to get to Killiney station to catch the 4 train so I rushed along in spite of my leg packing my bicycle and just got in, in time. That is why I was laid up on Sunday. My leg is all right again now.

I must write to Jack Y. now so goodbye my poor little changling be good and write often—I expected a letter this morning but didn't get one—

Your old Tramp

P.S.   How much money did *you* clear out of your Glasgow salary?

[*TCD*]   [*Glendalough House*]
Wednesday night
[*22 May 1907*]

Dearest Heart

You DIDN'T give me your address in your Glasgow letter so I couldn't have written any sooner. *I* was very disappointed at not hearing of you till Tuesday night. This is a mere line to make up for all the long time you have been without a letter. *I told you long ago* that I had been to the Exposition and how I liked it. I'm afraid you dont pay much attention to my letters!!! Be very civil to Miss Gildea[1] if you come across her it is the best way of showing you dont care a *"wag"* about her or her talk. Nothing has happened today I wrote to you this morning and then dodged about. I have got fresh cold or something and I dont feel well. Be sure to tell me *in time* what day you leave Cambridge and to give your address in advance this time. If you would post earlier if possible and convenient I ought to get your letter in the morning instead of evening, it seems slow

Your old Tramper

You'll have got no letter today either so you wont know what's happened. It is your own little fault however as you didn't *give me an address*

---

1. Miss Ida Gildea (later Mrs Hargreaves Heap), a very close friend of Miss Horniman, had volunteered to help the Players on tour by selling copies of the plays.

[*TCD*]

[*Glendalough House*]

Wednesday evening (late)

22.5.07

Dearest Heart

This is no less than MY THIRD letter to you today. What do you say to me now?

It is a wonderfully still beautiful evening and I feel as if I ought to write verses but I haven't the energy. There is nearly a half moon, and I have been picturing in my mind how all our nooks and glens and rivers would look, if we were out among them as we should be! Do you ever think of them? Ever think of them I mean not as places that you've been to, but as places that are there still, with the little moon shining, and the rivers running, and the thrushes singing, while you and I, God help us, are far away from them. I used to sit over my sparks of fire long ago in Paris picturing glen after glen in my mind, and river after river—there are rivers like the Annamoe that I fished in till I knew every stone and eddy–and then one goes on to see a time when the rivers will be there and the thrushes, and we'll be dead surely. It makes one grudge every evening one spends dully in a town. What wouldn't I give to be out with you now in this rich twilight coming down from Rockbrook or Enniskerry with strange smells and sounds, and the first stars, and the wonderful air of Wicklow? Is there anything in the world to equal the joy of it? And you, my poor changling, have to go to Birmingham next week, and I, poor divil, amn't well enough to go out to far-away places for even solitary walks. Write a nice *intimate* letter the next time and tell me how your little mind is feeling in its wandering.

I wrote to Jack Yeats today to ask if I might go there. I wonder shall I like it, if I go. I'll leave this now to see if there is anything new in the morning.

Thursday morning

Nothing new except an American Magazine with an account of the Irish writers—poor stuff enough. I am to go to the dentist today and see what he can do for me before I go away.

Write me a nice letter

Your old
Tramp

[TCD]   Glendalough House
Kingstown
23rd/5/07
Thursday night

My dearest Pet

I have just got your poor little Wednesday note. I tired of you indeed!! What a thing to say. Now I'm going to lecture you. If you'd brought a sheet of paper with you in the train and written three lines to say you were safe in Cambridge and to give me your address, and posted them when you arrived there, I would have got it on Monday and you'd have had an answer on *Tuesday*. If you couldn't do that you might have asked someone on Monday what time you had to post to catch the *Irish* Mail and posted your letter in time for it. Then I would have got it on Tuesday morning and you'd have had an answer on Wednesday! But you went and missed the Monday mail so I didn't hear till Tuesday night, and I wasn't able to write to you till Wednesday. Will you be wiser next time? I hardly know now whether to post this to you tomorrow (Friday) or not as I do not know what time you leave Cambridge, on Saturday, or whether it is not till Sunday that you go, and I'm quite sure you do not leave your next address in your digs in case anything comes after you are gone! That would be a bit of Wisdom far beyond you. Well that's lecture enough.

I was at the dentist's today and got my teeth settled up for the time being. They are not so bad as I feared. This is a most gloomy, dismal and dark evening—more like October than the end of May—and I feel wretched enough. I'd like to be away on some warm sunny hill—like the purple grapes hill—and to be warm, and well, and sun-burnt, and dressed in summer clothes, and to have you with me dressed in nice light summer clothes too, and a big hat so that we might be as happy as the day was long, instead of being boxed up here in this accursed place. Well I hope good times are coming

[*AS/encl*]   Friday morning
Dearest

Your letter came this morning, and I was glad to get it. I thought when I began to read it that you had not got my letter but then I found you had.

I am more pained than I can possibly tell you about your Glasgow 'digs', not the fact of your lodging together—though that is not de- sirable from many points of view—but that you should have deceived me, after all your promises. I find it hard to believe that you did not know all the last week in Dublin that you were going to lodge with the men. In fact you told me in the Park that you were going to do so, and then when I did not like it you said it was only a joke. Besides you promised to tell me everything, and then to keep me in the dark on this important point all that week———I cannot write about it, it is too painful. Cannot you see that you have cut away the very foundation of our happiness. Now when you are in America or God knows where I will never know whether you are not deceiving me or not in some matter that I have a right to know. ⟨Great Christ⟩ the thought of your writing so kindly last week when you were deceiving me all the time makes me sick with anguish. You said ⟨what is the use of talking to you. What is⟩ I am not scolding you, my poor pet, I do not think you understood what you were doing. Now even when you read this you will not understand why I feel ten years older than I did last week, and ⟨that⟩ why my whole life seems frozen up inside me, [*Synge's deletion*] Oh Why, why, why, do you torture me?

You know that I tell lies like anyone in small trivial matters to outside people, but you know, I think, that I would not deceive you on any matter. I lay awake nearly all night on Sunday brooding over this, then I thought it could not be true, my poor little changling, I am sure you did not mean to distress me the way you have done. I shall see you I suppose in a fortnight, the thought is not a joy to me now. I read some of your letters the other day that you wrote to me last summer. It is extraordinary how you have 'come on' in the whole turn and ease of letter-writing, I say to myself that perhaps you will learn to be open and be true with me also, when you get more used to my way of ⟨life and⟩ looking at things. I wrote a poem on you last night but I have not the heart to send it to you. Perhaps you will smile when I tell you that there are tears on the back of my eyes. I had begun to trust you so completely and————

I see you are spending all your money, but I thought you were looking forward to our getting married in July? How do you spend it? It is impossible to tell you how utterly broken and dejected I am feeling today

Your old Tramp.

Write to me soon and write lovingly if you want to cheer me. It is only because I *love you so deeply* that I feel all this so much.

[*TCD/tel*]   Stoneview Kingstown 25 May 1907 10.05 A.M.
Miss M Allgood c/o Petit 34 City Rd Cambridge
All right dont worry good luck for journey send next address Synge

[*Texas/GS267–68*]
Glendalough House
Kingstown
Sunday
May 26th/07

My own darling Changling

I got your little note this morning, and the sad ending you wrote to it distresses me. I did not mean to hurt you, but I could not write anything else if I wrote to you at all. I sent my telegram to cheer you up when I got your letter yesterday morning. I thought you would get it just after my letter and that it would brighten you up. You mustn't worry yourself my poor little pet, I know you did not mean to do anything, but that sort of thing has a dreadful effect on me. Love so strong as ours is, is a dangerous commodity and I think it will kill us if we do not get married soon. I am very unwell. All the anxiety and distress during this last week has had a very bad effect on me, I am afraid. I have not been able to walk or go about much so I have just been sitting here brooding all day, and I have had some terrible fits of depression. Write me a nice loving letter when you get this, that is the only thing that is the only thing that does me any good now. I meant this to be a bright cheerful letter to make you happy again, but I fear you will not think it so.

I have heard nothing of Jack Yeats so I think that visit is 'off'. I shall go to London (DONT SPEAK OF THIS) probably about Tuesday week, —I am not well enough for Oxford—and stay there till you come back, I do not know what day you will come. There are only three nights in Oxford so I suppose you will come back on Thursday. So–if I am well enough to go over at all—we shall meet now in about ten days. That is one comfort at any rate. It is of course an *immense joy to me* to think of seeing you again. I wish you weren't on the stage, the continual separations it will entail are not good for either of us. I was dreaming about you last night, but nothing very tangible that I can remember.

I wonder shall we be able to get married in the early summer. You, apparently, are throwing away your money as if you did not wish it anymore. What did you save in Cambridge? But I must not begin to scold you again. I feel very broken down, and I have a pain in my knee so I wont be able to have a walk today either.

I do not think the story you heard about *Playboy* in Birmingham was quite true. It was withdrawn for *political* reasons I believe.[1] I am not satisfied with the way things are going in the company, (—Miss H. is 'at' me again, so far in a friendly way, about some 'fit-up' that was to have been made last summer, and that I know nothing of—) and I wrote to Yeats yesterday proposing to resign my directorship. It does not do me or any one else any good, that I can see, and it is an endless worry to me. I will not do anything in a hurry, however, and please dont speak of this to *anyone*. I do not think things can go on much longer as they are, and I think I would have a freer hand to ask for what arrangements I want made for the working of the company if I was *outside it*. I will not desert W.G.F. if he wants me to stay on, so I must consult him.

My poor pet I love you more than I know myself　my life I think is in your hands, as I told you before. How I wish you were coming to see me this afternoon. I feel so down. I suppose you are travelling to Birmingham today. I wonder how you will do there. Are you all lodging together again?

I went to see *Frou-Frou* played by Jane Hading[2] at the Royal on Friday. I went to the gallery and sat with Connelly, Starkey,[3] Stewart, and Holloway. It was not very gay. I disliked the play very much and I didn't greatly care for J. Hading. I think the fashionable 'passionate' actress is a fraud. There is nothing inherently interesting or artistic in these violent scenes. I caught myself in the middle of a dismal yawn while the poor lady was flinging chairs about the stage. I found the French a little hard to follow for the first five minutes, then I got on all right.

Now be good and dont worry and we'll meet in ten days and be very happy again. Write me nice letters and write very often. I am sending you my last verses they are not good but they are sincere now I hope you feel all right my sweet love. When you come home you must go to some doctor here and get yourself seen to. You cannot be well. With a million blessings

Your old Tramp

1. *The Playboy* was produced with success in both Oxford and London, but because of licensing difficulties and fear of further rows among the Irish patriots, was not produced as Synge had hoped in Birmingham.

2. Jane Hading, or Jeanette Hadingue (1859–1933), a French actress with a popular following in Great Britain.

3. The Connolly referred to is probably Seamus O'Conghaile, Honorary Secretary of the Theatre of Ireland, not the 1916 rebel. James Sullivan Starkey (1879–1958), poet and essayist, who wrote under the pen name of "Seumas O'Sullivan," was a member of the original Abbey Theatre company but resigned in September 1905 on the foundation of the limited company. In 1923 he founded *The Dublin Magazine*.

[AS]
Glendalough House
Monday May 27th/07

My own dearest Love

I got your letter this [morning], and it upset me so much that I sat on my chair trembling all over, and I could hardly eat my breakfast. I have wired to you now to know how you are. It is a miserable business. You seem to have thought it a slight matter to tell me a lie, I, as I have often told you, and as you must see now feel it very differently. We will get to understand each other better by degrees I hope and believe so I think we need not be depressed. I dont think any good will come of discussing this affair any more in our letters. Let us drop it, and try and build up our old confidence again. When I said it would be no joy to see you in London I meant merely that I was so unspeakably hurt by the way you had treated me that for the moment I had lost the *joy* of our love, not (I need not say), the love itself. Further, what I meant about cutting away the foundations of our happiness was, of course, that without perfect, absolute confidence and openness ⟨that is the only thing⟩ all sorts of misunderstandings and doubts were sure to arise, and that you had made this confidence difficult. However do not let us discuss it unless you wish to. Oh my poor love if you know how I have suffered and am suffering still. Do not talk as if you thought we should separate. How could we do it? Dont you remember those evenings when we came down from our walks so perfectly happy in each other? Isn't it some peace to you to think that we shall have that again in three or four weeks now. Dont you look forward to lying up in the heather again and eating purple grapes? My poor sweet little heart I am sorry I have hurt you, but I have been hurt as badly or *worse* myself so you must not blame me. I am sure that when we are together we will understand each other better, and not have these fearful troubles. It seems so simple for you to tell me straight out all that [you] are going to do, and to let us talk it over together, then we would never have any trouble, but you will not do it.

Remember I am very nervous, very highly-strung, as they call it,— if I was not I couldn't be a writer—and the only way to keep things clear is to tell me everything at the beginning, not to keep me in miserable doubt for days till I find out what has happened. My dear love we have to learn by pain and trouble how to live our life together. We both have the deep true love, I am quite sure, that will bring everything all right in the end. Do be good to me, my sweet little pet, and tell me *everything* as you have promised so often. I heard from Jack Yeats at last this morning. He wants me to go over at the end of this week, for a week before I go to London. I dont know whether I shall be well enough now, I am going to the doctor today. There would be no use going to Yeats if I couldn't walk about with him, and see the country. I do not know yet how I shall go it is a very troublesome journey. If I go by long sea I shall leave Dublin on Wednesday and not get to his place till Friday, but I dont think I shall go that way. *Go on* writing here till I send you the new address I will write to you very often of course. My knee feels very bad today I doubt that I shall be able to go at all. Perhaps I wont be able to go to London even. That would be too bad. Now promise me, my little life, that you wont worry and make yourself ill. The thought of it makes me ill too. I wonder the answer doesn't come to my wire. I hope I have read your address right it was rather hard to read what you wrote. I wrote you a long letter yesterday. It wasn't a very cheerful one I am afraid still it was better than the last. I wish I could put my two arms round you and give you a good long squeeze, and then I know we would both be all right again. Wouldn't we? Write to me cheerfully. Your old

Tramp

[*TCD*]   Glendalough House
                                                  May 28th/07

My dearest Love

Your letter has come this morning and it has rolled the stone off my grave at last. You letter yesterday moved me in the morning, because you seemed so ill, but when I read it again (after I had written to you) I felt that it was very strange and unreasonable, and I got angry again. However I'll burn it today as you suggest. I was going to write you a very nice letter this morning, but I have just been answering a rather nasty letter from Yeats so I am not in a good humour for the moment.

I am as over-strung as you are, and when I got the wire yesterday tears of relief came into my eyes. It made me laugh this morning when I heard Sally had sent it. Dont tell her. I went to the doctor again yesterday he says I am to go away at once. He was astonished at the muscles of my legs, he said I must be as strong as a horse! So take care not to make me kick you!! After the doctor I went to Old Yeats and he drew me again.[1] We began to talk about Maire Walker[2] and then Sally whom he now admires very much. Then he went on to Sally's *sister* "Oh" he said "isn't she wonderful! I declare I think she is better than Sarah, though I always feel jealous when I see a younger sister beating an older one."!

I am going to Jack Yeats after all, I think, I shall leave here on Thursday evening and get there some time on Friday. So you may write here once more after you get this, and then I will send you his address so that you may write there. I shall stay with him for about a week and then go to London. If you get 'digs' address near Russell's Square or Russell's Street try and take them because I shall be somewhere about there. Be sure you get a 'decent' address as thousands of bad characters live in that neighbourhood. The man who translated *The Well of the Saints* into German is to be there and I shall have to see a good deal of him[3] but I will have some time to spare I suppose.

I feel indescribably sick of the continual worries of this company, worries with F.J.F. Miss Horniman, Lady G. Yeats, you never know where it will break out next.

Of course if you gave W.G. £1 that accounts for your Glasgow salary. I was sure you would not find it so easy to pay off that great debt as you thought. It is a pity. I am afraid this tour round by Jack Yeats will cost a good deal but I must get a change or I dont know what mayn't happen to me.

Did I tell you that Florence Ross has come to stay here again for a few days? She has been painting a lot and is getting on well.

I dont seem to have much to say this morning so good bye my dear love, it wont be long now till we meet again. You will like Oxford I think, it is a beautiful place.

Your old
Tramp

1. There are at least six drawings of Synge by J. B. Yeats in existence in addition to the oil painting of 1907. One drawing, unsigned, appeared in the December 1904 issue of *Samhain;* three further drawings were done in 1905, dated January, April, and December; the most frequently reproduced drawing, "Synge at rehearsal," is dated 25 January 1907, and, finally, the one dated May 1907, mentioned above. See the frontispiece for the December 1905 drawing.

2. Maire Nic Shiubhlaigh (d. 1958) and her brother Frank Walker had been members of the early dramatic company founded by Willie and Frank Fay; Maire left the company shortly after it became a limited company, but returned several times to perform in various roles. She first created the part of Nora in *The Shadow of the Glen.* Later, two other sisters, Eileen O'Doherty and Betty King, were members of the company. In 1928 Miss Nic Shiubhlaigh married Major General Eamon Price. She published her reminiscences in *The Splendid Years* (Dublin: James Duffy, 1955), by Maire Nic Shiubhlaigh and Edward Kenny.

3. Dr. Max Meyerfeld, whose correspondence with Synge was published in the *Yale Review,* July 1924. See also John Millington Synge, *Plays, Book One* (London: Oxford University Press, 1968), Appendix C.

[*Texas/frag*]   [*Glendalough House*]
                                                          Wednesday *night*
                                                          [*29 May 1907*]

Dearest
    I got your letter this evening at six o'clock. I hope you will post
today's letter in better time or I *wont get* it before I start tomorrow.
As I got no letter this morning I did not write to you, so—I have just
remembered—you will have no address to write to me tomorrow
(Thursday). I hope you are taking care of yourself.
    I have been in town and packing, and generally putting up my
books and things for the summer, today, so I am too tired to write
much. I was at the Abbey today getting some things. It looked very
deserted and queer. My knee is better. I am going over by the new
route Rosslare and Fishguard so I shall start off through Bray

[*TCD*]   Glendalough House
                                                          Thursday [*30 May 1907*]

Dearest
    I have just got your letter I am writing this in a great hurry as I
have a good deal of packing etc. to do and I am off at three o'clock.
I sail tonight from Rosslare just outside Wexford so I shall go down
the whole line where we went, on our first tour together and under
the old castle that we sat under so confidentially. It will seem strange.
I wish you had sent me a nicer letter to read and think over on my long
lonely journey; I do not reach Jack Y. till 1.15 tomorrow afternoon.
When you said that I should write to you every day to keep you 'good'
I got a "qualm of dread"! You little——do you find it so hard as that
to keep yourself 'good'? N.B. I'm writing this with a grin, so dont be
offended.
    I'm sorry to hear of bad business and rows in Birm[ingham]. I
knew the place would be a failure. If I resigned my directorship, I
would stay on in the company and leave my plays just the same. It
would make little difference except that I would be rid of all the endless
worry with Miss Horniman F.J.F. and the rest of them. However it is
not likely that I shall do it at present. When I said that things could
not go on much longer as they are, I meant that with the two managers,

F.J.F., W.B.Y. and myself and Miss Horniman, there are so many possible points for friction that one never knows when a bad row may break out. What part did the paper attack you for? You said you had been attacked. I am not surprised that *Baile's Strand* failed in Birm. We knew it would.

My address will be for the next week
c/o Jack B. Yeats Esq
Cashlauna Shelmiddy
   Strete
   Near Dartmouth
   South Devon

Give me your Oxford address as *soon as you can* and write it *very distinctly*. I could hardly read this last one you gave me. I shall try and write you a line on the journey and post it somewhere on Friday. Then I shall not be able to write again till I get the Oxford address as a letter from Devon on Saturday would probably miss you in Birm. Try and see as many of the Colleges etc. as you can in Oxford it is a wonderful place. Dont be alarmed or worried if you are some time without hearing from me. I shall do my best to write often but away there on a visit in such an outoftheway place, it is not always easy to manage. Now Goodbye my poor changling I have not given up the idea of being married in the summer. But we shall have to see how our money stands. I have not got my Doctor's bill yet. Good bye tomorrow anyhow we shall be in the same country.

Your old T.

[*TCD*]   [*30 May 1907*]
Dearest

I've started, out through our little tunnel past Killiney Strand past our *little lighthouse* then into Bray and on round the Head where we found the *puppy dog!* How it is all mixed up with you now. I am below Wicklow and the rain has stopped. The country is beautifully green under the clouds. I can hardly write the train is shaking so much. I wonder what I'll do with myself the three hours in Wexford before I sail. I feel lonesome and sad, here all by myself. The half lifted cloud is very beautiful and I'm seeing great sights all the same.

Arklow. My spirits are going UP. The country is wonderful, masses of bluebells, and wet green trees and ferns everywhere. It's wonderful after the long imprisonment I've had. I wonder could *we* come home by

[*Texas*]   White's Hotel Wexford.
                                                                    Thursday night

(*continuation*)

I am in Wexford now as you see trying to pass my evening I have two hours more to get through. I wish I could write to you for two hours I dont know what else I am to do. I have just had tea and plaice at the end of a big table, and there are three men at a table near discussing the world. I thought at first they were commercials but they seem to have too much information and knowledge for that noble calling. One of them has just told a fearsome tale on the effects of hypnotism—or mesmerism as you call it—I'll tell it to you by and by when we meet. Now they are on the Rebellion and they seem to know a lot about it.

It seems funny to me to be on the road again I have been so long shut up. Certainly there is nothing like travelling. I feel better already. It is one of the wettest nights I have ever come across, it is coming down in bucket-fulls so I cant walk about any where. This is like writing when you are hypnotised because I'm scribbling away as hard as I can and all the time I'm listening to the talk at the table behind me. I dont know how much this trip will cost, I like this route it has something out of the common. Did I tell you I am not to get to Jack Yeats' till a quarter past one tomorrow. Isn't that a good trot? By the way I had a funny incident today. You know my old breeches are in bits. 'Well'—as you say—I bought a new pair ready made yesterday to wear on my journey with my old coat and waistcoat   I hadn't time to try them on till an hour before I was to start. I put them on then and found them—I thought—mighty elegant. Then I sat down plump, to put on my shoes, and I heard a rend. The seam in the gable end had split right down and there I was! Fancy if that had happened when I was getting into the train after I had started. I dragged them off and got the cook to sew them up as best she could. Now I [am] walking about in great trepidation for fear they'll go again!—I have had a long talk with the waiter, he says they dont half know the bay yet on this line and they have run aground two or three times. I hope we wont be wrecked. If you get this you'll know I'm safe as it's going over with me!

[*TCD*]   c/o Jack Yeats
                                                    etc   [*Devon*]
                                            Monday morning 6 A.M.
                                            [*3 June 1907*]

Dearest

I hope you got my letter all right that I sent from Cardiff—did
you see the postmark?—I got two of yours on Saturday one from
Birmingham in the morning and the other in the evening sent on from
Kingstown. You do not give me your Oxford address so I must send
this to the Theatre. I dont feel very sure that it will find you,—or you
it, so I wont put in anything confidential. Let me know as soon as you
can what day you go on to London so that I may write to you there, in
case I am not able to write again in time to catch you in Oxford. The
post is difficult here, it only goes out once or twice in the day and we
are a long way from the village. Besides on a visit like this it is not
easy to find time to write. I shall go up to London on Saturday most
likely. I dont know where I shall stay.

This is a charming place, my room looks out across a little green
valley, with a little water mill at the bottom, and the birds sing so loud
they seem to waken me at 4 o'clock every morning. I went for a long
walk along by the sea with J.B.Y. on Saturday, so that we were out all
day from 11. till 7. Yesterday we puttered about, and today we are
going for another long expedition after Breakfast. He is a charming
fellow. I dont feel much better for the change yet, my cough is bad
still, and I'm not sleeping well, or in good spirits. J.B.Y. and his wife
seem a very happy couple after eleven years of it, and they must be
comfortably off as everything is very nice in a simple way. I wonder
how the Playboy will go in Oxford. How often was he rehearsed in
Birmingham?

I'll leave this now till the post comes.

Later

No letter from you today. Please let me hear soon. I could write you
a lot of nice things if I knew your address for certain. So now in four
or five days we shall meet again! That will be *good* anyhow! It seems a
long weary time since you went off do write me a nice letter I am
afraid I shall be very busy in London but of course I shall be able to see
you. I'm off now for a long country walk with Jack Yeats so I cannot
write much. Dont mind dullness of enclosed note I was lying awake
and in low spirits I hope you are all right again. Be good and cheerful
                                            Your old Tramp

[*TCD*]   [*c/o Jack Yeats. Devon*
                                                            4 June 1907]

Dearest Heart

      Many thanks for your two letters which I got this morning. I hope
you are better I am uneasy at all these bad accounts of your health.
I am not very well myself either I am sorry to say. My cough is troublesome. I do not go to London till Saturday and I dont know yet what
my address will be. Send me your London address as soon as you can
as this will be the last time I can write to you at Oxford. Excuse my
little scrawls from here, it isn't possible to write much. They are
delightful people to be with here, but I am out of spirits rather as I
am not well. I hope the second change to London will do me good.
Write as often as you can I wrote *you* yesterday to the *New Theatre* I
hope you will get it all right

                                    Ever your old Tramp

[*TCD/GS270*]   c/o Mrs Ward
                                                            4 Handel Street
                                                            Brunswick Square
                                                            W.C.
                                                            [*11 June 1907*]

My dearest Life

      It's too bad I have nothing to do this afternoon, but write letters,
so I might have had you out to tea with me if I had arranged it. It's
too late now as if I went round I would not find you. You were
CAPITAL last night in almost all of it, and everyone is speaking well
of you. Yeats especially.[1] He says also that you are excellent in *The
Shadow of the Glen* and that he withdraws all his former criticisms of
you.

      My poor pet I am sick of being shut away from you like this, and
I fear it will get worse as the week goes on as I am being asked to go
to all sorts of teas and things. Last night Yeats and I had supper with
a Mrs Meakin and Lord Dunraven[2] and his daughter. All the time I
was wishing I was away walking the world with my little fresh madcap
of a changling! I wonder shall I get a sight of you tonight. There isn't
much use going behind the scenes the place is so cramped and
crowded. Tomorrow you have the two shows so there is no chance, on

Thursday we are all going to the House of Commons to see Stephen Gwynn[3] I met him this morning, and he asked [me] to go with the company so I shall get a word with you then at any rate I hope. Anyhow we haven't much more of it. In four more days the tour will be over. Be good   dont think that I am neglecting you   I'd give the world and all to be with you but it is hard to arrange and it isn't very satisfactory in any case to go dragging about in the hot streets. Ten thousand blessings on my little heart and soul.

Your old T.

1. The company opened at the Great Queen Street Theatre, London, on 10 June with *The Playboy,* in which Molly again played the role of Pegeen.
2. The Earl of Dunraven and Mount-Earl, Windham Thomas Wyndham-Quin (1841–1926), and his daughter, Lady Ardee, who was married to the Earl of Meath. Lord Dunraven, who entertained Yeats at Adare House, Co. Limerick, later that year, had been war correspondent to the *Daily Telegraph* and from 1885 to 1887, Under-Secretary of State for the Colonies; he was chairman of the Irish Land Conference 1902–3, and President of the Irish Reform Association; in 1880 he published *The Irish Question.* His other guest was probably Annette Meakin (d. 1959), the first Englishwoman to cross Siberia by the Great Siberian Railway in 1900. A musician, travel writer, and translator of the classics, she published *Women in Transition* in 1907, and contributed to various journals and magazines.
3. Stephen Lucius Gwynn (1864–1950), novelist, travel writer, and M.P. for Galway city 1906–1919.

[*TCD*]

4 Handel Street
Brunswick Sq.
W.C.
Friday [*14 June 1907*]

Dearest

I have had a terrible night and I feel very ill. I want you to let me know at once, if you can, by what train and what day you go back to Ireland. If it is on Monday I will try and go with you—I suppose you would like me to do so?

Will you meet me tomorrow at *12 o'clock* sharp (Saturday) along the side of Brunswick Square that I showed you, and dine with me. I must talk to you and I will not say anything to upset you before your show.

I nearly fainted yesterday when I got back to my room, my despair was so intense. ⟨God⟩

I feel very ill indeed. Today I have to go to Greenwich to see Masefield.[1]

Oh Christ what will become of me if you go on like this

Your T.

Write at once for Heaven's sake.

---

1. John Masefield (1878–1968), poet and dramatist, had first met Synge in London in 1903 and was later to acknowledge the influence Synge had on his own early plays. After Synge's death he published his reminiscences, "John M. Synge," in *The Contemporary Review*, April 1911, pp. 470–472, and *John M. Synge: A Few Personal Recollections with Biographical Notes* (New York: Macmillan, 1915), and wrote the article on Synge for the *Dictionary of National Biography* (1912), pp. 468–471.

[*TCD*]   Glendalough Ho.
                                      Wednesday [*?19 June 1907*]

My little Heart's Core

I want you to find this in your little paw when you awake to-morrow morning to drive away your depression. I have had a long talk about you with my mother, and I feel cheered-up some how. She seems to have known a lot of cases like yours Mrs X. Mrs Z. and Miss Y and so on and they all got well and lived happily ever afterwards. I think it's only fair that you should have a turn at being ill too, if you were too well you wouldn't be able to sympathize with your poor old Tramp when he gets put up on the shelf. Now be very good and very cheerful and take care of yourself.

My mother—on second thoughts—seemed to think it would be rather improper for me to stay in the same cottage with you and Sally. So enquire about other places near by, when you get there. I shall go up on Friday—if it is fine and stay the one night anyhow and see how it suits me and then I can look round. Now be sure and be happy you'll find your poor little illness will only draw us closer together, and make us realize how much we love each other—if that is possible. (I mean I dont think we'll ever really know how dear we are to each other.)

For ever and ever my own poor darling
Your old Tramp.

[*Texas/frag*]   [*Glendalough House
? June 1907*]

The post has passed   I half hoped there'd be a line from you asking
me to go in today, however I am sure it is better for you to stay quiet.
A thousand loves and blessings on you my dear treasure.

                                                    T

[*TCD*]   Glendalough Ho. 26.VI.07
Dearest Love
     Thanks for your note, excuse this paper I have no other.[1] Dont
forget that you have to tell me *when* and *where* I'm to meet you tomorrow. I'll bring in the bag with me and leave it [at] Westland Row
for you, if you really want it.
     Remember to ask the doctor every thing I told you, ask him also
how much of his medicine you are to take, and if you are to take it
again when you get a turn. Ask him if cycling is better for you than
walking, and anything else you can think of.[2] I am ready to kill myself
for having let you walk so much last autumn. I thought you were old
enough to manage yourself—God help us!!!!! However I hope there's
no harm done. Isnt the weather awful. It is making my cough worse
again.
          Forever ever your old Tramp

Did you order my *Guardians* last night? If you didn't you had better
not as you wouldn't have time to get them before you go.

1. This is scribbled on the back of the first page of a draft of "In a Landlord's
Garden," first published 1 July 1907 in the *Manchester Guardian*.
2. Included among Molly's papers is a reassuring letter to Molly concerning her
menstrual difficulties from Arthur P. Barry, gynecologist of the National Maternity
Hospital, Holles Street, 26 June 1907, and the rough draft of a letter in Synge's hand,
evidently for Molly to copy, addressed to the doctor: "Mr Synge brought me your kind
letter last week, and I am extremely glad to know what you tell me. I fancied things
were much more serious and something I said frightened Mr S also. I feel quite easy in
my mind now and I am able to enjoy my holiday. . . . I dont know how to thank you for
all your kindness, but I hope you will believe that I am grateful to you indeed."

[*TCD/GS270*]

c/o Mrs McGuirk
Lough Bray Cottage
Enniskerry
July ? [*11*] /07

Dearest Life

F.J.F. overtook me today before I got back. I streeled along after
I left you and lay in the heather here and there feeling very 'lonesome',
and then when I was on the long stretch of road where we used to sit
in the evening I saw F.J.F.'s little figure appearing on the sky-line and
I recognized his walk at once. We went down then to Mrs Dunne's and
he arranged to stay there tonight, then we came on and had tea here.
After that we walked off the whole way to Sally Gap and didn't get
back till ten. I wish I could have taken you out there but it might have
been rather far for you at present. It would have been a good deal
further than any of the walks we took. I wonder how you feel tonight, little love, entertaining F.J. kept me from being as lonesome as
I expected to be; still it felt hard not to have you with me out on these
wonderful hills. F.J. talks of coming back here next week for a few
days. I told him he will have to amuse himself part of the time as I
am going to fish and cycle a good deal next week. I will be glad if he
comes, I think, it is wholesome to have someone to talk to, and he
was very pleasant this evening.

We you and I have had a good little time and we know each other
better than ever, take good care of yourself now and I hope we'll soon
be together for always, little sweetheart. I am tired now and cant write

Your old Tramp.

I am sending you one of my Wicklow articles with your song. Please
keep it safe for me. Tell me what you think of the other.

[*TCD*]

[*Lough Bray Cottage*]
Friday [*12 July 1907*]

Dearest

I haven't got my post yet as McGuirk hasn't been down and I
couldn't get away from F.J.F. So I am still looking out for your letter.

I have been up at the upper lake this morning with F.J.F. lying in
the heather, it was beautifully warm and summery, it is the world and

all of a pity that you aren't here still. F.J.F. is going back now 1 o'clock
after his dinner so I wont see him till he comes out again.

I am writing in rather a hurry as I have to write my mother and
Lady G. also before the post hour. I am going down on my bicycle
today down past the school-house where we saw the girl climbing the
tree and then back by our 'nook' road. I wish to —— —— you were
with me my dear love it's poor game to be alone up here

My poor dear love be happy and cheerful and take good care of
yourself for my sake

Your old Tramp

[TCD]

c/o Mrs McGuirk

Lough Bray Cottage

Enniskerry

Saturday [13th¹] July 1907

My dearest Pet

I got your poor little note yesterday and it melted my heart inside
me. I'm so sorry for you but we have to face what cant be got out of.
Only for your health, of course, I'd have kept you on here as long as I
am staying but, as it is, you have to be in Dublin now, so cheer up and
think what a good time we've had.

When I was going to the post yesterday after dinner I found my
bicycle was punctured so I had a long job putting it right, and I had
to send my letters down by McGuirk. I hope they were in time. After
that I rode round where we were last Saturday—you remember the
little lane—and on to the road where we had our wet walk before the
tour. Then I crossed the river and came home by the 'nook' road. It
was a heavy pull home and I got tired and out of spirit. In the evening
I walked up again towards Sally Gap—about as far as we went—and
then came in about nine. Today it is blowing a gale and is raining
very hard every few minutes so you haven't missed much of the fine
weather! It is a nuisance, I am so anxious to get well. I dont suppose
F.J. will come out again if this sort of thing goes on. I wonder if you
have sent me the envelopes! If you haven't you'll have to wait for your
next letter—*for this letter,* unless I can borrow one from Mrs McG.—so
I hope you've thought of it, little madcap! I'm going to write an article

on that back road to Sally Gap—or rather a chapter for my book, it would hardly have enough matter for a regular article.

I think F.J.F. seems better than usually. It is pathetic what a high idea he has of Sally, and her wonderful *nobility* of character. If he only knew how she speaks of him. I suppose that is the fate of many of us!

I dreamt about you a lot last night but only harum-skarum dreams that I do not remember. Yes though! I remember we had taken a little house two doors down from the man who wrote me the curious letter from Manchester. Tell me what you think of my Wicklow article. Poor old pet I wish you were here to make coffee for me and cheer me up today. The wind is howling in the trees of Jerusalem, and the stream is roaring with the rain God help us. You ought to go to Kingstown on top of the tram when it is fine and take a turn on the pier—you know the pier near my place—if you are *still quite well* write me long letters that I can *answer*.

Ever your old Tramp.

1. Synge misdated this letter Saturday 12th July.

[TCD]   [*Lough Bray Cottage*]
                                         Saturday later.
                                         [*13 July 1907*]

My dearest Love

I have got your second letter. Yes I felt nearly ready to cry—big ass that I am—when I turned away from you there on the road. It is very hard indeed to be pulled asunder so often, I did not say much of what I felt in my other letter as *we must be satisfied*. I do NOT think it would be a good plan to meet you tomorrow. You will certainly be unwell soon and it would be the worst thing in the world for you to be standing and streeling about all day or even sitting about in the wet. Remember it will only make our marriage more difficult if you keep up this delicacy and perhaps have to give up some of your parts in the theatre or Heaven knows what. Do for my sake—for the sake of our marriage—take real care of yourself till this turn is over—I implore you to do so—and then I will arrange to see you as often as possible.

I need not say how delighted I would be to meet you, but I am sure it would not be right, so we must put it off. I am not going to let you harm yourself again, and the Dr said you were not to walk before the attack.

When I left you that day I was wretched for a time then I said to myself "You bl---y old blitherer, you've been lonesome for thirty years and now you're sadder than ever because you've got a god-send of a changeling all to yourself." Then I brightened up again at the thought that I had you, and would soon be with you always. You must do the same. Get your health back and be cheerful then all will go well. Tell me more about the Timmy business. It's a queer story, and interests me.

A thousand kisses sweetheart

Your old Tramp

(Thanks for envelopes and pencil.)

[*AS*]   Lough Bray
                                                          Sunday night
                                                          [*14 July 1907*]

Dearest Love

I wonder how you have been getting on today? Cheerfully I hope. I suppose I shall hear from you tomorrow morning. Yesterday was the worst day there has been since I came out here, I got wet in the morning and in the afternoon I walked down to our little wood and got wet again on my way back. Today there was fog hanging about in the morning so I went up on the Sally Gap road and wandered about in the clouds, writing down my impressions as I went along. Then I came home and had dinner feeling very lonesome and down. After that I got my bike and went off over the Feather Bed mountain, in thick cold clouds again, to the place where I left you on Thursday. Then I turned to the right into Glen Dhu and up through it and Glen Cullen and back up Glen Cree from the Enniskerry end about 20 miles in all I suppose.

Mrs Dunne came out to speak to me as I was passing her cottage, and showed me a post card she had got this morning from F.J.Fay to say that there was some talk of "*the girls*" coming out again for a week so he would not yet decide about coming himself. Are you talking of coming? Have you discovered when the company are to begin work again? Of course you can decide nothing till you see how your health goes.

This evening it was very mild so I have been wandering and sitting about till ten o'clock. There has been a very wonderful white fog working about all through Glen Cree, and up the mountain opposite. It reminded me of old evenings long ago in Annamoe when I used to be watching "the light passing the North and the patches of fog." I am so sorry you did not see it. There was a Night-jar also whirring in the heather somewhere near our nook, altogether it has been one of the strange Wicklow evenings that have such an effect upon me. Poor Pet it is sad to think of you shut up in Dublin all this evening, when things are so beautiful out here. I'd like to write intimately to you tonight, but somehow I am tired and nothing very interesting comes under my pen. Your own little imagination, I expect, can read between my arid lines, and see me in Glen Dhu where we did our first flirtations, and passing the lane in Glen Cree where we sat so happily, and mooning about here in the twilight, with a changeling in my skull.

I hope you'll think over all the beautiful things you've seen out here and in our other walks and make a little fairy land in your own skull for you to live your changeling's life in when Mary Street is not tolerable. Read your G[olden] *Treasury* too and *Aucassin and Nicolette*. There has been a great deal that was unpleasant, my poor pet, in your little life—you have told me a lot now bit by bit—and I want you to get your little mind free and happy and confident and to forget all about the squabblings and uncomfortable moods that you have seen such a lot of. I think if you had more confidence in me you wouldn't be so *tiff*able. I dont mean to say that you haven't confidence, but you haven't got used to trusting me practically in little things. I am glad to think that for the last week we hadn't a single uncomfortable word. That shows that all we want is to be together out and out and then we'll get on *"magnifiquement"*

If you are still *quite* well when you get this trot off and have a look at the pictures in the National Gallery. Another time when you've nothing to do go to the Museum and look through the Case of Evolution, and see if you can make it out by yourself. If you [are] ill keep very quiet but if you are well there is always plenty to do without moping too much. Remember all the years I've mooned about Galleries and Museums by myself picking up my knowledge.

[*TCD/Encl*]   *Monday morning*
                                                       (I give up dates here)

Dearest

   I went down to Mrs Dunne's this morning at eleven and a minute after I got in the place was besieged with soldiers getting bread and minerals. In a little while I saw the post boy passing and *'chased'* out after him. He had my rod and three letters from you, my good little angel. Then I sat down under the tree and read your letters. When I came to F.J.F's offer I read 'pooed at' instead of 'jumped at' and I gave you a pat of approbation on the back!! Then when I got further on I found I had made a big mistake. Of [course] I'll be delighted to have you out here again if you come, but I'd rather you got the money from me than from him. Still I dont mind him much poor man. Remember if you are quite normal this time—which we must devoutly hope for— your day will be Saturday so dont make any definite plans till you see how things go. *You must not dream of hurrying up here* before you are quite well. Remember to find out when the company is to meet. I meant to go home on Saturday I am so dull here but if you are coming again of course I will stay on. I find it very hard to pass the long days here by myself, but now I'll be able to fish again. I got a cheque for my *Shanachie* article this morning for £3.10.0 so that will keep me going for a while. I think I'll give Mrs McG. 18/3d a week that is not too much as I eat a lot. Now I must post this

                                              Your old H. tramp.
Take care not to go too far in the Park where the roughs hang about.
P.S.   I had heard rumours of the Horniman-Payne scheme.

[*TCD*]   Lough Bray
                                                  Monday night [*15 July 1907*]

Dearest Love

   A very sleepy old tramp is writing to you tonight. I may be going to Annamoe tomorrow and if so I will not get your letter till I come back late at night. I will post this—if I go—in Roundwood or somewhere on the way and then I suppose you'll get it some time tomorrow night.

After dinner today I went down and fished again, and this time I caught *two* little wretches like the last, but I threw them both back alive. I began lower down than we stopped last day, and went on down. I got a lot of rises—some of them good ones—but it was [a] queer heavy day with low water and the fish were only jumping at the fly, not taking it. Still I enjoyed myself and lay about in the sun and thought about you. I never felt such heat when I got home my shirt—with respects to you—was as wet as if you'd dipped in a bucket. On my way home I met the gamekeeper and he asked if I had an order so I showed him the card. When I got back here I heard F.J.F. had called so I went down again to Mrs Dunne's after tea, and found him there. Then we walked back over the mountain—I went on till I could see the Hell Fire Club,[1] and then I came home.—I had my bicycle with me. I feel better today in my health than I have felt since I was in Kerry last summer. The warm weather is doing me good I think. I hope you are getting on well dearest pet. Good night

Your old Tramp

1. A ruined stone building on the summit of Mount Pelier, about 4 miles from Rathfarnham, which was the site of an eighteenth-century club.

[*TCD*]
Lough Bray
Wednesday July 17th [*1907*]

My dearest Love

I got a long letter from you last night when I came home from an expedition to Annamoe and now at 12 o'clock I have got your little note without a date saying that you want to come up 'tomorrow' that is today and asking me to write to say if I will meet you. You know that there is only one post in here in the morning and one out at 3.15 so that you *cannot possibly* get my answer till *tonight at 8 o'clock!* Putting Urgent on your envelope will not make the Post Office change their arrangements.

Now as to your proposal, my poor little love, I see you are longing to be in the country, but I need not say that YOU MOST CERTAINLY MUST NOT ATTEMPT TO COME. It would be sheer insanity. You are certain to be unwell between this and Saturday and if you took this long walk immediately before it you might lay yourself up for life. You have escaped once, and now you want to break the doctors orders and risk your career in the theatre and the happiness of our married life! For a few days pleasure!! What am I [to] say to you. I am terribly uneasy that you may start today without waiting for this and so injure yourself forever. Oh it is cruel of you to make me so unspeakably anxious. I'll have to go off now and sit on the mountain-road half the day to look out for you as the place is full of soldiers and queer tramps that have come about the camp. However your letter seems to imply that you will wait to hear from me. God grant that you will. I half thought of going to Enniskerry when I got your letter and now I wish I had. Great Christ I am so uneasy. You seem to think you are safe because you have escaped once, but for all you know the matter may now be wrong again and a long walk at the wrong time might ruin your health forever. I am very unwell today with asthma I was awake all night with it. If it continues I shall have to go home. If I get well again and if you get over your period all right you will be able to come up for some days at least. Do try and remember that you are a woman and not a baby. I dont know what to think when you write, as you have done again and again, and ask me to answer at once when it is perfectly obvious that it is not possible to get a letter sent in time. It makes me sad.

Dont think I am angry my dearest love and dont be angry with me. I bicycled up to Annamoe yesterday to see my mother[1] and came back the road across Sugar Loaf where we walked so often last summer and winter. It made me thrill and tremble with tenderness for my little god-send to be on those roads again that I walked so often with you last winter. I was wondering if we shall ever be able to walk so freely again. We certainly never shall unless you are careful. What in the world did you think would become of you if you came up now and got bad suddenly as you did the last time. That long jolty drive back would be the worst thing in the world and what a time you would have if you were laid up in bed in Mrs Dunne's with no one to look after you. I was going to write you a very long and very tender letter today all about my thoughts of you last night but now I am too upset. I may go to Kingstown tomorrow and if so I *may* wire to you to meet me in Dublin. I will if I can

Your old Tramp

My own God-send   Later

I'm afeard you'll maybe think I'm after writing a bit harshly in my other letter so just fancy you feel my arms round you making it all right again with a kiss in your little eye and a kiss in your little ear and forty kisses for each little heathen lip of yours. When I think what a joy it would be to me to have you here again, looking out for me, and making coffee for me, I get a pain with yearning for you, but this week, at least, it cannot be.

Do take good care of yourself if you get safely through this time it'll make such a difference. Remember if I wire to you tomorrow it will be in the forenoon so be in readiness, and remember if you are the least unwell you are *on your oath* not to come. I am very dull here now, if you were not coming I'd go home on Saturday I think, but I am not quite decided. Now with a thousand kisses and blessings my poor little madcap

You own old
T.

1. Mrs Synge was staying at Tomrilands House in County Wicklow for the summer.

[*TCD/GS272–3*]   Lough Bray Cottage
18.7.07

My poor darling

Your two letters came this morning. I am very sorry for my poor little pet, but I am glad it has come on before you had time to do anything foolish. I hope by today you are much better. Yesterday was very hot here too. I went over to Killikeen in the afternoon *to meet you*—as you asked me—though I hoped you would not come. On the way I met F.J.F. and Henderson and we lay for a long time in the heather and talked. Then Henderson went back to Dublin and F.J. came here to Mrs Dunne's for the night. This morning we have been sitting under the tree at Mrs Dunne's door talking since eleven o'clock. Now he is gone home. It is too hot to go out into the sun. This is not a very good place for such hot weather as there is no shade, one seems to get scorched with the continual hot sun. Tomorrow I am going to slip down to Kingstown if the weather permits and come back here in the evening, but I will not go to Dublin. Please when you get this tonight write me a little line to Glendalough House to say how you are getting on. Do you think you will come up here on Monday? I will send down the jennet[1] and trap for you if you do and I will stay on for the week of course. You could go back the following Sunday evening and be in time for the Theatre on Monday. I think tomorrow (Friday) you ought to write to Dr. B. and tell him how you have got on, and ask him if you should see him again. Tell him also that you are think-ing of going to the country again on Monday. You will have to use a little thought about our arrangements as there is no post here on Sunday, so that any thing you write to me on *Saturday* or *Sunday* I do not get here till eleven o'clock on Monday. Write to me on *Friday night* to this place to say if you think you can come. Then I'll tell the jennet man to keep himself open in case you come on Monday—he is often engaged—then you can write to me early on Sunday to say what time the trap is to meet you in Rathfarnham. You had better say four o'clock or so, so that there may be time for me to get him off after the post comes on Monday. I believe F.J.F. is coming up for Sunday so Monday would be your best day. I wonder if you will be able to see Barry on Saturday or Sunday it would be a relief to our minds I think if you could see him before you come back. Now do you understand what you have to do. Try and dont muddle things by writing contradictory letters as you did yesterday. There are so few posts here—and no telegraph—that if we once get muddled we'll never get clear again.

The purple grapes are ripe here now I got a lot of them last night on our nook road. The nightjar is singing every night also in the heather. I took F.J. to hear it last night, but he was so busy talking about pronunciation that he would hardly listen to it.

It is furiously hot today, and I hardly know what to do with myself. Tomorrow I'll be in Kingstown and on Sunday I'll have to entertain

Frank and that will pass me on to MONDAY then there'll be a change and a changeling please goodness.

I had a little asthma this morning but nothing to speak of so I hope it wont trouble me much. The bad attack I had was partly my own fault I drank a lot of whiskey that Mrs McGuirk gave me—not a great deal but a rather large dose—and a lot of tea and fresh bread after my long day at Annamoe, about ten o'clock, and that set me off

Now sweetheart be prudent and take good care of yourself for both our sakes and dont forget the line to Kingstown tonight, and the letter to this place tomorrow Have you anything to read? Get Sally to get you Scott's *Talisman* for /6d.

Your old Tramp.

If you have to see Dr B on *Monday* perhaps you should not come here till *Tuesday*

---

1. A small Spanish horse used to pull carts on mountain roads.

[TCD]   Glendalough House
                                              Friday [*19 July 1907*]

Dearest Love

I'm glad to hear you are getting on so well. Yes certainly see Barry if possible. You had better *not* decide to come up on Monday *till* you hear what day he wants to see you. If you fixed Monday and then were delayed by him you would have no way of letting us know. You dont seem to realize yet that there is *only one (morning) post to Glen Cree,* as you say in your last that you hope I got your letter in time to keep me from going to meet you at Killikeen. I did not—could not—get it till the next day at 11 o'clock. I think I'll have to take your education seriously in hand, Eh? This is not a scolding mind but I'm very hot and very hurried and in a very bad humour because I left two photo films with my nephew, three weeks ago, and asked him to leave them in some shop to be developed and he has left them lying, deliberately, for the three weeks under his nose, and never touched them. One's relations are the divil!

Of course I will send the trap for you, you *mustn't dream of walking so soon* after your attack it would be madness. Sally can drive up too if she likes, I pay the trap. I got your first letter this morning as I met the post man with it near Enniskerry, and then I found the second here. I hope you have written to me today;—to Lough Bray—of course. By the way I think you should put 'Co Wicklow' besides Enniskerry on your letters. Your 'Enniskerry' is sometimes so vague I dont know how they read it! I had a great evening on the Sally Gap road last night it was as warm as possible and I lay up in the heather long after it was dark. If this weather goes on we'll have great evenings next week. I am not looking forward to my ride up this evening, it is so hot and the road is so heavy. I broke a spoke in my cycle this morning, coming down the big hill into Enniskerry, but I was able to ride on to Bray and I have left it there to be repaired. The soldiers all went away from Glen Cree this morning they began marching past my window at five o'clock, and on up the Sally Gap road. This is a very dull letter but excuse it, dear heart. I cant do any better for the moment. I quite agree that some of my Western Articles are dull. It was very hard to write so many, always on the same subject—the distress in the West. Tell me by and by which you thought dull as I want opinions of competent people—or changelings—before I begin knocking them into a book.[1]

Did I tell you that I have just got £3.10 from the *Shanachie* so I can afford your jennet! I hope against hope that Barry will think well of you, I am sorry to write you such poor stuff when you want something nice to cheer you up. Poor little love I hope you'll soon have me to look after you and cheer you up always. Now sweet heart good bye I am looking forward, you can imagine how much, to having you in Glen Cree. I find Kingstown and the heat and the frowsy women *intolerable* today, what must it be in Mary St, you poor little pet its no place for changelings, is it?

Your old Tramp

1. Synge did not complete his revisions before his death; *In Wicklow, West Kerry and Connemara* was published in Volume IV of the 1910 *Collected Works*, a decision which caused Yeats to withdraw his support in protest (see Oxford *Prose*, pp. xiii–xiv).

[*TCD*]   Lough Bray
                                         Saturday 20th [*July 1907*]

Dearest Love

    I have just got your note. I was down waiting at Mrs Dunne's for it for half an hour before it came. I am afraid this letter will be dull too, I cant help it, as I had asthma last night and I am dull myself in consequence. I have told Mrs Dunne that you are coming on *Monday or Tuesday* and asked her to tell her brother to keep himself free to go for you on the afternoon of either day. You must write *tomorrow (Sunday)* and say which day it is to be. If there is *any doubt* about Monday you had better fix Tuesday as there is no way of letting us know on Monday if you cannot come, and it would not do to send the little man down for nothing. I am looking forward very much to having you here again but I am too uncomfortable and too hot to write you a nice letter today. Excuse me dear heart, I cant help it. I hope I wont have asthma next week, I feel as if you would charm it away if you were here. If you see Barry after getting this ask him if you may LEARN the bicycle now. It is a very [different] thing *learning* from riding when you know how, and all the straining of flopping about might not be good for you. Yes if Barry allows it, you can get Kerrigan[1] to teach you by all means, but I doubt Sally will lend you her new bicycle to learn on. It is very bad for a new bicycle so she will be foolish if she does. There is heavy thunder rolling all round the glen today but no rain, the air is very heavy and has given me a headache.

    There is my dinner now. I cant write any more Remember to write tomorrow *decidedly* about Monday.

        Thanks for paper
        Your lonely old
            Tramp

Dont forget to tell me what *hour* the man is to be in Rathfarnham. I dont think F.J.F. will come today it is too thundery.

N.B. This is the last letter you will be able to get from me if you come on Monday. So good bye till we meet Dearest Life I'll be looking out for you. I wish it was Monday now. Bring me a box of matches and bring some coffee if you like.

---

1. J. M. Kerrigan (1885–1965) joined the Abbey Theatre company in 1906, making his first appearance in Yeats's *Deirdre;* in 1916 he went to the United States, where he continued to act on stage and in films.

[*TCD*]   Lough Bray
                                Monday [*22 July 1907*]

My dearest Love

I got your two letters half an hour ago, and I have ordered the jennet to meet you at Rathfarnham at a *quarter* to *three tomorrow (Tuesday) wet or fine.* So that is settled. It is just as well you are not coming to day as the roads here are very nearly impassable after the floods yesterday. The Reformatory was struck twice by lightning in the afternoon and the foundation of the bridge at Smiths just below Mrs Dunne's was washed away. I am very glad to hear of Barry's verdict. You must tell me all when you come. I feel it hard to have to get through another day without you. F.J.F. sends a card with your message, and says that he and Montgomery[1] are coming out on Tuesday *bad cess* to them. He didn't come on Saturday because of the thunder. I have had two more bad nights with asthma, and I feel very depressed today. You'll cheer me up I hope.

I dont know when or where I shall see you tomorrow, I suppose I'll have these two wretched fellows hanging after me all day. I am writing F.J.F. a terrible account of the thunder to frighten him if possible. Bring me a little note paper please tomorrow if you can afford it. Goodnight dearest

                                               Tramp

P.S.   I dont think you read my letters I'll tell you why tomorrow.

1. James Montgomery (1870–1943), who became Ireland's first film censor in 1923; his name recurs frequently in Joseph Holloway's Diaries.

[*Texas*]   [*Glendalough House*]
                                Tuesday. July 30th. 1907

Dearest

Did I ever write to you with this thing before? I haven't a pen handy so I am using it now though it doesn't not seem to lend itself to this kind of note.[1]

I am going to the dentist tomorrow at a quarter to three and after that I'm free, are you free too? Or do you rehearse in the afternoon as well as the morning? Would you like to meet me? I dont know where we could meet......A card has come from Henderson to say I am wanted at the Abbey tomorrow so I'll probably go in about twelve, and if so we can lunch together and arrange about the afternoon. I dont know yet what time F.R[oss] is going on Thursday, she doesn't know herself. I have written to my ma that I am asking you down for lunches and teas. It is very uncomfortable here for the moment as my mother forgot to leave any knives and forks etc. so F. and I are hard up.

Yes we had a great time yesterday. It's wonderful how we always amuse ourselves when we are together. I'm better glory be to.....so we'll hope for the best.

This machine wont write sentiment so good bye till tomorrow sweetheart.

TTTTTTTTRRRRRAAAAAMMMMMPPPPPP

---

1. Synge has written this letter rather inexpertly on the typewriter.

[*TCD*]   [*Glendalough House*]
                                                    August 7th 1907
Dearest Love

It seems quite curious to write to you now, it is so long since I have written. It is so showery tonight I dont think I shall go to the Yeats' after all, I dont want to get wet. I went for a ride last night after you had gone, and I felt a little 'down' as I always do after one of our bad days when we do not get on very well. It is lucky we have so few of them, and that they are getting fewer as we go on. Will you meet me tomorrow at Tara St at *twenty minutes* to *four if it is fine.* We can have a turn in the Park and tea together, I think that is as much as you should do. If it is a wet day I will not go up there would be no where to go. If you are at all unwell or for any reason cannot meet me write to say so *before eleven.* I do not think I shall stay on in town for the night show, I cannot "STICK" these plays any more.[1]

I have nearly finished my article now and I will show it to you to-morrow if it is presentable enough.[2] I hope, my old heart, that you are taking good care of yourself I think you ought to go home and go to bed after *Kathleen.* I wonder will you get this tonight no, I think, it will be tomorrow morning when you wake up out of your dreams.

I am sorry your visits here dont "go" I dont know why it is. I am rather out of spirits today, I dont know why unless it is because I am not to see my little heart's Treasure, that is enough to make me wretched surely.

I want to go through *The Tinkers* again before I send it to Granville Barker as some cuts have to be made,—I have just been writing to them about it,—and I want also to read it to you, or let you read it to yourself.[3] This is a dull letter, my dear heart, but I am dull today. It is lonely in this house by myself—Next summer please God things will be different.

I went for my usual ride today around through the Scalp and home by the 'Brides Glen' but it came on to rain on my way home so I had to change when I got in. Do you want the little bag for this tour I will send it to you by the tram if you do. I am sorry you will not get this tonight—I suppose you will be looking out for it—I was too tired to write this morning when I had finished my article. God bless you my thousand loves and give you good luck and good health.

Your lonely old Tramp.

1. The theatre was open for one week, playing revivals only, before the company left on 11th August for a two-week tour of Waterford, Cork, and Kilkenny.

2. Presumably one of the articles on West Kerry for *The Shanachie;* Synge published one in each of the Summer, Autumn, and Winter issues for 1907.

3. Harley Granville Barker was interested in producing *The Tinker's Wedding* at the Savoy Theatre in London, but after reading the play reluctantly decided his company would not be able to "capture" "the Irish atmosphere."

[AS]   Glendalough Ho
                                                        August 12 [1907]

Dearest
I got your letter this morning. I fervently hope that you are getting on well and not the worse for your knocking about. I hate to think of you knocking about in Kilkenny yesterday with no one to take care of you! Poor pet.

I was very bad all day yesterday, hardly able to open my eyes with a heavy feverish cold, but I am better today I only hope it wont go to my chest and make my cough worse again. I think about you a very great deal, but I am a little afraid to put much of my heart into this letter for fear it might go astray and be lost. I am VERY lonely.

I heard from Lebeau this morning that he has taken a room for us with two beds for a month.[1] I dont much fancy sharing my room with a man I know, after all, so slightly especially when I am not very well. It is a nuisance. I am too heavy today to write much, let me know every day how you are my poor love

T.

1. Synge was considering joining Henri Lebeau on a tour of Brittany.

[*TCD*]   [*Glendalough House*]
                                                August 13th [*1907*]

Dearest Life

I got your letter—last night, and I was very much distressed to hear of your bad time on Sunday evening. I cannot understand why *you* went with Sally and Fay, when they could have looked for digs *just as well* without you. However it is too far away and I am too wretched myself to scold you. Let me know again as soon as you can how you are. I am of course exceedingly anxious about you.

I have one of my regular influenza-ish turns with my usual cough as bad as ever, but not at all so bad as in the winter. It is *very* disheartening; but nothing new, of late years I seldom get through a summer without a turn like that. Last year I had it in Glasgow and Aberdeen, when we were on tour. It is very lonely and wretched sitting here all day by myself, I am not able to go out yet. I wish I could write you a nice letter but I'm too miserable in myself, and too uneasy about you to have any little sentiments left in me. I expect you will find me here when you come back. I wont be able to face that long journey for some time yet. Perhaps I wont go at all—or wont go till after the operation. Then I could pick up for both at the same time.

I often think of your story of the moth,—I delight in all your little ways—there's a sentiment at last by grace of God. Do put down your foot and swear once for all that you will take care of yourself come what may—even though the theatre and the Fays and every thing else—except me—should go to pot. I cant help thinking it is a sort of bravado that makes you do things like going out the other night when there was no need. Are you sure of your Cork digs? Is it Opera House Cork? for letters. This will of course be my last to Waterford.

T.

[TCD]   [*Glendalough House*]
                                                        August 14th [*1907*]
Dearest Treas.

I got your letter (Tuesday's) this morning—it was a very charming little one, but I am sorry to hear that things are not going well in Waterford. At least I am sorry and not sorry—*too* much touring in little Irish towns would be a dog's life for you, and it would mean doing our *un*intellectual work, L. Gregorys etc., only.[1] I was out for a short time yesterday but I wasn't much the better for it so I am staying at home today. The days seem quite endless here in this empty house and it is not easy to keep up my spirits. However I really am not at all bad this time—I have had no fever except the first day which is a very good sign—so I hope this little attack wont make any further change in our plans than to throw off my Brittany voyage for a week or so. Curiously the last time I was going to Brittany from Paris—in 1900—I had influenza too, and I remember lying all day in my little room wondering whether I should go or not. I had a turn like this too one year in Aran and it did not leave any trace behind it.

I am glad to see by your letter that you seem pretty well. Do you think you are none the worse for your experience on Sunday? I always feel a little doubtful whether the letters I send to the Theatre will reach you—I am sending this to the Opera House—so I am afraid to put much *depth* into them. Perhaps if I sent this to Waterford you might [get] it but I'm afraid to risk it. I wonder shall I see you before I go away.

Your T.

I bought a book when I was out yesterday, Thackeray's *Esmond* which has passed a good deal of my time. I will leave it for you. It is quite readable though very 'flat' in places. You ask if I was ever in Waterford. Dont you remember my voyage there last year with Miss T[obin]?

P.S.   Give me your address in Cork very *legibly* written. Did you get my letter of yesterday?

---

1. Only one of Synge's plays, *Riders to the Sea*, was being performed on this tour.

[*TCD*]   [*Glendalough House*]
                                                       August 15th 1907

Dearest Love

   Your letter came all right this morning. There was a post card in the box so I thought for a minute it wasn't there, and I nearly collapsed. I'm sorry Waterford is failing. Dont mind W.G's talk, it is natural enough for him to try and run up his wife. I agree with him that the additional £1 a week all round makes some of the salaries too high. Mrs Fay wouldn't get two pounds a week in any other show in Europe, neither would O'Rourke. This is between ourselves. I wonder what gave you hysterics. I found a book on nursing the other night in a cupboard so I turned up hysteria at once that I might know! They say the patient must resist the attack *herself* that is the great thing, and she might drink a glass of cold water—be sure it is clean if you try it— when an attack threatens.

   I think I am better today but I'm not sure. I'm going out for a while I cant stand another long day in here. I thought yesterday would never end,—sitting in these empty rooms from 9 in the morning till 11 at night. I dont know at all when I shall get away, I have a good deal of loose cough still, and I'm very pulled down. I'd give the world and all to have you here these days, little sweetheart. I always have an ocean of beautiful things to say to you when I'm in bed or sitting alone in the evening, but now somehow—I'm in a fuss to go out—they've all disappeared out of my poor old skull! I have been thinking very often of those late evenings we had up on the mountain road in Glen

Cree, and feeling to you as I felt to you then in that wonderful solemnity and calmness. Many people, little Heart, have never been as happy [as] we were then, at least with a happiness of such a good quality as ours. I feel that we are a great deal nearer each other now, than we were when the last tour was on, I hope you feel so too, and that you are remembering all your promises.

What a long time it seems since we were in Glen Cree, and what a good time it was. Dear little life write me a long letter the next time.

I hope you are getting proper food and keeping yourself well. Do please. I believe if I was *put to bed* and kept there when one of these colds is coming on—as it was last Saturday when I went to the Abbey—that I'd never have a cough. Will you do that for me. It is amazing how many of my illnesses the last few years have been made serious by my doing something foolish the first day of them.

We're a pair of old crocks I'm afraid. I dont feel too bad today, and I hope I'll soon be all right write to me nicely Sweetheart. I wrote yesterday to the Opera House. Have you got it?

Your old T.

[TCD]   [*Glendalough House*]

August 17th [1907]

D----t L---e

I got your letter this morning, but of course none yesterday which made me a little uneasy. I am a good deal better and out again as usual, but I expect you will find me here when you come back. Could you come and see me I wonder on Wednesday afternoon. Find out what time you are likely to get back to Dublin and let me know. You dont tell me where to write today or when you are going to Kilkenny so I dont know whether this will find you. I am going to *rush* off with it now to the general Post Office in Kingstown and then it *may* catch the Cork Mail and reach you tonight.

I have no time for more—if you had given me your Kilkenny address I could have written a better letter but perhaps you are not settled yet, I dare say not. Send me your new address as soon as you can and then I'll write again.

T———

I wonder will you think of leaving your address in the Hotel if you go before this comes!¹

1. The envelope is addressed to "Miss M. Allgood Innisfallen Hotel Cork" and on the back Synge has written "If not found please forward to c/o National Theatre Company 'The Theatre' Kilkenny."

[*TCD*]   [*Glendalough House*]
                                                                          August 18 [*1907*]

D.L.

 I wrote to you yesterday to Cork but I have not any idea whether you will get it or not. Now you write to say you are extraordinarily anxious to hear from me and I am to write at once and then you give me NO ADDRESS. I will send this to the Theatre Kilkenny and perhaps you will get it. I am much better I am glad to say, and I expect to get off in a few days. I had almost decided to go on Thursday morning— so that I might see *you* on Wednesday *evening* before I start—but as you are going back to Cork I may go sooner. It is not clear from your letter whether you are going back or not, but that is what I gather.

 I would like to write you a fuller letter, but it is impossible when I do not know where to write. I have written every day except the day I did not hear from you. Excuse this note I have a head ache today, and I am not some how in a humour for writing. Send me your Kilkenny address *at once,* also tell me when you leave there on Wednesday and whether you are going to Dublin or to Cork. If you dont make things clear we may miss each other on Wednesday if I am still here.

P.S. Thanks for cuttings I am glad things are doing so well in Cork. I would write you five pages today if I felt quite sure you would get them but it is intolerable to me to think of my letters knocking about, and perhaps in the end being opened and laughed at in the post office. I am a little hurt that when I am so ill and lonely your last letters are so scrappy and short. Write me a better one please before I go. This illness has taken all the pleasure out of the thought of my trip to France I wish I wasn't going now. Be sure to tell me by return what your movements will be. I asked you long ago if you are any the worse for Waterford and you have not answered!

This is a scolding sort of letter, dont mind it Je t'aime beaucoup! et Je n'aime que toi!

[TCD/GS273–4]   [*Glendalough House*]
                                        August 18/07

Dearest

I wrote a grumpy letter to you this morning as I was a little 'put-out' by the uncertainty you left me in, as to your movements and addresses. Forgive it.

I have had another long lonely day—how different from this day a fortnight or three weeks ago—the day we left Glen Cree—but I took two walks, one of them through the rocky furzy place where we sat one evening when you were down here, so I have got along. I am much better again and my temperature is lower than it has been for a long time a good sign—a proof almost I think that there isn't much the matter. I met Dr Gogarty[1] the other day and he says I ought to get the glands out as soon as ever I can and that I will be all right then. So there is a good hope that I may shake off the delicate condition I have got into the last couple of years. You know I haven't been always like this. One thing is certain I'm not going to kill myself anymore for the Theatre, I get no thanks for it, on any side, and I do no good—at least as things are going now. If the company becomes a success after all as a touring company, and you have to spend half your time fagging round England and Ireland, I fear we will be separated a great deal. It will be worse for me, I think, as you have the variety of moving about and the excitement of playing, but I find being left behind here again and again a very trying and disheartening experience. However there is no use crying over what cant be helped at present.

I find it very desolate by myself here now without my little change-ling, I'm *unused* to being lonesome and I'm not happy for an hour when you're off walking the world. I have just lit the lamp, as old Mary[2] has gone to bed, and I am writing in the silent house. How happy we'd be if you were here with me, little Sweetheart, I never thought that I would come to take anyone into my life so utterly as I have taken you, and how many chances, if they were chances, there have been in it all. It is a great thing that we had those quiet evenings and days in Glen Cree, they will be with us all the winter, the little stream, and the crying birds and the wonderful stillnesses in the evenings. I think sooner or later we'll come to spend a great deal of our time in the country. I wish you'd become a writer, and then we could both have our career living on a hill-top by ourselves. As long as your career is on the stage, of course, we will be tied to towns. I dare say this is all blather that I'm talking, but one's mind likes to look forward into a beautiful and intimate future. I sometimes wonder what your 'ambition' is like or if you have any. Is it chiefly a desire to get applause and get talked about, or is it a real love for acting good plays, and a real desire and determination to do it well. You have real talent I think and real talent of any kind is a very priceless thing so I would be sorry to see you give up the stage unless you could use your talent in some other way.—Suppose you and I write a play together!! Wouldn't that be great! You could supply the actual stage experience and I'll supply the fundamental ideas. Then you can write all the men's parts—I know you like men—and I'll write all the female's. We'll do a play at once about life in Switzer's[3]—with an Act II laid in Miss Fluke's—Then we hire the Abbey and stage it ourselves and make our fortunes and live happily ever after. Now I'm going to bed as that's settled.

Monday morning

No letter from you this morning. I dont know what to do. I have just read yesterday's letter again, but you do not say whether you are all going back to Cork—only that the manager has *proposed* it. It is really *exasperating* not to know as I have to make my plans today. I suppose I had better fix on Thursday for my journey as I could not bear to go away on Wednesday morning without seeing you if you are coming to Dublin that day. You will get this I suppose on Tuesday sometime. If you have time to write on that day, tell me if you can come down here on Wednesday and *what time.* If you get it too late to write on Tuesday *wire* to me on Wednesday morning. Of course if you are too tired after your journey up from Kilkenny to come out here, I could go up for an hour or two in the afternoon if it is fine. I am still coughing a good deal but it is not a bad cough

I am sending this to 'The Theatre' Kilkenny I have no idea whether it will reach find you.[4] I cannot write to you again till I hear where you will be on Wednesday. If I hear you are coming home I will write to Mary Street.

Tramp

---

1. Oliver St. John Gogarty (1878–1957), poet, surgeon, and "Buck Mulligan" of Joyce's *Ulysses,* later with Yeats a Senator of the Irish Free State, contributed three plays to the Abbey Theatre: *Blight* in 1917, *A Serious Thing* and *The Enchanted Trousers* in 1919.

2. The housekeeper, Mrs. Mary Tyndall.

3. A large department store on Grafton Street.

4. On the back of the envelope he wrote "If not found please forward to The Abbey Theatre, Dublin."

[*TCD/GS274*]   [*Glendalough House*]
                                                              Monday Night
                                                              19/VIII/07

Dearest

The post has just come and made my heart jump with delight—for an instant—till I found he had brought a circular for my mother only and nothing from you. Are you getting tired of writing to me? I dont want to be a bother to you, but if we are to keep up during this long separation without drifting, or at least seeming to drift a little apart— as you said we did the last tour—we must get into the way of writing *intimately* and fully. I cannot help feeling a little 'lonesome' tonight— I had a few lines only from you yesterday and nothing today though I have watched for every post. These days have been among the most dismal I have ever spent. It has been too showery to go far, as I am afraid to get wet, so I have been wandering in and out all day, and then wandering about this empty house. I am too restless to read, and too heavy to write so the time hangs terribly.

I am going into town tomorrow to see Roberts about my 'agreements'—which I have never signed—and perhaps old Yeats. I wrote to Lady G. the other day about various matters, and got an answer from *Yeats*—and I fancied rather a stiff one. There is no word of R.G.'s engagement. I wonder if his mother is against it.[1] I wonder what you are doing, and if you are very good? When I think I wont even get answer to this for nearly a week—if you go back to Cork—I get a queer qualm of uneasiness, and lonesomeness. It is a mercy you aren't going to America this autumn—you couldn't go away from me just now I think, we are too united, and still not united enough. There is no good in writing more I may hear tomorrow that you are to be home on Wednesday and that I shall see you I hope to Heaven that I shall. Tonight I hate the thought of going away at all. Are you remembering your promises?

Tuesday morning

Dearest Life

Your letters—two of them came today. I dont know whether to send this to Kilkenny or Cork I suppose Cork is the safest,—you do not tell what hour you leave tomorrow or where I am to write. By the way it would save a great deal of worry if you would put at the bottom of

(the address)

every letter when you are on tour—"Write next to —— ———", or "Write here till (Thursday night)" etc. It is always done when people are moving about.—Of course you would have to calculate roughly how long it would take to get answer. If you get this early on Wednesday and write in time for the night mail, I may get it—I ought to get it— before I start on Thursday morning. Please write me a good letter I'll write to you tomorrow to give you my French address. I dont feel well, I wish now I wasn't going away at all, but I suppose it is best to go. I had a friendly letter from Lady G. this morning, and she tells me of her son's engagement. They are to be married in the autumn, and spend the winter in Paris,—at least that is what it looks like though one is never sure of her letters.

By the way I got a *great* qualm of uneasiness when you said casually you are going to leave Sally and 'dig' with someone else. PLEASE dont, Dear Heart, it is better for you to be together, I think, and I will be very anxious and worried if you leave her. What do you know of the other people you suggest? I dont want *my* WIFE to be mixing with Music Hall artists. Now wont you be good? I wish you would tell me more that you are doing, you always promise to and then the moment you get on the road you keep me absolutely ignorant as to what you are doing, who you are going about with, and how you are passing your time, this isn't a scold, my poor little heart, I'm far too lonesome to scold, but I wish you'd write more fully, writing fully of external things leads on naturally into intimate things

Old Mrs Tyndall only spent 8/6 on my food last week, and when she was giving me the change she said she could easily keep two people for the same price. I have four fresh eggs—we have found fresh ones—every day, and two big chops, and cabbage, and marmalade and everything I want. I wonder if we ought to have her. She's a great old gossip and I think she'd think it wasn't proper to attend on an actress, but she manages very well and she['s] "mighty knacky".

Oh God this cough is a fearful worry I am not getting on very well I am afraid, at least there is no change from day to day.

I feel very depressed and wretched, and lonesome. Be a good changeling and write to me nicely my dear old Heart

Your T.

I am uneasy now till I hear where you are staying you ought certainly to be with Sally, I think. Tell me what you decide and please be very good my O.h's L.

1. Robert Gregory (1881–1918), Lady Gregory's only son, married his fellow-artist Margaret Parry in 1907.

[*TCD*]
                                        [*Glendalough House*]
                                        Kingstown
                                        August 21 (evening) [*1907*]

Dearest

I got your note this morning. You dont say how your eye is. I am anxious about [you], so dont forget to let me know. I was in town yesterday and I coughed so much and felt so ill that I almost decided to give up my French trip altogether—for the present at least—Today I am better, I think, but I find it very hard to decide, I wish you were here to advise me. I am not going in any case till Friday, so I'll have a day longer to think matters over. You see Lebeau and I are to sleep in a Breton village and have our meals at the house of some friends of his who have very kindly invited me. At present however I feel too unwell for that sort of thing so I hardly see the good of spending £10 on a trip that I am not likely to enjoy and that is more likely to do me harm than good. I have more cough now than I had when I went to Jack Yeats, and I was miserable there too ill to enjoy myself in the least. Lebeau wants to take me about touring on our bicycles and I am not well enough for that either, and if I do it I may regularly knock up again. What is more if I go now it will put off the operation till very late, and then the weather will be getting wintry and it will be harder to pick up. On the other hand I am sorry to disappoint Lebeau.

Well, I think the *case* for *staying at home,* now that I state it at length, is overwhelming. I think Lebeau will have to do without me. What do you think? There is not much use asking you as I shall have to decide before I get an answer to this. If I stay at home I will see you on Monday, then if possible I'll go away for *a week* to somewhere near in Wicklow or to Lucan. Then the first week in September I'll have the operation, and go away about the middle of the month for a couple of weeks to pick up—and *then* if I am all right!!!!!!!!!!!!

I might go to Paris and see Lebeau if he is there at the end of September that would be more possible. However I'll take another night to think things over, perhaps tomorrow morning I'll feel keen to go.

I have been to Bray by train for a walk this afternoon, and I am not very bad still I get turns of coughing and wheezing that are most distressing.

This is a dull letter all about my poor ailments, I was awake last night for a long time and I was 'brimming-over' then with things to say to you. Well you'll have them some other time. I am glad *Riders* is going well; after *Longford* Yeats said it was quite useless for the provincial tours. I saw a book copy of *Deirdre* at Roberts' yesterday at 3/6d. There is an extraordinary note at the end giving a page of the play that he had cut out, and then found that it was necessary after all. He makes himself ridiculous sometimes.[1] Roberts says about 600 *Aran Islands* have gone, that is very good I think. God bless you my little life
Your T.

---

1. The theatre edition of Yeats's *Deirdre* was published in August 1907.

[*TCD/GS274*]   [*Glendalough House*]
                                         Thursday 22nd.VIII/07
Dearest
I got your wire this morning and your note. I wrote you a long intimate letter on Tuesday *to Cork* (Opera House) and posted it early so that you should have found it when you arrived on Wednesday. I also wrote to you yesterday to same address I hope they haven't gone

astray. I dont feel very certain about sending letters to these country theatres.

I am glad to hear that your eye has recovered. You dont tell me what you have done about your lodgings. Are you with Sally, or who are you with? You might have told me that I think, perhaps you for got. I have given up the French trip finally. I am not well enough to go. I met a youth this morning who has just been in Aran. He says the people are deeply offended by my story about the tea being kept hot for three hours!

There is no use writing now till I hear if you are getting my letters I am looking forward to seeing you on Monday. I am very down and very lonely.

Your T.

[*TCD*]   [*Glendalough House*]
Friday 23rd VIII/07

Dearest Pet

I got your letters one last night one this morning. Last night's did me a world of good I was getting very depressed stuck here with nothing to do after I had finally given up my trip. It is good to write me a warmhearted letter now and then.

This will be my last letter to you on this tour—you will leave I suppose early on Sunday. Write to me on Saturday and then send a line when you arrive on Sunday to say what time you will come and see me on Monday. Old Mary T. has just put her head in to the door and told me I look 'lovely' 'splendid' again now.—I suppose writing to you does me good! I sent the *Tinkers* to Barker yesterday and I am working now on the MS. as Roberts wants to print it soon. I am longing to see you again I have had an utterly miserable fortnight since you went away.

I have made no plans about next week. I ought to go somewhere I suppose to pick up a bit before they operate on me, but I dont know where to go. I am going to have tea with my niece Ada Synge[1] this afternoon to meet some old man relation of hers who wants to make my acquaintance. I am getting better I think but I am up and down. I was wise probably not to go to France now. Till Monday—I hope.

Your old T.

I may write a line to Mary St to bid you welcome when you arrive. Your old T.

---

1. Ada Synge (1888–1960) was his brother Edward's only daughter.

[*Texas*]   [*Glendalough House*]

Saturday 24th VIII/0'

Dearest

I got your note this morning so I am writing again to Cork as you tell me—I wonder am I to write to Miss O'Neill or to you?—though I haven't much to say except that I'm longing to see you. You had better come by the quarter to two I think on Monday, you will want a good rest after your long journey, and I am busy in the morning getting *The Tinker's Wedding* ready for the press.

I am much better again and I have been out today for a turn on my bicycle. That is a good sign. I had tea with my niece yesterday   my brother has a fine big house, and a nice drawing room. Ada was out on the Fleet in the afternoon[1] so she left a note asking me to wait a few minutes till she came back with her friends, so I had plenty of time to poke about their room and look at their curiosities. They have photos of every member of the family on both sides young and old except *me*. It is funny how I am a sort of 'outsider' with them all.

Be very good on your journey and have a good sleep and dont miss your train on Monday. I would die of despair if you did.

Your old T.

---

1. The Atlantic Fleet, consisting of five battleships and three cruisers, had arrived in Dublin in August 1906 and was scheduled to visit Galway during the Galway Exhibition the following year.

[*TCD*]   [*Glendalough House*]
                                                        August 28th/07

Dearest Child

What about tomorrow? The charwoman is not coming till Friday
so I would like you to come here for tea if you can afford it. Will you
come down by the quarter to two? If you'd rather come out on Friday
we could go to Bray that day or we could do both. Please write tomorrow morning (Thursday) and post it before *eleven* to say what
you'd like.

I had a cycle ride today but it was very dusty and unpleasant.
I feel very well. I dont know what day I shall go to town, I am waiting
till I have finished the Tinkers so that I may take them in to Roberts.
I feel twice the man since you came home again, sweetheart, and I
grudge every day I dont see you. So I hope you'll come tomorrow.

I have been typing my verses today but I am not working very
hard. I got a letter from the *Manchester Guardian* last night asking me
to do them a series of articles on 'Types of Irishmen'! If we can bring
it off that will be £10 to £20 into my little pocket.

                                              Goodbye Dear Heart
                                                        T.

Be sure to write tomorrow morning

[*TCD*]   [*Glendalough House*]
                                                        Thursday night
                                                        [*29 August 1907*]

Dearest

I found a letter from Miss Tobin, when I got back here this evening,
asking me to call on her brother *at once* at the Shelbourne Hotel, so I
suppose I must go there tomorrow afternoon. I am sorry that our
excursion is off. I shall probably see you at the Theatre *before* one, and
if I am not whipped off by Yeats or someone we might dine together—
I needn't go to this man till three or four o'clock

                                              Your old T.

[*TCD*]   [*Glendalough House*]
                                                        Saturday night
                                                     [*31 August 1907*]

Dearest

Dont come till tomorrow afternoon *a quarter to two* please as I
feel rather done up and I'm a bit feverish I'd better take things easy
tomorrow.

                                                                    T.

[*TCD*]   [*Glendalough House*]
                                                      September 2nd/07

Dearest Treasurette

You'll want to hear what the doctor said I suppose   He thinks
pretty well of me—but as I am still a little feverish from Saturday's
turn he thinks it better not to have operation till next week. I am to go
to him next Monday to make arrangements. Tomorrow I'll take a day at
home as I've not given myself much chance of shaking off this last turn.

Then on Wednesday morning I'll go and see Roberts, and look in at
the Abbey afterwards about 12 or half past. Of course if you aren't well
dont come down I'll have plenty of time to see you towards the end of
the week. Write and be careful of your little self.

                                                          J. M. Synge (T)

[*TCD*]   [*Glendalough House*]
                                                     Sept. 4th [*1907*]

Dearest Old Pet

Sally told me today that you weren't well so I hope you are staying
safe *in bed* this time and taking care of yourself. There is no need at all
for you to go to the Theatre as no show is near. Tell me how you are
getting on. You will be well again I suppose by Sunday so that we'll
meet again before my turn comes. I was in with Roberts today talking
over the proposed American edition of my work. Every-thing looks
promising I think. He (Roberts) thinks very well of *The Tinkers* but its
publication may be delayed if the American edition comes off. I hope

you aren't very bad this time, let me know as soon as you can how you are, I am anxious to know.

My mother and Miss C.[1] came home all right yesterday and the house is very much upside-down, for the moment, as everything is getting put in order for the winter. My mother enquired very particularly for "Molly". By the way the other night old Mary Tyndall was telling me about some lady in the country and she [said] "She was a nice pretty girl, the best of her family, and indeed the young lady, you had sitting there the other day put me in mind of her. A nice cut of a lady she was."! Now do you feel flattered? You *ought,* because old Mary is mighty critical. I am sending you one of my American notices to read, do you want more books? Or is there anything else I can do for you? This is a hurried letter so that is why it isn't very intimate. I've heard nothing of Tobin I must write to him I suppose and see if he is still in town. I half meant to go to him today, but then I thought I might as well come home early and save my money. My mother is giving me two pounds towards my house-keeping expenses while she has been away. So I wont come off too badly. Now I'll post this and you ought to get it at six.

Ever your old Tramp

DONT get up tomorrow unless you're very much better, and in any case DONT REHEARSE
Keep the cutting for me.

1. Rosie Calthrop, who later married William Godwin, was a cousin of Synge's sister-in-law, Mrs Samuel Synge, and a close friend of the family. She frequently spent the summer in Wicklow with Mrs Synge and was a long-time cycling companion of Synge's.

[TCD]

[*Glendalough House*]
Sept. 5th [*1907*]

Dearest Love

I got your letter this morning I think it was [a] very great shame for you to go to rehearsal yesterday—YOU PROMISED me you'd stay in bed the whole day, however I wont scold you now, as you aren't in good spirits. Let me know how you are getting on—I imagine if you take care now for three or four months you may make yourself all right again, but of course if you WILFULLY break the doctors orders you can expect nothing but a LIFETIME of suffering and ill health. Now it's out —Dont mind me *too* much.

I've nothing very new to tell you I'm just getting along and waiting for my day next week—I dont feel at all uneasy about it, but I wish it was over. I'm sending you some stamps so that you may write to me tonight. You *dont* tell if you would like any books—so I suppose you dont want them—or perhaps you hadn't time to think of asking for them. I was very depressed last night about everything or nothing but I'm cheerful today and so I hope are you. I had a great hunt yesterday for *MS.* of P.B. but I found him at last. If *that* comes off I'll get you a bicycle! Remember it is a profound secret. The Abbey Co. will very soon have to make up its mind one way or other as to what they are going to do with me and my work, I'm not going to hang up my career on the good pleasure of any of them.

I might see you on Saturday I suppose if you are well enough. What do you think?

I have a number of letters to write this morning so I must stop good bye my own little heart, think about Glen Cree and keep yourself cheerful and take good care of yourself—it's a pity I'm not having my job done this week too so that we would both be laid up, and get it over, at the same time.

I have to write to Quinn,[1] and Gregg—the man who wrote the notices in America,[2]—and Lebeau and to the friend of his who invited me to stay over there. All troublesome letters. I hope you pity me. Goodbye again my own treasure

T

1. John Quinn (1870–1924), New York lawyer, collector, and patron of the arts, had already financed American copyright editions of *The Shadow of the Glen, The Well of the Saints,* and *The Playboy of the Western World* and now offered to buy the *Playboy* manuscript for his collection.

2. Frederick James Gregg (1864–1927), an old school friend of W. B. Yeats, had published notices of Synge's plays and *The Aran Islands* in the *Evening Sun* (New York), which Quinn forwarded to Synge.

[*TCD*] [*Glendalough House*]
Sept. 6th. 07

Dearest Treasure

I got your letter this morning and I am glad to hear that you are getting on so well. Take care now you dont make yourself bad again. I will go up tomorrow by the train that gets to Tara Street at *five minutes past two* so meet me there then, and we can go to the Park or somewhere. If there is anything to stop me I'll wire to you at Mary Street before one. My little old cousin—who first took me abroad is to be in Kingstown tonight and it is just possible that she may annex me tomorrow, but that is not probable.¹ I've got a very sore eye again, but it is the lid and not like yours. I hope it will get better soon.

I have been out riding with Miss C[althrop] the last two days, round the lane between the Chimney and the Scalp yesterday and round through the Scalp today. My mother told her all about you so we have been talking about you, and she wants to meet you. How would you like that? I might take her to the Abbey next week, if there is time before the operation. You wont get this in time to answer about to-morrow, so if you are not a[t] Tara St I'll take it for granted that you aren't coming. Dont come if you do not feel well, and do not come, of course, if it is wet. I must post this now so that you'll get it in the morning. I was doing other things this morning sorting my papers so I did not write.

For ever and ever
Your old T.

P.S.   Your letter has just come. Yes the letter was from Tobin, he says he was at the Abbey one night and was delighted with the show.

Do not on any account, please, have anything to do with Mrs Vaughan   I blushed red all over at the very thought of it. It could be of no use to you and would finally ruin your health. Who is paying Mrs Vaughan?² Is Sally? Or Who? Isn't it splendid that you have got over this turn so well? Now when I'm spliced up too we'll be grand. I am going off to see my old cousin now   I dont know when I saw her last. By the way Tobin went off to Killarny the day I called on him and when he came back old Yeats told him I was in *Wales!* So he did not try and see me. Old Yeats must be doting.

Now till tomorrow, sweetheart   isn't it an age since we met.

T.

1. Mary Synge (b. 1840), a concert pianist and music teacher, had persuaded Synge's family to allow him to study music in Germany in 1893, and introduced him to the von Eikens, with whom he stayed at Oberwerth, near Coblenz.

2. I have been unable to trace Mrs Vaughan or any other reference to the training she was apparently giving Sally and Molly.

[TCD]   *[Glendalough House]*
                                                                    Sept. 9th/07

Sweetheart

I'm sending you *Macbeth,* Hans Anderson, and the little book of old Welsh stories—written 900 years ago—that you once asked me for.[1] I hope you'll read them and like them, though they'll need a little bit of an effort from your lazy madcap head to lift out of Mary Street into that wonderful and beautiful old world. Hans A. I know you'll like. I coughed a great deal this morning, so I'm not going to the doctor till tomorrow. I have been doing a good deal all last week so one day of rest will be good for me. Let me know how you are and if you are well of your cold.

I am sending these early so I haven't much to say.

Please take great care of the *Mabinogion,*—as you did of *Aucassin and Nicolette.*

I'll write to you again when I've seen the doctor tomorrow

                                                                    Your old T.

1. The books referred to are apparently Hans Christian Andersen's fairy tales, first translated into English in 1846 and frequently reprinted in various editions, and *The Mabinogion,* a collection of eleven Welsh tales from the "Red Book of Hergest," translated by Lady Charlotte Guest, 1838–1849.

[Texas]   *[Glendalough House]*
                                                                Tuesday Sept 10 '07

Dearest

I am surprised at not hearing from you today I hope that you got the books all right and that you are all right yourself.

I have to put off my affair another day—worse luck—as I have a threatening of a little cold today—the merest threatening only—so there is no use fixing for the job as it could not be done unless I am quite well, and it would be a great bother to fix the day and hour and then have to put it off. I hope to go without fail tomorrow. This cold was brought on by a bungle the servants made about not airing my night garments. My eyelids are sore again today. How are yours? I am eaten up with impatience now to get this business over, these days of waiting are intolerable   I cant write

Your old T.

[*TCD*]   [*Glendalough House*]
Tuesday evening
10th.IX.07

Dearest Life

I have just got your letter I am *furious* with *myself* for having frightened you by my silly talk. I do not think there is practically any danger in this operation—I would put it stronger only that I dont want to boast—so cheer up and keep a good heart. I heard today that the surgeon is away and wont be back till Thursday so there is another delay. I must see you again of course. Will you meet me tomorrow (*Wednesday*) at Tara Street at *20 minutes* to *three*. If you cannot, *write before eleven* if I cannot—if I am stopped or not well I will wire to Mary Street. Of course I wont go if it is wet.

Now my poor sweetheart be happy we ought to be very thankful that it is possible to get rid of this beastly ailment that is upsetting me so much. How are you. I dont mind O'Rourke's teaching you to cycle, but I confess I get a qualm when I think of you going for walks with a tailor! *Take* care he doesn't see this! Till tomorrow your old

T.

[*Texas/tel*]   Westland Row Dublin 11 September 1907 4.04 P.M.
Miss M. Allgood 37 Mary Street Missed you Tara please write Synge

[*Texas*]
                                            Glendalough House
                                            Sept. 11th 07

Dearest Love

Your letter did not come till *six o'clock it is stamped 1.P.M.* You
must have posted it *late* for the eleven post. I went off to town and
stood about Tara Street for half an hour or more I felt very uneasy
about you and I got a great headache from anxiety   I thought you
must have been run over or something. I hope I may not be the worse.

If I am all right tomorrow as I hope—I shall be at Westland Row,
at 25 minutes to three if you are able to get there to meet me.

If there was any doubt about your letter being in time you should
have enquired at the Gen. Post Office, and wired instead. I feel shaken
all over by the anxiety I have been in, I dont know what would become
of me if anything *did* happen to you, I'd never survive I think. I must
post this now I suppose you will have got my wire. You deserve a good
scolding for dragging me off to town by your carelessness I suppose to
stand about in the damp when it is so important for me to keep in good
health   however I'm so overjoyed to hear that you are all right I haven't
the heart to say anything to you. Dont ride *too* far at first.

Your old T.

I wont wait tomorrow so be in time if you come to W. Row.

[*TCD/GS276*]
                                            [*Glendalough House*]
                                            September [*12th*¹] 07

Dearest Treasure

I saw the doctor and surgeon all right and the operation is fixed
for 12 o'clock on Saturday so I am to go in tomorrow evening. I got a
qualm when I left you today and sat down in the doctors waiting room,
but as soon as I saw him and started off for the surgeon's I felt as gay
as if I was going to order a pair of boots. When I had seen Ball² I went
off to the hospital and engaged a room. Then I got some tea in O'Brien's
and went off and saw old Yeats and came home by the quarter to six.
Tomorrow I shall have to stay quiet so I fear I will not be able to meet
you—I cannot ask you here as people are coming—perhaps it is just
as well for us not to be together   we would feel queer and uneasy all
the time and then when I see you getting uncomfortable I begin to get

'qualms' myself. Ball says the glands will come out 'beautifully' and that I will be much the better for it, so cheer up now and dont *dream* of being *uneasy*. You can enquire for me about 2.30 on Saturday the address is "Elpis" 19 Lower Mount St.

You must write me a very nice cheerful letter when you get this. I hope I didn't depress you about the bicycle I hardly know what to advise. It seems *foolish* not to take a little time and make sure you are getting the best value for your money when your comfort and safety for the next five years or so depend on your choice. Besides you will want clothes and you have very little money to spare with your debt in the theatre and your "trousseau"! coming on. However I dont want to be a spoil sport, but I would be very anxious about you if you went riding much now without me to look after you, and I am afraid you might over-do it if you hadn't me to warn you.

You'll get this, my own heart's treasure, tomorrow morning, so write to me if you can in time for the evening *6 o'clock* post here. When I'm in Mount St. I'll write to you to the *Abbey* when I'm able to write of course I wont be able for *some time*. (Do please take care of yourself I feel anxious about leaving you so long)

It is *just possible* I may wire to you tomorrow to come down by the *quarter to three*, if it is very fine and I feel very well. You will find the wire at Mary St about one if I wire. I would meet you at Glenageary and have a little walk   dont be disappointed if I dont wire as it is quite uncertain.

Post Script.   Now I've had supper. I think I have told you everything. Be cheerful and well when I come out again—you weren't looking at all well today—and then we'll have great times. Of course I'll write to you again tomorrow if I dont wire you to come down here. Read your books and learn your parts and be happy my sweet pet, I feel worse about you moping and making yourself miserable than I do about my own affair.

Remember it is very doubtful about tomorrow so dont count on seeing me. I must be careful now. A thousand blessings your old Tramp. If you come down we'll have tea out so dont worry about your 'get up'.

1. Synge misdated this letter the 11th.
2. His surgeon was Sir Charles Ball, Regius Professor of Surgery, Dublin University, of 24 Merrion Square North.

[Texas/GS276]　　　　　　　　　　　　　　Glendalough House
　　　　　　　　　　　　　　　　　　　　　Sept. 13th. *[1907]*

My own dearest Love

　　I couldn't get you out to me today, I was inclined to sneeze and the weather was threatening so it would have been madness to run the risk of giving myself cold. I am very sorry not to have seen you, yet in some ways it was better not, I feel perfectly hard, and fearless and defiant now, but if I saw your little sweet face looking mournfully at me I'd get sentimental and qualmish at once. I'm really not at all uneasy the doctors and nurses and all of them take it so utterly as a matter of course, they reassure one. You mustn't think of being uneasy either. I'm going in there to be cured I hope, and it isn't at all as if I was going to the wars. How would you like it if I was a 'gaudy officer' getting potted at by the Boers or some one? Did I give you the address? It is "Elpis" 19 Lower Mount Street. If you like to come down there at about 3 o'clock tomorrow and inquire for me you can, but perhaps the telephone is the simplest way. Perhaps they will call me 'singe' you'll have to spell it S.y.n.g.e. as Fay does in his article. The little skit, by the way, isn't at all bad. It's six o'clock now and I'm looking out for a letter from you. I hope one will come. Dont forget you've promised *not to ride in traffic!*

　　I feel wonderfully gay! I'm going in by the quarter past eight this evening so I haven't much longer to wait. The worst time will be tomorrow morning waiting about without any breakfast till 12 o'clock at the hospital. I dont believe you'd like me a bit if I was a kind of cast-iron man who didn't know what it was to be ill? If I was like that I wouldn't be able to sympathize with you, when you aren't well.——

　　Your letter has come　do try and be happy. If you know how I am counting the hours till I can get you for my very own! Meanwhile try and keep philosophical and cheerful—a certain amount of wretchedness is good for people when they're young—I wouldn't be half as nice as I am if I hadn't been through fire and water!!!

　　My spirits are going up, and up, and up, they always do when I get into a good tight corner. The only weight on me now is the thought that you are unhappy. Of course I'll have qualms tomorrow but after all it's an interesting experience to break the monotony of one's daily. I believe if I was a woman I'd have a big family just for fun! I wish you could see me grinning over this letter and you'd get as cheerful too, by this time tomorrow of course I'll be pretty flat. Now Good bye for a few days my own pet, treasure, life, love, light and all thats good

Your T.

[*TCD/GS276*]   [*Elpis Nursing Home*
                                  18th September 1907]

Dearest

Going on splendidly Write to me as often as you like. It is a good plan for you to come with F.J.F., I'll tell you when Of course I'm rather weak still

I mustn't write more, I think of you a lot

T.

[*TCD*]   [*Elpis Nursing Home*]
                                  Sept 20th '07

Dearest L

I got your note yesterday and I hope will get one tomorrow. How are you, my little pet, I'm getting on very well, but it's terribly slow. I'm afraid of having people in to see me JUST YET as I'm a bit too weak still, and I dont want to give myself a longer time than necessary Sir C. Ball is going to take off the dressings tomorrow and then if all is well perhaps he'll let me up. Write me a good letter now. I got the one you gave W G. all right. Dont cycle *too* far. A thousand blessings

T.

[*TCD*]   19 Lower Mount St
                                  Dublin
                                  21 Sept 1907[1]

Dearest

I'm in a great hurry, writing this. I'm up today and better but I'm ANXIOUS about you You oughtened to be unwell *now*. It's not the time

I hope you haven't done too much cycling. For my sake don't go to-morrow. *I'm very distressed*

Your old T

I hope to see you about Tuesday. Blessings on you. I heard today they were all right not tubercular in any way I am overjoyed.

---

1. The address and date are written in another hand.

[*TCD*] [*Elpis Nursing Home*]
Monday
Sept 23rd/07

Dearest

I got your two little notes all right I am relieved to hear that you aren't unwell.

I was out in the garden yesterday for half an hour, and today they have taken the stitches out of [my] neck, so I shall soon be all right now I hope. I am very shaky of course still.

Will you come and see me tomorrow with F.J.F., about 4 would be a good time.

Dont be disappointed if I seem queer and flat, in this sort of a business one feels worse the first days one is trying to get about again than any other time. Please bring me an ounce of Three Castles and some papers, – I dont know whether there is anything in the Theatre Library that I haven't read, and that is readable, ask F.J.

Your old T.

[*TCD*] [*Elpis Nursing Home*]
Sept.25th/07

Dearest

Sir C. B. has just been in and says, I am *well* and may go home as soon as I like. I think I'll go tomorrow morning so you can write to me here if you write *tonight* or to *Kingstown* otherwise. Remember the time has come now for *you* to be careful of yourself. I feel in great trim today and ready for any thing. Your grapes were *magnificent* I was enraged when I opened them that I had not done so when you were here so that you might have had some too. I was so full [of] the pleasure of seeing you I could think of nothing else. Isn't it *great* that all this wretched business is over!

T.——

The only thing this pencil can do is *underline* so I do it OFTEN!

[*TCD*]

Glendalough Ho.
Sept [27¹] 07
Friday

Dearest

I got your nice little note all right yesterday morning.

I came back here before dinner, and, of course, felt very tired all the evening so that I couldn't write to you. Can you come and see me tomorrow (Saturday) afternoon? If you can, and *if you are all right,*— come down by the quarter to three and come to the House. Write BEFORE eleven tomorrow to say if you can come If anything happens here to make it impossible for me to have you I will wire to Mary Street in the morning.

I feel a good deal better now, but I am rather shaky still. That is to be expected. I dont know at all yet when I shall get away for my change. I am sorry to have to leave you again, but of course it is quite necessary now that I should have a good change before the winter. Goodbye old pet

T.

1. Synge has written 25th with a question mark.

[*TCD/GS277*]

[*Glendalough House*]
Sept 30th 07

Dearest Love

I got your letter this morning and I was delighted to hear that you are getting on so well, remember to go on taking care of yourself. I am doing very well indeed, I wear a collar now when I go out, and I was able to take quite a good walk this morning, round through the furzy place where we sat one evening near Killiney Hill, and I am going out again now. I am beginning to think that I will only go to Kerry for my change after all, I dont feel very much inclined for Brittany while my neck is at all sore. However we'll see. Yes I hope we'll soon be 'fixed' as you call it. I dont know what to advise about the table linen. If you get it you'll have to pay for it and I dont think you've any money. Anyway dont get much, as we may have to go into lodgings, after all, and then we'd have no need for it at once.

By the way I want *you* to get a *Note Book* and write down everything you read, who it is by, when he lived, and any particulars that you think you would like to remember. I have a wheelbarrowful of such notebooks (every one who reads seriously keeps them), and you will find it no trouble, and the greatest use. Do try,—to please me, because you know I'm ill still! Wont you? You are reading a lot of books that very few ordinary people read and it is a pity for you to let everything go in at one eye and out at the other. In a few years you'll be the best educated actress *in Europe,* and I want you to take a pride and pleasure in your progress. 'Nish,[1] dont you feel that I'm nearly well again, as I'm setting off to lecture you? Be good, write soon, take care of yourself, and we'll have great times presently.

T.

1. Apparently one of Molly's favorite expressions; it probably comes from the Irish admonitory "now!" (*anois*).

[*Texas*]   [*Glendalough House*]
Oct 2nd 07

Dearest

I am most distressed at not hearing from you this morning. Are you ill or what has happened? Please write by return. The last line I got was written on Sunday and this is Wednesday. You never left me so long without news of you before, and as I'm not very strong yet, I have worked myself up into a fuss.

I am getting on all right but I am very much bothered by this numbed finger they have given me. It annoys me more than the glands ever did all the time I had them. I am going to Sir C. Ball today if it is fine. I dont know [whether] I shall go away at all after all. My mother is making me pay for my time in Elpis so I dont know if I can afford a trip. If you dont write today I'll go in and see you to find out what is the matter.

> Your old T.

[*TCD*]
> [*Glendalough House*]
> Saturday night
> Oct 5 [*1907*]

Dearest Love

I'm very fond of you tonight. I've managed to have tomorrow clear—thanks be to God—so come down by the quarter to two dont miss it. I'll meet you at the train if I can and take you on to Bray but if I'm not there come down to the house. I wish it was tomorrow.

I'll tell you then all about the play as I understand it and criticize the acting.[1]

> Your T——

---

1. *The Country Dressmaker,* by a new playwright who greatly admired Synge, George Fitzmaurice (1877–1963), was first presented at the Abbey on October 3rd; Molly played two small parts, "Min Dillane" and "Maryanne Clohesy."

[*TCD*]
> [*Glendalough House*]
> Monday Night
> Oct 7th 07

Dearest Life

How are you tonight? I wonder what you've been at all day, I've been very busy and I'm very tired now. First I typed my new Kerry article from 9.30 till 11, then I cycled till 1, then I had dinner and a smoke and cycled again till 4, then I typed till 5.30 and went up to my sister's to bid my cousin goodbye, till 7. Then supper and now its 8, and I'm writing to you. Have you done as much as that? I'm beginning to wish you weren't so lazy. You'll have to stir up one of these days and give up snoozing till one o'clock, *soon,* I hope. Nish! are you wounded in your tenderest feelings? This is a silly letter, but I'm too tired to write; that is why. Do you know what I've been thinking you ought to write some Irish Theatrical Articles for the *Evening Telegraph* and make enough to get a bicycle. I'm sure you could write as well as Henderson—you've no idea how easy it is till you try and how soon your ideas begin to stream out of your mind—and of course I'd help you to put them in trim. I wish you'd try; you'd find it much more amusing than 'Nap'.[1] And you'd get money instead of spending it.

Hadn't we a great time yesterday? I wasn't at all tired or the worse, I hope you weren't either. I was thinking last night it's rather remarkable how well we seem to know now, how we're getting on at a distance. I felt 'as sure as sure' on Saturday night that you and Dossy were talking or something, and there you were, playing him off for Lady G's benefit. That feeling for people at a distance is quite a well-known fact between people who are in close sympathy. It's called 'telepathy', as I dare say you know. I think we'll be married by Xmas, as we're long enough like this. I wonder if I should go out in the cold to post this or if I should leave it till tomorrow. I think I'll go so that you'll have it when you wake. Blessings Dear One

Your T

N.B.   This is a long letter because I've written very small.

1. The players frequently whiled away the time off stage by playing cards.

[*TCD*]   [*Glendalough House*]
                                                                    Oct. 9th. 1907

Dearest Love

Jack Yeats didn't come yesterday after all, so I had a very long day here by myself. Didn't I tell you it was going to rain 'cats and dogs', I hope you realized what a damn fine prophet I am! I got your little note yesterday morning all right. Yes Sunday is a delightful memory, may we have *many many many* more like it. I'm going in to see Parsons today and I'm going to Ventry on Saturday, tomorrow there will be a Directors' meeting I think, and on Friday the matinée[1] so I dont quite know when and how we're to meet. It's a great nuisance, and I suppose after the matinée on Friday they'll have all sorts of business to do and people to see. It's high time to put an end to these snatched interviews. Write at once and tell me what *times* you are free on Thursday we might meet for a lunch or tea before the meeting if it can be managed. I'll wire to you tomorrow if I can when I hear from you and Lady G. So tell me what hours you'll be at home and what at the Abbey. Good bye my own love, I've written five (5) letters this morning, business ones.

Your T.

---

1. The players held a professional matinée for Beerbohm Tree's company on 11th October.

[*TCD/GS277–8*]

c/o Mrs Kevane
Sea View
Ventry
Dingle
Co Kerry
Oct 13(?) 07
Sunday
night!

Dearest Love

At last I have got to work at a letter. I sent you a card yesterday with my address which I hope you got—I gave it to [a] clergyman to post in Killarney as I could not get at a post-office myself. Today there was no post from here so this will go tomorrow and you'll get it on Tuesday. I hope you wont be very disappointed tomorrow when the post man goes by.

I did not get here till ten o'clock last night, the trains were so late. Then at Dingle I found they had only sent a little flat cart with a jennet for me and my luggage and bike so I had to ride four miles in the dark on very wet muddy roads. However I got here in great spirits and I wasn't anything the worse. Today I've been walking nearly six hours on the mountains in heavy showers of rain—like the ones we had at Glen Cree—and I feel very well except that I am a little inclined to have asthma, but I hope it may keep off. I enjoyed my day's walking here very much, but I had qualms of loneliness every now and then. Still it wasn't like the old loneliness—the loneliness before I knew you—as in a way now you seem to be with me even when you're miles away.

I wonder how you got on at Darley's today, tell me all about it.—I ate too much duck for my dinner today and I've got a pain—so I can't be emotional! I had a very amusing journey from Tralee on to Dingle with a quantity of country people. The carriages are like tram-carriages, and there was such a crowd—mostly of women and girls—that I and an old man had to sit on a flour sack, at the end. We had a great talk and every one in the carriage stopped and leaned out to listen. They couldn't make out who or what I was—here everyone is known by sight—sitting up on my sack with my typewriter on my knee. The old man said I was a Kerryman, that I was dressed like a Kerryman, and talked like a Kerryman and therefore I must be a Kerryman. Then he asked what was my calling—I put him off and talked vaguely about my travels. Then an idea struck him, "Maybe you're a rich man" he said. I smiled as much as to say I was, "And you're about 35?" he said. I said I was. "And not married?" I said no. "Well" he said, "you're a damn lucky man travelling the world with no one to impede you." Afterwards he got out and I fell into the hands of another old man who had got in. We talked about the fishing season, and the Aran fishing etc. Then he turned a knowing eye on me "Begob" he said, "I see you're a fish-dealer!"

Now I've given you a guinea's worth of "article" so never say I'm not generous![1]

The sea is right under my window with a beautiful moon shining on it.—How I wish you were here. I am delighted to have seen this place in winter—it is winter here—as I will be able to strengthen my Kerry book very much. My poor little pet try and be happy. If you [have] nothing to do all day you ought to go to the National Gallery

or the Museum, it would be a variety you will make at home. Now
I've to write up my book diary so goodbye dear love. The lodgings
are comfortable 1000 blessings

Your old ⟨T.⟩ Fishmonger

---

1. Synge later used this material for his own article in *The Shanachie,* see Oxford
Prose, pp. 277–279.

[*TCD*]   c/o Mrs Kevane

[*Ventry. Kerry*]

Tuesday [*15 October 1907*]

Dearest

I have just got your note. I could not help the delay in writing. I
was dead tired on Friday night and had all my packing and settling to
do. I started before eight on Saturday. I have been very bad indeed
with asthma so I am leaving here again at once. It is too bad. I hoped
so much from this trip. I may be a couple of days at Killarney or somewhere on my way home so you cannot write till you hear from me
again. I shall be home by Saturday I expect at the latest.

Certainly I am an afflicted poor devil. I am all right now however
fortunately it only takes me at night.

Goodbye dear Heart

Your T.

[*TCD/tel*]   Ventry 15 October 1907 2.50 P.M.

Miss M. Allgood 37 Mary St. Dublin. Leaving Dont write here again
Synge.

[*TCD*]   *Glendalough House*
                                                       Oct 17th/ 07

Dearest Pet
      I got home last night after all. The asthma has rather renewed my
cough—for the time being—so I thought it wisest to come home and
get myself better as fast as I can. I wrote to you on Tuesday to say that
I was leaving Ventry and I gave the letter—with one to my mother—
to the people in the Hotel in Tralee to post but they must have forgotten them or something as my mother's letter did not come till this
morning! When did you get yours? The letter you wrote me on Saturday only reached me *this morning*—my mother sent it on late so that
it did not get to Ventry till after I had started. It made me feel very
penitent—my poor love—for not writing to you on Friday, but I
couldn't have written anything worth while. Are you glad to hear that
I'm home to you again? I'm glad to think I'll soon see you again, but
of course I dont like being driven home by asthma. I've a nasty cough
still, but I'm not at all ill, and I hope it wont last. My sweetheart I'm
looking forward so much to seeing you. Write me *by return* when you
are free tomorrow *if you can.* I might wire to you to meet me tomorrow afternoon, if it is fine and I am well enough. Do not count on it
however, I will go to the Saturday matinée to see the new *Shadow of
the Glen,* so I'll see you then in any case, and then SUNDAY!
      My trip cost me about £3.10.0 but I'll get it all or most of it back
by articles I hope, now my dear treasure goodbye till very soon I hope
you're very good, and thinking of me and that you forgive my not
writing on Friday.
                        Your old T.

[*TCD/GS278*]   Glendalough House
                                                       22.X.07

Dearest Heart
      I didn't write to you yesterday as I was waiting to hear from Lady
G. but no letter has come. I dont know how we're to have our 're-
hearsal' unless we have it in the Abbey.[1] I suppose I'll hear from her
Ladyship tonight

I got a 'Deirdre' fit yesterday and I wrote *10* pages of it in great spirits and joy, but alas I know that that is only the go off. There'll be great anguish still before I get her done if I ever do. Write to me. How are you. I'm afraid to propose to meet you anywhere for fear you may be unwell. I had a little bicycle ride yesterday afternoon, and enjoyed it, but I croaked a good deal in the night. By the way I saw houses advertised in yesterday's *Irish Times* for 6/0, 8/6, 9/0, 10/0 a week. I wonder where they are. The address was Tully, House Agent, Parliament St. would you like to send a line to enquire. They'd stick on the price or something if I enquired from this address. However I'm sure they're hovels.

I have worlds of work to get through now. I was so tired last night I kept falling asleep in my chair—a rare thing for me. Write dearest.

Your old Tramp

1. Molly was playing the role of Nora Burke in *The Shadow of the Glen,* for a professional matinée on 25 October in honor of the English actress Mrs Patrick Campbell (1865–1940) and her company who were performing in Dublin.

[*TCD*] Glendalough House
Oct 23rd/07

Dearest Child

I was delighted to get your note last night. I didn't fix on a rehearsal for a number of reasons, the first that it is *probably* better for you to stay quiet today as you will have to work in the evening. Further it would have cost 0/6 for a wire 1/0 for my train and 2/0 for teas, that is 3/6 in all and we wouldn't have had much to show for it, so I am staying at home. You know I'm to be married soon! I am not at all sure that you are not better without a rehearsal with me—*one* so soon before the show would be more likely I think to embarrass you than anything else. I would rather you went through the part yourself (I mean rehearse yourself) using your own intellect and taste and let us see what you can do with [it]. All you have to do is to be *simple and natural* as you used to be.

I dont think I'll go to *Hedda Gabler* tomorrow I dont like being out in the late train till this cough is better. I'll go to her Matinée on Saturday and see *Magda,* that will do me very well, I'm sure I wont like her at all—from what I have heard and seen of her. By the way if you are unwell tomorrow night I HOPE YOU WONT GO. It would be very very bad for you rushing down to the Gaiety.[1] *Please* dont, *remember* what you've been *through* and dont have it, or worse over again.

I expect to have MacKenna out here to see me tomorrow afternoon and then he'll be at the show I hope on Friday I'll introduce you to him afterwards so wash off your make up well and dont powder your-self before you come down!! And also have on your best face and get into some part of the Green Room where your left profile will [be] very telling. Nish! It's too bad to go through all this week without seeing you, but what's to be done I cant take you out to walk, and I must have fresh air myself. By the way if you'd really like me to hear Nora before the show we could run through it at the Abbey perhaps at 1.30 on Friday or earlier if there is no rehearsal. What do you think of that? This is an extra long letter as I'm not seeing you today. I was very lonesome after you went away on Sunday. Yesterday I went to Killiney in the train and walked up to the church where we once quarrelled I enjoyed part of it, and part of it I was lonesome. Today I'm going on my bicycle. I'm printing the films today. They aren't much good. I must have left them too long. This isn't very intimate I'm afraid, Dear Heart, but I've just eaten a big dinner and that's against sentiment. Be good and be happy and for *Heavens sake take care of* yourself.

Later
　　Post Man
Just heard from Mackenna to say he's coming tomorrow, so we wont meet till Friday hard luck! Of course I'd have you out walking with me only that this is not a time for you to walk. With Mountains of love
　　　　　　　　　　　　　　　　　　Your old T.

---

1. Mrs Campbell had invited the company to her performance of *Hedda Gabler* at the Gaiety Theatre on Thursday evening, 24 October.

[*TCD*]   Glendalough Ho
                                    Tuesday Oct 29th [*1907*]

Dearest Love

I have just got your letter thanks.

Meet me at Tara St tomorrow at *twenty-five* minutes to *three* if it
is fine, and bring my cape with you. I'd better not go up I think if it
is wet. I coaxed another thread of smoke out of the fire when I got
home but that was all. My mother didn't say anymore about you, I
didn't expect she would. That will come in good time. MacKenna said
more nice things about you and Sally yesterday. I had tea with him
and then dinner and then we walked out as far as Booterstown. He is
coming to Ireland I think in the spring so we'll have them for neigh-
bours in Rathgar.

I walked round by Loughlinstown today at a great rate as I am trying to get rid of my stomach!

Yes Sunday was a great day. I hope tomorrow will be fine enough
for us. I have been slaving at my Kerry article all day I hate putting
the last touches and getting the spelling and punctuation right it
bothers me.

                                    Till tomorrow Your old T.[1]

1. Molly has written on the back of the envelope *What is the meaning of an otiose epithet.*

[*NLI*]   [*Glendalough House*]
                                    Nov 1st 07

Dearest Love

This a hurried *after-dinner* line only, to wish you good day and
many of them. I hope I'll hear from you tonight with news of *Dervorgilla* there was a cold notice in the *Irish Times.*[1]

I worked hard and I think well at Deirdre this morning if I go on
like this I may have it done for this season if I only escape illness. I
walked round by Kilmacanogue—or *Kilmaconick* as we call it—all
round Little Sugar Loaf and back into Bray through Wind Gates yesterday in 2½ hours! When I got out of the train at Glenageary I was so

stiff I could hardly walk. I haven't gone so fast for years. Our black-berry lane—where we fought—was full of blackberries, and all the country was fine. It's a pity you weren't with me. I'll be in tomorrow I hope. It's just possible that I'll go away with Lady G. and W.B.Y. after the show as there may be things to discuss. I'll see you of course on Sunday. How seldom you write to me now! A little while ago you wrote every day

Your old

Tramp

1. Lady Gregory's play, in which Molly played the role of Mona, the old servant, was first produced on 31 October 1907.

[*TCD*]   Glendalough Ho
                                          Saturday night Nov 2 [*1907*]

My poor little Pet

I have felt very bad ever since I had to run away from you, and saw you ducking in behind the scenery. I couldn't help it my sweet genius—you are a genius after your Mona and that's no lie. Will you forgive me? I heard nice things about [you] that I'll tell you tomorrow.

Come down by the *quarter* to *two* dont miss it, and if its fine we'll go off and have tea in Enniskerry and come home slowly under the stars—in the balmy beautiful night. Wont that be great. If its *wet come here*. I'll be counting the hours till I see you. I'm afraid I'm a great fool to be so upset by missing my little talk with you and disappointing you. Never mind my treasure soon we'll be together for ever with the help of God Dont be late dear Heart tomorrow

Your old T——

[*TCD/GS278*]   Glendalough House
                                          Nov. 9th 07

Dearest

I haven't had dinner today yet; but I've been working at Deirdre till my head is going round. I was too taken up with her yesterday to write to you—I got her into such a mess I think I'd have put her

into the fire only that I want to write a part for YOU, so you mustn't
be jealous of her.

I am very glad you came down on Wednesday and gave me a little
glimpse of you, I am *living* on that. I suppose I wont see you now till
Sunday. I will not go to [the] Matinée, there is no use.

I am keeping pretty well but I am very tired, worn-out, with
anxiety about Deirdre. Since yesterday I have pulled two acts into one,
so that—if I can work it—the play will have three acts instead of
four, and that has of course given me many problems to think out.
As it is I am not sure that the plan I have is a good one. Ideas seem
so admirable when they occur to you and then they get so doubtful
when you have thought over them for a while.

Write me a full intimate letter, my dear love, I am weary and depressed, and lonesome. I wish we were together.

Florence Ross came yesterday and there is some talk of Ada Synge
coming also as one of her brothers is ill. Remember we go out *early*
on Sunday if it is fine and get a good long day together. I hope it may
hold up but the glass is coming down again. I wonder shall I hear from
you today before you get this. I hope you have written me a nice letter
it would put heart into me

Your old Tramp

[TCD/GS278]

Glendalough Ho
Saturday Nov 9th/07

Dearest Heart

It looks as if it would be fine tomorrow, if it is be sure to come
down by the *quarter to eleven* and we'll have a great day with the help
of G__. I had a long ride this afternoon—the country was radiantly
bright wonderful and I was as happy as seven kings. I had nearly
forgotten what it was like to be in good health, and to have hearty
spirits. I only wished that you were with me—but though you weren't,
you were putting a glow into my heart of hearts all the same, my blessings on you. I finished a second rough draft of *The Sons of Usnach*
today.[1] So I have the whole thing now under my hand to work at next
week.

If it is not fine tomorrow come here as usual by the quarter to two.

I hope against hope that it may be fine tomorrow so that we may have a royal radiant day together.

I must post this now. I wrote to another address about lodgings in Terenure today. It does no harm to enquire.

> Till tomorrow
> Your old T.

1. Synge was undecided what to call this play until four or five months later, when he finally decided on *Deirdre of the Sorrows.*

[*TCD*]   [*Glendalough House*]
                                                      Monday Evening
                                                      Nov 11?/07

Dearest Pet

I am a little disappointed and uneasy at not hearing from you to-night you promised to let me know how you were after the long walk, I hope I shall hear tomorrow morning. I am going to post this to you tomorrow early so that you may get it in the afternoon to make up a little for the 'Ball' you've given up for me. I was wonderfully happy last night thinking how good you had been to me, my dear heart, I'm afraid I've often written to say you'd put me in the blues—do you remember the horrid incident this time last year before I went away? —but this time you've made me OVERFLOW with delight. I hope I dont seem very unreasonable, I'm sure by and by you'll be glad that you've chosen a good *style* of life, there is a 'style' in life as there is in acting, or painting or writing—but this is dry stuff I didn't mean to write.

I hope you aren't too tired today, why didn't you send me a line? I never felt better than I did this morning and I had a long satisfactory time at Deirdre. Afterwards I went out on my bicycle but it was very damp or something and I got a headache and didn't enjoy myself much. What a day we had yesterday!!! The people I wrote to about the rooms did not answer me at all, which is queer, so I wont be able to go and look at them tomorrow as I intended. This is a very dull letter I'm afraid and I wanted to write a particularly nice one today when I am so full of love and delight in you my little treasure—I am tired, so shut your eyes and imagine I've got my arm round you and am just resting my poor old head on your little shoulder.

Tuesday

No letter this morning I am dreadfully uneasy about you, if I have made you ill again I will never forgive myself. WRITE BY RETURN

Your old T.

P.S. I'm just off to Rathgar for the lunch with this good man.[1] It is a bother as we might have met today, but I daresay it is better for you to be quiet today as your time of rest is coming near.

I want to show you my Deirdre some day soon perhaps I can on Sunday.

My blessing on you, little Changling, you have made me very happy, you are so good to me now, giving up your ride with O'R[ourke], and now your Ball.

T.

---

1. Probably E. A. Stopford, who had recently moved to Dublin.

[*TCD*] Glendalough Ho
14/11/07

My dearest Love

I got your two letters on Tuesday and was very much relieved. It is hard not to see you this week, but I could not appoint to meet you today or yesterday as your time was so much taken up and you must be tired out. I shall be at the Matinée but I fear I am nearly sure to be carried off by the Directors as I have not seen them for nearly a fortnight.[1]

I cannot live this way any longer—I nearly died of loneliness and misery last night while you ought to be here to comfort me and cheer me up. Do take care of yourself this *time* if you get a pain in your back or anything we will be afraid ever to take a long walk again, and our long walks are such a delight to us. I was very depressed last night, were you? I suppose you were at *The Merry Wives,* I wonder if you liked it. I am working myself sick with Deirdre or whatever you call it. It is a very anxious job. I dont want to make a failure.

On Tuesday I lunched with my friends at Rathgar and then we went to the lecture on Japanese art at the Alexandra College. It was interesting enough but heavily delivered. If you get this in time please write me a line. I think it is a *bad* plan you have started of writing so seldom now. I get sad for the want of a little sympathetic line that wouldn't take you a minute.

Your old T.

1. The Abbey players gave a professional matinée on 15 November for John Martin Harvey and his company who were performing in Dublin.

[NLI]   Glendalough House
                                                             Nov 15/07
Dearest Love

How are you today? I was tired after all the compliments, but I am as usual now. About tomorrow; if it is *wet* come by the quarter to two or the quarter to three, as you find it most convenient, and if it [is] *fine* come by the quarter to *three,* so that I'll have time for a little walk. That will leave us three hours together. No great thing but I suppose we must be satisfied. Of course I DEPEND on you not to come out at all if you are not well *enough.*

I was too busy with Deirdre to write to you this morning so—as you can see—this is an after-dinner note. I wonder which of my letters it is that you like so much. You mustn't mind my letters being a little dry these times, because I am pouring out my heart to you in Deirdre the whole day long. I am pleased with it now, but that doesn't mean much as I go back and forward in my feelings to my work every second day—at least when they are in this stage. I am half inclined to write to Old Yeats and ask him straight out to sell me your picture. Would that be a good plan? If it goes to the Abbey we'll see no more of it.[1]

Now do take every possible care of yourself my own treasure of the world.

Your old Tramp

[*TCD*]

P.S.   Your notes have just come. My poor Changling to worry your little self about nothing! Dont you trust me?

I am very sorry to see by the first that you speak of being very ill. Perhaps we should not walk tomorrow if you aren't feeling well dont bother about it! *I hope you'll feel well!*

1. I have been unable to trace this picture; the portrait of Molly by J. B. Yeats now hanging in the Abbey Theatre is dated 1913.

[*TCD*]   Glendalough House
                                                    Tuesday night
                                                    Nov. 19th [*1907*]

My dear Hearts Love

I went to the Abbey today to meet Poel[1] and was sorry to hear that you are unwell. I am in a fever of anxiety to know how you are I nearly telegraphed to you but then I thought you would write. Write at once for Heaven's sake. I am eaten up with uneasiness. I never know how much you are the very breath and soul of my life till something goes wrong. Are you worse than usual? Or are you only being wise and taking care of yourself?

I was greatly pleased with Poel who is most enthusiastic about my work. We dined together Poel and the three Directors—every now and then Poel launched out into praise of my work, and it was amusing to see Lady G dashing in at once with praise of Yeats' work. They have put off *The Well of the Saints* till *Lent* I feel angry about it, and sick of the whole business I wish you were here, I feel lonely tonight. I am going off to Kingstown with this in the hope that it may reach you tonight—it is five o'clock now. Good-bye, Dearest Love. If no letter comes from you this evening I will be WRETCHED INDEED.

                                                    Your old T.

P.S.   Is there any possibility of getting the sketch, please let me know, also send me news how you have been this turn it is not fair or right to keep me in distress and anxiety.

1. William Poel (1852–1934), actor and producer famous for his emphasis on verse-speaking and reinterpretation of Shakespeare in terms of Elizabethan techniques.

[*TCD*]   Glendalough House
                                                                       Nov 20th/07
Dearest
     I have got your two letters—the one this morning seemed a most bitter and cruel one, and upset [me] so that I could hardly do my work. I got home yesterday at a quarter-to-five (with a headache and coughing worse than I have done for months)—and as soon as I got a cup of tea I wrote to you and rushed off with it [to] the Post Office at *Kingstown Station* where I found after I had posted it that I was three minutes late. I could do no more.
     Your second letter does not tell me how you have been [*Synge's deletion*] so I am uneasy and miserable still. I am afraid I am not so well as I have [been], or else it is the worry—on top of my fatigue with *Deirdre*—that is knocking me up.
     I believe that I am go to to tea with Poel after the lecture tomorrow, so perhaps I can see you on Friday afternoon I heard them saying that you are not going till Monday after all. So we may have Sunday[1]
     I am BITTERLY DISAPPOINTED that we have lost the sketch of you, why did you stop me writing to him—you promised to write. L.G. I should think has paid for it.
     Excuse this letter I will be a long time before I quite get over the blow you gave me this morning. I am glad you are better. *Be cheerful* and take care of yourself
                                                                       Your old T.

1. The company went on a tour of Manchester, Glasgow, and Edinburgh from 24 November until 15 December.

[*TCD*]   Glendalough House
                                                    Nov 23? /07

My dearest Heart,

 I have a queer lonesome qualm in me today all the time I am
working—I dont [know] how we would get on if you went to America!
How are you my dear child? I am watching all the points of the compass to see if you'll have a fine day tomorrow, I hope the gods (I mean
the saints) will be kind to you.

 I am not going to *John Bull*[1] or the Abbey today. I haven't been
quite so well this week so I'm going to be very careful now for a day
or two till I recover the lost ground. I do not feel the slightest in-
clination to go and see Shaw—I'd rather keep my money for Esposito's
concert tomorrow and hear something that is really stirring and fine and
beautiful—though I dont suppose I shall go there either—that would
quiet my poor lonesome gizzard. It is queer how *hollow* I feel today,
my poor changeling, but still I have been working well and hard and I
am not unduly depressed. I know you wouldn't like me to be *too*
cheerful.

 Write me full satisfying letters every day please that will keep me
well. I am kicking myself today because I forgot to make you *swear*
yesterday that you'd write your promised article on this tour I mean
while you are on tour. F.Ross has got her article on Skerries quite clear
and good now after three corrections. Why wont you do the same?
There is dinner Goodbye dear love.

J. M. Tramp.

I shall write to [you] as M. O'Neill on Tour. I hope you wont forget to
send me the Manchester address in a legible form.
P.S. I've opened your letter again to remind you to put on your warm
under garments for the journey. It makes the greatest difference travelling I know by experience. Its very cold out here today and I expect
you'll have it very sharp tomorrow Remember all your swears Goodbye
again old Heart

---

 1. William Poel's company was performing in *John Bull's Other Island,* the play Shaw
had originally written for the Abbey Theatre but which was rejected by the Directors as
unsuitable for their company to act.

[AS]   Glendalough House
                                                    Sunday 24th Nov. 07

Dearest Love

    Your little scrawl, your *charming* little scrawl I should say, has just
come and cheered me up very much though I dont like the thought of
going off for a cold lonely walk today in our old haunts. I wont go till
after dinner. Yesterday afternoon I walked out through Loughlinstown
—I [wonder] if you've remembered to remember where Loughlinstown
is? and on to Killiney and back by train from there, in time for a bout
at Deirdre.

    I heard the boat blowing its horn this morning at a quarter past
eight and I got hollow again at the sound of it. However I'm not really
unhappy this time because I trust you very fully ⟨to be good,⟩ and
three weeks wont be long going over as we're both so busy.

    I have been building castles in the air this morning to no end—
a sign I suppose that I am really in good spirits. I saw the Abbey coming to grief—I sometimes think it is doomed in its present shape—then
I saw Martin Harvey or someone taking up my work and money beginning to come in by the wheelbarrow full! Then in about ten years I saw
us starting a little Dublin company of our own with you as leading lady
of course and first Stage Manager! Then by that time Dublin will be
better educated and I saw big houses coming in, and a real Irish Drama
getting on its legs at last thanks to the enthusiasm of the extraordinarily
gifted and subtle actress *Mrs* J.M.Tramp! That is what we must live for,
and to do that you must keep off the English Stage which would destroy your peculiar and subtle talent which I am getting to understand
better than you do.

    I think if the Abbey breaks up soon we might go to Paris for a
while, and then you could be my literary secretary and at the same time
study the French stage and the French art of speaking.—of course your
French blood predestines you to be the bringer in of the essence of the
French tradition for the Dublin stage! Nish*!!!!!!!!!!!!!!!!!!* I hope you
will not keep up your feud with F.J.F. first because he is a man—with
all his drawbacks—that deserves sympathy and friendship rather than
anything else; and also because you *can* learn, and *ought* to learn, a
great deal from him—taking of course nothing he tells you for granted,
and testing everything by your own intuition.

I wonder will you think this a dull letter. I suppose you are nearly half way across the Channel by this time, I hope you are not sick. Be sure to write every day and to write fully telling me how you are and everything else.

I suppose you will get this tomorrow (Monday) morning, and probably the next of my letters will reach you on Wednesday. Now I must write to Lebeau. Many blessings on you, my dear treasure,

Your old Tramp.

[*TCD*]
Glendalough Ho
Nov 26th 07

Dearest Life

Your letter came this morning a very good one too, I'm afraid I haven't much to tell you today. I went up on Sunday to Kilmacanogue and up our little lane round little Sugar Loaf and on to Bray. There was snow on the back Hills and a gray whitish cloud stretching round the horizon, with the Sugar Loafs black against it, that made me very mournful. Before I got to Bray it got quite dark and rained a cold drizzling rain, and I felt as lonesome as the Almighty God—out in the night by myself and you far away talking and laughing with the company. Yesterday (Monday) I went into town and spent a while in the National Gallery and then paid for my fishing-rod at last! In the evening I was very depressed it seemed as if I was put down at the bottom of a black well for three weeks of solitude.

This morning I got your letter which did me good, also a card from MacKenna to say that he is over again and wants to see me tomorrow. That will make a little break.

It is very wet today, *pouring,* but I have written 7 pages of *Deirdre* this morning and I am very cheerful but very tired. My mother's friend came last night. It is a nuisance trying to keep up small talk at meals. I am to go to the Dentist on Thursday and I'll enquire about you. I got a rather favourable answer to an enquiry about a digs at 39 Rathgar Rd. I may go and look at it on Thursday. It is furnished, so I am not sure that it will do.—Excuse this scrap of paper it is all I have in my *reach.*

By the way I looked into *Riders to the Sea* the other day and I saw a stage direction (*in a whisper*) before your speech "Is it (B) it is?" No wonder I am not pleased when you wail it out.

Do you remember your first show of Nora at the Midland? And how you sent me a message that you wanted to see me after it, and beamed with delight when I praised you for it? It is unfortunate that our life separates us so much—"I am not used to being lonesome," now, and I feel it very much more than I did.

Dont let this letter depress you, I am [all] right and working hard, so the time will slip away. Be very good my dear Heart, and write very often and very fully.

Your old lonesome
Tramp

P.S.   I wouldn't think badly of Poel—it is age and nerves most likely that makes his eyes 'shifty', with highly strung people, passing expressions are often misleading. There is a great storm rising it is well you aren't on the sea today. I dreamt last night I was introducing you to my nephews.

[AS]   Glendalough House
                                                        Nov 27th/07

My own dearest Life

I am writing you an extra line today as I could not write to you anywhere tomorrow. I will write on *Sunday* to Glasgow—I suppose you will get it there sometime during the day, dont be disappointed if it does not reach you in the morning.

My dear child I'm at my wits end to know what to do—I am squirming and thrilling and quivering with the excitement of writing Deirdre and I *daren't* break the thread of composition by going out to look for digs and moving into them at this moment. Meanwhile my mother's visitor drives me nearly to distraction though I only see her at meals. One thing is absolutely certain as soon as ever we find a digs now we must be married *even* if you *have no holidays*. Let me get Deirdre out of danger—she may be safe in a week—then Marriage in God's Name. Would you mind a *registry office* if that saves time? I dont know whether it does or not, but we might be married *here* in a registry

office perhaps when you come back if I have not got 'digs'. Write very
often I am so eager to hear every day. I went to the dentist yesterday,
but there was nothing serious to be done. He gave me the name of a
young but reliable and cheap dentist where you can go and use his
(my man's) name so that you will be sure to be well treated.

Your old Tramp.

I have got your picture (photo) framed and put it up in my little
study. It looks very nice, *of course.*
Send Glasgow address I am not sure where I have put yours.
I have a letter to Lady G. on my table and I have just written this
last message on her letter by mistake!!!

[*AS*]   Glendalough House
Nov 28th 07

Dearest Life

What a chapter of accidents. I am *proud* of you, for coming out so
brilliantly and saving the reputation of the company forever. Let me
know as soon as ever you can how everything is going, and how you
are yourself.[1] Dont knock up. I am all right. Yesterday I spent the
afternoon with MacKenna first at Bewley's[2] and then at the Arts Club.
I made a lot of enquiries from him about the way one gets married,
but he did not know things very definitely as he was married in
England. He thinks you must register yourself *three* weeks before hand
with the registrar of your district and fix the day. I can do nothing
till I find a digs, but I am going off to Rathgar tomorrow to look
round. By the way if things go the same as last time you will be
unwell the week between Edinburgh and Christmas. What are we to
do? I am going out of this as soon as ever I can, and then we'll have
to do our best. If the worst comes to the worst, we can get married
on a Saturday to Monday while our shows are going on.

We had a long talk with Count Markiewicz at the Arts Club yesterday. There seems to be some scheme in the air—*this* is absolutely
private not A WORD of it to SALLY or the COMPANY—of buying up the
old Queens [Theatre] and starting a sort of municipal theatre to play
all the *good* plays of the day on a wide basis, not mainly Irish ones,
but including Irish ones. If that comes off there will be a hope for *us*

after the Abbey is buried. I am going to frequent the Arts Club and see what is going on. It may be all talk.[3]

I am writing this in a hurry as I am going to the Dentist at 2 o'clock. I corrected the final first proofs of *The Tinker's Wedding,* yesterday and this morning I have finished (?) the Preface to it. The play is good I think, but it looks mighty shocking in print.

Tell Sally I hope she is better, and to take care of herself for her sake and ours

With many blessings

Your old Tramp

Send me your Glasgow address again.

1. Sara Allgood fell ill in Glasgow and the company doubled on parts, Willie Fay blotting his copybook with the Directors by allowing his wife to go on in Sally's major parts without informing the audience or the press.
2. The coffee house on Grafton Street.
3. The plans must refer to the Independent Dramatic Company, founded later that year with Casimir Dunin-Markiewicz (1874–1932), husband of Constance Gore-Booth, as producer, director, and resident playwright; the company's early productions were · presented at the Abbey until a confusion over identity while on tour caused the Directors to refuse permission for Markiewicz's company to hire the theatre.

[*TCD/GS278*]   Glendalough House
                                                          December 1st 1907

Dearest Love

Your little note came this morning, you dont say if Sally will be able to play in Glasgow, is she better?

This is a grey cool Sunday morning, I wish we were going off for a day in the mountains I am tired and I haven't the heart to go by myself.

Yesterday I went out on my bicycle and when I got as far as Carrickmines just as I was mounting, after a hill, the wheel bent into the brake and jammed, so I had to take off the brake and wheel the thing home. There was a spoke broken apparently that I had not noticed, if the wheel had gone when I was spinning down a hill I'd have got a fine come down! I am beginning to feel the strain of this hard work very much, I wish you were here to take my thoughts off it, and cheer me up for a while. I didn't go to sleep till two last night my

poor nerves were so excited—indeed I'm sleeping badly nearly every
night. I finished the (G) i e the 7th revision or re-writing of the III Act
yesterday. It 'goes' now all through—the III Act I mean—but it wants
a good deal of strengthening, of *'making personal'* still before it will
satisfy me. I wish you'd read a lot of the best things—G[olden] *Treasury*,
Shakespeare and so on—I'll have to rely a good deal on your criticism
and if you dont read what is good you wont know what is good—
you wont know really and surely, no one can—and what'll I do then?
Anyone with a quick taste and intelligence—and you have them ten
times over—who reads and knows the masterpieces of literature can
very soon tell whether some new work is rubbish or a masterpiece too.
Nish. That's your Sunday lecture!

I hope you're very good my own dear dear life, not rolling your
dear little eyes, or playing cards and remembering your swears! By the
way do you know you've spent £25 since this time last year on
Nothing? You gave your Mother £25 we'll say—you didn't really give
so much—I bought you two dresses and paid for all your outings.
Dossy paid for your amusements on tour and going to theatre, F.J.F.
paid for one of your weeks in Glen Cree and I paid for the jennet.
What's become of the other £25. For that you should have got two
beautiful dresses £10 and a bike £5, and £10 pocket money, but I dont
know where it's all gone. I'm afraid you're not old enough to be trusted
with money! This is not a scold my poor sweet treasure, but a little
gentle kind of a warning. That is harmless isn't it.

I'm going to Parsons tomorrow to show him my neck, its swelling
a little again, but nothing much.

My cough is keeping nearly all right which is a good sign. I hear
Lady Gregory has had influenza so I'm afraid to go in there for fear of
catching it.

We'll easily get 'digs' of some kind when we want them tempo-
rary furnished ones if necessary till we can settle into our permanent
ones. Did I tell you I have got Jack Yeats' sketch of the stoker framed
and the glass put into the etching? I am quite proud of them, I have
them in my little study and they look very nice. That is my first step
towards furnishing! Nish! *I'm* as unpractical an ass as you are—that's
the worst of it—fancy marrying and setting up with no furniture but
three pictures and a *suggan* chair[1] and a fiddle! Yet that's what I'm at
now. This is a long rambling letter with not much in it I'm afraid. Is it
too long?

I am not seeing anyone and I have nothing interesting to write about. I got the last 'page' proofs of the *Tinkers* last night   it will be out in a few days now. That will be my *third* book published this year.

                    Your old Tramp.

Write at once

By the way you've worked out a *most elegant* 'hand' for the outside of my envelopes at least, is it a fine pen or what?

1. *Sugan* or *suggan* is the Irish term for a hard twisted rope made of straw or heather.

[*TCD/GS278–9*]   [*Glendalough House*]
                                             December 3rd/07

My dearest Life

I am looking out for a letter from you—it is a quarter past one and the post passes at half past. If none comes I— I— I— I'm writing this beforehand that I may have something to send you in any case. How are you all? I was in, with Lady G. and Yeats yesterday and they told me that Sally had been left behind in Manchester—poor wretch —it is too bad.

Lady Gregory went out to call on Mrs Russell in the afternoon and Yeats set to to find out my stars. He says there is a very big event coming off in my life in the next month—a good one on the whole though with unusual circumstances and some breaking of ties. Isn't [it] curious? He evidently had no idea what it was—and I pretended not [to] know either—he thought it had something to do with the theatre or going to America. At the end he said "If you were a different sort of man, I'd say it was a wild imprudent love-affair." Nish!

No post yet I'm very anxious—it is the hour now I must watch out —— Here he is, a letter!

I am so very sorry to hear of rows, do try to keep cool and quiet it is not worth while to make yourself ill or uneasy for anything our friends may say. There is nothing like keeping a check on one's self then no one can gain a point anywhere. I am very uneasy about you, my poor dear Life, away there with no one to advise or help you. Try and be happy and quiet and do your work and let the rest slide. You'll be coming home to me in 10 days now, and then we'll be together all ways my dear love.

I told Yeats the story of my Deirdre last night. He was very much pleased with it I think. *He asked* me to get the hour of your birth and date, I think he believes in you a great deal—we all do—I could say more that would please you perhaps but I had better not. I wonder when you will get this I shall be *very anxious* for further news.

Does the rug keep you comfortable? I am so glad you have it this cold weather, it is very cold here. I must go to the post now. Good bye my hundred treasures remember you are my little wife and keep as quiet as I did when I had words with our friend.[1]

Your old Tramp.

P.S.   Curiously I dreamed on Saturday night that Fay was in some way scoffing [at] Sally's illness. You see I keep an eye on you! I have got the £3 from Prague, all right at last.

---

1. During this tour the antipathy between Willie Fay and the company was becoming more and more obvious, leading at last to his demand that the Directors give him complete control over the company; when they refused, he resigned five weeks later.

[*TCD*]

Glendalough House
Dec.4th/07

My dearest Love

How are things going? I hoped there would be a letter today to reassure me—yesterday's was so stormy but none has come. I do not wonder, you must find it hard to get time to do anything.

Dear Love do write me a nice letter. I am uneasy about you somehow. I am *glad* Dossy is there to look after you. Nish! Never say I am jealous again.

Little Heart you dont know how much feeling I have for you. You are like my child, and my little wife, and my good angel, and my greatest friend, all in one! I dont believe there has been a woman in Ireland loved the way I love for you a thousand years. When that is so, what do the Fays matter? Be punctual and polite, and do not lose your temper, then nothing they say can have any power over you.

Now I am going to town.

Write a lot to

Your old lonely Tramp.

[*TCD/GS280*]   Glendalough House
                                                    Dec 6th/07

My dearest Treasure

   I got your letters and the cuttings yesterday but I did not manage
to write to you as I had written the day before and I was very busy.
I have several rather important things to tell you. I have had long
talks with the Directors and we have come to some important decisions
which you will hear of in good time. Meanwhile you are to stop
Kerrigan leaving the company—if he is taking his notice seriously—
just tell [him] to stay on till he has seen the Directors this PRIVATELY
from me. If he is not really meaning to leave dont say anything
about it. You know, I suppose, that we are to have Miss H[orniman's]
subsidy for *three full years* more—if nothing unforeseen happens—that
is great news for 'US-TWO'—as by three years I ought to have a much
better position than I have now and I think we'll come through all
right—so that it is really worth while to fight the battle on and we
the Directors are going to do it at all risks. We have just got a really
excellent play from a new young man—in many ways really clever and
good so that we wont run short of work this season.[1] I was at the New
Arts Club *debate* with Yeats the other night and I was delighted to find
him the favourite and star of the evening with a crowd of young men
hanging on his words—new clever young men who have nothing to do
with all the worn out cliques. Trinity College also is becoming vehe-
mently interested in Irish things so that if we can only get *good plays*
we may strike a new audience any day. Remember the Abbey is so small
and our expenses are so small that quite a few people out of the crowds
who go to Martin Harvey, say, would put us on our feet. So keep your
spirits up and Sally's up, for my own have come up greatly. MacKenna
is coming over very soon and he will be of the greatest use to us
I think on the Irish Press. I remember I spoke gloomily about the
Abbey a few days ago, but somehow the new play and the new sympathetic people at the Arts Club have given me new hope. Long may it
last.
   Yeats got a wire on Wednesday night to say Sally was taking
Dervorgilla. Did she get there in time. I think the Directors must know
that we are getting married, they probably have no idea it is so close.
We talked about you and the communications I have with you, quite
frankly of course. Now be discreet and dont let Kerrigan or anyone

leave. THIS IS VERY PRIVATE it is likely that on any further tours one of the Directors will go also—so perhaps you and I will be on the road again together before too long. Nish!

I wonder shall I hear from you today. I have written you two extra letters and you haven't written one *extra letter* to me. You little *B. Rose!* I was touched and obliged and grateful for your list of the Chaucer. I think the 8/0 or rather 6/0 one is the one I want. If it is complete and fairly good print that is the one. If not probably the one in three vols 3/0 net would do, but the 6/0 one I imagine is many times the better.

I went to Parsons the other day he thinks I am *"grand"*, my neck and chest are very satisfactory. I had not been quite well this week with queer pains in a portion of my inside, but he couldn't find anything the matter so I hope it is nothing. I am very anxious now of course as the time—our time is coming on—I am better today. Remember not to over do yourself *next week.*

I hope you understand Dear Heart that when I write about money-matters, it is for *our sakes* not for my sake.

I am going in to see Roberts today to try and arrange a copy-right reading of the *Tinkers,* we may publish it next Tuesday if all goes well. I have written a preface I wish I had you here to advise me about it.[2] Good bye my one treasure

Your old Tramp

Send me your *Edinburgh address* again please, I'll write there next on Sunday.

P.S.   Your letter has just come I am sending on cutting to Lady Gregory. It was a *very great shame* to do *what they did.* I mean Vaughan[3] and Fay.

---

1. Probably *The Piper* by Conal O'Riordan (1874–1948), who wrote plays under the pseudonym "Norreys Connell" and at Synge's death became Managing Director for a short time. Two other plays, *Time* and *An Imaginary Conversation,* were produced in 1909, but after this he left the Abbey and later concentrated on novels.

2. *The Tinker's Wedding* was copyrighted on December 23rd and finally published three days before the end of 1907. The Directors thought it "too dangerous" for the Abbey, and it was first produced in London after Synge's death.

3. Ernest Vaughan became business manager after Payne left the company; a member of W. G. Fay's Comedy Combination in the 1890's, Vaughan's name first appears on Abbey Theatre programmes in April 1907, and he resigned when the Fays did in January 1908.

[*TCD/GS281*]   [*Glendalough House*]
                                                         Dec 8th [*1907*]

Dearest LOVE

This is the second day without a letter and I need not say that I
am ⟨greatly⟩ disappointed and ⟨most anxious and upset⟩. (I'm *not
now* as I understand Dear Heart.) I have not got your Edinburgh
address—you gave it to me but I am afraid I have lost it—so I will
not be able to send you this till I hear from you. ⟨I wish you would
[write] me the merest line——two words rather than leave me without
news. I make myself ill with uneasiness.⟩ (Amn't I a born ass?) I dare
say you were very busy your last day in Glasgow and perhaps missed
the post—and that has spoiled my day. (I will be cheerful in spite of it,
but I got an AWFUL *qualm* when the post passed!) It seems *years* since
you went away, I feel like a blind man or a deaf man, or something
queer and horrible ever since. I cant *live* now without you. Thank
Heaven in a week now the tour will be over.

I am getting better I think, but I'm not altogether flourishing yet.
Nothing much is the matter but I've queer pains in my inside. They
are going away I think. I got a letter from Brodzky[1] yesterday asking
for particulars for an article he is doing on *my work* for Australia.

                                                      Your old Tramp

P.S.   I realized that *I'm* a fool, your letters never come till midday
from Glasgow so I could not hear from you this morning if you posted
yesterday as usual. I ought not to send this perhaps but you wont
mind my being lonesome.   T.

I've found your address so this goes. Good Luck!

P.S.   I wonder how all your affairs are going now. Keep every body
quiet till the tour is over, then there will be opportunities of saying
anything that has to be said.

I told Lady Gregory about Sally—she *very* STRONGLY disapproves of
what was done—I mean about letting Mrs Fay appear in Sally's name.
This is *private,* but you can tell Sally if you like that we disapprove
of the course that was taken, but there is no use, for the moment,
crying over spilt milk—it will not happen again.

I hop with delight when I think how nearly the tour is over. I have
never known such a long fortnight.

                                             Your very lonesome old Tramp.

Take care of yourself my own dear Treasure. Be cheerful.

1. Leon Brodzky, an Australian journalist who later changed his name to Spencer Brodney; his article "The Lesson of the Irish Theatre," describing his first encounter with the Irish players on tour at Hull, appeared in *The British-Australasian*, 9 August 1906. Synge's letters to Brodzky are in Trinity College, Dublin.

[*AS*]   Glendalough House
                                                  Dec 10th [*1907*]

Dearest Love

I wired to you this morning to look for the letter I wrote on Sunday to the address you gave me before the tour—you must find it somehow. Try the General Post if it is not at the 'digs' Mrs Strathdee 26 Grindley Street, and if that won't do write to the Dead Letter Office— they will tell you where at the G.P.O. Edinburgh. It is intolerable to think of my intimate letter to you being opened and laughed at in the Post Office and then sent back to me here "Tramp", Glendalough House ⟨I feel more humiliated at the thought than words can tell you. I shall be the laughing stock of the servants and the whole family, and all because you didn't think it worth while to send me a post card with your address,⟩ and because I —⟨poor fool⟩—thought you would be lonely getting into Edinburgh and finding no letter for you on Monday. I thought you valued my poor letters, such as they are, but now you have left me half a week without your address. You could have written on Sunday I suppose if you had cared to. However this is not to scold you, only I feel sad somehow. Dont, for a moment get it into your head that I am writing crossly my poor little heart. I dont want to make you unhappy for a quarter of a second. You are my whole life remember.

[*TCD/GS281*] ⟨Your address I am sorry I have written at such length.⟩ The Chaucer came yesterday it is charming Dear Heart and I'm *very grateful indeed.* I am enquiring about a 'digs' and will have one soon I hope. I am better I think, but I've queer pains still a little. I am off to town now 1 o'clock to arrange about *Tinker's Wedding* copy-right show which is on tonight I believe.

I needn't say that what you write about the money—the money I lent you—*is nonsense.* All I have is yours now and you know it. Why is it that you get so get so careless about my letters when you have been such a little time away? It makes me a little low Dear Heart though I dont suppose you mean it. I'm afraid you've taken up what I said about the money quite wrong I never wanted you to send me any, *I never give it a thought.*

The Chaucer was only 5/0 post free so they sent me 1/6 back I've bought another book with it   you are a good little changling after all. I was in Lane's new gallery today. They have my portrait by old Yeats *not* a good one.[1]

Be sure to read this cheerfully it isn't a scold.

Take care of *yourself this week*

P.S.   *Deirdre* is getting on I think, but slowly now. I over-worked myself for a while and I'm taking it a little easier now. In any case at this stage one cannot go fast. I am so glad to think the tour will be over now in four days it has seemed interminable—months since you went away.

Please write by return to say if you have got my letter. Dont let this letter upset you in any way I am writing in a very great hurry Dearest Treasurette.

Your old Tramp with many blessings.

---

1. Lady Gregory's nephew, Hugh Lane (1876–1915), had been primarily responsible for the new Municipal Gallery of Modern Art, 17, Harcourt Street, which was officially opened on 20 January 1908. Synge wrote an article about it for the *Manchester Guardian,* 24 January 1908 (see Oxford *Prose,* 390–392). The portrait by John Butler Yeats referred to here was commissioned by Hugh Lane and presented to the Municipal Gallery.

[*TCD*]   [*Glendalough House*]
                                                          Dec 11th/07

Dearest Little Heart

Your letter has come   I am so glad you got the other I felt upset about it yesterday. I wrote part of my letter yesterday to you twice over I was so afraid of saying something that might upset you   I hope it was all right.

I am counting the hours till we meet. This is a most lovely day and I am just off on my bicycle for a ride to the Scalp or somewhere. By the

way when do you get home and what day do you leave your present address. There should not have been 'card' in the wire I put "Letter sent etc". Write to me every day now I cant hold out any longer. In a hurry your old
> Tramp

Yes I *often* dream of you.

[*TCD/GS281*]   Glendalough House
Dec 13th/07

Dearest Love

Your letter came last night at six o'clock and gave me a pleasant surprise, they dont generally come at that hour.

I laughed at your cranky morning scrawl. You little B. rose you ought to have more sense! I am overjoyed to think that I shall see you so soon again. If you are very tired after your journey on Monday and *unwell* perhaps you ought not to come down on Monday. It might be too much for you. I could meet you in town perhaps. Of course we must meet as soon as ever we can, but you must not start off by making yourself ill. My inside is making me uneasy—I was rather worse after my bicycle ride the other day. I hope it is only fancy, but I think I'll have to go to Parsons again. Yes I see they are doing A.E.'s *Deirdre* at the Abbey tonight. Madame M. is Lavarcham I think. There was an absurd "puff" about the play in the *I. Times* today written evidently by one of themselves. They should have more sense.[1] I can hardly believe that this is the last letter to you on tour I cant write now you are coming so soon take care of yourself on the journey and be *very good*.
> Your old Tramp

Let me know of course if there is any change in your time for arriving.
J. M. S.

1. *Deirdre,* by the poet, painter, mystic, and economist George Russell ("Æ") (1867–1935), was first produced by the Irish National Dramatic Society in 1902 and was frequently revived by amateur companies around Dublin; this production by the Theatre of Ireland was presented in the Abbey Theatre with Constance Markiewicz playing the role of the old Nurse/Druidess.

[*TCD*]   Glendalough House
                                                   Kingstown
                                                Dec 14 [*1907*]

Dearest Heart

I got your letter (Friday's) last night, I am glad you had one pleasant day at least during your tour.

Isn't [it] grand that you're coming back at last—I am counting the minutes till tomorrow—This tour has been intolerable and interminable, I seem to have been sitting here making myself old with looking on the days and they passing me by for the last ten years.[1]

I wonder how you are. It is likely to be foggy tonight so you may be late getting in tomorrow morning. I think Tuesday would be a better day for you to come out here. My mother's friend goes away on Tuesday morning early, so she'll be fussing about all day on Monday. Will you meet me in town tomorrow Monday afternoon and have tea somewhere, I couldn't let a day pass without seeing you. If you are tired and not up for much I could meet you at *twenty* to *four* at Tara St. and just go as far as the D.B.C.[2] Or if you are pretty fit I could meet you at *twenty to three*. Of course if you are *feeling done up you* had better stay quiet, and wait till Tuesday. I wont go up unless I get a letter *posted before eleven,* or *a wire* to say the hour and place. A wire would be the safer perhaps as the post is getting clogged with Xmas letters. If you do not meet me will you please write as soon as you can to say how you are. Also please tell me if Kerrigan still means to leave, and if so give me his address and tell him I would like to see him before he does anything definite. You need not, of course, say anything of this to the Fays.

I wish to————————it was tomorrow. I'm better I think, I haven't got digs yet I'll tell you why tomorrow, a thousand blessings

                                                Your old T.

1. Synge is parodying Nora Burke's speech in *The Shadow of the Glen.*
2. There was a Dublin Bread Company tea room in Sackville Street (now O'Connell Street) which would be fairly near Molly's home in Mary Street.

[*TCD*]   Glendalough House
                                                  Dec 18th/07

Dearest Heart

What about tomorrow? Where shall we meet? Can we meet? I wonder if you are rehearsing in the evening? You had better write to me before eleven and be sure to post in time to say if you will come out or if I should meet you in town. If I am to meet you I might not catch the quarter past two train if the post is late. Then I would go by the next write anyhow. If there is any put off I'll wire.

I saw Kerrigan and Fay today
I must run with this to the post
                    Your Old Tramp

[*AS*]   Glendalough [*House*]
                                                   Saturday
                                                   21/12/07

Dearest Life

The doctor says I'm all right so come down tomorrow by the quarter to eleven—dont miss it—if its fine. The doctor made me nervous the last time I was there, thats why I went back today. If its wet tomorrow of course, come by the quarter to two. If I'm not at the eleven train—by any chance—come to the house.

By the way I heard from Quinn today. He is going to take the *Playboy* MS after all and send me whatever he thinks it is worth! He is also going to guarantee an edition of all my plays in America next spring.[1] Nish! This is all between ourselves of course. So till tomorrow
                                        Your old Tramp

1. Although Synge was discussing the possibility of an American edition of his plays with George Roberts of Maunsel and Co., the plan did not materialize.

[*TCD*]   Glendalough House
                                                                              Dec 22nd/XII/07
Dearest Love

   I see that the carols are on tomorrow at [St.] Patricks and I think
we'd better go to them. Will you meet me at Tara Street at 20 to three
tomorrow (*Tuesday*) afternoon and we'll go. If its wet—very wet—I
wont go. My mother says I ought to give you an umbrella for Xmas
would you like that?

   Hadn't we a great day yesterday This was a magnificent day here
but I'm told it was wretched in town.

   I rode round near the Scalp and through Loughlinstown and I've
done a great day's work also—I *must* work again, but I've got lazy
somehow. I'm very well I hope you weren't too tired If you cant meet
me tomorrow send me word. If its wet come out here if you can.

                                                              Your old Tramp
Only dont miss me.

[*TCD*]   Glendalough House
                                                                              Dec 28th /07
Dearest Love

   I was too busy and too tired out afterwards to write to you yesterday. Are you all right? I think it is too cold and wretched to go out
for a long day tomorrow. Come down by the quarter to two—and if it
is very fine perhaps I'll meet you at [the] train and take you for a walk
or else we can be here. Come here of course if I'm not at the train.
Dont bring rug or picture with you in case I meet you.

   I have no fresh news since except that I'm hard at work as
usual and that I'd pains in my inside last night. I think it's the cold.
Keep yourself as warm as you can the wind is very bitter.

   We'd a nice little time on Thursday hadn't we? I heard your train
passing up after I got home, and I pitied you for having to wait so
long. No word from Mrs Cassidy yet.[1] Till tomorrow

                                                              Your old
                                                              Tramp

   1. Another enquiry about digs.

Molly Allgood, about 1907

Spreading the News, *1907*

Molly Allgood, about 1909

[*Texas*]   Glendalough House
                                                  Jan 3rd 08

Dearest Child

    I have come to the conclusion that you MUST have warmer clothes
before you go away[1] You'll get some bad illness if you dont. Please buy
yourself some warm things tomorrow morning and I'll lend you the
price you can pay me off when you are clear of the theatre. Shall I send
you in my rug by the tram tomorrow. You *must* have it. There were
five degrees of frost outside my window this morning so it is quite
too cold for you to be dressed as you are.

    Another thing can you lock up your picture *really safely* before you
go away or would it be safer with me? We must not lose it.

                                             Your old Tramp

I have been working at Kerry stuff today and found it a pleasant
change. Remember this is quite serious you know what will *happen*
next week and if [you] get a chill you may get very seriously *ill*.

---

1. The company went to Galway for a week on 5 January.

[*TCD/GS282*]   [*Glendalough House*]
                                        Tuesday [*7 January 1908*]

Dearest Heart

    I was surprised and delighted to get your little letter last night—I
did not expect it till this morning—and to hear that you are down
safe. The weather changed here too on Sunday evening and it has been
very mild since, it will be cold again in a day or two. I heard from
Mrs Cassidy on Sunday and I'm going out to see her rooms tomorrow
I think, her house is in Upper Rathmines. That would be all right.

    Sunday was a long day without you—I went for two little walks,
and then wrote to Quinn and other letters in the evening. Yesterday
Fraulein von Eiken—the German lady—came to see us in the afternoon, so that made a little variety.

    I am working at Deirdre again—I cant keep away from her, till I
get her right. I have changed the first half of the first Act a good deal,
by making Fergus go into the inner room instead of Conchubor, and

giving C. an important scene with Lav[archam]. Then D. comes in and
Lav goes out and D. and C. have an important scene together. That—
when it is done—will make the whole thing drama instead of narrative,
and there will be a good contrast between the scenes of Deirdre and
Conchubor, and Deirdre and Naisi. It is quite useless trying to rush it,
I must take my time and let them all grow by degrees. I wonder have
you seen Lady Gregory. Be very careful of yourself and dont go out in a
boat with the company or do anything foolish. If all goes well I may
move into Mrs Cassidy's next week. Wont that be fun.

The two pictures have come at last, but they are not well done
and I am not happy about them. He has put the mounts too close in
so I am afraid they are ruined *forever*. I have hung you up too opposite
my table—where the pampooties¹ were—you look very nice, but I get
tired of your cigarette. Its a pity you're smoking. He has also put in
your glasses and that makes you look as if you'd a black eye at a little
distance. However, you're charming all the same. Write me a long letter
about every thing.

Your old
T.

---

1. Traditional footgear of the Aran Islander; Synge describes how a pair were made
for him in *The Aran Islands,* Oxford *Prose,* pp. 65–66.

[*TCD*]   G.H.
                                                  K. 9.I.08

Dearest Heart

I got your two letters all right thanks. I'm sorry to hear you've been
coughing. Tomorrow night you'll be done with Galway, I suppose, so
you'll be home on Saturday, and we'll meet on Sunday. Tell me what
time you leave on Saturday, but I suppose in any case there will not
be time for me to write to you again. I didn't go to Mrs Cassidy
yesterday as it was a very bad day, but I'm going this afternoon as
it is fine again. I'm sure I told you about the German Lady. She is an
elder sister of the mug one—and she called here to see me weeks
ago but I was out, then I called on her but she was out, so at last

we invited her here to tea. She is going away again in a few days! and she's about 50.[1]

The blotting paper was a feeble attempt to make your letter 'fat', but evidently [it] didn't serve its purpose. I think you're losing your sense of humour. Nish! You've written me very nice letters this tour I hope I'll have another tonight.

It is queer that Lady G. hasn't turned up. I wonder if her son is at home I haven't heard. I had a letter from Yeats yesterday he'll be over soon. I dont seem to have much to tell you today—it has been so wild I haven't been doing anything. Florence Ross is in town today getting lodgings for herself I wonder how she'll get on. I sent the P.B. MS. to Quinn yesterday—that is private remember—I wonder what he'll send me for it. I am working quietly and slowly at Deirdre and gradually improving her, I think. There is no use doing much at her now at a time, as what I have to do can only be done when I am fresh and clear.

I wonder what I'll think of Mrs Cassidy and her place. I feel in a fuss, as it is a difficult bargain to make. I wish you could do it for me In future that'll be your—*one of your*—little jobs. Let me know when you are to be home dear Heart and leave your address behind you in case I write again and the letter does not catch you.

Your old
T.

I am *very glad* your flannels are comfortable.

1. One of the von Eiken sisters with whom Synge stayed on his first trip to Germany in 1895 and who were to remain good friends until his death; "the mug" refers to a gift decorated for him, probably by the youngest of the sisters, Valeska, with a violin and a scroll with the German anthem written on it.

[*TCD*]   [*Glendalough House*]
Jan 10th 08

Dearest Heart

I'm not sure that this will find you, as you didn't tell me when you leave, so I'll send a line only to show that I'm dutiful![1] I got your letter last night, and I'm sorry to hear of bad houses. I went to Mrs Cassidy's yesterday but she was out and had left a message that I was to wait for her for an hour. I went over the house with a small boy who let me in, and then I went off. I dont much like either the house or neighbour-hood—Upper Rathmines—so I'm putting an ad. in the *Times* tomorrow, and writing to another place besides. Florence Ross has given—or at least lent the bed—so that's all right, but there's no use dragging one's things into a dreary house where one would not be cheerful. I'm just off for my walk, it is very cold I've written 5 letters and a card this morning.

> Your O T.

1. Synge has written on the envelope "If not found please forward to the Abbey Theatre, Dublin."

[*TCD*]   Glendalough [*House*]
                                                          11.I.08

Dearest Heart

I didn't write to you this morning as Yeats was in town and I had to see him. I'm in great spirits and joy to think I'll see you tomorrow come by the quarter to two as you say. Did you get my letter this morning in Galway? I'm writing this in a hurry I've been in town with Yeats and Lady G. all the afternoon, and just got home to supper.

L.G. told me how bad the House was on Friday, you seem to have had ill luck.

I had another good go at Deirdre this morning I think she's coming on. Yeats says Masefield has written a wonderful play the best English play since the Elizabethans so I'll have to look out,[1] but perhaps he excepts me because I'm Irish.

Dont miss your train tomorrow and be in a very good humour. My ad is in the *Irish Times,* I wonder what answers I'll get

> Your old T.

1. *The Tragedy of Nan,* published in 1909.

[*TCD/GS283*]   [*Glendalough House*]
                                                                    13.I.08

Dearest Child

It has occurred to me that the best thing you could do—*much* the
best thing I think for many reasons—would be to take a room on
business footing, paying usual rent, from your brother-in-law T.
Callender, for the few weeks till we can finish our arrangements. It
would simplify matters in several ways—I feel strongly so—and it
would be convenient as we would then, I think, be in a range of Peter's
Church where the curate is an old friend of mine.[1]

I am writing this in a hurry to catch you in the morning.

                                                              Your old T.

1. The Dublin City Directory for 1908 names Rev. S. F. H. Robinson, M.A., as senior
curate of St. Peter's Church of Ireland, Aungier Street. Synge may have met Robinson
through Rev. T. A. Harvey, curate at St. Stephen's Church and later Bishop of Cashel, a
friend of Robert Gregory and Jack B. Yeats, and a frequent visitor to Coole.

[*TCD*]   Glendalough Ho
                                                              Jan 14th [*1908*]

Dearest Heart

I was greatly relieved to get your note yesterday to say that all
was quiet—keep it so at any cost, for the present.

I hoped for a note this morning to tell me what had happened last
night—you have heard the great news of course about the Fays[1]—
perhaps I shall hear by the middle of the day post. I am going to the
doctor this afternoon, and then to the Directors, and tomorrow morning
I am to see Lane at his gallery as I am to do an article on it for the
Manchester Guardian so I dont know when I'll be free   I may wire to
you about the middle of the day to make an appointment somewhere.
I have had an answer to my advertisement that seems very promising
indeed in Rathgar—I'll have to go out to it, too, sometime. It is a
thousand pities I am so busy this week as you are free on the three
latter days I hope we may be together. This is all I can write now till
I see if a letter comes.

No letter—I am a little uneasy please write at once and fully

Your old T.

I was in with the Directors yesterday they wired for me.

J. M.

1. Willie Fay had finally tendered his resignation on 13th January; his wife Brigit O'Dempsey, his brother Frank, and Ernest Vaughan also resigned. Throughout the discussions, Synge had been acting as liaison between the Directors and the players.

[*TCD*]   [*Glendalough House*]

Jan 15/08

Dearest Nish

I'm as sorry as you are for difficulty in seeing you—I will *wire* to you today to come down if I am free in the afternoon. I'm just off to town now.

We feel very confident about the Abbey now—I have some things to tell you that will interest you. I wonder what F.J.F. wants to do with Sally.

I dont think you're at all fair in calling yourself a *little* ass—I think you're a BIG one. Nish!—I write to you to say I am going to be with [you] the three last days of the week, in any case, and you write a hullabuloo about the *whole* dreary week! Nish.

Please Heaven I'll have you today we might have a good walk somewhere be ready for your wire. Though I cannot be sure yet— tomorrow *I am* sure of. Now I've just time for my train.

J.M.S.T.

The doctor says I'm 'grand'.

[*TCD*]   Glendalough Ho

Jan 15th /08

My dearest Little Treasure

I am very lonely tonight, and I am longing to have you here to rest and comfort me. I was at business of various kinds all day and I am giddy with weariness. I could not go out to Rathgar so I am writing to the people to say I'll go tomorrow. Dont be annoyed about it—it was quite impossible for me to go. The day was extraordinarily close and heavy and I feel utterly fagged—that'll pass of course.

There is the usual treasury call tomorrow morning   you'll find Yeats and J.M. Synge doling out the money. Afterwards we W.B.Y. and I have newspaper men to see so I wont be free for you. Please dont be unreasonable or annoyed, I may see you in the evening though it's not very likely—and I'll see [you] on Saturday I hope and of course on Sunday. Dont be depressed about it, I'll soon have you always.

It's out about Sally and Tree—the Editor of the *Mail* told Yeats and me about it at 1.30, and another man—who is a secret told *us* at 2.15—that's the way secrets are kept in this country. I'm glad it's known.[1] I thought I would have had a letter from you today   perhaps one will come tonight I hope you weren't too tired. Be nice and helpful tomorrow and believe I'm dying down dead to be with you. I feel as if I hadn't been nice enough to you yesterday. Was I?

Your old T.

---

1. Beerbohm Tree had asked Sara Allgood to act in one of his Shakespeare productions in February; although this request was not granted, the Directors did allow her to act the part of Isabella in *Measure for Measure,* directed by William Poel, at the opening of Miss Horniman's theatre in Manchester the week of 11 April 1908, and on 21 and 22 April at Stratford-on-Avon.

[TCD]   [*Glendalough House*]
                              Friday night.   Jan. [*17. 1908*]

Dearest Heart

I saw the rooms today three—one with place for gas-cooker—*with attendance* and cooking for 12/6 a week. I dont *very* much like the house and the landlady has a sore nose—those are the drawbacks—I wish you'd come down tomorrow and talk it over with me. Come by the quarter to two unless I wire some other hour—If you cant come send me a card.

In haste your old T.

[*TCD*]   Glendalough House
                                           Jan 21st [*1908*]

Dearest Love

I got a cheque for £6. last night—returned Income Tax—and I want
you to make out a list of what we want most up to that amount. I
suppose you could get some of the things for us, I expect you're a better
hand than I am. I feel in great spirits today. It's funny the qualms we
get but natural enough I suppose.

I believe I'm to go to a supper at the Nassau tonight in honour of
Hugh Lane, and I'll probably be in the Abbey tomorrow morning. On
Thursday evening we must meet and talk over our affairs. I wish you'd
get Whittaker![1]

Now I must write to [?Mme MacKenna] I was too late and too tired
last night—and then I have my article to write and post today—God
help me—

          Your old T——

1. Perhaps the solicitor H. T. Whitaker, whose office is listed in Thom's Directory as
42 Fleet Street, Dublin.

[*TCD*]   [*Glendalough House*]
                                           Wednesday Jan 22nd [*1908*]
                                           3 P.M.

My own dearest Child

I'm sure you thought I was 'horrid' today, there were many things
to think of so I couldn't well help it. I got away just before two and
slipped down here by the 2 train. You looked very nice and quiet and
pretty this morning I felt proud of you though you didn't guess it!
Isn't it a pity, though, to wear out your nice new dress by hacking it
down at the theatre. It'll be shabby in a week! It is trying for both of
us to be half seeing ourselves, and not able to talk, next week when
I move it will be better I hope. Poor Yeats with his bad sight and
everything is very helpless, and I have to look after him a bit. The
question you spoke of about 'Stage-Management' is serious enough,
we'll feel our way for a day or two and see what can be done. Casey is

a nice fellow I think, like you I'm not quite sure how much I like his play, it has good scenes especially in the first act.[1] I suppose I shall go in tomorrow again but I'm afraid I wont be able to get away with you —it is just possible however—perhaps on Friday afternoon I might get you down here.

I dont know what I am going to do about moving. I must get your advice. I wonder if you're depressed, my poor changling, because I ran away from you today, if you could look into my little bosom and see how I am yearning for you, you'd forgive me write me a nice letter

Your old T.

I have just finished my article and I am posting it with this that is something done.

1. *The Man Who Missed the Tide*, by William Francis Casey (1884–1957), was first produced by the Abbey Theatre 13 February 1908, and a revised version 21 October 1908; a second play, *The Suburban Groove*, was produced 1 October 1908. In 1913 Casey joined the staff of *The Times*, of which he was Editor from 1948 to 1952.

[*TCD*]   Glendalough Ho
                                                            Jan 28th '08
Dearest Heart
    Will you please send me your basket tomorrow morning. I think I will not be able to get on without it. I am having the cart on Thursday and I suppose I'll get over myself on Friday or Saturday or Monday at the latest. Did you get Whittaker?
    By the way I've a crow to pluck with you about today. Why didn't you come with me? I waited as long as I could at the scenery room door then I streeled along half thinking you might come after me. Then I saw you and when I went back to meet you, you ran away. I felt upset for the moment, and I couldn't eat my dinner when I got home. Somehow, changeling, you dont try and make things easy for us—for you

and me, I mean—at the Theatre. It is a difficult position for the moment, and—well there's no good bothering about it now.

I dont know where to begin my packing it's a rather ghastly job. I think I'll [go] out and see Mme [MacKenna] tomorrow, I may not, however and I may wire to your house to ask you down, but I am not sure. There is a lecture in town in the afternoon I rather want to go to.

I am sad somehow today. Why do you tease me so much? It is easy to give me pain. Your old

Tramp

[NLI]   [*47 York Road Rathmines*[1]
                                                            early Spring 1908]

Dear Little Heart

Come to tea, and bring eggs with you I was *overjoyed* to get your note this morning—

My poor pet!

No time for more

Your old T.

1. In preparation for their marriage, Synge had taken rooms on 2 February 1908.

[AS]   [*47 York Road Rathmines*
                                                            Spring 1908]

My Dearest Love

Henderson kept me so long today that I am only getting down by the quarter to one. I will come back as soon as ever I can, but I may not be back till five. Type and amuse yourself, my poor heart, till I come, perhaps I'll be back at four.

Your old T.—(Its a long time since I've written that.)

[*TCD*]   [*47 York Road Rathmines*]
                                                           Tuesday [*24 March 1908*]

Dearest

   I have developed a big cold in my head. Will you bring me some
eggs, butter and marmalade if you can, and the Molière script[1] I'll be
here all day. I'm not very bad.

   Come early
   Yours *affectionately*
      J. M. S.

---

   1. Now that the Fays had left, Synge was a great deal more active in the management
of the theatre; Lady Gregory's translation of *The Rogueries of Scapin* was first produced
under his direction on 4 April, Molly playing Zerbinette.

[*Texas*]   [*47 York Road Rathmines*
                                                           25 April? 1908]

Dearest

   Dont be uneasy about me. Henderson told *me* about six times that
I had a tumour, but he knows about as much about it as a tom cat.
I'm to see Ball on Monday I believe and we wont know much till then.

   I'm going out now three o'clock its a pity I cant meet you. Wait
for me tomorrow Saturday between 3 and four at the Abbey and I'll
come over if I can and we can go to the Park. Nish

                                                           Your old T

[*TCD*]   [*Elpis Nursing Home*
                                                           4 May 1908][1]

Dearest

   Will you come and see me here at four today as I am not to go out.
The operation is to be tomorrow.[2]

                                                           Your old T

1. Synge wrote Molly a second letter on this date, addressed to her c/o the Abbey Theatre with the instruction *to be sent in cover in case of death;* Molly received it a year later, see p. 317.

2. The doctors had located a lump in Synge's side, and he entered Elpis on 30 April for examination.

[*TCD*]   [*Elpis Nursing Home*
mid-May 1908]

Dearest Heart

Sorry to hear you are not well, I hope you will get all right soon.

I have been *very bad* for last 24 hours with my stomach, but I am a little easier to night though still in bed with a poultice all over me. I am afraid, Dear Heart, we must put off your visit again for a day or two. I shall be in bed tomorrow again, and in this state we could get no good of a visit. Dont be uneasy about me, I think I am over the worst now, but I have to stay very quiet indeed.[1] Write plenty of nice letters to me to keep me going

With endless love
Your old Tramp.

1. On 12 May Mrs Synge reported to her son Robert, "Ball had no hope of our dear boy's life . . . the tumor or abscess is still there as it cannot be removed. . . . He has no idea he was in danger—the Drs. hid it from him completely."

[*TCD*]   Elpis
Thursday [*11 June 1908*]

Dearest

This is a line only (as I'm rather tired from one thing or other) to tell you I'm getting on very well. I've been up since 12.45 and it's 7 now.

I got your note last night and I hope I'll have a longer one this evening. I'm sorry your weather is so bad.[1] I haven't many visitors now, F Ross today and my younger nephew. S. Gwynn called this morning but I didn't see him as I was in bed. He wrote me a very kind note. Lady G. is gone, I haven't seen Henderson yet.

Goodby Dear Heart,

J. M. S.

---

1. Molly and Sally had gone to Balbriggan until 16 June for a brief holiday after the theatre closed for the season.

[*TCD*]   [*Elpis Nursing Home*]
                                                    Saturday [*13 June 1908*]

Dearest

I have had two more *little* notes from you—one without a stamp but I only smiled—why dont you write me a good long letter, as I thought you promised, of three or four sheets? I hope you haven't made yourself ill doing too much rowing or anything. Why do you go to the W[rights] so often, that sort of thing gets a great nuisance after a day or two. Are you coming home on Tuesday? I had a visit from my mother yesterday and then Henderson came, and nearly wept over me when he talked [of] my bad times. I got him to lend me a book *Tristram and Iseult* that I wanted very much to read, so he left it round this morning and I am happy with it for the day.

I seem to have lots of things to write to you, but I wont write them as you are treating me so shabbily. Nish. Are you ashamed of yourself! Sirrah! d— little b.

My gap is still closing slowly but nothing is settled about going away

Give my love to Sally

                                                    Your old
                                                        T.

[*TCD*]   [*Elpis Nursing Home*]
                                                       Sunday
                                                  June 14/08

Dearest Child

I got your note this morning and I nearly got tears in my eyes—
you know I'm shaky still—it was so short and scrappy and external.

I'm very sorry you are feeling so unwell, I hope you're taking care
of yourself. You needn't have taken the stampless letter so much to
heart, you poor child, I'm afraid I'm a great tyrant, you are in such awe
of me. I dont mind that sort of thing a bit.

I suppose you ought to stay on longer if you feel inclined It is a
pity to have had such a poor holiday.

I am much the same, but I've got my beard off

                                                   Your old
                                                     T.

[*TCD*]   [*Elpis Nursing Home*]
                                                 June 16 [*1908*]

Dearest

I got your letter last night—a much longer and better one, as usual
however you dont tell me where to write today so I must send this to
your old address on chance. There is nothing very new to tell you here.
I heard from Q[uinn] in New York the other day with £20 for the MS.
It is cruel that it will all be lost in the expenses of this present business. He also invites me to go to New York for a fortnight and offers
to pay my way out and back. I dont think I'll go however.

I go for a walk down the passage every day now and look out of
the window.

Later

Henderson has been to see me again. He tells me U. Wright has
been staying in Balbriggan too. Is that true?

It makes me feel—I do not know how. Your

                                                   T.

Please answer question at end BY RETURN I feel queer and shaky

[*TCD*]   [*Silchester House Kingstown*
                                             7 July 1908]

Dearest Pet

I got your note this morning all right.

I got down here last night, and I am rather knocked up by the fatigue so I am staying in bed and may not write.[1]

A thousand blessings Dont be uneasy.

Your old T.

1. As his mother had gone to Tomrilands House in County Wicklow for the summer, Synge was convalescing at his sister's house on Silchester Road. Molly had packed up his things and vacated the flat on York Road on 25 May.

[*TCD*]   [*Silchester House*]
                                                 Wednesday
                                                [*8 July 1908*]

Dearest Love

I am better again today, but I'm still in bed. I was so feverish yesterday my sister went in and told Sir Charles Ball and he came down to see me in his motor. He couldn't find anything wrong so I hope it was only the fatigue. I slept like a top last night, and I feel "grand" today, perhaps I'll get up this evening. I am dying to see you but I'll have to be up and about first I'm afraid. I meant to have you down for this afternoon but now that cant be done

How are you? You dont tell me if your back is all right. I hope you *aren't* going to Miss Dickinson today.[1]

This is a stupid letter my poor love but I cant manage much while I'm stretched here. Be good and be happy and go to your picture galleries and write me nice *long* letters

Your old T.

1. Possibly Miss Emily Winifred Dickson, B.Ch., M.D. M.A.O. (Royal University of Ireland), the first woman Fellow of the Royal College of Surgeons in Ireland; she practiced gynecology from 1895, but after 1900 her name no longer appears in the Medical Directory.

[*TCD*]   Silchester [*House*]
                                               Thursday [*9 July 1908*]

Dearest Love

I got two notes from you yesterday as your morning's note came at
midday, and so I had none this morning.

I got up yesterday about 4.30 and went into my nephews room to
sit there for a while. Five minutes afterwards my sister came up to
say that two nurses had come down from Elpis to see how I was as
they had heard I was ill. They came up and brought me downstairs
and stayed with us for a good while. Then they went away and I went
back to my bed. Today I am better, but I'm still "a bit" shaky. I wanted
to wire for you this morning, but my sister thought it would be better
to have you tomorrow when I'm stronger. So come down tomorrow by
the quarter *to* 2 unless we wire to the contrary. You can go back by the
¼ past five. I hope it'll be fine so that we may sit out in the garden but
in any case I've a quiet little corner where we can be for part of the
time anyhow. I wonder how you are today. It is beautiful weather as
far as I can see I haven't been out yet. I have no further news.

                                                   Your old T.

I heard from Agnes [Tobin] the other day, and from Quinn again.
P.S.   Your letter of today has just come. I suppose you'll be well
enough to come tomorrow if not send me a line. Dont let Miss
D[ickinson] talk you over into doing anything foolish. If you do not
need the drill as she says, and if it hurts you, why do it? Has your
back recovered?

I feel "mighty flat" today, sitting here by myself in silence and
solitude. Aren't [you] glad you weren't Kerrigan?

                                                   T.

Blessings as usual.

[*TCD*]   Silchester [*House*]
                                               July 11th/08

My dearest Love

I meant to write you a particularly intimate and tender note today—
because you were so good yesterday—but now I have been writing

semi-business letters till I am tired out so I can only send you a line, to say that I think you are very nice—when you like.

I have written to Quinn and Lady G. and I have 21 more letters to write but I cant do them. (sings) Oh K. H.

Oh "   "

Oh "   "

etc.

How are you today I hope the gooseberry didn't disagree? I wonder if Sally will get down today. There is supposed to be a tennis-party here today—T. of course not visible—but [it] is half wet and they dont know what to do.

Oh —— ——

——————

Your O.T.

[*TCD*]   [*Silchester House*]
July 12th /08

Dearest Love

This is a short line only to thank you for your charming—Nish— letter that I got this morning, and to tell [you] I'm going on well. I've been out in the garden all day from 11 to 7 except for my meals so I'm "a bit" tired now and I'm going to bed. I wish you'd always write as fetchingly as you did yesterday—if you did I'd have to buck up or you'd beat me at letter-writing and that wouldn't do, would it?

It has been a lovely day here in the garden with the birds and Brunettes[1] it is a pity you weren't here.

God help me I've wind enough in my poor belly—saving your presence—this evening, to drive a mill.

Be good and let me know all about your arrangements with Poel.[2]
Your old T.

---

1. Presumably puppies as the family dog was called Bruno.
2. William Poel had been invited by the Directors to give some classes in verse-speaking to the company and to rehearse them for a contemplated production of Cal- deron's *Life's But a Dream*.

[*TCD*]   [*Silchester House*]
                                                 Monday [*13 July 1908*]

My Dearest Child

I got your poor little note this morning with my breakfast—it is hard to see so little of each other. I am getting better I suppose but it's very slow and I get very dull. I'm writing in the garden now on the back of a book so I cant make much of a letter—I stay out all day they say its good for me.

I wonder when we'll get another drive. I hope to hear particulars about your hours tonight or tomorrow morning. Then we'll see.

I am getting very anxious for a view of the world again, and of course of you.

F. Ross has come out this evening. She is going to Greystones in a day or two so she came to say goodbye. I wonder how you are getting on with Poel today. I am anxious to hear all about it. Goodnight my dear Heart.

                                                 Your O.T.

[*TCD*]   Silchester [*House*]
                                                 14/July/08

Dearest Child

I got your little note as usual this [morning]. Of course I cant fix anything about your coming down again till I know when you are free. Why do you say you have only a fortnight to get up *The [Country] Dressmaker?* I dont think [it] is on till the Horse Show and that is towards the end of August, so you have a long time.[1] You should get as much as possible out of Poel while you have him. I wonder what part he'll give you. I'll be interested to hear all about him when you come down again. I'm waiting to have another drive till I can have you with me. I walked out at the back-gate today and round by the church and in at the front, I am getting on well I suppose but I have pains and aches that alarm and annoy me. I hope your mother is better, you ought to get a doctor if she is really ill.

This is a wet tedious day, and I feel very dull. Perhaps I'll hear from you again this evening. I heard from Lady G. this morning just to say she was glad I was out. Goodbye dear Heart

Your O.T.

1. The Theatre did open for Bank Holiday Monday, 3 August, with performances of *Riders to the Sea* and Fitzmaurice's *Country Dressmaker.*

[*TCD*]   [*Silchester House*]
                                                                 15th July/08

Dearest Love

I am very glad to hear you have a good part. It is inconceivably small-minded of Sally to refuse Rosaura[1]—you would have done the same I'm afraid if you had been in her shoes all through—it is an attitude I cannot understand.

I hope everything is going smoothly. I have asked you FOUR TIMES to tell me what hours you are free so that I may ask you down, but you have never alluded to the matter.

I am glad to hear Dr Barry thinks well of you. Did Miss D. go with you? Did you give him a fee?

I am not very well. It is hard to manage the wound without any skilled advice. In my efforts to keep it clean I have made the opening larger than it has been recently. Today I have asked my nephew to call on Sir Charles and ask him about it. It is cold and raw and wretched out here. I am all by myself this afternoon the others are out—as often happens. I have nothing cheerful to write, sitting here day after day is nearly intolerable. They have a tennis party here tomorrow to make things worse. They are all very kind but what can they do for me?

Your O.T.

How is your mother?

1. One of the female roles in Calderon's *Life's But a Dream.*

[*Encl*]

My dearest Love

My poor child, your second letter has come. I am ill with anxiety about you. For my sake do not have any unpleasantness, give what is necessary, and keep with Sally. Promise me this. For my sake have no rows, it would kill me. Do promise!

In great anxiety

Your O.T.

By the way, another matter, were you told to tell me to send on that play to Yeats?

[*TCD*]   Silchester [*House*]
                                                             Friday [*17 July 1908*]

My dearest Love

I think you are treating me very badly—I suppose you are so busy, you have no time to think of me now. I am very lonely and very wretched and not very well.

On *Wednesday* at 7 o'clock I got your note about your troubles, and your promise that you would write again that same day. Then *all day yesterday* I got no news of [you] till I was perfectly sick and ill with anxiety and had a very bad night. *Then this morning* I hear from you and you promise to come down and tell *me for the first time what* hours you are free. Then *at 2.30*—after I have been out to meet the train I get a line from you to say you are not coming down at all. I am to be alone today for six hours and I feel most wretched and broken down. ——
—— —— —— —— —— If I write anymore I will say things that I do not wish to say. I am profoundly wounded that you have prevented me asking you down this week and left me so long in such great anxiety. I see you are busy tomorrow afternoon by your list of hours so we cannot meet till next week.

Your O.T.

Why do you tell me nothing of what has happened in your home, God knows it would not be much to spare ten minutes to write to me.

[*Texas/tel*]   Kingstown   18 July 1908   11.47 A.M.
M. Allgood Abbey Theatre Dublin Yes tell Henderson you are coming
Synge

[*TCD*]   Silchester [*House*]
                                                     Monday [*20 July 1908*]
Dearest Child
     I wasn't able to write to you yesterday—when I came in to do a
letter in the evening I found my brother-in-law hard at work in the
little study so there was no place for me to go. I got your little note
this morning—you dont say a word about going to Poel yesterday—I
wonder if you went or what happened.
     I am much as usual but I feel rather flat as I didn't go properly to
sleep till 5 o'clock this morning my nights are nearly always bad now.
     I'm half thinking of going to Bray this afternoon to get out of this
perpetual garden—it is baking out there today. This is a foolish note
but what can I do—I'm red hot and I've a pain in my b—— stomach I
mean. I've just got a hankering to go up and stay a couple of weeks at
Lough Bray I dont see why I shouldn't.

                                                     Your old T.
I'll write better the next time.

[*TCD*]   [*Silchester House*]
                                                     Tuesday [*21 July 1908*]
Dearest Love
     I got your letter about 2 o'clock today. It was taken to Glendalough
House and the old woman brought it up to me. It is better to put
c/o Mrs Stephens on the envelopes or else the postmen think they know
more about it than you do.
     You and Sally are a clever pair not to know where you were to see
Poel—that sort of thing is a mistake; if it can be helped. (It puts people
against you I mean.) I got a qualm when I read of your visit to the
Green—remember if what she told you is true the *danger* goes on *for
years* no matter how well she may look. It is a terrible matter.[1]

I went to Bray today and sat on the esplanade for an hour and then came home again. I was very bored but I suppose it was good for me. I suppose Saturday would be the best day for us to meet again. They are having a tennis party here so I will want to be out of the way. We might go to Bray and have a drive and tea, and sit on the Esplanade. Nish! I suppose you will be free on Saturday. I haven't gone to Ball yet I'm going tomorrow or Thursday—I thought I told you I was going.

Your O.T.

1. In a letter to Yeats about his poems on 7 September 1908, Synge wrote: "There is a funny coincidence about the Curse you will find among them;—the lady in question has since been overtaken with unnamable disasters."

[*TCD*]   [*Silchester House*]
Wednesday [*22 July 1908*]

Dearest Child

I got your little note—one of the *charming* ones—this morning. You mustn't mind my notes being so short I haven't anything to tell you. I wont write to you tomorrow till after my visit to Ball so that I may tell you what he says. My nights are bad now and they make me uneasy but I hope it is nothing. It is very hot today and I feel exhausted and wretched enough. You poor child you must be nearly dead with such long rehearsals. It is well you have only four days more. Find out if you are free on Saturday so that you may come to me if we can manage it. It will depend a little on how I am. Oh —— —— — —— I'm so —— —— —— —— hot.

Take care of yourself and be good

Your O.T.

[*TCD/GS288*]   [*Silchester House*]
July? Thursday [*23 July 1908*]

My Dearest Child

I got your little note with its huffy beginning this morning,—the idea*r*! I was in with Ball today. He seems to think I am all right now, and says I may do what I like—only I am not to go to the Blaskets! He told me about the operation but I'm not much the wiser. I'll tell you what he said when I see you. I am glad Peggy's matter is well over—remember—if you have to go there—all I have said to you.

Dont forget to tell me in your next if you are free on Saturday—as usual I have asked you two or three times and you have taken no notice. Now you must write and tell me early tomorrow or I'll hardly have time to arrange. Nish!

I'm not very well with all Ball's talk and I had a worse night than ever last night. I think I'll go and see Parsons on Monday I suppose you'll get this tomorrow before you're up.

Your O.T.

[*TCD*]

[*Silchester House*]

Friday July [24¹] /08

Dearest Child

Thanks for note. I was in town again today with Sir Charles as my wound was in a new stage—the skin closed too soon—that I did not know how to deal with.

I haven't heard yet for certain if you will be free tomorrow—I suppose you dont know yet yourself. If you are free my plan is that we go to Bray by the *quarter to Three* (I'll meet that train, if its fine), and if it's not fine we'll go down to Glendalough House and look through my books and *our* furniture and get tea from Mary Tyndall and have a good time. Nish! It will be my sister's At Home day so I dont want to be here. Now is that all quite clear? You come down by the *quarter to three* and if I meet the train we go on, and if not you come to the "little gate" and we go to Glendalough [House]. Dont miss the train—if you are coming—as I would have to go on to Bray by that train if I was there. Of course if you are not free I'll be all forlorn, trying to get along by my poor unfortunate self—I think you all deserve the afternoon's rest but of course you'll have to do what Poel says. I've no news I'll wait now and see if there's a letter by this post it is due in 20 minutes.

No letter, well I heard this morning so I cant copy you and say——.

If you can let me know before *eleven* tomorrow if you are coming, and come by the quarter to three that will give you time for your dinner

Your old T.

---

1. Synge misdated this letter the 23rd.

[*TCD/GS288*]

[*Silchester House*]
Monday July 2? [27] /08

My dearest Child

When I got your charming little letter this morning I felt very guilty for not having written to you yesterday. Somehow it isn't easy to write here on Sunday. My brother-in-law was in the little study all the evening and I had no place to collect my thoughts. It was well you wrote so particularly nicely as I'd have given a great scolding about your bicycle. As it is I feel a [little] hurt that you let them knock about my present to you, the way you do—a fall does a bicycle more harm than six months riding. I hope you will make quite sure that the brake is quite secure. It is a *fatal* mistake to let anyone mend a bicycle except the makers or someone you know and can rely on a clumsy workman can do an extraordinary amount of harm in five minutes. I have had axles split and screws stripped and nuts twisted so I speak from sad experience. Nish! I wont scold you any more, you poor child. I'm very lonely and very low and not very well yet. I may go to Bray after lunch but I'm not sure. I have been reading your Chaucer all the morning, its a pity the print is so small. By the way, if your brothers take your bicycle without leave it is easy to get a chain and padlock (*at a cycle shop*) for about 1/0 and then you can put the chain through the wheel and head and lock it and then you are safe, and no one can ride it. If you are in any doubt about the brake being all right take it to the maker I will pay if you like. You had better show it to O'Rourke or someone.

I was dreaming of Wright last night but nothing very sensational. This is [a] dull external letter to send in answer to your nice one, my

God if we could only be well again and out in the hills for one long
summer day and evening what Heaven it would be. I feel ready to cry
I am getting better so very slowly.

Good bye dear Heart
Your old T.

This is a beastly letter but forgive it and me I've a pain.

[*TCD*]   [*Silchester House*]

Tuesday July 2? [*28 July 1908*]

My dearest Child

I got your nice little note with my breakfast this morning, and it
made me very gay. You will not get this till tomorrow morning, as I
went to Bray today and have missed the post. I took paper and envelope
with me and I meant to write to you in the train, but at the last moment
I forgot my pencil. I have turned over fifty plans for meeting you tomorrow but I haven't hit on anything satisfactory so I suppose it'll have
to be Friday or Saturday. I think you said you are going to Miss D.
tomorrow so I dare say that will be enough for you. It was very hot at
Bray today and I felt quite 'done up' with the glare on the esplanade
and now I have a pain as usual, God help me!—I nearly wrote God with
a small 'g'!

How do you get on with Swift? He was over 40 I think when he
wrote those letters. Have you sent *Lady May* to Miss Grierson, Elpis?
I hope you've got your bicycle settled properly.

I heard from my mother today. She is only middling it seems. My
nephew and brother-in-law have gone out to Aran again so we are a
small party.

Your old T.

[*TCD*]   [*Silchester House*]

Wednesday
July 29th [*1908*]

Dearest Child

Your letter came this evening at 7 I was looking out for it all day.
Well we'll meet on Saturday I'll write you what train tomorrow. I was
very lonely and miserable in Bray yesterday by myself, and today I went

to Blackrock and sat in the park and was lonelier again. Dr. Parsons has gone away and Ball too so I'll have to get on as best I can till they come back. I had a wretched sort of night again last night. Still I hope it may be only the effects of the operation, and general indigestion. I am very lonely too, we must try and meet oftener after this once a week is far too seldom.

I am writing this in a hurry to catch the post tonight so that you may have this tomorrow morning. Have you got your brake settled yet? My second nephew came home today he has been up with my mother for a month.

Now be good and cheerful Dear Heart

Your Old T.

[TCD]   Silchester [*House*]
                                               Thursday July 30th [*1908*]

Dearest Child

Your note came this morning. What is the splint? Is it to make both sides of your face what, *Eh?* That['s] a nice way you keep me informed of your doings! Nish. I'm beginning not to wonder that you sometimes find it hard to write—these last days as you see I'm not up to much. I've been in Bray again today from 5 till 7, it was less hateful than it is earlier in the afternoon. I suppose the quarter to three train would be the best for you to come by on Saturday. If its fine we'll go to Bray and if not to Glendalough [House] I suppose. I've been invited to go and stay at my brother's house while he is away, his daughter and F. Ross are to be there. I suppose I'll have to go as they'll be getting this place ready for the wedding[1] soon so I'd be in the way. My wound is just the same and I still have the bad nights. Now good night dear Heart I'm very lonely and wretched without you.

Your O T.

1. The marriage of Synge's brother-in-law's sister, Elizabeth Stephens, to Thomas Franks, in August.

[*TCD*]   [*Silchester House*]
                                                               Friday
                                                            July 31st/08

Dearest Child
    Well the week is gone by at last and I am to see you tomorrow.
Come down by the quarter to *three*—dont miss it for Heaven's sake and
we'll go to Bray or Glendalough House. I got your little card this morning—it doesn't seem to be weather for letterwriting somehow.
    I sent off the little play to Lady Gregory today at last. It might pos-
sibly do [if] it was altered a good deal. I certainly agree with you that
it is most mean and unfair of Sally to put you out of *Scapin*. She
wouldn't do it if I was about. It is a pity with all her fine qualities that
she is so queer.
    I hope we'll have a good time tomorrow. You had better be early
enough to get a seat next the window so that I may see you in the train
tomorrow—and dont go too far up the train. If I'm not there come on
here.
    Till then goodbye dear Heart
                                                            Your old T.

[*TCD*]   [*Silchester House*]
                                                          August 3rd [*1908*]

My dearest Child
    I forgot somehow that there would be only one post today or I'd
have written to you yesterday—now I'm afraid you'll be two days without a letter. I got your little note this morning yes Saturday was
good Eh?
    I had a pretty good night too and wasn't tired. However to make up
I was very bad last night and I feel shaken and wretched today. There
is no news. It is too hot and too crowded to go out so I am loitering
about trying to pass the day, and to forget my miseries, God help me.
    I'm too flat to write nicely it is impossible, so believe how much I
love you and how I long to see you again
                                                            Your O.T.

[*TCD/GS288*]   Silchester [*House*]
                                               Tuesday Aug 4/08

My dearest Child

There are several pieces of news to tell you today. My mother is so
unwell that she is coming home on Friday or next Tuesday, so I shall go
down there instead of going to my brothers. We are anxious about her.
Next I am very unwell myself so I am going in tomorrow I think to see
young Ball and have a talk with him. I cannot let things go on like this.
I dont know what is going to become of me, I wouldn't be surprised if
they send me back to Elpis for a while. You need not say anything
about this to Henderson or the others they are too much given to
gossiping. Anyhow I hope I'm not very bad as I was so well on Saturday. I meant to ask you down tomorrow but that is off now, and I dont
know what time I'll be in town so I cant ask you to meet me. Then on
Thursday afternoon I suppose you rehearse—what time do you finish?
Please thank Henderson for his letter and tell him I'll write and fix a
day but that I'm going to the doctor tomorrow. Dont be downcast my
little Heart there are bound to be ups and downs I suppose in my re-
covery.

                                               Your O.T.

[*TCD*]   Silchester House
                                               Wednesday
                                               August 5th/08

My dearest Child

I got your poor little note last night and your card this morning. I
am not going to the doctor today so I am sending a line to Yeats to ask
him to be sure and come. I had a very much better night last night, and
other ways I am better so I want to wait a day or two to see how things
go before I go to the doctor. In any case going to young Ball is not very
much good, unless it is absolutely necessary. I hope you are not very
unwell let me know how you are as soon as you can.

I dont know what day I'll go down to my mothers yet, it seems
strange going back there after so long when I thought I had left it
forever. My nephew heard from his 'fancy' by the same post that I
heard from you last night. He had three big sheets closely written on

both sides so I felt that I had only come off second best. However of course she is in Wales so that they have to live on correspondence God help them.

"Oh, Johnny Gibbon
You're over the say!"   (the splash is an extra dont mind it.)

Nish amn't I better. If I get a good night today I'll be "grand". Amen

Your O.T.

[Silchester House]
Thursday
August 6th [1908]

[*TCD*]

Dearest Child

I was delighted with your little note this morning. I am not so well today however and I'd bad pain in the night so we must[n't] halloo too much till we're out of the wood. I was very glad to see Yeats yesterday and talk over things with him it seemed like getting back into the current of life again. I suppose Saturday will be the best day for us to meet again we can go to Bray or Glendalough House according to the weather. My mother is not coming home till Tuesday next so I suppose I'll stay on here till then. If you were rich you could come down on Sunday too and have tea with me in Glendalough [House] but I suppose two days together would be a bad division. I have been in Bray today but I did not enjoy myself a bit.

Your O.T.

[Silchester House]
Friday [7 August 1908]

[*TCD*]

My dearest Child

I've had no news of you today. How's that, Eh?

Come down tomorrow by the quarter to three—unless you get a wire to put you off—and I'll either meet you at the station and go on to Bray, or else on the road and we'll go to Glendalough [House]. *Dont be late.* I had a very good night last night and thought I was 'grand' but I've not been quite so well today. I'm afraid I must go to young Ball on

Monday. If I should have a *very* bad night tonight I might have to go to him tomorrow, so you need not be distressed if I wire to you; as we would meet on Sunday instead. But that's not likely I hope.

My mother comes on Tuesday—did I tell you that before I think I did. I have been to Bray again today for the good of my health, it's rather a fagging job going there alone. The regatta was on there again and rather a crowd in the train so it was hot. I hope I'll hear from you tonight

     Your old
     T.

[*TCD*]   [*Silchester House*]
                                           Monday 1 P.M.
                                         August 10th
                                             1908

My dearest Child

I couldn't manage to write to you yesterday so I am writing early today. I am sorry to hear about Peggy[1] for *my* sake, my dear child, be careful about these matters and make Sally be careful. I am going in to Dr Ball today at a quarter past two to see what he says to me. I was a good deal worse yesterday I am afraid than I have been yet, but I had a good night and I was better this morning, though the pains are beginning again now all up my back.

Florence Ross and Ada Synge were here all day yesterday, but I didn't see very much of them. When I am not feeling very well I find the large party here rather trying.

Yes I am not seeing you half often enough you must come much oftener now. I dont think I shall go down to Glendalough [House] till Wednesday—as my mother does not get in till pretty late tomorrow, so that the house will be upset. Goodbye there is lunch now. Remember what I have asked you

          Your O.T.

Tell Sally I'll be very glad to see her some day I'll let her know.

1. Mrs. Callender was suffering from illness and marital troubles.

[*TCD*]   Silchester [*House*]
                                                           11th August/08

Dearest Child.

I was in with Dr Ball yesterday but he did not find much that was
very definite. He found, he thinks the cause of the discharge—an *unim-*
portant one if he is right—but he does not really know what my severe
pains are from. I liked him very much and I am to go back to him in a
few days if I am not better. He takes more trouble and is much gentler
than the old man.

I got your post card this morning I suppose it was better than nothing. Write me a better letter tonight. I move down to Glendalough
[*House*] tomorrow and then we must arrange to meet oftener. I had a
line from MacKenna last night asking if I was still in the land of the
living—I never answered his last letter.

I hope my mother will have it fine for her drive down this evening
—she is two hours drive from the railway in Wicklow town, and she is
to have a two-horsed landau to bring her down.

This is one of the days when I am not able to write. With ten
thousand blessings—somehow I can always bless you—your

                                                           O.T.

[*TCD*]   Silchester [*House*]
                                                           Wednesday [*12 August 1908*]

Dearest Child

I'm here still. My mother came home yesterday but is so unwell
that she has to stay in bed so they thought it better for me to stay on
here another day. There is a lady staying with my mother so now I suppose I'll have to entertain while my mother is ill. That will be a job.

Your little line came this morning—poor Maire—that woman passes
anything. I'm only very middling still. I went for a little walk today for
half an hour but it makes me tired very soon when I have to walk without sitting down.

What did you see at the Gaiety? I'm afraid I cant fix a day for us to
meet till I get down to Glendalough [*House*] and see how things are.
I lay—or rather wriggled—awake last night till four o'clock so I do not
feel very bright.

Good luck dear Heart

                                                           Your O T

[*TCD/GS288–9*]   Glendalough [*House*]
                                   Friday
                                   14/8/08

Dearest Child

I am sorry to have left you a day without a letter but it could not very well be helped. I came down here yesterday about 6 and found your letter waiting for me but I was too tired then to write to you and go to the post. Your second note has just been brought me now from Silchester—It was a nice one.

My poor mother is not at all well and is in bed still. This illness seems to have aged her in some way and she seems quite a little old woman with an old woman's voice. It makes me sad. It is sad also to see all *our* little furniture stowed away in these rooms. It is a sad queer time for us all, dear Heart, I sometimes feel inclined to sit down and wail. Come down to me tomorrow, say by the *quarter* PAST TWO from *West. Row*—a Saturday train. I will either meet you, or else you can come here. Dont miss it or I will be lost. I heard from MacKenna today I will show you his letter tomorrow. Oh Mother of Moses I wish I could get well. I have less pain at night I think than I had but I'm all queer inside still.

It is kind of Sally to want to give me more books[1]—I'll think of one. She is good-natured in her own way. I'd like to go and have tea in the Abbey some afternoon next week—wouldn't that be fun?

By the way *dont* bring the typewriter tomorrow as we may be going on to Bray. I wish I had you coming down today—I feel so flat and sad.

Goodby now and dont be late tomorrow a *quarter* PAST *two*

                                   Your O T

---

1. Among Synge's possessions was a copy of A. E. Housman's *Poems* (London: Grant Richards, 1907) with the inscription "J. M. Synge from Sara Allgood June 5th, 1908."

[*TCD/GS289*]   Glendalough House
                                   Kingstown
                                   Monday [*17 August 1908*]

Dearest

I got your note this morning. I wish it was Wednesday I feel very dull and wretched, it is very hot and my mother is still very poorly and Miss Massey—the guest—is lying down with a headache.

I went to Merrion [Square] yesterday on top of the tram and walked along a bit and came back again. It was very hot and I hated it. Today I am going to Bray God help me.

I got a card from Lebeau this morning he is going to Canada in three weeks for good. He has got a post there to teach French literature in Montreal—in the university. I sat down this morning after breakfast and wrote to him and Musek and Meyerfeld—the German *Well of the Saints* man—and then I got fagged. I think I'll go in and see young Ball again tomorrow and then God send Wednesday.

They are in a great fuss at Silchester today getting ready for the Wedding tomorrow. I'm glad you had a spin yesterday. Where did you go.

Oh me God I'm as flat as a mangled pancake. Write me a nice letter. I found *Gulliver's Travels* today I'll bring them to you on Wednesday

Your O T

[TCD]   [*Glendalough House*]
                                    Tuesday [*18 August 1908*]

Dearest

I haven't gone to Ball today after all. I am going to him because he said I was to go back and because the worries in my inside aren't by any means gone. I'll go on Thursday perhaps.

Florence Ross and Ada were in here a little while ago in white dresses on their way to the Wedding. They looked very nice, and for the first time I felt a little qualm of regret that you would not have a nice white brilliant wedding too. However any colour would do us. If you only knew how much I am longing for our day to come. I am afraid to think about it, God help me. I am going to try writing crooked the way you do to see if you admire it as—oh damn where shall I go now. Do you follow this joke I'm not drunk but your letters have been getting skewier and skewier and I'm beginning to get hypnotised into doing the same. It's rather fun when you try it.

My mother is a little better today, she is beginning to come round I think. I am sorry to hear that the men of the Company are giving trouble. Sally had better report them to the Directors if they get too bad.

I had a wretched time in Bray yesterday all by myself. Come down tomorrow (Wednesday) by the quarter to *three*. I'll join you at Glenageary as usual. If not come here. Of course if it is a *wet* day dont come. It wont be wet please God

Your O T

[*TCD*]

[*Glendalough House
21 August 1908*]

Dearest.

This is the only bit of paper I can find. I was 'a bit' disappointed not to hear from you this morning, and I suppose you were the same not to hear from me. Serves you right. I didn't go to Ball yesterday it was so wet so I'm going today instead, to see what he says. Tomorrow is Saturday I believe, God be thanked, so come down if it is fine by *the quarter* PAST TWO, we'll go to Bray or perhaps Dalkey—but you'd better not come if its wet.

Miss Massey—the visitor—is going away on Monday, so you can come here more easily after that. My mother is getting a little better by slow degrees. I am much the same. It's funny how a little piece of paper makes me write little sentences—I feel as if I'd no room for big ones.— This is a longer letter than usual, I am writing so small, so dont turn up your nose at it.

My mother will have to get a nurse I think after Miss Massey goes —it's a pity you aren't trained, and you could come. I feel, as you see, perfectly incapable of writing today I wish I was going to meet you in town today.

Your O.T.

[*TCD/GS289*]

[*Glendalough House*]
Monday August 24th [*1908*]

Dearest Child

I wasn't at all the worse I think for our great little walk on Saturday. Henderson came in the evening and I talked business as spry as possible till ten and then I went to bed and slept very well. If it was[n't] for that bloody blood I'd be damn fine now Eh?

Magee came to see me yesterday afternoon—I like him—and then afterwards I went for a little walk and met the red-headed Abbey enthusiast I've told you about, and he walked with me out and back again.

My eldest brother came back from America this morning I am very glad as Miss Massey has gone away and I felt anxious here alone with my mother. I think he will stay here till we get someone to look after her. The pretty young nurse cant come you'll be sorry to hear.

I've been working at Deirdre this morning—Nish—I've decided to cut off the second act (you remember Jesus Christ says if thy second act offend thee pluck it out, but I forgot you're a heathen and theres no use quoting Holy Scriptures to you), so that I can take the one good scene in the II and run it into the third when D and Naisi are together. It will be useful there as Naisi['s] part was so weak in the last Act. Now what do you say to me.

You must come down soon with my type-writer I'll tell you when soon. By the way do you rehearse tomorrow afternoon? I suppose not I think I'll go and see MacKenna this afternoon. Goodbye Dear Heart.

O.T.

[*TCD*]   [*Glendalough House*]
                                                        August 25th 08

Dearest

I got your letter at half past one so that wasn't too bad. I'm glad to hear the House was so good. What is wrong with Morgan? at the other show he was quite good—even very good in places. What's happened to him.[1]

You had better come down tomorrow (unless I wire to put you off —to the Abbey) by the quarter to three or the quarter to two if it suits you and bring me my type-writer. Then if its fine we can go somewhere.

Is the British Association *next* week? I thought it was further off.[2]

I had a letter from Jack Yeats this morning, not a very interesting one. He is at Coole, but leaves tomorrow. I heard from Lady Gregory also. This is [a] flattish kind of note because I'm to see you tomorrow I suppose so I'm too lazy to put energy into my letter—

I found our pictures today and I've put myself up in our parlour over the chimney-piece. I wish you hadn't that cigarette it makes your picture a little common. I found the mug also so nearly everything has turned up now, so till tomorrow good bye and good luck

O.T.

1. Sydney J. Morgan (1885–1931) had joined the company early in 1908 and remained with the Abbey for almost twenty years, afterward moving to London where he acted in many of Sean O'Casey's plays.

2. The British Association met in Dublin for a week from 2 September; the members visited the Abbey Theatre twice, at a special matinée on September 4, when Yeats delivered an address on the Theatre, and on Tuesday evening, 8 September. The company played for the entire week.

[*TCD*]   [*Glendalough House*]
August 28th /08

Dearest Child

I got your nice little note last night at six—I am delighted that the Abbey is going so well. I am going to Sir Charles today, so I will have news for you the next time, let me know if you are coming out tomorrow or on Sunday. I heard from Nurse Mullen[1] putting off our party till the weather is more settled. My mother is getting on well, but I've a pain today—my dinner wasn't a success yesterday and I've been the worse for it ever since.

I've just had a wire from Roberts to say that he is coming out today.

I'm very glad you like Gulliver there's great stuff in him. You see I cant write today

Your old T.

1. One of the nurses from Elpis Nursing Home.

[*TCD*]   Glendalough Ho.
August 28th [*1908*]

Dearest

I've been with Sir Charles, he says I'm not to mind my inside and that I may go away and ride my bicycle and do what I like—Nish!

I had Roberts out here today we have very complicated business to do over this American Edition. I hate this haggling over money. I wonder what you'll write to me about tomorrow, and if you'll have had the good sense and forethought to make definite arrangements—I'm sure you will you're *so good at that!* Nish!

Your old T.

I walked up from Merrion Square today round through College Green and back to the Station by Brunswick Street. If I'd known where to find you I'd have got you for tea somewhere.

NISH

[AS/GS289]

Glendalough [*House*]
August 31st [*1908*]

Dearest

I am very glad to hear that you are better though it gave me a sorry qualm to hear of your expedition—especially as you let him pay for you. I had a very pleasant afternoon at the MacKennas—they have a charming old house full of excellent things that they have picked up, among other [things] a little bronze statuette by Rodin—you have seen his work at Harcourt [Gallery]—which he gave to Mrs MacK. I envy them—there is no one else in Ireland probably who possesses such a thing. They have admirable furniture also and a lovely view of the mountains. They want me to bring you to see them as soon as I can shall we say next Sunday or when?

I didn't go out with my nurse of course today—she wired to say she was too busy and of course with this weather it wouldn't have been possible. I hope you are feeling as well today, I've been playing round and round my verses this morning—I cannot do any work as I have no paper—isn't [it] too bad I asked you to get it on Wednesday and I have lost nearly a whole week—I might have written an act of Deirdre. However you haven't been well so I'll forgive you this time. I'm a bit *belly-some* today—isn't that a fine word—as I ate a whole dish of cabbage yesterday. When I'm by myself I gobble up everything without thinking. I suppose you'll come to me on Wednesday Eh. Write again

O.T.

[*Texas/GS290*]   [*Glendalough House*]
                                                      Sept 1st 1908
Dearest
    I have had no news of you today so far. I got impatient this morn-
ing so I trotted off into town and bought my paper and a book and
went to the bank. Then I came home on top of the tram in time for my
dinner.
    Will you come down tomorrow by the quarter to three? We'll go
to Bray if its fine I rather think there is a travelling circus there which
would be fun.
    Roberts is coming out here tonight for me to read him my poems it
gives me a big 'D', as you call it. I dont know how I'll ever face showing
them to Yeats, but it'll have to be done, God help me.
    I felt nearly quite myself dodging about in town. Will you write
tomorrow before 11 or tonight to say if you'll come tomorrow.
    I'll leave this now to see if I hear from you at six.
    No letter so good-bye Dear Heart till tomorrow. If it is wet you can
come here.
                                                      O.T.

[*TCD*]   [*Glendalough House*]
                                                      Sept 4th /08
Dearest Heart
    You little —— not to write me a nice long letter yesterday! I am
getting on very well indeed getting rid of my —— symptoms I think.
But I'm so well I'm afraid to go to the Abbey for fear of bringing things
on again. It's not worth the risk. Isn't that so? I am writing to Lady
Gregory to ask if I can see her tomorrow. If she says I'm to go, I wont
be able to see you till Sunday. I'm beginning to think in that case we
wont go to the MacKennas till another day, so that we can go out on
Sunday to Bray or somewhere.
    What did you do yesterday. It was too wet for my expedition that
is the third time it has failed. Did you see about the woman who shot

herself in Rathmines. I used to know the man a little and his brother quite well. Do you see what comes of flirting, Eh?[1]

I am going out now as I was at home all day yesterday

Your old Tramp

1. The *Evening Mail* for 1 September reported the suicide of a solicitor's wife after she had separated from her husband and been jilted by her lover.

[*TCD*]   [*Glendalough House*]
Sept 5. 08

Dearest

For three days I have heard nothing of you—I do not know when you left me so long before—I need not tell you that I am troubled and uneasy. You could find time to write me a line no matter how busy you are.

I have just come back from seeing Lady Gregory and Yeats. They seem very well. I am not quite so well today I have a pain under my wound. Will you come down by the quarter to three tomorrow. I will join you at Glenageary if it is fine and I am well enough. If I do not, then you come down here. A post is due now I wonder shall I hear from you. I am beginning to worry myself sick.

The post has passed I dont think ever since I knew you you have left me so long. Why do you do it? You seemed as usual when I saw you on Wednesday

Your O.T.

[*TCD/GS289*]   Glendalough House
Sept ? [7] 1908

Dearest Pigeen

I hugged myself with delight when I got your offended card this morning. Nish! Miss Changlingette Miss Changlingeen, how do you like being neglected the way you neglected me last week? You used to write to me every day and I used to do the same but now you've taken to writing twice a week and Begob if you dont write to me I'll not write to you. Nish Nish, *N I S H !*

I'm going up to see Parsons tomorrow and I'll be in Westland Row at 25 *to* three. Will you meet me there and walk up? I dont suppose he'll keep me very long if you like to wait for me in the Museum and then we could have tea. I was with Yeats yesterday afternoon and we had a long talk about the Poems. He is thinking of putting them with Dun Emer[1] after all.

Your O.T.

P.S. My dearest. You have given me a lot of misery, but perhaps what you did was mere carelessness, and if so I suppose my letter hurt you in turn. In that case I am sorry but when you do not write to me how can I know what to say to you.

However in a few days with the help of God we'll be out in the glens again and then we wont be in danger of getting at cross purposes as we are in these accursed letters. Remember always it is because I am so wound up in you that I am so sensitive about all that you do. That is a good symptom isn't it?

Your old T.

1. The original name for the Cuala Press run by Yeats's sisters.

[*TCD*]   [*Glendalough House*]
Wednesday Sept 9th/08

Dearest

Your letter came last night, just in time to save you from another scolding! Nish. I got a letter from Yeats yesterday morning to say that some of the poems were *very fine,* (no less) and ask me to go in today to talk about them so, I am going in after dinner. I may write to you a line tonight to fix something for tomorrow—no I think I wont the weather is so bad. Perhaps Friday will be better.

I was very much tickled by your story about Sally and the curse. I was sure it would 'fetch' Yeats. I wonder what he will advise. I would not be surprised if he still wants to put me off publishing them for the present. We'll see.

My mother goes into our little room now for a while in the afternoon, and she seems a little better Still she is so unwell we are getting another doctor down from Dublin for a consultation tomorrow or next day I think.

I was in Dalkey Park the last two evenings from 5 to 6 and it was so bright and wild and magnificent over the sea it almost reminded me of the West. You must come there some evening. I have decided to put my Wicklow and Kerry stuff into one book and publish it as soon as I can, though there is a good deal of work to do on it still. I have typed three pages this morning and I feel rather tired. It is another Wicklow [article] for the *Manchester Guardian* and then for the book afterwards. I wish I could get you down to type for me we'd have the book done in no time. You say no more about your head so I suppose it is all right. Isn't this what you call a stupid letter?

Your old T.

[TCD]   [*Glendalough House*]
Sept 14th 08

Dearest Been
I dont know whether this will get to you tonight or tomorrow, but I must do it now. I am on the edge of a *bad cough* today, and my chest is very sore, but it may not come to much—if I have luck. You'd better take some warm things with you to Galway as its likely your home journey in the night will be very cold.[1] Look round in Galway for lustre jugs or Irish curios—*that are cheap*. When you're going away any where I always feel like God Almighty dictating the ten commandments to Moses. However you ought to know my commandments by heart—why do we say by heart and not by liver or kidney?—before this so I'm d'ed if I'll repeat them—Nish—

I got my poem right last night about midnight—when I suppose you were snoring—

every
There's snow in ⟨all the⟩ street⟨s⟩
Where I go up and down
And there's no man or dog that knows
My footstep in the town

I know the shops and men
French Jews and Russian Poles
For I go walking night and noon
To spare my sack of coals.²   (!)

I wonder if it
is right after all?
Anyhow its better.
Be careful of this
M.S. and maybe you'll
be able to sell it
to an American collector
for £20 when
I'm rotten.

This would be a nice sheet to put up in the Museum over our skulls, by and by when we go up to keep Swift and Stella in countenance. Begob I think I'm feverish I'm writing such bosh—and I've no thermometer.

Didn't we have a good day yesterday. Think of it, Little Heart, and be very wise—Think of me, sweet Kidney, and dont be frivol—How the deuce do you spell it?—lous.

Your O.T.

1. The company went to Galway on 16 September to take part in the Galway Agricultural Exhibition.
2. See Oxford *Poems,* p. 63, for the final version as published in the Cuala Edition in 1909.

[*TCD*]

[*Glendalough House*]
Thursday [17] Sept. 08.

Dearest

I was very glad to get your letter this morning—I thought the post had passed and I was getting very cranky, but when I came down there was your letter. My brother-in-law is in Galway today I wonder if you will meet him. I'm sorry to hear of your discomfort, but that was almost to be expected in Exhibition time in a small town in the country. It's not for long anyhow. It is very fine here this morning so I hope it may be the same with you. I've had a bad enough sort of turn but I might have been worse. I haven't been out yet, and I dont think I'll get out today. It is a very great nuisance as it will put off my trip to Germany for a week and so run me in for the cold weather there. I'm afraid you'll never learn to take care of me, little scatterbrain; it was folly for me to go and sit by the sea so late on Sunday when I was so bad. This is the first cough I have had since the operation on my neck last year—but now I've started I'll have them all the winter, unless Germany does wonders.

I have a headache still, little Heart, so I cant write you a very nice letter. I mean well as always, and I think about you a great deal. I hope your cold isn't bad, take care of yourself whatever you do. I'm afraid you'll be disappointed at not hearing from me sooner but as usual you gave me no address so I could not write sooner. My mother is still very poorly. I have been working at my Kerry book yesterday and today—it gives me a headache but I must do something. Goodbye and be very good indeed. I'll write to you again tomorrow, to reach you on Saturday, that will be my last to you there. By the way I had a long friendly letter from *Musek* last night! He must have heard us in Bray! I think you had better *not* ask Lady G. and W.B.Y. to sign the card, they might think it below their dignity. I can sign with the Co. or send one by myself.

—— —— —— —— ——

—— —— —— Your O.T.

[TCD]   [*Glendalough House*]
                                               Friday Sept ? [*18*] 08

Dearest

I got your letter this morning. What a catastrophe about the scenery! I wonder whose fault it was, I can imagine Yeats' delight in making his announcements.[1] Which arm of Dossy's did the dog bite? If it was the arm he gave you in London I'll say good dog and God speed you!

I haven't been out yet, I'd go today, but it is too wet. I've made my inside sore with the shaking of the coughs, and I feel very wretched. I'm not happy about your poor little nose, you'll have to show it to a doctor at once when you come back.

I dont know whether to laugh or cry over you for expecting me to write to you when you knew you had not given me an address. Did you think that half an hour after you posted your letter a little angel with

John M. Synge to Molly Allgood, 14 September 1908

Sept 14.ᵗʰ 08

Dearest Beer

I dont know whether this will
get to you tonight or tomorrow, but I must
do it now. I am on the edge of a bad cough
today, and my chest is very sore, but it may
not come to much — if I have luck. You'd
better take some warm things with you to Galway
its likely your home journey in the night will
be very cold. Look round in Galway for lustre
jugs or Irish curios — that are cheap.

When you're going away any where I always
feel like God almighty dictating the Ten commandments to Moses, However you ought to know my
commandments by heart — why do we say by heart
and not by liver or kidney? — before this so I'm
sed if I'll repeat them —

Nest —

I got my poem right last night about
midnight when I suppose you were snoring—

    There's snow in every street
      where I go up and down
and there's no man or dog that knows
    my footsteps in the town.

    I know the shops and men
    french Jews and Russian Poles
For I go walking night and noon
  to spare my sack of coals. ①

I wonder if it
is right after all
anyhow its better
Because fond of this
M S. and maybe you
be able to sell it
to an american coll[ege]
for £20 whe[n]
I'm rotten.

This would be a nice sheet to put up in the [room]
over our skulls, bye and bye when [we're going?] to keep
Swift and Stella in countenance. Begob I think I'm
feverish I'm writing such bosh— and I've no
thermometer.

Didn't we have a good day yesterday. Think of it,
little Heart, and be very wise— Think of me, sweet
kidney, and dont be proud— How the deuce do
you spell it?—louse.   Jim O.

an air-ship would sail in to Glendalough House to give it me, and then sail back with my answer?

I'm very lonely and miserable, I've been four long days—this is the fifth—sitting in this room seeing no one God help me! and I'm not really a bit better yet.

You dont tell me much about your doings. I wonder if my brother-in-law and nephew got beds yesterday they went down in the afternoon. Oh be —— —— I'm very flat. Take care of yourself and be very good on your return journey I wonder if you'll have my people in the same train. If I can I'll write you a little note to meet you in Dublin and then on Monday thank God I'll see you.

Your old T.

1. The stage arranged for the company was too small for their scenery, so it had to be draped with hessian hangings at the last minute.

[*TCD*]   [*Glendalough House*]
Saturday Sept ? [*19*] /08

Dearest

I'm afraid I cant wait till Monday, so if you feel quite rested come down by the quarter to three tomorrow (Sunday) and come to the house. If you'd rather stay quiet of course do so and come to me on Monday instead, by the same train. I wont expect you tomorrow unless you come by that train.

Your letter this morning was a very charming one—I laughed till I coughed at the sentence you over-heard it was *magnificent.*

I was out a little yesterday and a little this morning but I dont feel very much the better yet. It is very trying. I am glad the weather is mild so that you will not be frozen tonight coming home.

I dont seem to have much to say today, except that I'll be in great spirits and joy to see you again. I wish I was there to hear Mac's speech! It would be a treat.[1] Did Henderson stay with you all the time?

Your O.T.

1. At the closing performance on 19 September Sara Allgood and Arthur Sinclair, as leading actress and actor of the company, were presented with gold medals by the Exhibition Executive.

[*TCD*]   Glendalough House
                                                    Sept 24/08

Dearest

   I got your letter last night, and the telegram came all right. I dont
know who the goodman is who is so anxious to see me. I'm getting
better I think by degrees, so I need not go to Parsons. I got a thermometer and my temperature is all right so I needn't bother. I hope to
get away to Germany about the first of Oct. Will you come down tomorrow (Friday) by *the quarter to three?* If you'll do some typing for me
I'll pay half your train, Nish, isn't that generosity? Joking apart it is a
pity not to see each other when I'm going away so soon. I had Jack
Yeats with me all the afternoon yesterday—It was a very heavy day and
we both seemed to find it rather hard to keep up a flow of conversation.
It isn't easy when you're not very well to be suddenly confronted with a
man you haven't seen for a year or so. Still I was very glad to see him,
and I think he was glad too.

   I have no other news, except that I have nearly finished an article
for the *Manchester Guardian.* It will go off today or tomorrow I hope.[1]
If you can and will come tomorrow you needn't write, but if you *cant*
please send me a line tonight or BEFORE 11 in the morning. I hope you'll
come. It is very bright and sunny here today I wish you were here
                                                    Your O.T.

---

   1. The last article Synge published in the *Manchester Guardian* was "In Wicklow. On
the Road," 10 December 1908.

[*TCD*]   Glendalough [*House*]
                                        Saturday [*26 September 1908*]

Dearest

   I got another wire from that wretched man this morning at 7.30
asking me to supper with him tonight at 11 in the Shelbourne. I wrote
to say that I could not go, but I would lunch with him tomorrow if he
liked but that I was only free till *2.30.* So *if* I go (—I will not go unless I
hear in the morning—) I may be in your train. If I should miss it—by
any chance you had better come on and wait here, or would you rather
come by the three to make sure. If I go to the beast I'll go down again

as soon as ever I can you may be sure of that. If he sees me to the station you needn't be alarmed he wont be coming here I told him I couldn't have him as my mother is ill. D——D——D—— him. I am much better today. How are you Isn't this a scrappy note.

Your old

T.

[AS/GS291]   [*Glendalough House*]

2.X.08

Dearest

I am not going to the Abbey today as I have been in town every day since Sunday and I think it is time to take a good day's rest— though I am feeling well enough. I have got all my bills in now £114. or thereabouts, God help me. Parsons £20. Elpis £37. and Sir Charles £57.

I handed over the MS. of my poems to Yeats yesterday so I hope that will go all right now. I did one new poem—that is partly *your* work —that he says is *M a g n i f i c e n t*

> I asked if I got sick and died would you
> With my black funeral go walking too,
> If you'd stand close to hear them talk and pray
> While I'm let down in that steep bank of clay.
> And, No, you said, for if you saw a crew
> Of living idiots, pressing round that new
> Oak-Coffin—they alive, I dead beneath
> That board—you'd rave and rend them with your teeth.[1]

By the way did you ask about Marine Lodge and what did they tell you. I think they ought to give it to me for nothing, because after we have lived there and written verses about it, it will become so famous that they'll be able to sell it to an American for £50,000. Did you tell them that? I'll be in town tomorrow and I'll see you then if I can. In any case I'll see you on Sunday of course.

Write me a line today if you can.

Your O.T.

1. An earlier version in his notebook is dated 28.9.08; see Oxford *Poems,* p. 64, for final version published in the Cuala Edition, 1909, and Yeats's notes on the poem in *Autobiographies* (London: Macmillan, 1955), p. 519.

[*TCD*]   Glendalough [*House*]
                                           Oct [*6th*[1] *1908*]

Dearest Child

This is a little line to bid you goodbye. It is ten o'clock and I'm very tired, with fussing and packing. I was in town this morning till the 1.30 train. Then I got back here and did some packing. Then out comes Roberts—though I had just left him—over some business about the poems, then I do some more packing then at 6 out comes Colum and settles down to talk, and stays till eight. Then I pack more—Isn't this a model of a sentimental lover's goodbye letter? I'm too tired to write. Thats what it is. I am writing with my new fountain pen. God help me I feel down and lonely going off this way. Good bye sweet Heart be very good.   T.

1. Synge misdated this October 8th.

[*TCD*]   City of Dublin Steam Packet Company
                               Royal Mail Steamer "Leinster"
                                    [*6 October 1908*]

Dearest

Here I am on the boat. We are near Holy Head now so I've run down to write you a line. It is rolling "a bit" so I cant write very much. I feel very well—the sea has been clear and calm couldn't have been better.

Write me a letter with nothing *very* confidential for fear of accidents to address on other page

                        c/o Fraulein von Eicken
                              Oberwerth
                              Coblence
                              Germany

I'm thinking of you a lot.

                                           Your old T

[*TCD/GS292*]
London. Wednesday
evening. Oct 7th/08

Dearest

    I am just beginning to pack up for my start to Germany at 8.35 to-night. I was very tired when I got here last night—I was turned away from three hotels—so I had to go to a sort of Boarding House. I have taken a very quiet day today however and I feel fairly fit again. I sat all the afternoon on a chair in Hyde Park and then had tea in the Express Tea Shop where I went with you last year. So I've been thinking of you a great deal. I hope this trip will set me up—I am only beginning to realize what a wreck this business has left me. However I wont be downcast—though it has been a depressing sort of day sitting about here by myself. I hope I shall find a letter from you when I get to Germany—I must stop now. I may have to post this letter without a stamp. Will you think it worth /2d?

Your old Wreck.

[*Texas/GS292*]
c/o Fraulein von Eicken
Oberwerth
Coblence
Germany
Thursday
Oct 8th?/08

Dearest Child

    I have got safely to my journey's end, and found the letter you wrote to Glendalough House waiting for me. You poor little animal to be making yourself unhappy because I did not run in to the Abbey in the Middle of a Rehearsal for an unsatisfactory half minute!!! When am I to have a letter from you to me here? I have been thinking about you to no end all this journey God bless your poor little soul. This place is a good deal changed but very pleasant still. I have been out by the Rhine till six o'clock—it was very clear and beautiful. I hope this will make a man of me again. As soon as ever I got into the train last night I felt better, and I got on as well as possible on the journey I got here a little after two this afternoon it was very hot the last part of the way and through a very uninteresting country

Oh how I hope I'll soon get back to you as well as ever my own little treasure of the world. Write me a really nice letter please.

Your J.M.S.

[*Texas/GS292*]   [*Coblenz. Germany*]
                                                   Friday [*9 October 1908*]
Dear Child
    There is no letter for me this morning—it is very strange that you have not sent me a line—I gave you this address in time surely.
    I'm sitting by the Rhine now about ten o'clock. I wish I could make you see it. The river is so wide the people look quite small on the opposite bank, and big steamers are going up and down. It is often very foggy in the morning—it is so now—and then about 12 or 11 the sun comes out and it is a beautiful day. At the other side of the Rhine I can see masses of trees, with bits of hilly vineyard behind them, and clumps of houses—ugly houses, yet quaint and German, in a way-
    Now a whole bevy of boats and steamers are coming up out of the fog on my left, and the sun is beginning to glitter in an extraordinary way on the water under the opposite side. The Rhine is a wide steady sweep of water, but when steamers pass waves begin curling up the bank.
    A little steamer has just galloped by—Police boat No VII on it. Now a big tug with two funnels is coming up & towing a string of barges nearly a quarter of a mile long—two little fellows with mops are leaning over the edge of the tug washing her sides. The barges all have little houses on the lower end of the deck, and you can see the women smacking their children just as if they were on land. It is all interesting and unlike what we are accustomed to. Does this sort of stuff bore you Eh? If it does mind you tell me. I must wander on now I'm getting a coldness where I'm sitting on the stones.

                                                   10.X.08
                                                   Saturday
Dearest
    Your little note of the 7th has reached me this morning—it was a wee bit long coming and I was getting uneasy; dont bother reading all the blather on the back of this[1] I wanted to show you this place and I

haven't brought it off. Its not easy; when I start describing anything I feel as if I was writing an article and then I get impersonal, and then its a ⟨bloody⟩ bad letter—⟨That's personal anyhow. Nish!⟩

Evening

I've been knocking round here all day—it's wonderful autumn weather —and lying under the acacias. The last half hour I've been sitting out on the balcony in the dark wondering what you were at, and if you missed me much—I felt desolate enough.

Yesterday at dinner one of the von Eickens plumped out that Mrs Vanston had told them that I was engaged to an actress—and then they popped out their eight heads to see what I'd say. So I told them the story and now they know all about you. Of course I'd have told them in any case. The married sister and her daughter have been here for the last couple of days and when they were going away the good lady made me a long speech of congratulations and good wishes for my marriage and so on, so on, so on! So you see you aren't forgotten.

All the von Eickens are very kind—by the way its Fraulein—not *Fraw*—but poor things they are most of them getting old. My friend[2] is nice still but you needn't be uneasy, I am beginning to count the days till I can get back to you. I am still a little knocked up from the journey. I wonder are you writing me long letters too get a little book like this and write in it whenever you've a little time. That will be good for both of us. Now I must wash my hands and get ready for supper. I wish you could have seen that German girl—not a bit pretty—she was something quite different from anything I've ever seen. Her mother had admirable gestures—I think you could learn a great deal here on the Continent. I'll never go abroad again without you. Nish!

Sunday

No letter today—one little hurried line only the six days I am out of Ireland You must write to me better than that. I am disappointed.

I suppose you'll get this on Tuesday—this is my 4th letter to you since I left Kingstown I wonder if you have got them all, one on the boat, one in London and two here. I hope you are well and taking care of yourself.

Your old J.M.S.

1. Synge wrote this and the following letter on the leaves from a small notebook similar to the one he had used the previous year in Kerry.

2. Valeska von Eicken, the youngest of the sisters, whom he had nicknamed "Gorse," see Greene and Stephens, *J. M. Synge,* pp. 36–40 et passim.

[*Texas/GS293*]   [*Coblenz. Germany*
                                                          12 October 1908]
                                                          Monday

My dearest Heart.

I got your little letter this morning and it nearly wrung my poor guts out with delight. I cant tell you how I liked it, you little blasted Changling!

I have come away into the woods this morning by myself. It is inconceivably wonderful—so still my breath sounds like a foghorn, and nothing but masses of trees everywhere. Towards the sun it is misty and silvery, and looking away from the sun it is all gold and green. I have been wandering on for an hour squatting down on every seat I came to (every quarter of a mile or so) to rest my poor ripped belly. The weather couldn't be better. Now I've come out of the trees into the sun on a big cliff over the Rhine, and I'm sitting in front of a Restaurant with a bottle of beer. It is perfectly blue and sunny over head, but there is fog down on the river so that I can not see the steamers.

I think this knocking about in the woods may help me with Deirdre in a way. I have written no more verses since I came here. I am not alone enough for one thing and for another the confusion of images one gets travelling about does not help one to write. A friend of the von Eickens, that I used [to] know, is an actress now and has played some good parts—leading female in *The Red Robe*[1] for instance. They tell me she only gets £6 a month and has to buy *all* her costumes out of her salary. How would you like that, you little Been!

How are your lessons with George[2] getting on, or was that *all talk?* I wonder if you are able to read this stuff that I scribble down so from one minute to another? On Saturday night a friend of the von Es. sent in a present of a great dish of oysters. They wanted me to have some, but like a wise man I didn't, glory be to God, for the family began to pewk yesterday and nearly split themselves! N.B. *Dont eat oysters!*

Evening

I am down by the Rhine and the lights are coming out all along the banks. When I think of you and all the nice things you've written to me I get a ripple of delight all through me. I'm reading a play of Sudermann's—the author of *Teja*³—now but it isn't very much good.

Tuesday 13.X.08

I'm just going off to the town of Coblence—we are outside—to buy some books so good morning to you meanwhile. How are you getting on with the Galleries? It is a week today since I left Kingstown so a *quarter* of my time is over. The pewking ladies are better again today. It is funny when I'm down by the Rhine all the signs the people make to me from the barges going by. Yesterday there was a woman beating a cushion, and when she saw me lying on the stones she held it up and patted it as much as to say—Would you like that to put under your—self! Another girl waved her bowl of soup at me. So my own little heart goodbye till the next time By the way, dont say by*e* the way.⁴

Your old T.   J.M.S.

1. *La Robe Rouge,* a satire on the law written in 1900 by the French playwright Eugene Brieux (1858–1922).
2. Probably Molly's favourite brother, who was killed in action in 1915.
3. Produced at the Abbey on 19 March 1908, in Lady Gregory's translation; the play was directed by Synge, and Molly played the role of Bathilde.
4. A mistake Synge usually made himself in his letters to Molly.

[*AS/TCD*]

c/o Fraulein von Eicken
Oberwerth
Coblence
Wednesday
14/X.08

Dearest Herzchen (little heart)

I suppose I'll hear from you tomorrow—and of course you'll tell me all about the Galleries you've been to! I'm getting on well I think on the whole. Yesterday I went into Coblence and ordered books Walter von der Vogelweide, and Hans Sachs—two old German poets—I want to do some translations from them if it goes, like the ones I did of Petrarch and Villon. Today I took a long walk into the woods to a bierhouse and drank my bottle of beer. I'm beginning to wish I was home again. Do you? Eh? I've just been down on the Rhine in the twilight, with a big bat gadding about me, and partridges making a great stir in the acacias. Do you know what acacias are? If you dont go to Glasnevin and look in the garden   one of the men would show them to you. I lie under them here half the day. I am more alone now as my novelty has worn off—they [are] still very good and kind. They are always enquiring about you. Now we'll see what tomorrow's post brings—

Thursday evening

No letter today, so I was a little disappointed I went out this morning to a place called Rhens one of the oldest little towns on the Rhine with little [houses] exactly as they were in the time of Aucassin and Nicolette —or a couple of centuries later. I'll try and get you some photos before I go back. I was too tired when I got there to do more than go into a Wirthhaus and drink a bottle of beer which cost /1½d. On my way out in the tram—the tram took me half way—they were gathering the grapes along the Rhine for the wine making. In one place there was a big barrel of grapes on the side of the road, so they stopped the electric tram, and the conductor and driver rushed over and came back with their hands full of grapes, and gave me a big bunch—I was [the] only passenger. We have jam here made of *our* little purple grapes—the fraughans—its great stuff. There are no heathy mountains here but they grow in the woods. I'm looking forward to hearing all about your gallery-visits. I suppose you play the 'Squeal' for the first time tonight. I wonder how it'll go.[1] I wish I was *home*. Nish! Nish.

Friday morning.

No letter! You wrote to me last on Saturday the letter which I got on Monday. Now Sunday, Monday, Tuesday, Wednesday you have not written—though I have been writing to you so much I am profoundly hurt and uneasy. ⎯⎯⎯
I came skipping down the stairs today absolutely certain that you would have written, but instead I only had the news that my mother is not getting on well so my good spirits are gone—

Saturday.

Still no letter—It is a fortnight tomorrow since I saw you and, you have written me only one line before I started and then one letter? I cannot conceive what has happened. I am ill and giddy with anxiety. ⟨In the two years we have known each other you *never* did anything like that before.⟩ If you are ill *get Sally to write. If I do not hear by return of post* I will go home.

J.M.S.

c/o Fraulein von Eicken
Oberwerth
Coblence. Germany.
Can you have made any mistake with. Great Christ I am sick with wretchedness.

1. On 8 October the Abbey Theatre gave the first performance of Lennox Robinson's first play, *The Clancy Name;* Molly played the part of Mrs. Spillane. Robinson (1886–1958) was appointed manager of the Abbey Theatre for a short time in 1910, until he too roused the wrath of Miss Horniman; he returned in 1919, became a director in 1923, and remained one until 1956. Twenty-two of his plays were produced at the Abbey.

[*Texas/GS293*]

c/o Fraulein von Eicken
Oberwerth
Coblence
20/X/08

My dearest Child

I was very much relieved to get your letter on Sunday—you shouldn't have left so long.

I am very sad tonight as I have just got very bad news of my poor old mother—she is much worse I am afraid—if she does not soon get better I shall have no one in the world but you—one's brothers and sisters though mine could not be kinder—are never the same as one's mother or one's wife. I have a lump in my throat as I am writing—She is in bed again now too weak to read or write, Her life is little happiness to her now and yet one cannot bear the idea of not having her with us any more. If she gets worse I will go home, perhaps, very soon I do not like to think of her all by herself in the house

Oct. 21st.

Your letter has just come. We wont quarrel about the number of your letters—at any rate you left me six days without news—and you said yourself in your last that you were *"a beast"* to have left me so long. I dont think any of your letters have gone astray as you have ac- knowledged all mine date by date,—one from my brother however *has* gone astray. I think I had better send you this today as I want you to know what I tell you in it. You mustn't think I'm crusty because its so short, I'm not but it's too cold to write in my room and I have to go out early. I sent you a card yesterday to acknowledge the Sunday letter. I cannot find any very interesting cards. Is Yeats back in Dublin yet? A thousand blessings, write soon again, and so will I. I had asthma the last two nights and I'm rather knocked up.

Your old T.M.S.[1]

---

1. Molly has written at the top of this letter *answered 24.X.08.*

[TCD]

Coblence etc.
23/X/08

Dearest Child

I have just got your letter of the 21st. It came very quickly, it is stamped Dublin 5 A.M. 22nd Coblence 4 P.M. 23rd and I have got it at 5. I am very sorry my card didn't please you. I thought that as I had scolded you, you would like to know I had got your letter and I thought the Irish would do as Tom could read it. He cant know much Irish as there is quite a different word for the cold one gets. I wrote that it was cold here. I got the card in Coblence and wrote it on a seat by the Rhine and sent it off.

I hope you are quite well again   I am uneasy about you, so you must write again by return and tell me how you are. I wrote you a

letter on Wednesday too, I suppose you have got it by this. I have had
no further news of my mother I shall probably hear tomorrow morning
before I post this. I feel lonely and sad here now and I am counting
the days to get home. At the latest I go home, all being well, on Thursday week so I have only about 12 more days here. I think I am much
better, and I can walk quite a good deal. The weather has been very
cold, but with bright, sometimes magnificently bright, sunshine.
Yesterday I went a bit up the Rhine to where another river the Lah⟨n⟩
joins in, and I sat on a seat in the sunshine opposite a little hill with
a big mediaeval castle on it, and read a modern German translation of
the Tristram and Isolde that you read the other day. The English version
is very much cut down, and things the good lady didn't approve of are
left out. Today I went to Rhens—the little old town again—it is extraordinarily quaint. There are houses that were built in 1400, with ordinary peasant people living in them still. I wish I could get some photos
of them, I'll try tomorrow.

Saturday 24th.

I have heard from my sister this morning that my mother is a little
better again, so I am in better spirits. Dont *you* get ill now, and be sure
you write to me by return to say how you are.

It is still bright and cold here. This morning I am going into
Coblence to get stamps and to see if I can find any interesting post-
cards for you. I hope you feel very penitent for having scolded me for
sending you the picture p'card as a little joke for you, you little Been!

I got a post card from Lebeau this morning from Canada—he is
still very lonely and unhappy I must write to him soon. Good God
I'm freezing I'll die of cold if I dont go out soon and get warm. I'm
writing in my room with the double window wide open and the frost
coming in. There is a lovely view, by the way, from this window of a
queer old German farm first, and then of the Rhine hills with woods
on them. If you were here we'd have great times but by myself, it's no
fun. I'm going to the Market in Coblence this morning to look at the
peasants etc.

Now be sure you write a nice and long letter, little Been, to cheer
me up again. In twelve days—damn them—I'll be on my way back to
you. So now take care of yourself goodby dearest

J.M.S.

[*AS*]   Coblence
                                          Monday [*26 October 1908*]

Dearest Heart

    I wrote a long cheerful letter to you yesterday and this morning but I do not care to send it to you tonight[1] as I have just got the bad news that you have probably heard. When I came in from my walk today one of the von Eickens came up to my room to say that a telegram had just come to say that my poor mother had passed away. I am hardly able to realize it. I wish I had you near me, now I have you to live for only. The von Eickens are exceedingly kind. Write to me here again when you get this—I cannot write much, I am very sad when I think of all my life and how endlessly kind and good she has been to me.

                Yours, my own heart,
                J.M.S.

    1. See letter below dated 25/X/08.

[*TCD/GS294–5*]   Coblence
                                          SUNDAY 25/X/08

Dearest Child,

    I am sitting up in my little room reading Walter von der Vogelweide and waiting for supper. I wonder what you're at! This has been a *diabolical* day, cold raw and wet, with snow in the morning—the first bad day since I left home. It reminded me of the speech in *The Well of the Saints* about the Almighty God looking out on the world bad days etc etc. I'm lonesome, it is absolutely silent up here except for an odd whiff of piano. The man who is playing is the landlord of Oberwerth—a baron—and lives in a big house stuck on to this one. He was married a long time ago and had one daughter, then he got tired of his wife, and when I was here last she was a faded poor creature who used to go streeling about by herself. The next thing was he fell in love with one of his farm girls and 'kept' her in Coblence. The wife heard of it and went off to Vienna and sent for the Baron. He went to her, and she asked him would he break off his connection. He said divel a bit, and came back here! The next day he got a telegram to say his wife had poisoned herself. He put the girl into a convent for six months and then married her. Now she is the lady baroness going about in furs and furbelows, and the men she used to make hay with are still working in the yard. The baron is cut by everyone and shuts himself up and plays the piano and composes all day. He is grey haired now, but a fine musician. They have three children—fine ones too.

Monday morning

I have just got your letter written on Saturday, and also a letter from my brother to say that my mother is still a little better. She is quite too ill to see anyone so she could not see you if you called, but you can call and enquire if you like. She is so ill I dont suppose they would even tell her you'd been there. So you have got a house with a nice view! I'm very glad you are leaving Mary Street but I hope you wont be very long in the new place.[1] How are you, I am nervous now when I hear of you getting unwell in your side after all I have gone through myself. My asthma is gone again, but I'm a little queer inside still. What a bit of news about Old Yeats![2]

I did *not* know about Sally—It must have happened since I left and I have not heard from the Directors—I forgot as a matter of fact to give them my address. I am sorry you think Sally a fool for doing what is honorable. I can only hope you wrote that without thinking, I'd like to give you a good scolding but I'll let you off as you have been ill. Please tell Yeats that I am going home on Thursday week—the time is coming near at last thank God. I'm weary to death of being here though they are all very kind. It is very foggy again today but not so cold as it has been.

Wednesday evening

Dearest Child,

I have had two very sad days since I wrote to you, but I am trying to be cheerful again, and to think happily of my poor old mother as I know she would have wished. She was 73 or 74 I think and unless people are exceptionally robust—which she never was—life after that age is mere fatigue and suffering. She often said she would rather die with all her faculties still clear than drag on into real old age. I wonder how you are   I am a little uneasy as I wrote on Saturday and asked you to write by return but you haven't. Do take good care of yourself —remember you are the whole world to me now. I wonder if you heard the sad news before my letter came to you. It must have been in the *Irish Times* on Tuesday and I should think some of you must have heard of it. My going home now will be very sad—I can hardly bear to think of going to Glendalough House she was always so delighted to see me when I came back from a journey—I cant go on.

Thursday *morning*

I expected a letter from you this morning—perhaps you think I am on my way home. I shall get a letter from my brother tomorrow, and then I will let you know what day I go home. I may stay on here for the week   my health is now all important. Do be careful of yourself
Your J.M.S.

Thursday
N.B. This is the letter I had written to you before I got the bad news when I thought all was going so well.

1. Molly had moved to 2 Vincent Terrace, Glasnevin.
2. J. B. Yeats decided to emigrate to America, and despite the arguments of family and friends on both sides of the Atlantic, sailed in November 1908 with his daughter Lily; he never returned to Ireland.

[TCD]
[Coblenz. Germany]
Friday [30 October 1908]

My dearest Treasure

I must just write you a line to thank you for your little letter and to tell you what an inexpressible comfort it is to me. You could not have written anything more tender or beautiful.

I am going to stay on here till Thursday so please write to me again. I do not know whether I shall go back to Glendalough House or to Silchester. My poor sister has not written to me yet. I had a kind letter from my brother this morning.

I am doing my best to be cheerful, and to pick up my health for your sake and mine.

Yours forever
J.M.S.

[*TCD*]   Coblence
Tuesday Nov 3rd/08

Dearest Heart

I was glad to get your note last night—the one you wrote on Saturday. This is a line merely to tell you that I leave here on Thursday —the day after tomorrow—and stay Friday night in London, so that I get to Kingstown at five o'clock on Saturday. Please write to me to Glendalough House.

I shall write to you on Saturday evening to arrange where to see you on Sunday. I suppose it will be at Glendalough House.

This last week here has been interminable. I can hardly sit quiet I am so anxious to be off. It will be very sad going to Glendalough House, still I shall have the great joy of seeing you again.

So—you will not hear again till Sunday morning.

Yours ever and always
J.M.S.

[*TCD*]   Montague Hotel,
2 & 3, Montague Street,
Russell Square,
London, W.C. Nov 6th 1908

Dearest

I have got as far as London on my way back—and my journey has been satisfactory so far. I have just had breakfast and now I have to loll about and rest myself all day. I left Coblenz at 4 P.M., got to the boat at 11 last night, and reached England at six this morning. The sun rose over low boggy tracts and arms of sea just after the train started.

It was indescribably wonderful. We must often get up early and see the sun rise.

I am infinitely glad to be on my way home—though at times a wave of sorrow comes over me that nearly breaks me down. You will get this I suppose on Saturday morning, please write then to say if you can get your dinner early enough on Sunday to come down by the quarter to two! The days are so short now the quarter to three would leave us little time. I think this first day we will be happier out walking than in Glendalough House. I hope I shall find a nice letter to cheer me when I arrive. I can hardly realize how empty the house will seem

Your old T.

[TCD]   [*Glendalough House*
                                                7 November 1908]
Dearest

I am home at last. I am inexpressibly sad in this empty house. You had better come by the quarter to *three* tomorrow (Sunday) otherwise you could not dine. I will meet you at Glenageary and we can go to Bray for a while. It is too sad here. I hope you were not hurt by your fall. I am sorry to hear you are not feeling well again.

Till tomorrow—I am too unhappy to write you anything that is not gloomy.

Your O.T.

[TCD/GS295]   Glendalough House
                                              Kingstown
                                              Nov 9th /08
                                              five o'clock
Dearest

I have just been in town and ordered my black suit. I have to try it on tomorrow so you will not be able to come and see me here. Will you meet me at *Tara Street* at twenty minutes to three. I am to try on at four so we could take a little turn and then have tea.

It is very dreary coming back to this empty house. Last night when I came home I found I was locked out. The little donkey of a servant had gone out and left both the latch and lock on. She had the lock key and I had the latch key so she couldn't get in either. I found her and got in about half past seven. I wasn't very well last night. I woke up feeling very queer and I thought I was going to get very sea sick, but it didn't come to anything.

My sister told me all about the money affairs today. I am to have £1500 share (at 5%) out of the property, that with what I have will make £110 a year, so—if only my health holds we will be able to get on now. My sister says that apart from my share of the things—I can have all the little things I need for a house if I take one carpets, saucepans linen etc etc. I will not get any money for six months. You need not repeat these particulars. The £1500 is I think really mine, not for my life only, so I will have that to leave you. Otherwise I should have had to save closely. If the Abbey breaks now we will have enough to live quite comfortably in Dundrum or somewhere in the country.

Your old T.

If you're not at Tara St. I'll understand you cant come. I hope you'll take care of yourself tonight.

[TCD/frag/GS295]

[Glendalough House]

Monday night [9 November 1908]

Dearest Child

I have just been out and posted a letter to you and then walked up and down in the dark. As you are not here I feel as if I ought to keep writing to you all the time though tonight I cannot write all that I am feeling. People like Yeats who sneer at old fashioned goodness and steadiness in women seem to want to rob the world of what is most sacred in it. I cannot tell you how unspeakably sacred her memory seems to me   There is nothing in the world better or nobler than a single-hearted wife and mother. I wish you had known her better, I hope you'll be as good to me as she was—I think you will—I used to be uneasy about you sometimes but now I trust you utterly, and unspeakably. I am afraid to think how terrible my loneliness would be tonight if I had not found you. It makes me rage when I think of the people who go on as if art and literature and writing were the first thing in the world. There is nothing so great and sacred as what is most simple in life.

[*TCD/GS278*]   Glendalough [*House*]
                                    Saturday [*14 November 1908*]
Dearest
    I may see you tonight at the theatre but I'm writing this in case I dont. Come down tomorrow by the quarter to three—I suppose it's the best—and come here. We may go for a little walk but not to Bray. I'm getting on pretty well, but I'm very lonely. Yesterday was the first day I've had here all by myself.
    I did a good [deal] of work on Deirdre not on the MS. but just notes for a new scene in it. I'm going in to Lady G today at five. I didn't ask you to meet me earlier as you should not walk and I should not sit, and there's no good knocking ourselves up. Excuse this hasty line—I was going to write to you an hour ago but my sister came in and I couldn't
            Yours ever and only
            J.M.S.

[*TCD*]   [*Glendalough House*]
                                    Monday [*16 November 1908*]
Dearest Love
    I haven't much to say since yesterday except that its mighty cold and I've got into my warm garments. Air yours tonight and put them on, it is far more comfortable. I believe all my inside misery has come from cold.
    Come down by the quarter to eleven tomorrow if its fine and if it isn't come by the quarter to two and come to the house. If there's any

change of plan I'll wire to you at cock-crow   I hope you're warm and
good and happy.

Your old

Tramp

I enclose the cutting for Sally bring it back to me

[*TCD*]   Glendalough [*House*]
Nov 17th 1908

Liebes Kind

Ich habe belly-ache. How are you getting on and why do you
never write to me now?

Will you come and see me tomorrow by the quarter to three? I
think I've got a good scene now for the beginning of Act II, Deirdre,
altogether between Lavarcham and Deirdre.

Have you heard from Sally?[1] I have rheumatism in my back and
neck today and I'm not at all happy.

So I cant write still I have written a whole sheet eh?[2]

J.M.S.

1. Sara Allgood had gone to London to act with Mrs. Pat Campbell in a brief run of
Electra and Yeats's *Deirdre* in which Mrs. Campbell had appeared with the Abbey Theatre
9–16 November.
2. Synge has scrawled this in large writing across the second side of the page.

[*TCD*]   [*Glendalough House*
21 November 1908?]

Dearest

I'm just off to the Abbey. This is to say you're to come down tomorrow (Sunday) by the quarter to *three*. If it's fine I'll meet you and
we'll go on to Bray, if not come here.

I was very glad to get your letter this morning—I was just thinking
last night of the time you used to write to me every day—when we
were young.

I'm better inside I think

Your old T J.M.Synge

[*TCD/GS297*]   Glendalough [*House*]
                                           Nov 24th/08

Dearest Child

   Will you come down to me on *Thursday* by the quarter to three?
I am going to MacKenna tomorrow and he forgot to ask you—I told him
what you'd said about them but he took it (from the way I put it) to
refer to his wife only—you remember you said what a lovely world
it would it would be if there were many like them.

He writes—"It was really good of you to tell me that pleasant remark
                          J.M.S.
upon my Lady, of course it is true (!) but also it was pleasant to hear.
My wife too was greatly pleased with Miss O'Neill, greatly attracted
(no less! J.M.S.) to her, and greatly enjoyed pleasant talk in the garden
and over the house. We both hope to have many such pleasant talks
round the friendly table." Nish! He probably feels that after all that has
happened here I might like to go there alone the first time and sit with
him quietly in his book room. I am really delighted that you've 'cap-
tured' Madame. Why wouldn't you, but still women are strange beasts,
and she's capricious in her likes—the same as your own self. I suppose
you're very hard at work this week.

   I strained my knee getting in to the tram yesterday—the fellow
started full tilt before I got up and then my foot slipped off the step
as it was slippery with the mud. So my knee is stiff and queer. I have
very nearly got a full version now of the second act of Deirdre. I wish
I could see a show of *The Well of the Saints*. The third act used to go so
well, and I thought I had improved it, but now you say it drags. At
Cambridge Fay got round after round of applause during the last half
of the third act.[1]

   I suppose you'll be at the Theatre of Ireland this afternoon.[2] Write
me a nice letter to say you'll come on Thursday.

                                           Your O.T.J.M.S.

I wrote another poem on you last night.
Did you find the House? in Glasnevin.

---

   1. A revival of *The Well of the Saints,* with a revised third act and new costumes and
setting designed by Charles Ricketts, was performed on 14 May 1908; Synge directed the

first rehearsals himself but had to call in Lady Gregory to take over when he entered Elpis.

2. The Theatre of Ireland produced *The Turn of the Road* by "Rutherford Mayne," pen name of Samuel Waddell (b. 1878), and *The Flame on the Hearth* by Seumas O'Kelly (1881–1918), 23 and 24 November in the Abbey Theatre.

[*TCD*]
Glendalough [*House*]
Saturday Nov 28th/08

Dearest Child

I feel very lonely this wet day thinking that I'll have no more of you for ten days. I wrote to Lady Gregory yesterday to ask if I should have my talk with her after the matinée or this morning, and she has replied 'after the matinée', so I will not be able to be with you. This weather I am quite sure it would be foolish to bring you down here tomorrow before your long journey, so there is no chance of seeing you. Be sure to send me your address when you get to Belfast and to tell me how you have got on.[1] You must write very often—a post knock even is a relief in this empty silent House. I got [a] letter from my aunt in Greystones[2] asking me to bring *you* down there to lunch some day —I have answered that you are very shy (!) (little brassy!) but that I would do my best. So we can do whatever we like. It is very kind of her. There is a sentence in her letter I will quote to you the next time I have not got her letter with me now. My poems have come back from *The Nation* as "not quite suitable" I'm not much surprised.

I wrote to a houseagent yesterday and got a list of a lot of little houses in Rathgar—all in Red Terraces I am afraid—from £34 to £45 a year.

Excuse the paper I am getting very economical. I am sad. Be *very good* on your tour, and take care of yourself

Your old Waif,
J.M.S.

Am I to address you as Miss O'Neill on tour?

1. The company was appearing at Theatre Royal, Belfast for the week 30 November to 5 December.
2. Mrs. Harriet Traill Dobbs, Mrs. Synge's sister.

[*Texas*]   Glendalough Ho
                                                      Nov 30th/08

Dearest Child

You are very good—I have had two letters from you today—I
laughed over Mac and the four porters, I wish I had seen it. I think
I am a little better I took a hard quick longish walk with my nephew
yesterday and I think the exercise did me good. After that I came home
here and had tea and then wrote a lot of letters that I have had lying
over for a long time.

Today I went to town after my dinner, and went to the National
Gallery—I'M not an old stick in the mud—and saw a new picture that's
there lent by Hugh Lane a Titian a wonderful thing that filled me with
delight.[1] I also saw portraits of Swift and Stella, and I wondered how
we'll look when we're stuck up there!

So you saw a Turner sunset! That was very clever of you. Nish.
After the N.G. I went to Roberts on business and had a long talk with
him. Then I had a D.B.C.T.—(isn't that smart)—down stairs, and on
my way to the train I met Miss Garvey.[2] She says she hears that Frank
Fay is to get the sack after Christmas. I dont know who she heard it
from   it evidently wasn't from Frank.

I wonder how you are doing tonight. Hone saw Mrs P's[3] Deirdre
in London. He says it was not so well done as in the Abbey, but that
it was very well put on and the men were tall and fine-looking.

I think I have got the first scene in A.II right now—so the Act may
be nearly finished when you come back. Yes I'll go to Parsons this
week, God help us.

I've been working at the Preface to my poems tonight. Be very good
and write very often
                    Your old T.J.M.S.

1. Titian's portrait of Baldesar Castiglione, later bequeathed to the National Gallery
of Ireland by Hugh Lane.
2. Mary Garvey (Maire Ni Gharbhaigh) joined Fay's Irish National Dramatic Society
in January 1904 and was one of the co-signers of the original agreement with Miss
Horniman over the gift of the Abbey Theatre. She resigned when the company became a
limited society in September 1905 and acted subsequently with the Theatre of Ireland
company.
3. Mrs. Pat Campbell performed in Yeats's *Deirdre* in London, with Sara Allgood as
First Musician.

[*TCD*]   Glendalough [*House*]
                                         Dec 2nd/08

Dearest Child

Your little note came today by the second post I am sorry your business is so bad—I am not so sure that it is all *Scapin*'s fault. Why didn't you send me a cutting or two? I am not surprised that *The Shadow of the Glen* wasn't a great success—Kerrigan does not suit the tramp and without the tramp there is no play. I suppose Sally is with you today. Perhaps the end of your week will be better.

I haven't been to Parsons yet, but *I'll go.* Yesterday I went to Bray and walked up as far as the 'little woodland path' as you used to call it, and back by that road. It was a most wonderful evening. Today I took a walk from here round the golf-links and round a road you've never been. The only excitement I had—it was a vile muggy day—was that I saw a squirrel fall out of a tree!! He was high up skying along from one tree to another and he missed his poor little shot and down he came head over tail with a thud behind the wall. I ran across and looked over, but he was gone, so he was killed out-and-out.

I feel pretty wretched, and very lonely tonight. Anyhow you've only three days more. I'm glad you are dull as you'll be all the gladder to come back. Did you see the letters in today's *Irish Times* from Miss Horniman and Connolly? She's not going to give them the theatre any more and they are naturally raging! If any one talks to you about it up there—the Ulster people I mean—you'd best say that it is Miss Horniman's affair—it is her theatre and she can do what she likes.[1]

I haven't anything to make this letter interesting. I am always over-joyed to hear from you.

My brother was in for a few minutes this morning except for him I've seen no one all day—it isn't very cheerful.

Deirdre's going well I think D— her.

                        Your old T————————!

---

1. The Theatre of Ireland company was advertised as "members of the Abbey Theatre Company" when they moved their productions to the Gaiety Theatre for 26–28 November; despite a published apology by the Theatre of Ireland Secretary, Miss Horniman refused to allow the group to hire the Abbey Theatre again.

[*TCD*]   Glendalough Ho
                                                               Dec 4th/08

Dearest Child

Your little note came today—it was very short and hurried and
scrappy with very little to cheer me up in my solitude

I have just come from Dr Parsons. I will tell you all he said when I
see you. Is it you and Sally or you and Dossy who are stopping at the
Wrights? in Balbriggan? You can do what you like.

Henderson has sent me one paper each day. It is silly stuff they
write even when they praise. Hendersons booming of Sally has not had
a good effect. I am glad you are to be home so soon. I am very lonely.

I hope you will enjoy the supper tomorrow night.

I seem to be unable to write, this evening. Blessings on you. Come
home safe

       Your old T.J.M.S.y.

You'll not hear from me again of course till you get home.

[*TCD*]   Glendalough House
                                                          Saturday Dec 5/08

Dearest Child

I'm afraid my letter yesterday wasn't very agreeable—I was dis-
couraged and sad and lonesome, and your proposal to stop at Balbriggan with U. Wright and his people of course hurt me. What would
you think if I was travelling with [the] company and I got out at a
station with Miss Gildea to stay with her and her relations. I can
imagine the sneers and jokes there'd have been at *me* among the
company if you had done it. I didn't mean to allude to it all, in this
letter but I've done it surely.

I am glad to see by the papers today—that Henderson sent—
how well things have gone after all. It is very unfair how the booming
of Sally has influenced the papers. For instance Mac in the Sergeant[1]
—or you in Nora Burke are certainly better than she is in *The Man who
Missed* [*the Tide*]. Yet look at the papers!

Will you come down here on Monday! I believe there is a fire
rehearsal at the Abbey—I dont know what time. You can come here
any time you like, but send me a line to say.

I was at the Municipal Gallery today but it [was] too dark to see anything with comfort. God help me I'm afraid I'm not very well.

I met Roberts and Miss Garvey in Grafton Street. They looked very beaming.

      So till Monday I hope

                Your O.T.

1. In Lady Gregory's *The Rising of the Moon.*

[*TCD*]   Glendalough House
                                 Dec 11th/08

Dearest Child

Why didn't you come down today—or at least send me a line to say you couldn't come.

I am not at all well and I feel deserted and wretched. A week of holidays is over now and you've only come to me once. Will you come tomorrow? Please write by return.

The servant is just going out so I will send this by her.

                Your old T

                J.M.S.

I met the train today fully certain that you'd be in it.

[*TCD*]   [*Glendalough House*]
                        Friday Dec 18th/08

Dearest

Will you come down tomorrow (Saturday) by the quarter to three for a good long afternoon. If you cant come let me know and if you can write and say so.

I've spoken to no one since I left you except Brigit—and a beggar man. How did you get on last night? I wonder will you *have had* the grace to write to me about your adventures, before this reaches you.

I heard from Agnes Tobin today. She had seen Sally and Mrs P. She [said] Mrs P had lovely moments but was spoiled by a bad com-

pany and a poor mise-en-scène. I dont take her criticism very seriously.
That's all that's happened I think—I've done the usual amount of
Deirdre, and had the usual belly-aches and taken my usual little walks,
—bad cess to the lot of them.

Be sure and come tomorrow. I feel like a watch that wants to be
wound when you dont come. Henderson is coming on Monday

Your O T
J.M.S.

When is Sally coming back?

[*TCD*]   Glendalough House
Dec 21st/08

Dearest

Brigit wants to go into town for a day's shopping tomorrow so
I'm afraid you'd better *not* come for lunch. She'll be in a great fuss all
the morning. Come by the quarter to three, of course, and make my
tea for me here.

I've had Henderson here for two hours, and I've told him my mind,
or some of it. I'll tell you more tomorrow.

So good night Dear Heart
Your O.T.

I hope you enjoyed the Municipal Gallery!!

[*TCD/GS298*]   [*Glendalough House*]
22nd/XII/08

Dearest

I remembered your pupil last night (after I had written) and wondered if you'd come. Will you come to lunch tomorrow—you do not
say what day you rehearse—if you will come let me have a line by
return or there'll be nothing to eat. If you are rehearsing in the morning
come in the afternoon will you? Anyhow let me know. I dine with my
brother in the evening, but that wont interfere.

It is frightfully damp out here now   I dare say it's dryer in Glasnevin. I wish I was out of this house. I've nothing much to tell you. I've

pretty nearly gone on to the end of Deirdre and cut it down a little. It is delicate work a scene is so easily spoiled. I am anxious to hear you read it to me.

You ask *me* to write you letters and then what is it I ask you, that you write yourself? I dont see any notice of the Carols this year I wonder if they are coming off. If they do I suppose we should go.

Your ———

————

——

—

J.M.S.

Give my love to Sally.

[*Texas/GS298*]   [*Glendalough House*]
Dec 24th/08

Dearest

I feel humiliated that I showed you so much of my weakness and emotion yesterday. I will not trouble you any more with complaints about my health—you have taught me that I should not—but I think I owe it to myself to let you know that if I am so 'selfpitiful' I have some reason to be so as Dr Parsons report of my health, though uncertain, was much more unsatisfactory than I thought it well to tell you. I only tell you now because I am unable to bear the thought that you should think of me with the contempt I saw in your face yesterday.

Your O T

[*TCD*]   [*Glendalough House*]
Dec 25th/08

Dearest Child

Your letter reached me today and was a great relief to me. I am not sure if I will be at the Abbey tomorrow. I haven't been very well the last couple of days, and I will not be able to go in unless I am better. You needn't be uneasy it is nothing new, only the same troubles inside somewhat worse than they were.

I am here alone all this afternoon, Brigit is gone to Lucan for the day.

Your present hasn't come yet or if it came the house was empty so I hope I'll get it tomorrow. I got *one* Xmas card—from Martin Harvey of all people in the world!

I heard also from Florence Ross   she says she will be very glad if you'll go out to see her.

Will you come to me as usual on Sunday—come here if I do not meet you—

Your old T.

AGREEMENT made this the 14 day of *February* *1908* between The National
Theatre Society Limited of the one part and *Miss M. O'Neill*
of the other part .

WHEREBY it is agreed that in consideration of the sum of *£1"5"0*
paid weekly by the said National Theatre Society Limited to the said
Miss O'Neill the said *Miss O'Neill* agrees to rehearse
and perform to the best of his skill and ability such parts as he may
be cast for in plays performed by the Society and carry out such
other duties as he may be called on to perform.

IT IS ALSO AGREED that the said salary shall be inclusive of seven
performances weekly if required.

THIS ENGAGEMENT to commence on *the 14 February 1908*
at *the Abbey Theatre* and continue in force one month's notice on
either side.

THAT should the said *Miss O'Neill* be imperfect (provided
a reasonable time has been allowed for rehearsals) and not speak the
AUTHOR'S lines at any performance he shall be subject to suspension
and have no claim for salary beyond the proportion due up to such
imperfect performance till decision of the Directors on the matter
shall be given.

That should the said *Miss* conduct *her* self in or out of
the Theatre in a manner calculated to bring discredit upon the
SOCIETY he shall be liable to instant dismissal and have no claim
for salary whatever.

That said *Miss O'Neill* shall conform to all rules of the Society.

Molly Allgood (M. O'Neill)

Maire O'Neill's contract

Molly Allgood, about 1908

John M. Synge, from
the painting by
John Butler Yeats, 1908

[*TCD*]   [*Glendalough House*]
                                              Jan 1st 1909

Dearest Child

A Happy New Year to you and many of them! I was very pleased
to get your nice little note today,—it was a nicer one than I've had for
some time. I was in bed by that hour though I could just hear the steam
whistles roaring through my sleep. I dont think you would find
Saturday a good day to go to the Miss Yeats'—*unless* they said so—as
they are likely to give their girls a halfholiday and shut up their work
rooms—which you are going to see. If you *do* go tomorrow you'll have
to go by train—it is too long a walk for you from the tram.

If you dont go then you'd better come here, and if you do send me
a line before 11. G.P.O. to say you're coming. If you cant come tomorrow come on Sunday of course. Have you acknowledged Miss White's
cheque? You should do so at once if you haven't.

I have been trying to keep myself busy the last couple of days to
see how that will work. I went to MacKenna yesterday. He was out
when I went and I'd a long talk with Madame—then in came Master
Stephen with his hair on end and a mass of mud down from his ear to
his heel—you never ever saw such a sight. He'd fallen in a tram-line
and nearly been decapitated by a motor. Then we chatted till 6.30 and
he walked down to the tram with me. They renewed their invitation
for you to go as often as possible.

Today I took a long walk in the morning, and then I went in on
top of the tram and saw Roberts on business, and came home. I couldn't
have arranged to meet you as I was quite uncertain if I'd go. Nish!

A thousand blessings and come soon—*Dont kill* yourself trying to
write in the morning if it [is] not easy I'll be about here in any case
if you come.

[*TCD*]   Glendalough House
                                              Saturday Night [*2 January 1909*]

Dearest Child

Hell and Confusion and Brimstone! I have just got a post card
from Magee to say that he and Best[1] are coming out to see me tomorrow
afternoon at 4 o'clock ———B———G. ——— Ch———H———Y

That means I am afraid that you cant come tomorrow. What a pity. I have tried to think of some alternative plan but there is none so you must come on Monday or Tuesday instead. What a great evening we had today and tomorrow we'll be lonesome O be C   Oh——B   Oh
     Write to me a long letter instead
            Your old T.

1. Richard Irvine Best (1872–1959) had known Synge in his Paris days; Synge reviewed Best's translation of H. D'Arbois de Jubainville's *Le Cycle mythologique Irlandais* in *The Speaker,* 2 April 1904. Best was at this time on the staff of the National Library of Ireland; he became Director of the Library in 1924, holding that post until 1940 when he became Senior Professor of the School of Celtic Studies in the Dublin Institute for Advanced Studies. From 1948 until 1956 he was Chairman of the Irish MSS. Commission.

[*TCD*]   [*Glendalough House*
                                                              5 January 1909]
Dearest Child
    I went to Parsons today but he was running off to the country to somebody and could not see me so I am to see him tomorrow. Then I went up the Quays and looked at the book shops for a while and came home by the quarter to four. I met Starkey—and he seemed amazed to see me; he said he had heard that I was ill again. Remember if any one asks you how I am you are to say I'm all right   I dont want to have people condoling with me.
    I suppose you'll go to the Miss Yeats' tomorrow and then I think you had better come down to supper on Thursday however I'll write to you tomorrow and fix up.
    I am better than I was yesterday and I have done a good deal of Deirdre today
          Your old T———
Excuse this shabby line I'm in a hurry for the post—I only wrote because I thought you might be on the look out for news of Parsons.

[*TCD*]   Glendalough House
                                                      Jan 6th/09

Dearest

I saw Parsons today—there were 17 people waiting in his room but he took me first as I had an appointment. He does not think I am worse than I was a month ago, and he has given me some medicine and he says he thinks I'd better look in and see Ball and see what he thinks of me.

What about tomorrow evening? Do you feel you would be fresh enough and energetic enough to come down so late and for so short a time? I'll be delighted if you'll come but try and let me know by the early post if you are coming—That is to say dont ride under a tram or do anything rash in order to get to the G.P.O. on time—but write if you can.

Parsons says I may cycle a little if I like   I think I'll begin soon I've been working at Deirdre a lot but I'm not satisfied at all.[1]

                                                      Your old T

If you come tomorrow it would have to be by the quarter to five—later trains would be too late—if it was as fine as tonight we might go and walk on the pier by moonlight after supper.

                                                      J.M.

---

1. *Deirdre of the Sorrows* was never finished to Synge's satisfaction. After his death Yeats, Lady Gregory, and Molly assembled a final text from the thousand typescript pages; this text was the basis of the Abbey Theatre production with Molly in the title role, on 13 January 1910, and the Cuala Press edition in July 1910.

[*Texas*]   [*Glendalough House*]
                                                      Jan 11th/09

Dearest

I am writing this in a hurry—merely to tell you that I've seen Ball and that he is hopeful, and has ordered me a big dose of Castor Oil to clear me out. I forgot that my cousin will probably be here *tomorrow* so do not come down unless I wire for you.

This must go now so God bless us. I met Columb[1] today in town, he's a queer looking little creature now.

Your O.T.

---

1. Padraic Colum (b. 1881), poet and playwright who left the Abbey Theatre with the dissenters in 1905, transferring his plays, *Broken Soil* and *The Land,* to the Theatre of Ireland; he returned to the Abbey with *Thomas Muskerry* in 1910 and in 1914 emigrated to the United States.

[*AS/GS298–9*]
Glendalough House
Tuesday Jan 12th [1909]

Dearest Heart

This is another mere line to tell you I am getting on well I think—though for the time being I'm more wretched than ever. Sir C.B. was evidently right in what he thought—or part of it—but I'm not cured yet, so I'll have to give myself more doses, God help me. However if that will set me right then may Heaven's eternal fragrance fall on Castor Oil. I wonder if you can follow all this. I've been thinking about you a great deal with your little socks for me, and all your little attentions and I'm ready to go down on [my] knees to your shadow—if I met it in a dry place—I think I'm drunk with Castor Oil!

My cousin was out with me today for a long time and he's coming again—tomorrow Wednesday afternoon, so I wont see you I fear till Thursday. Write me a nice letter—there's a bit of hope for us still Glory be to God.

Your old Tramp.[1]

---

1. Later Molly mistakenly wrote on the envelope *my dear ones last letter to me.*

[*TCD*]
Glendalough House
Saturday 16.I.09

Dearest

I've had such a take in. That wretched man wrote that he was coming down this afternoon. Then at 20 to three he drove up on a car, left his car outside, came in for ten minutes, and then off again, leaving me here for a wretched lonely day. I took more Castor Oil this morning but it is no use I'm afraid.

Of course you'll come down tomorrow by the quarter to three. I wonder if you are skating today—if you are happy and amusing yourself that's one good thing at any rate. I haven't been out at all today

Your old T.

I am watching every footfall in hopes that you may come still. It is only four thirty. How shall I get through the evening?

[TCD]   *[Glendalough House*
                                                1 February 1909]

Dearest

I am going in to Elpis tomorrow to get there about one. I'll be very tired and they'll probably put me to bed and keep me very quiet.

I am certainly a little *better* today so that is a great thing. Eh, Mister?

Will you please send me *The Mill on the Floss*—or else *Silas Marner* (both by George Eliot), both published by Nelson /6d—I think—to Elpis some time any time tomorrow. I'll let you know how I do. Now I must stop.

Your old Tramp

                                        [Elpis Nursing Home]
                                        May 4th *[1908]*[1]

My dearest Love

This is a mere line for you, my poor child, in case anything goes wrong with me tomorrow to bid you good-bye and ask you to be brave and good, and not to forget the good times we've had and the beautiful things we've seen together

Your old Friend.

1. On the day before his operation the previous year, Synge addressed this letter to Molly at the Abbey Theatre and wrote on the envelope *to be sent in cover in case of death;*

it was stored with his papers until his death 24 March 1909. Lady Gregory, who had also received a letter written at the same time, wrote to Molly from Italy, 22 May 1909: "I have just been sent a letter written to me by Mr. Synge just before the operation last year. He tells me of his having hoped to marry at Easter, and asking me in case of his death to do what I could for you—I know you will be touched by this proof of his thought for you, as I am touched by his having written as it were a farewell to me . . . . I hope you are keeping well, and keeping your courage, as he would have wished you to do." The original of Lady Gregory's letter is in the possession of Miss Elizabeth Coxhead.

Maire O'Neill as Deirdre of the Sorrows

Index

Index

Abbey Theatre, xi, xiv, xvii, xx; "At Home," xxvi; chronicle of events, xxv–xxx; company tours, xvii, xxv, xxvi, 3n, 14n, 26, 36, 132ff, 141n, 173n; 173ff, 216n, 217ff, 236n, 237ff, 276ff, 303, 303n; matinees, xxvii, xxviii, 65, 66n, 203, 206, 207n, 211, 213; possibility of American tour, 93, 106, 110n, 113, 114, 116, 143, 181, 217

Aberdeen, xxvi, 36n, 174

Allgood, Molly (Maire O'Neill), xi ff; as Bathilde (*Teja*), 289n; as Cathleen (*Riders to the Sea*), xvii, xxvi, 83 (illus.); as Decima (*The Player Queen*), xxi; as Deirdre (*Deirdre of the Sorrows*), xx, 319 (illus.); as Kitty (*The Mineral Workers*), 42n; as Mary (*The Gaol Gate*), 31, 32n; as Maryanne Clohesy (*The Country Dressmaker*), 201n; as Min Dillane (*The Country Dressmaker*), 201n; as Molly Byrne (*The Well of the Saints*), xxix; as Mona (*Dervorgilla*), 210, 210n; as Nora Burke (*The Shadow of the Glen*), xvii, xxvi, 37n, 207n, 208, 220, 306; as Pegeen Mike (*The Playboy of the Western World*), xii, 1 (illus.), 85, 88n, 90; as Mrs. Spillane (*The Clancy Name*), 291n; as Zerbinette (*The Rogueries of Scapin*), 246; death of, xxi

Allgood, family, xii; George (Molly's father) xvi; George Junior (Molly's brother), xvi, 259, 288, 289n; grandmother O'Neill, xvi, 40; Harry (Molly's brother), xvi, 259; Johanna (Annie, Molly's sister), xvi; Margaret Harold (Molly's mother), xvi, xviii, 14n, 27, 69, 72; Margaret (Peggy, Molly's sister), *see* Callender; Sara (Sally, Molly's sister), xii, xiv, xvi, xvii, xxi, xxix, 4, 4n, 7, 9, 14, 14n, 17, 39, 72, 88n, 111, 122, 125, 134, 139, 148, 156, 160, 161, 168, 169, 170n, 174, 183, 185, 191, 192n, 209, 221, 222, 222n, 224, 225, 226, 228, 241, 242, 242n, 252, 254, 255, 256, 262, 265, 267, 267n, 268, 276, 291, 295, 300, 301n, 305, 306, 308, 309; Tom (Molly's brother), xvi; Willie (Molly's brother), xvi

Andersen, Hans Christian, 192, 192n

Annamoe, 162, 163, 164, 165, 168

Aran Islands, Co. Galway, 132, 185, 204, 237n, 248n, 260

Aran Islands, The (J. M. Synge), 46, 47n, 68, 128, 184, 190n, 237n

Aucassin and Nicolette, 46, 49, 162, 192

Australia, 228

Balbriggan, Co. Dublin, xxvi, xxix, 1, 4, 8, 9, 248n, 249, 306

Ball, Sir Charles (JMS's surgeon), 194–195, 195n, 197, 198, 201, 246, 250, 254, 257, 258, 261, 271, 283, 315; Dr. Ball, Junior, 263, 264, 265, 266, 268, 269

Ballybrack Hill, Co. Dublin, 116, 134 (see map)

Barker, Harley Granville, 66n, 173, 173n, 185

Barrie, James M., xxvii, 110n

Barry, Dr. Arthur P., 157n, 167, 168, 170, 188

Belfast, xxix, 303

Best, Richard Irvine, 313, 314n

Birmingham, England, 132n, 141, 145, 150, 151, 153

Birmingham, George, xxi

Blasket Islands, 3, 20, 257

Blunt, Wilfred Scawer, xxvii, 114n

Bourdillon, F. W., 46

Bourgeois, Maurice (JMS's first biographer), 135n

Boyle, William, xxv, xxvi, xxvii, 42, 122, 123n

Brawne, Fanny, xxii

Bray, Co. Wicklow, 9, 30, 31, 33n, 42, 57, 78, 79, 100, 125, 127, 128, 134, 139, 140, 151, 184, 187, 201, 209, 219, 256, 257, 258, 260, 264, 269, 273, 300, 301, 305 (see map)

Brayden, William, 100n

Brides' Glen, Co. Wicklow, 126, 131, 134, 173

Brieux, Eugène, 289n

Brigit (JMS's housekeeper), 307, 308, 310

Brittany, 174n, 175, 200

Brodzky, Leon (Spencer Brodney), 228, 229n

Broken Soil, The (Padraic Colum), 316n

Building Fund, The (William Boyle), xxv

Burke, Dan (*The Shadow of the Glen*), 4n, 79

Burke, Nora (*The Shadow of the Glen*), 79, 149n, 232n; *see also* Molly Allgood as Nora Burke

Cahirciveen, Co. Kerry, 20, 21
Calderon de la Barca, Pedro, 252n, 254n
Callender, Margaret (Peggy, Molly's sister), xvi, 14n, 17, 18n, 48, 59, 86n, 89, 107, 116n, 117, 119, 256, 258, 265
Callender, Tom (Molly's brother-in-law), xviii, 17, 18n, 59, 86n, 240, 292
Calthrop, Rosie, 189, 189n, 191
Cambridge, England, xxviii, 136, 137, 139, 140, 142, 145, 302
Campbell, Mrs. Patrick, xxviii, xxix, 207n, 208n, 301n, 304, 304n, 307–308
Canavans, The (Lady Gregory), xxvii, 74
Cardiff, Wales, xxvi, 4, 36n, 43, 60, 153
Carrantvohill, Co. Kerry, 18
Carrickmines, Co. Dublin, 6, 38, 40, 131, 222 (see map)
Casey, Sarah (*The Tinker's Wedding*), 112n
Casey, W. F., xxix, 243–244
Catriona (Robert Louis Stevenson), 22, 22n
Chaucer, Geoffrey, 227, 229–230, 259
Clancy Name, The (Lennox Robinson), xxix, 291n
Coblenz, Germany, xx, xxix, 284–297
Colum, Padraic, xxv, xxvi, xxvii, 9, 10n, 20, 21n, 284, 316, 316n
Connell, Norreys (Conal O'Riordan), xx, xxix, xxx
Connolly, James (Seamus O'Conghaile), 146n, 305
Conrad, Joseph, 27n
Coole Park, Gort, Co. Galway, xxvi, 2, 2n, 3, 270
Cork, xxviii, 173n, 175, 178, 178n, 181, 182, 184, 186
Corsican Brothers, The (Dion Boucicault), 51n
Country Dressmaker, The (George Fitzmaurice), xxviii, 201n, 253
Court Theatre, London, 66n
Cousins, James, xxvi
Coxhead, Elizabeth, xvi, xxiii, 76n, 135n, 318n
Craig, Mary, 88n
Crossroads, The (Lennox Robinson), xxx
Cuala Press, 315
Cuchulain of Muirthemne (Lady Gregory), 46, 47n, 49, 113
Cullen, Philly (*The Playboy of the Western World*), 88n

Dalkey, Co. Dublin, 269 (see map)
Dana Magazine, 39
Dante Alighieri, 81
Dara, Michael (*The Shadow of the Glen*), 7
Darley, Arthur, 7, 31, 131, 204
Darragh, Florence (Letitia Marion Dallas), xxvii, 40, 41n, 48, 68n, 71
Deirdre (George Russell, Æ), 231
Deirdre (W. B. Yeats), xxvii, xxix, 41n, 44, 44n, 68, 111n, 170n, 184, 184n, 301n, 304, 304n
Deirdre of the Sorrows (J. M. Synge), xiii, xx, 47n, 207, 209, 210–211, 212n, 212–213, 214, 216, 218, 219, 220, 223, 225, 230, 236–237, 238, 270, 272, 300, 301, 305, 308, 309, 314, 315, 315n
Dervorgilla (Lady Gregory), xxviii, 209, 226
Devon, England, xxviii, 151–154
Diarmuid and Grania (W. B. Yeats and George Moore), 52n
Dickson, Dr. Emily W., 250n, 254, 260
Dingle Bay, Co. Kerry, 20, 203, 204
Dobbs, Mrs. Frank (JMS's cousin), 91n
Dobbs, Mrs. Harriet Traill (JMS's aunt), 303n
Doctor in Spite of Himself, The (Molière-Gregory), xxvi
Don Giovanni (Mozart), 72
Doul, Martin (*The Well of the Saints*), 20, 21n
Dundalk, Co. Louth, xxvi
Dun Emer Press (later, Cualla Press), 275
Dunne, Mrs., 158, 161, 163, 165, 167, 170, 171
Dunraven, Lord, 154, 155n

Edinburgh, Scotland, xxvi, xxviii, 36n, 129, 216n, 221, 227, 228, 229
Eglinton, John. *See* W. K. Magee
Eicken, Valeska von, xiii, 288n
Eiken, von, family, xxix, 192n, 236, 237–238, 238n, 284, 287, 294
Electra (von Hofmannsthal-Symons), 301n
Eliot, George, 317
Eloquent Dempsey, The (William Boyle), xxvi
Elpis Nursing Home, Dublin, xi, xviii, xxviii, xxix, xxx, 195, 196, 201, 247n, 251, 260, 263, 271, 283, 303n, 317
Enniscorthy, Co. Wexford, 3
Enniskerry, Co. Wicklow, xix, 13n, 32, 33n, 50, 70, 134, 141, 161, 165, 169, 210 (see map)

Esposito, Madame, 2n, 124
Esposito, Michèle, 1, 2n, 217
Esposito, Vera (Emma Vernon), 2n
Epipsychidion (Percy Bysshe Shelley), 132
Eyes of the Blind, The (Winifred M. Letts), xxvii

Fand (W. S. Blunt), xxvii, 111n, 113
Farrell, Jimmy (*The Playboy of the Western World*), 88n
Fay, Frank J., xvii, xxv, xxviii, 1, 7, 8n, 30, 59, 86, 88n, 91, 93, 103, 109, 114, 116, 120, 125, 127, 132, 135, 137, 149, 149n, 150, 151, 158, 159, 160, 161, 163, 164, 166–167, 168, 171, 174, 175, 197, 198, 218, 223, 225, 240, 241, 241n, 304
Fay, William G., xvii, xxv, xxvi, xxvii, xxviii, 2n, 3, 4n, 8n, 17, 21, 25n, 32, 33, 38, 40, 45, 45n, 48, 56, 85, 86, 87, 88n, 96, 107, 108, 109, 112, 113–114, 115n, 121, 139, 145, 149, 149n, 175, 176, 197, 222n, 225, 227, 232, 233, 240, 241n, 302
Fay, Mrs. W. G. *See* Brigit O'Dempsey
Featherbed Mountain, Co. Dublin, 161
Fishguard, Co. Wexford, 150
Fitzmaurice, George, xxviii, xxix, 201n, 254n
Flame on the Hearth, The (Seamus O'Kelly), 303n
Fluke, Miss, 100, 180
Fraughans, xix, 11n
Frohman, Charles, xxvii, 110, 110n, 112n, 114, 123n
Frou-Frou (Meilhoc & Halévy), 146

Gaiety Theatre, Dublin, 27n, 266
Gaiety Theatre, Manchester, 41n
Galsworthy, John, 66n
Galway, xxvi, xxviii, xxix, 14n, 26, 186n, 236, 237, 239, 276, 277, 277n
Galway Exhibition, 277, 281n
Gaol Gate, The (Lady Gregory), xxvi, xxvii, xxviii, 32n, 34, 42
Garvey, Mary, 304, 304n, 307
General John Regan (George Birmingham), xxi
Gildea, Ida, 140, 141n, 306
Glasgow, Scotland, xxvi, xxvii, xxviii, 36n, 115, 132, 132n, 136, 139, 140, 143, 149, 174, 216n, 220, 221, 222, 228
Glenageary Station, Co. Dublin, 9, 10, 42, 54, 80, 123, 125, 195, 209, 269, 274, 298 (see map)
Glenbeigh, Co. Kerry, 20

Glencree, Co. Wicklow, xx, xxviii, 32, 127, 161, 162, 168, 177, 179, 190, 204, 223 (see map)
Glencullen, Co. Dublin, 6, 37, 93, 100, 161 (see map)
Glendalough, Co. Wicklow, 119, 120n (see map)
Glendhu, Co. Dublin, 107, 161, 162 (see map)
Gogarty, Dr. Oliver St. John, xiv, 179, 180n
Golden Helmet, The (W. B. Yeats), xxix
Golden Treasury of English Lyrics (Francis Turner Palgrave), 162, 223
Gordon, D. J., xxiii
Gore-Booth, Constance (Countess Markievicz), 222n, 231
Gort (See Coole Park, Co. Galway)
Greene, David (JMS's biographer), xi, xvi, xxii, xxiii, xxxii, 288n
Gregg, F. J., 190, 190n
Gregory, Lady Augusta, xi, xii, xvii, xx, xxi, xxiii, xxv, xxvi, 1, 2n, 3, 4, 9, 10n, 26n, 32n, 35n, 40, 41, 45, 48, 49, 53, 74, 74n, 77, 88, 91, 95, 110n, 113, 115n, 120, 122, 124n, 126n, 128, 134, 137, 159, 175, 181, 182, 202, 203, 206, 210, 210n, 215, 216, 221, 223, 224, 228, 237, 238, 239, 241, 241n, 252, 254, 262, 270, 273, 274, 278, 289n, 300, 303, 303n, 307, 315n, 318n; *Cuchulain of Muirthemne*, 46, 47n, 49, 113; plays, xxv, xxvi, xxvii, xxviii, xxix, 32n, 34, 42, 74, 114, 137, 173, 209, 226, 246, 246n, 262, 289, 289n, 305
Gregory, Major Richard, xxiii
Gregory, Robert, 126n, 181, 182, 183n, 240n
Greystones, Co. Wicklow, 253, 303
Guest, Lady Charlotte, 192n
Gulliver's Travels (Jonathan Swift), 268, 271
Gwynn, Stephen, 48, 155, 155n, 248

Hading, Jane (Jeanette Hadingue), 146, 146n
Hague, Mrs. Morton, xiv, xvi
Hardon, Margaret, xiii
Harris, Philly, 23
Harvey, John Martin, xxviii, 51, 51n, 52n, 214n, 218, 226, 310
Harvey, Rev. T. A., 240n
Hayden, Christine, xxiii
Hedda Gabler (Henrik Ibsen), 208
Hell Fire Club, 164

Henderson, W. A., xxvi, xxviii, 32n, 47, 111, 112n, 166–167, 172, 202, 245, 246, 248, 249, 263, 269, 281, 306, 308
Henry Esmond (William Makepeace Thackeray), 176
Hillis, G. R., 8n
Hodgkin's disease, xiv-xv, 97n
Hofmannsthal, Hugo von, 301n
Hogan, Robert, xxii, xxiii
Holloway, Joseph, xxii, 88n, 100n, 112n, 146, 171n
Hone, Joseph Maunsell, 98n, 304
Horniman, Annie Elizabeth Frederika, xvii, 10n, 20n, 41n, 96, 107, 112n, 139, 141n, 145, 149, 150, 151, 163, 226, 242n, 291n, 305, 305n
Hourglass, The (W. B. Yeats), 111n, 126
Housman, A. E., 267n
Hull, England, xxvi, 36n, 229n
Hyacinth Halvey (Lady Gregory), xxvi
Hyde, Douglas, 2n

Ibsen, Henrik, 66n, 208
Interior (Maurice Maeterlinck), xxvii, 111n, 115
International Exhibition, Dublin, 132, 133n, 140
Irish Dramatic Company, 4n
Irish National Literary Society, Dublin, 100, 100n
Irish National Theatre Society, xxv, 102n, 123, 124n
Irish Players of the Abbey Theatre, xvii
Irish Players, 1916 company, 71n
Irving, Sir Henry, 52n
Ivanhoe (Sir Walter Scott), 132, 134

Jackdaw, The (Lady Gregory), xxvii
Jackson, Holbrook, 129, 130n
James, Michael (*The Playboy of the Western World*), 88n
John Bull's Other Island (George Bernard Shaw), 217, 217n
Joy, Maurice, 20, 21n
Jubainville, Henri d'Arbois de, 314n
Julleville, Petot de, 46n
Juno and the Paycock (Sean O'Casey), xxi

Kathleen ni Houlihan (W. B. Yeats–Lady Gregory), 114, 173
Keats, John, xxii
Kelleher, D. L., xxx
Kenny, P. D. ("Pat"), 91n
Keogh, Shawn (*The Playboy of the Western World*), 88n
Keohler, Thomas, xxvi

Kerrigan, J. M., 88n, 170, 170n, 226, 232, 233, 251, 305
Kerry, County, xxvi, xxviii, 46, 94, 95, 124, 164, 204, 209
Kettle, Thomas, xxvi
Kidnapped (Robert Louis Stevenson), 22n
Kilkenny, Co. Kilkenny, xxviii, 173, 173n, 177, 178, 180, 182
Killarney, Co. Kerry, 191, 203, 205
Killikeen, Co. Dublin, 166, 168 (see Killakee House, map)
Killiney Hill, Co. Dublin, 116, 125, 126, 132, 133, 139, 140, 151, 200, 208, 218 (see map)
Killorglin Fair (Puck Fair), 19
Kilmacanogue, Co. Wicklow, xix, 40, 72, 209, 219 (see map)
Kilternan, Co. Dublin, 6, 40, 50, 131, 136 (see map)
Kincora (Lady Gregory), xxv
King, Betty, 149n
Kingstown (Dun Laoghaire), Co. Dublin, xxv, xxvi, xxix, 54–55

Laird, Helen, xxvi
Land, The (Padraic Colum), xxv, 316n
Lane, Hugh, 110n, 230n, 240, 243, 304
Lang, Andrew, 46
Laragh, Co. Wicklow, xx (see map)
Lebeau, Henri, 130, 131n, 174, 174n, 183–184, 190, 219, 268, 293
Leeds, England, xxvi, 129
Letters to My Daughter (Samuel Synge), xxiii, 11n, 43
Letts, Winifred M., xxvii
Life's But a Dream (Calderon de la Barca), 252n, 254n
Limerick, Mona. *See* Payne, Mrs. Ben Iden
Liverpool, England, xxvi
London, England, xxviii, 72, 107, 132n, 135, 147, 153, 154, 285, 297
Longford, Co. Longford, xxvi, 2, 184
Lough Bray, Co. Wicklow, xx, 169, 256 (see map)
Loughlinstown, Co. Dublin, 131, 140, 209, 218, 234 (see map)
Lucan, Co. Dublin, 114, 122

Mabinogion, The, 192n,
"Mac." *See* Arthur Sinclair
Macbeth (William Shakespeare), 192
MacDonagh, Thomas, xxix
McDonnell, Francis Quinton. *See* Arthur Sinclair, "Mac"

McGuirk, Mr. and Mrs., Lough Bray Cottage, 158, 159, 163, 168
MacKenna, Mrs. Stephen (Marie), xi, 21, 22n, 243, 245, 272, 273, 302, 313
MacKenna, Stephen, xi, 21, 22n, 208–209, 219, 221, 226, 267, 270, 272, 273, 302, 313
Maeterlinck, Maurice, xxvii, 111n
Magda (Hermann Sudermann), 208
Magee, William Kirkpatrick (John Eglinton), 38, 38n, 270, 313
Mahon, Christy (*The Playboy of the Western World*), 32, 88n
Mair, G. H. (Molly's first husband), xx
Mair, John D. (Molly's son), xxi
Mair, Mary Marguerita (Pegeen, Molly's daughter), xxi, xxiii, 76n, 135n
Man Who Missed the Tide, The (W. F. Casey), xxix, 244n, 306
Manchester, England, xx, xxviii, xxx, 160, 216n, 217, 224
Manchester Guardian, xx, xxv, 33n, 47, 133, 136, 157n, 187, 240, 276, 282
Markievicz, Count Casimir Dunin, 51, 221, 222n
Markievicz, Countess Constance Gore-Booth, 222n, 231
Martin, Mrs. Katherine, 8, 8n
Martyn, Edward, xxvi, 10n
Masefield, John, 156, 156n, 239
Massey, Miss, 268, 269, 270
Master and Man, The (Leo Tolstoi), 99, 100n
Master of Ballantrae, The (Robert Louis Stevenson), 98
Matheson, Cherrie (Mrs. C. H. Houghton), xiii
Maunsel and Company, 98n, 102, 233n
Maurya (*Riders to the Sea*), 87
Mayne, Rutherford (Samuel Waddell), 303n
Meakin, Annette, 154, 155n
Measure for Measure (William Shakespeare), 242n
Meredith, George, 46
Merry Wives of Windsor, The (William Shakespeare), 213
Messiah, The (George Frederick Handel), 81
Meyerfeld, Max, xxv, 131n, 149n, 268
Meynell, Alice, 27n
Mill on the Floss, The (George Eliot), 317
Milton, John, 102
Mineral Workers, The (William Boyle), xxvi, xxvii, 42n
Miser, The (Molière-Gregory), xxix

Molière, Jean-Baptiste Poquelin, xxvi, 246
Montgomery, James, 171, 171n
Moore, George, 51, 52n, 98n, 111
Morgan, Sydney J., 270, 271n
Morte D'Arthur (Sir Thomas Malory), 16, 22
Musek, Pan Karel, xxvi, 1, 2, 2n, 3, 4, 7, 9, 10, 79, 129, 130n, 268, 278

National Literary Society, Dublin, 32n, 48
National Theatre, Prague, 7
Nesbitt, George, xxvi
Nethersole, Olga, 27n
New Arts Club, Dublin, 221–222, 226
Newcastle, England, xxvi, 36n, 139

O'Casey, Sean, xxi, 271n
O'Dempsey, Bridget (Mrs. W. G. Fay), xxvii, xxviii, 6, 7n, 24, 25n, 26, 45, 45n, 87, 88n, 101, 112, 139, 176, 222n, 228
O'Doherty, Eileen, 149n
Oedipus (Sophocles), 38, 39n
O'Kelly, Seamus, 303n
Old Mahon (*The Playboy of the Western World*), 87, 88n, 108
On Baile's Strand (W. B. Yeats), xxv, 111, 111n, 114, 151
O'Neill, Maire. *See* Molly Allgood
O'Neill, Michael J., xxii
Ordeal of Richard Feverel, The (George Meredith), 46
O'Riordan, Conal. *See* Norreys Connell
O'Rourke, Joseph A., 70, 71n, 88n, 176, 193, 213, 259
O'Sullivan, Alice, 88n
O'Sullivan, Seamus. *See* James Starkey
Oxford, England, xxviii, 107, 131–132, 132n, 145, 151, 153, 154

Paris, France, 114, 175, 182, 184, 218
Parsons, Dr. Alfred R. (JMS's doctor), 54n, 54, 57, 91, 96, 97, 104, 105, 106, 114, 121, 122, 125, 134, 147, 151, 194, 203, 223, 227, 231, 258, 261, 283, 304, 305, 306, 309, 314, 315
Paterson, James, 135n
Payne, Ben Iden, xxvii, 111n, 125, 126, 130, 134, 163, 227n
Payne, Mrs. Ben Iden (Mona Limerick), xxvii, 111, 112n
Pearse, Padraic, xxvi
Petrarch, Francesco, 81, 290
Pie-Dish, The (George Fitzmaurice), xxix
Pinero, Arthur Wing, 27n
Piper, The (Conal O'Riordan), xxix

Playboy of the Western World, The (J. M. Synge), xii, xxvii, 4n, 12, 14, 28n, 32, 33, 44, 45, 47, 48, 49, 50, 51, 52, 52n, 53, 57, 59, 60, 62, 67, 69, 71, 74, 76, 79, 80, 81, 84, 86, 87, 88n, 88, 89, 96, 97, 100n, 102, 111, 112n, 113, 116n, 119, 129, 130n, 145, 153, 155n, 190, 233, 238, 249; *see also* Synge

Player Queen, The (W. B. Yeats), xxi

Plough and the Stars, The (Sean O'Casey), xxi

Plunkett, Horace, 21n

Poel, William, 215, 216n, 216, 220, 242n, 253, 256, 258

Poorhouse, The (Gregory-Hyde), xxvii

Power, Ambrose, 21, 22n, 39, 87, 88n, 108, 119, 125

Price, Alan, xiv, 10n

Puck Fair, 19n

Queens' Theatre, Dublin, 221

Quin, Widow (*The Playboy of the Western World*), 88n

Quinn, John, 190, 190n, 233, 236, 238, 249, 251, 252

Racine, Jean Baptiste, 27n

Rea, Hope, xiv, 27n, 27

Red Robe, The (Eugène Brieux), 288, 289n

Rhens, Germany, 293

Ricketts, Charles, 302

Riders to the Sea (J. M. Synge), xvii, xxvi, 2n, 49, 51, 52n, 87, 88n, 113, 114, 176n, 184, 220, 254n

Rising of the Moon, The (Lady Gregory), xxvii, 307

Roberts, George, 101, 102, 109, 128, 181, 184, 185, 188, 227, 233n, 271, 273, 284, 304, 307, 313

Robinson, Lennox, xx, xxi, xxix, xxx, 8n, 291, 291n

Rodin, Auguste, 272

Rogueries of Scapin, The (Molière-Gregory), xxix, 246n, 246, 262, 305

Ross, Florence, 10n, 11, 53n, 80, 84, 90, 101, 149, 172, 211, 217, 238, 239, 248, 253, 261, 265, 268, 310

Rossbeigh, Co. Kerry, 23

Rosslare, Co. Wexford, 150

Rostrevor, Co. Down, 122

Roundwood, Co. Wicklow, 163 (see map)

Russell, George (Æ), 102n, 231

Russell, Mrs. George, 224

Ryan, Frederick, 39n

Sachs, Hans, 289

Sally Gap, The, Co. Wicklow, 158, 159, 160, 161, 169 (see map)

Sandycove, Co. Dublin, 9, 10, 15 (see map)

Savoy Theatre, London, 173n

Scalp, The, Co. Dublin, 13, 50, 134, 230, 234

Scheming Lieutenant, The (Richard Brinsley Sheridan), xxix

Scott, Sir Walter, 111, 132, 134, 168

Second Mrs. Tanqueray, The (Arthur Wing Pinero), 27, 27n

Shadachie, The, 16n, 24n, 52n, 91n, 98, 98n, 99, 102n, 122, 163, 169, 173n, 205n

Shadow of the Glen, The (J. M. Synge), xix, xxvi, 2n, 4n, 7, 37n, 79, 80n, 114, 149n, 154, 190n, 206, 207n, 232n, 305

Shadowy Waters, The (W. B. Yeats), xxvii, 41n

Shakespeare, William, 22, 216n, 223, 242n

Shaw, George Bernard, xx, 66n, 217, 217n

Shelley, Percy Bysshe, 132

Sheridan, Richard Brinsley, xxix

Shewing-up of Blanco Posnet, The (George Bernard Shaw), xx

Shiubhlaigh, Maire nic (Mary Walker), 10n, 149n

Sigerson, George, 100n

Silas Marner (George Eliot), 317

Silver Tassie, The (Sean O'Casey), xxi

Sinclair, Arthur ("Mac," Francis Quinton McDonnell), xxi, 16, 16n, 20, 70, 71n, 88n, 119, 281, 304, 306

Skelton, Robin, 63n

Sligo, Co. Sligo, 1

Sons of Usnach, The (early title of *Deirdre of the Sorrows*), 211, 212n

Spreading the News (Lady Gregory), xxv, 114, 137

Starkey, James (Seamus O'Sullivan), 146, 146n, 314

Stephen Gray (D. L. Kelleher), xxx

Stephens, Annie Isabella (JMS's sister), xv, 4, 4n, 10n, 11, 53n, 80, 250, 256, 258, 297, 299

Stephens, Edward M. (JMS's nephew), xi, 11, 53n, 80, 84, 124n, 261

Stephens, Francis Edmund (JMS's nephew), 11, 53n, 80, 84, 260, 263, 281

Stephens, Mrs. Lily M., xxiii, 135n

Stevenson, Robert Louis, 22n

Stewart, Bob, 39n, 146

Stopford, Edward A., 77, 78n, 213n

Suburban Groove, The (W. F. Casey), xxix, 244n

Sudermann, Hermann, 289
Sugarloaf Mountains, Co. Wicklow, 12, 47n, 116, 165, 209, 219 (see map)
Swanzy, Henry R. (Molly's eye specialist), 105, 105n, 121, 124, 128
Swift, Jonathan, 268, 271, 304
Switzers Department Store, Dublin, 180
Symons, Arthur, 27n, 301n
Synge, John Millington, attempts to educate Molly, xviii-xix, 6, 13, 22, 46, 67–68, 72, 81, 98–99, 102, 107, 132, 134, 162–163, 168, 192, 200, 204–205, 223, 268; attitude toward his family, 13; considers resigning directorship of Abbey Theatre, 145; convalesces at Silchester House, xxix; death of, xx, xxx, 317; discusses new scenario with Molly, 116; enters Elpis Nursing Home, xxviii, xxix, xxx, 195–199, 246; fears tuberculosis, 106; form of address to Molly, xviii; friends of, xiii, xiv, 27, 156, 156n; horoscope read by W. B. Yeats, 224; illness of, xiv–xv, 91, 97n; jealousy of Dossie Wright, xvii, 6, 24, 127, 202, 225, 249, 278; marriage plans, xviii, 220; moves to mother's home in Kingstown, xxv, xxvi, xxix; portraits of, xxiii, 135n, 149n, 230n; possibility of American edition of plays, 188, 233; quotes poetry to Molly; 121, 132; readings, 16, 22, 46, 176, 227, 248, 259, 267n, 317; shows W. B. Yeats his poems, 273; suggests he and Molly write a play together, 180; suggests Molly write theatre articles, 137–138, 202; takes rooms in Rathgar, xxvi; takes rooms in Rathmims, xxviii, 245; tells mother about Molly, 56, 57, 58, 64, 69, 71, 72; visits Cousin Edward Synge in Surrey, xxvii, 64–78; visits Co. Kerry, xxviii, 15–26; visits von Eickens in Germany, xxix, 284–298; visits Jack Yeats in Devon, xxviii, 131, 140, 142, 147, 149, 150–154
Synge, family of, xii, 53, 80, 130; Ada Synge (JMS's niece), 80, 84, 185, 186n, 211, 261, 265, 268; Edith Synge (JMS's niece), xxiii; Edward Synge (JMS's brother) xv, 53n; Edward Millington Synge (JMS's cousin), xviii, 56, 57n, 58, 65, 67, 70, 73, 123, 316; John Hatch Synge (JMS's father), xv; Kathleen M. Synge (JMS's mother), xv, xxix, 4n, 6, 10n, 43, 49, 55, 56, 59, 74, 77, 79, 80, 94, 99, 102, 108, 115, 156, 166, 172, 189, 189n, 191, 209, 232, 234, 247n. 250, 264–

265, 266–267, 268–269, 276, 278, 291–295, 299; Margaret Bertha Synge (JMS's cousin), 69n; Mary Synge (JMS's cousin), 191, 192n, 202; Robert Anthony Synge (JMS's brother), xvi, 53n, 104, 104n, 247n, 261; Rev. Samuel Synge (JMS's brother), xi, xv, 4n, 11, 11n, 35, 35n; see also Stephens entries
Synge, J. M., works of: The Aran Islands, 46, 47n, 68, 128, 184, 190n, 237n; Deirdre of the Sorrows, xiii, xx, 47n, 207, 209, 210–211, 212n, 212–213, 214, 216, 218, 219, 220, 223, 225, 230, 236–237, 238, 239, 270, 272, 300, 301, 305, 308, 309, 314, 315, 315n; essays, 16n, 24n, 51, 52n, 91n, 98, 99, 102n, 122, 124, 136, 157, 159, 160, 163, 169, 169n, 173n, 187, 201, 205n, 236, 244, 276, 278; The Playboy of the Western World, xii, xxvii, 4n, 12, 14, 28n, 32, 37, 44, 45, 47, 48, 49, 50, 51, 52, 52n, 53, 57, 59, 60, 62, 67, 69, 71, 74, 76, 79, 80, 81, 84, 86, 87, 88n, 88, 89, 96, 97, 100n, 102, 111, 112n, 113, 116n, 119, 129, 130n, 130, 145, 153, 155n, 190, 233, 238, 249; poems and translations, xii, 36, 40, 62, 63, 76, 117, 118n, 123–124, 135, 137, 138n, 144, 257n, 276–277, 283, 290, 303, 304; Riders to the Sea, xvii, xxvi, 2n, 49, 51, 52n, 87, 88n, 113, 114, 176n, 184, 220, 254n; The Shadow of the Glen, xix, xxvi, 2n, 4n, 7, 37n, 79, 80n, 114, 149n, 154, 190n, 206, 207n, 232n, 305; The Tinker's Wedding, xxi, 112n, 173, 185, 186, 188, 222, 224, 227, 229; The Well of the Saints, xii, xxv, xxix, 20, 21n, 44, 45, 52n, 110, 131n, 149, 190n, 215, 268, 294, 302; When the Moon Has Set, xiii

Talisman, The (Sir Walter Scott), 168
Teja (Sudermann-Gregory), xxix, 289, 289n
Tess of the D'Urbervilles (Thomas Hardy), 134
Thackeray, William Makepeace, 176
Theatre of Ireland, The, xxvi, 10n, 302, 303n, 304n, 316n
Theatre Royal, Belfast, 303n
Theatre Royal, Dublin, 51n
Thomas Muskerry (Padraic Colum), 316n
Time (Conal O'Riordan), xxx
Tinker and the Fairy, The (Douglas Hyde), 2n
Tinker's Wedding, The (J. M. Synge), xxi, 112n, 173, 185, 186, 188, 222, 224, 229
Tobin, Agnes, xvii, 27, 57, 68, 69, 72, 77,

Tobin, Agnes (*cont.*)
80, 110, 113, 114, 115, 176, 187, 251, 307;
brother of, 189, 191,
Tolstoi, Leo, 49, 100n
Tragedy of Nan, The (John Masefield), 239n
Tralee, Co. Kerry, 204, 206
Tramp, The (*The Shadow of the Glen*), 4n
Tree, Herbert Beerbohm, xxviii, 36n,
203n, 242, 242n
Trench, Dermot, xxvi
Trinity College, Dublin, 226, 229n
Tristan and Iseult, 248, 293
Turn of the Road, The (Rutherford Mayne),
303n
Turner, J. M. W., 304
Tyndall, Mary (Mrs. Synge's house-
keeper), 179, 181n, 182, 185, 189, 258

Unicorn from the Stars, The (Yeats-Gregory), xxviii

"Vagrants of Wicklow, The" (J. M.
Synge), 51, 52n
Vaughan, Ernest, xxviii, 227, 227n
Vaughan, Mrs., 191, 192n
Vedrenne, J. E., 66n
Ventry, Co. Kerry, 203, 206
Vernon, Emma (see Esposito, Vera)
Villon, François, 290
Vogelweide, Walter von der, 289, 294
Von Eicken (see Eicken, von)

Walker, Frank, 149n
Walker, Mary (see Shiubhlaigh, Maire nic)
Wareing, Alfred, xxvi, 35, 36n
Waterford, Co. Waterford, xxviii, 27, 173n,
175, 176, 178

Well of the Saints, The (J. M. Synge), xii,
xxv, xxix, 20, 21n, 44, 45, 52n, 110, 131n,
149, 190n, 215, 268, 294, 302
Wexford, Co. Wexford, xxvi, 136, 150, 151,
152
When the Dawn Is Come (Thomas Mac-
Donagh), xxix
When the Moon Has Set (J. M. Synge), xiii
Whitaker, H. T., 243, 244
White Cockade, The (Lady Gregory), xxv
Wicklow County, xii, xiv, xix, 4n, 120,
136, 141, 151, 169, 189n
Workhouse Ward, The (Lady Gregory), xxix
Wright, Udolphus (Dossie), xvii, 1, 2, 3,
4, 6, 24, 127, 202, 223, 225, 248, 249, 259,
278, 306

Yeats, Anne Butler, xxiii
Yeats, Elizabeth, 275n, 313, 314
Yeats, Jack Butler, xxv, xxviii, 32, 33, 33n,
34, 128, 131, 135, 140, 142, 145, 147, 149,
150, 152, 153, 183, 202, 223, 240n, 270
Yeats, Mrs. Jack Butler, 153
Yeats, John Butler, xxiii, 59, 60n, 79, 148,
149n, 181, 191, 194, 214, 230n, 295, 296n
Yeats, Lily, 19, 275n, 313, 314
Yeats, Michael Butler, xxiii
Yeats, William Butler, xi, xii, xx, xxi, xxv,
xxvi, 2n, 3, 10n, 32n, 41n, 42, 44n, 45,
48, 52n, 68n, 76, 77, 88, 90, 93, 98n, 111,
111n, 113, 114, 118, 120, 124n, 126n, 145,
148, 151, 154, 169n, 170n, 181, 184, 184n,
187, 210, 215, 224, 225, 226, 239, 241,
241n, 242, 243, 255, 257n, 271n, 273, 274,
275, 276, 278, 292, 295, 299, 301n, 304,
304n
Yeats, Mrs. W. B., xxiii